This book comes with access to more content online.

Choose from hundreds of practice questions
to create quizzes on every concept!

Register your book or ebook at
www.dummies.com/go/getaccess.

Select your product, and then follow the prompts
to validate your purchase.

You'll receive an email with your PIN and instructions.

1,001 ASVAB AFQT
Practice Questions

by Angie Papple Johnston

1,001 ASVAB AFQT Practice Questions For Dummies®

Published by **John Wiley & Sons, Inc.** 111 River Street Hoboken, NJ 07030-5774, www.wiley.com

Copyright © 2017 by John Wiley & Sons, Inc., Hoboken, New Jersey

Published simultaneously in Canada

For general information on our other products and services, please contact our Customer Care Department within the U.S. at 877-762-2974, outside the U.S. at 317-572-3993, or fax 317-572-4002. For technical support, please visit https://hub.wiley.com/community/support/dummies.

Wiley publishes in a variety of print and electronic formats and by print-on-demand. Some material included with standard print versions of this book may not be included in e-books or in print-on-demand. If this book refers to media such as a CD or DVD that is not included in the version you purchased, you may download this material at http://booksupport.wiley.com. For more information about Wiley products, visit www.wiley.com.

Library of Congress Control Number: 2016958951

ISBN 978-1-119-29148-0 (pbk); ISBN 978-1-119-29149-7 (ebk); ISBN 978-1-119-29150-3 (ebk)

Manufactured in the United States of America

SKY10034091_040722

Contents at a Glance

Table of Contents

Introduction

The Armed Services Vocational Aptitude Battery — affectionately called the ASVAB by military personnel — is the test that military recruiters use to determine whether you're eligible for service in the U.S. Armed Forces. Don't let that scare you, though. With the right preparation (and this book), you'll be well-prepared to take the test and join the military branch of your choice.

Four sections of the ASVAB determine your Armed Forces Qualification Test score, or AFQT: Word Knowledge, Paragraph Comprehension, Mathematics Knowledge, and Arithmetic Reasoning. The military calculates your score on these four subtests to find out whether you qualify for service. Your recruiter will use your AFQT score and your scores on the other five subtests (which are all covered in *ASVAB For Dummies*) to zero in on the jobs you're most qualified to perform in the Army, Marines, Air Force, Navy, or Coast Guard.

This book gives you 1,001 carefully crafted practice questions to help you prepare for the ASVAB AFQT. The questions are similar to those you'll see on the actual ASVAB, so by the time you're finished working your way through them, you'll be confident in your ability to ace the AFQT portion of the test . . . and you'll be well on your way to becoming the military's latest and greatest recruit.

What You'll Find

The first four chapters of this book cover all the essentials of the AFQT. There are 250 of each question type, except Arithmetic Reasoning. (There are 251 Arithmetic Reasoning questions, because who *hasn't* wished for just one more math word problem?) Here's what each subtest covers:

>> **Word Knowledge:** If you want to be successful in the military, you'll need a strong vocabulary that gives you the ability to communicate clearly and concisely. That's why you find Word Knowledge in the AFQT, which asks you about definitions, synonyms, and antonyms.

>> **Paragraph Comprehension:** There's an old saying in the military: "You don't have to know all the answers. You just need to know where to find them." Once you find the answers, though, you have to understand them; that's why Paragraph Comprehension is part of what determines your eligibility for military service.

>> **Mathematics Knowledge:** Your knowledge of arithmetic, algebra, and geometry will be put to the test when you're taking the ASVAB. The military wants to know if you can do more than count on your fingers (it's tough to count on your toes when you're wearing combat boots), and basic math ability is a necessity if you want to claim your place in the world's strongest military.

>> **Arithmetic Reasoning:** Sure, you can read, write, and do arithmetic, but can you do them all at the same time? The Arithmetic Reasoning subtest measures your ability to extract mathematical concepts from word problems and find the answers.

After you've answered as many questions as you can stand for one sitting, flip to Chapter 5 to check your answers. Every answer includes a complete explanation. The math problems include steps for reaching the correct solutions. That way, you can see exactly where you went wrong — or guessed right! The vocabulary and reading questions include definitions and the reasoning behind the correct answers. Make sure to spend some time studying the answer explanations because doing so can help you better understand the questions you struggle with.

Beyond the Book

In addition to the book you're reading right now, be sure to check out the free Cheat Sheet for a set of quick reference notes on general test-taking tips for the ASVAB and specific hints for each of the AFQT subtests. To get this Cheat Sheet, simply go to www.dummies.com and search for "1,001 ASVAB AFQT Practice Questions For Dummies Cheat Sheet" in the Search box.

The online practice that comes free with this book contains the same 1,001 ASVAB AFQT practice questions and answers that appear in the book. The beauty of the online questions is that you can customize your online practice to focus on the areas that give you the most trouble. So if you need help with Paragraph Comprehension questions or Arithmetic Reasoning problems, just select those question types online and start practicing. Or if you're short on time but want to get a mixed bag of a limited number of questions, you can specify the number of questions you want to practice. Whether you practice a few hundred questions in one sitting or a couple dozen, and whether you focus on a few types of questions or practice every type, the online program keeps track of the questions you get right and wrong so you can monitor your progress and spend time studying exactly what you need.

To gain access to the online practice, all you have to do is register. Just follow these simple steps:

1. Register your book or ebook at Dummies.com to get your PIN. Go to www.dummies.com/go/getaccess.

2. Select your product from the dropdown list on that page.

3. Follow the prompts to validate your product, and then check your email for a confirmation message that includes your PIN and instructions for logging in.

If you do not receive this email within two hours, please check your spam folder before contacting us through our Technical Support website at http://support.wiley.com or by phone at 877-762-2974.

Now you're ready to go! You can come back to the practice material as often as you want — simply log on with the username and password you created during your initial login. No need to enter the access code a second time.

Your registration is good for one year from the day you activate your PIN.

Where to Go for Additional Help

This book gives you 1,001 practice questions to help you ace the AFQT portion of the ASVAB. It's designed to help you zero in on the areas you need to improve, but if you find that you need more help, head to www.dummies.com to find books and articles that can give you an extra push in the right direction.

You can use this book to simulate your ASVAB test-taking experience, but if you need more in-depth study of the AFQT or the other sections of the test, you can pick up the following *For Dummies* products:

>> *ASVAB For Dummies:* This book walks you through the entire ASVAB, gives you practice tests in each subject, and even helps you understand the requirements for specific military jobs so you can study the right material.

>> *ASVAB AFQT For Dummies:* This book gives you an in-depth look at the AFQT portion of the ASVAB and comes with plenty of practice questions you can use to further your knowledge and get the best possible score.

>> *1,001 ASVAB Practice Questions For Dummies:* This book gives you 1,001 practice questions that cover all nine ASVAB subtests, and it's broken down into easy sections that let you focus on the right places.

1 The Questions

IN THIS PART . . .

Find out just how big your vocabulary is with Word Knowledge questions.

Test your understanding of what you read with Paragraph Comprehension questions.

Review fractions, percentages, scientific notation, algebra, and geometry problems with Mathematics Knowledge questions.

Practice converting math word problems into solvable equations with Arithmetic Reasoning questions.

Chapter **1**

Word Knowledge: Putting Your Vocabulary to the Test

The Word Knowledge subtest on the ASVAB measures your ability to communicate by gauging your vocabulary level. To do well on this subtest, you don't have to be a walking dictionary. However, you *do* need a good grasp on the English language, which means having a solid knowledge of words and their meanings. You also need to be able to determine what words mean based on their context within a sentence.

When you're working through these 250 practice questions, you may encounter words you use every day, words you hear occasionally, and words you've never seen before. When you come across a word you don't know, give it your best guess — sometimes your knowledge of other, similar words will kick in and you'll get it right. (You can use that strategy on test day, too, when you have 8 minutes to answer 16 Word Knowledge questions on the computerized version of the ASVAB or 11 minutes to answer 35 questions on the paper version.)

The Questions You'll Work On

You find three types of questions on the Word Knowledge subtest:

>> **Synonyms:** These questions ask you to find the word closest in meaning to the underlined word.

>> **Sentence context:** Sentence context questions give you a sentence and ask you to find the find the word that can best replace the underlined word without changing the meaning.

>> **Antonyms:** These questions ask you to select the answer that's most opposite in meaning to the underlined word.

What to Watch Out For

English isn't exactly known for being the easiest language in the world, which means you may have to implement some strategies as you prepare for the Word Knowledge subtest. Keep these tips in mind:

» When you find a word you don't know, try to figure out its root and see whether that sets off a spark of recognition.

» Pay attention to context clues. Sometimes the sentence will give you clues about a word's meaning.

» Remember to read the questions carefully. Some ask for the meaning of the word, and some ask for a word's antonym — the word most opposite in meaning.

Synonyms

1. <u>Accord</u> most nearly means
   - (A) agreement.
   - (B) theory.
   - (C) judgment.
   - (D) attempt.

2. <u>Establish</u> most nearly means
   - (A) set up.
   - (B) foundation.
   - (C) give.
   - (D) receive.

3. <u>Obtain</u> most nearly means
   - (A) hold.
   - (B) work.
   - (C) get.
   - (D) top.

4. <u>Brazen</u> most nearly means
   - (A) dim.
   - (B) obnoxious.
   - (C) timid.
   - (D) bold.

5. <u>Vain</u> most nearly means
   - (A) vessel.
   - (B) useless.
   - (C) nice.
   - (D) condescending.

6. <u>Fortitude</u> most nearly means
   - (A) strength.
   - (B) bravado.
   - (C) inconsistency.
   - (D) difficulty.

7. <u>Plausible</u> most nearly means
   - (A) deceptive.
   - (B) believable.
   - (C) ignorant.
   - (D) lagging.

8. <u>Persuade</u> most nearly means
   - (A) deter.
   - (B) encourage.
   - (C) lead.
   - (D) convince.

9. <u>Dialogue</u> most nearly means
   - (A) leader.
   - (B) text.
   - (C) conversation.
   - (D) soliloquy.

10. Exempt most nearly means
   (A) underprivileged.
   (B) excused.
   (C) untenable.
   (D) taxable.

11. Buttress most nearly means
   (A) support.
   (B) arch.
   (C) matriarch.
   (D) object.

12. Bizarre most nearly means
   (A) strange.
   (B) extreme.
   (C) fierce.
   (D) futuristic.

13. Liable most nearly means
   (A) typical.
   (B) slander.
   (C) immune.
   (D) responsible.

14. Optimistic most nearly means
   (A) short-sighted.
   (B) preferential.
   (C) hopeful.
   (D) likely.

15. Affect most nearly means
   (A) result.
   (B) change.
   (C) signify.
   (D) define.

16. Labyrinth most nearly means
   (A) system.
   (B) path.
   (C) maze.
   (D) connector.

17. Blatant most nearly means
   (A) subtle.
   (B) obvious.
   (C) unclear.
   (D) noisy.

18. Maneuver most nearly means
   (A) movement.
   (B) achievement.
   (C) reach.
   (D) simulation.

19. Disclose most nearly means
   (A) tell.
   (B) hide.
   (C) shut.
   (D) teach.

20. Quarantine most nearly means
   (A) annotate.
   (B) identify.
   (C) insinuate.
   (D) isolate.

21. Adept most nearly means
   (A) considerate.
   (B) careful.
   (C) thoughtless.
   (D) skilled.

22. Recede most nearly means
   (A) move.
   (B) compel.
   (C) retreat.
   (D) wax.

23. Volatile most nearly means
   (A) changeable.
   (B) confusing.
   (C) sickened.
   (D) broken.

24. Intrepid most nearly means

    (A) nervous.

    (B) clever.

    (C) fearful.

    (D) brave.

25. Wrath most nearly means

    (A) revenge.

    (B) anger.

    (C) expulsion.

    (D) flux.

26. Proliferate most nearly means

    (A) create.

    (B) grow.

    (C) generate.

    (D) decline.

27. Vacate most nearly means

    (A) keep.

    (B) relax.

    (C) abandon.

    (D) inform.

28. Pathetic most nearly means

    (A) pitiful.

    (B) hopeless.

    (C) disgusting.

    (D) terrible.

29. Refuge most nearly means

    (A) entrance.

    (B) chamber.

    (C) dwelling.

    (D) sanctuary.

30. Scour most nearly means

    (A) detour.

    (B) scrub.

    (C) frown.

    (D) petrify.

31. Aversion most nearly means

    (A) opposition.

    (B) advocate.

    (C) dislike.

    (D) animosity.

32. Strife most nearly means

    (A) conflict.

    (B) suffering.

    (C) attack.

    (D) accordance.

33. Nourish most nearly means

    (A) administer.

    (B) entrust.

    (C) sustain.

    (D) proffer.

34. Tread most nearly means

    (A) step on.

    (B) steer.

    (C) try.

    (D) hurry.

35. Console most nearly means

    (A) ascend.

    (B) rejuvenate.

    (C) bolster.

    (D) comfort.

36. Banter most nearly means

    (A) taunt.

    (B) repartee.

    (C) ridicule.

    (D) reproach.

37. Credible most nearly means

    (A) believable.

    (B) secretive.

    (C) annoyed.

    (D) unlikely.

38. Erode most nearly means

   (A) chop.

   (B) deteriorate.

   (C) scrub.

   (D) repair.

39. Generate most nearly means

   (A) consider.

   (B) create.

   (C) boil over.

   (D) take.

40. Mode most nearly means

   (A) resource.

   (B) alone.

   (C) octave.

   (D) way.

41. Foil most nearly means

   (A) wrapping.

   (B) confer.

   (C) aggravate.

   (D) prevent.

42. Chamber most nearly means

   (A) enclosed space.

   (B) passageway.

   (C) trough.

   (D) shelf.

43. Aide most nearly means

   (A) abet.

   (B) teacher.

   (C) creator.

   (D) helper.

44. Stump most nearly means

   (A) confuse.

   (B) chop.

   (C) pound.

   (D) clarify.

45. Insist most nearly means

   (A) continue.

   (B) assert.

   (C) wish.

   (D) demand.

46. Bland most nearly means

   (A) uninteresting.

   (B) tiny.

   (C) dramatic.

   (D) rough.

47. Sentinel most nearly means

   (A) aggressor.

   (B) lookout.

   (C) coward.

   (D) reveler.

48. Repeal most nearly means

   (A) yell.

   (B) hold.

   (C) ignore.

   (D) cancel.

49. Labor most nearly means

   (A) think.

   (B) illuminate.

   (C) market.

   (D) work.

50. Aberration most nearly means

   (A) anomaly.

   (B) commonplace.

   (C) disgusting.

   (D) revered.

51. Winsome most nearly means

   (A) hardy.

   (B) difficult.

   (C) windy.

   (D) charming.

52. <u>Initial</u> most nearly means
 (A) first.
 (B) exception.
 (C) new.
 (D) tragic.

53. <u>Rabid</u> most nearly means
 (A) generous.
 (B) sickly.
 (C) fanatical.
 (D) deepen.

54. <u>Mobile</u> most nearly means
 (A) movable.
 (B) fixed.
 (C) cellular.
 (D) turning.

55. <u>Solicit</u> most nearly means
 (A) decry.
 (B) evoke.
 (C) drag.
 (D) request.

56. <u>Fallacy</u> most nearly means
 (A) misnomer.
 (B) misconception.
 (C) truth.
 (D) ersatz.

57. <u>External</u> most nearly means
 (A) during the night.
 (B) after the fact.
 (C) outer surface.
 (D) transcendental.

58. <u>Vociferous</u> most nearly means
 (A) noisome.
 (B) vehement.
 (C) plant-like.
 (D) strong.

59. <u>Convert</u> most nearly means
 (A) change.
 (B) prevail.
 (C) belie.
 (D) track.

60. <u>Consider</u> most nearly means
 (A) tarry.
 (B) dawdle.
 (C) defy.
 (D) think.

61. <u>Prompt</u> most nearly means
 (A) arrogant.
 (B) slow.
 (C) fast.
 (D) bright.

62. <u>Turpitude</u> most nearly means
 (A) depravity.
 (B) strength.
 (C) justice.
 (D) piousness.

63. <u>Makeshift</u> most nearly means
 (A) permanent.
 (B) adversarial.
 (C) substitute.
 (D) difficult.

64. <u>Comprise</u> most nearly means
 (A) create.
 (B) is composed of.
 (C) track.
 (D) herald.

65. <u>Spurious</u> most nearly means
 (A) prickly.
 (B) dangerous.
 (C) nonsense.
 (D) bogus.

66. Expanse most nearly means
    (A) cost.
    (B) growth.
    (C) area.
    (D) beat.

67. Fearsome most nearly means
    (A) menacing.
    (B) calming.
    (C) noxious.
    (D) teary-eyed.

68. Sophomoric most nearly means
    (A) afraid.
    (B) pretentious.
    (C) emotional.
    (D) defiant.

69. Exasperate most nearly means
    (A) infer.
    (B) confuse.
    (C) drag out.
    (D) infuriate.

70. Scarcity most nearly means
    (A) majority.
    (B) shortage.
    (C) surplus.
    (D) abundance.

71. Resist most nearly means
    (A) withstand.
    (B) hold.
    (C) divide.
    (D) conduct.

72. Ersatz most nearly means
    (A) fake.
    (B) genuine.
    (C) authentic.
    (D) green.

73. Portend most nearly means
    (A) surprise.
    (B) contrast.
    (C) vicissitude.
    (D) be a warning.

74. Lucid most nearly means
    (A) relaxed.
    (B) incoherent.
    (C) understandable.
    (D) confused.

75. Ostracized most nearly means
    (A) brought in.
    (B) excluded.
    (C) parted.
    (D) captivated.

76. Allure most nearly means
    (A) tempt.
    (B) trick.
    (C) tease.
    (D) sneak.

77. Gleeful most nearly means
    (A) delirious.
    (B) joyful.
    (C) displeased.
    (D) derisive.

78. Tranquilize most nearly means
    (A) sedate.
    (B) trick.
    (C) deride.
    (D) overdose.

79. Oppose most nearly means
    (A) irk.
    (B) cooperate.
    (C) resist.
    (D) argue.

80. Mores most nearly means
   (A) customs.
   (B) types.
   (C) anomalies.
   (D) data.

81. Chap most nearly means
   (A) tangle.
   (B) expose.
   (C) irate.
   (D) become chafed.

82. Overbearing most nearly means
   (A) overwhelming.
   (B) bossy.
   (C) grouchy.
   (D) tough.

83. Equity most nearly means
   (A) fairness.
   (B) devaluation.
   (C) privacy.
   (D) earnings.

84. Subtle most nearly means
   (A) understated.
   (B) conspicuous.
   (C) suggestive.
   (D) harsh.

85. Pecuniary most nearly means
   (A) strange.
   (B) out of place.
   (C) economic.
   (D) disjointed.

86. Temporary most nearly means
   (A) permanent.
   (B) impermanent.
   (C) drafted.
   (D) sticky.

87. Insightful most nearly means
   (A) blind.
   (B) ignorant.
   (C) dull.
   (D) perceptive.

88. Superficial most nearly means
   (A) without depth.
   (B) thorough.
   (C) genuine.
   (D) sensible.

89. Render most nearly means
   (A) fail.
   (B) win.
   (C) deliver.
   (D) hold.

90. Constant most nearly means
   (A) intermittent.
   (B) unchanging.
   (C) dreadful.
   (D) periodic.

91. Commission most nearly means
   (A) delegation.
   (B) force.
   (C) recreation.
   (D) assignor.

92. Venture most nearly means
   (A) cower.
   (B) inaction.
   (C) endeavor.
   (D) persevere.

93. Range most nearly means
   (A) part.
   (B) end.
   (C) movement.
   (D) vary.

94. Scheme most nearly means
    (A) plan.
    (B) schedule.
    (C) suggestion.
    (D) theory.

95. Plea most nearly means
    (A) demand.
    (B) answer.
    (C) request.
    (D) offer.

96. Stake most nearly means
    (A) meat.
    (B) post.
    (C) steal.
    (D) embellish.

97. Attribute most nearly means
    (A) guilt.
    (B) characteristic.
    (C) thing.
    (D) roast.

98. Awesome most nearly means
    (A) extreme.
    (B) radical.
    (C) impressive.
    (D) tricky.

99. Provoke most nearly means
    (A) ignore.
    (B) curtail.
    (C) emulate.
    (D) annoy.

100. Cite most nearly means
    (A) earmark.
    (B) quote.
    (C) target.
    (D) place.

Synonyms in Sentences

101. Mrs. Jenkins turned and addressed the class.
    (A) lectured
    (B) divided
    (C) embarrassed
    (D) interrogated

102. Shelly wanted to analyze the results from the tests on her own.
    (A) combine
    (B) determine
    (C) synthesize
    (D) examine

103. The cacophony was almost unbearable for the adults, but the baby slept through it.
    (A) silence
    (B) music
    (C) racket
    (D) hissing

104. A good press release needs to include quotes from industry professionals.
    (A) place
    (B) contain
    (C) share
    (D) subordinate

105. The advertising team took the concept to the company president, who gave her approval.
    (A) idea
    (B) create
    (C) storyboard
    (D) drawing

106. Designing a new solution can be difficult, but it's usually worth the effort.
    (A) words
    (B) answer
    (C) chart
    (D) breach

107. The pearls on the <u>strand</u> seemed to glitter in the sunlight.

(A) satchel
(B) bucket
(C) hair
(D) thread

108. Renee put together a <u>coherent</u> argument that convinced the entire jury.

(A) logical
(B) ordinary
(C) jumbled
(D) confusing

109. Jackie made her <u>selection</u> based on the options offered on the cafeteria menu.

(A) position
(B) choice
(C) population
(D) semantic

110. The photos the squad submitted didn't match their commander's <u>narrative</u>.

(A) confession
(B) ilk
(C) imposture
(D) commentary

111. Nothing the woman said was <u>relevant</u> to the incident police were investigating.

(A) pertinent
(B) acceptable
(C) apt
(D) timed

112. The boys went to the <u>rally</u> together.

(A) restaurant
(B) store
(C) activation
(D) assembly

113. The generals followed a <u>divide</u> and conquer strategy.

(A) separate
(B) tool
(C) classify
(D) fight

114. The meteor's <u>velocity</u> dropped after it entered the atmosphere.

(A) temperature
(B) speed
(C) resistance
(D) girth

115. It was always hard to <u>differentiate</u> among the triplets.

(A) generalize
(B) relate
(C) change
(D) distinguish

116. The man pulled the sleeping bag over his head when he felt the <u>draft</u>.

(A) drawing
(B) current
(C) text
(D) drive

117. If the president takes the time to call you, he probably has something <u>significant</u> to say.

(A) distracting
(B) obvious
(C) important
(D) loud

118. She told me not to put so much <u>emphasis</u> on the last syllable.

(A) stress
(B) weakness
(C) focus
(D) stroke

119. Cherise made more than one error that ultimately led to her poor grade.

(A) correction
(B) perfection
(C) truth
(D) mistake

120. The excerpt detailed what it was like growing up in Germany on an American military base.

(A) passage
(B) pieces
(C) exception
(D) entirety

121. Preheat the oven before you combine the ingredients.

(A) cook
(B) bond
(C) mix
(D) dissolve

122. The kids were extremely resourceful when the teacher asked them to find solutions.

(A) prompt
(B) skillful
(C) inept
(D) aspiring

123. Julia proceeded to enumerate all the reasons she wanted to join the Army instead of the Air Force.

(A) acquiesce
(B) concede
(C) tell
(D) itemize

124. The doctor determined the underlying cause of the man's symptoms.

(A) foundational
(B) critical
(C) necessary
(D) transient

125. You can refer to the chart for the latest statistics.

(A) appearance
(B) data
(C) finish
(D) ideas

126. Many people find it difficult to assimilate in a new culture.

(A) unlearn
(B) misinterpret
(C) conform
(D) correspond

127. It is crucial that you understand the directions before you begin.

(A) dire
(B) superior
(C) essential
(D) significant

128. New laws come about with the emergence of new nations.

(A) materialization
(B) classification
(C) opening
(D) stoppage

129. Psychologists are attempting to understand the genesis of human instincts and how they have evolved.

(A) finality
(B) beginning
(C) explanation
(D) causation

130. Maher decided to have a simple breakfast comprising only oatmeal.

(A) small
(B) delicious
(C) foolish
(D) uncomplicated

131. Ulices valued Marta's <u>counsel</u>, so he did what she told him to do.

(A) negligence
(B) foresight
(C) advice
(D) reprimand

132. The investigators found that Jimmy was able to <u>corroborate</u> Justin's story.

(A) eviscerate
(B) establish
(C) authenticate
(D) disprove

133. Katie told Lilly she could <u>achieve</u> results if she worked a half hour every day.

(A) obtain
(B) negotiate
(C) perform
(D) stop

134. Doug told Trenton he'd <u>reimburse</u> him for the damage.

(A) penalize
(B) compensate
(C) collect
(D) convert

135. In a caste system, it's rare for people to move from one <u>milieu</u> to another.

(A) condition
(B) element
(C) environment
(D) ambience

136. Mallory said she would prefer someone with <u>egalitarian</u> beliefs in the Oval Office.

(A) unbiased
(B) dispassionate
(C) distinctive
(D) nondiscriminatory

137. Ty followed the <u>narrow</u> river to its end.

(A) thin
(B) wide
(C) slow
(D) bubbling

138. Yoli gathered her <u>meager</u> belongings and left.

(A) insufficient
(B) many
(C) adequate
(D) wealthy

139. Forty-three people had <u>adverse</u> reactions to the medication.

(A) opposite
(B) auspicious
(C) unfavorable
(D) dignified

140. For many parents, saying, "We'll see" is <u>tantamount</u> to saying, "No."

(A) proportionate
(B) oppositional
(C) paramount
(D) equivalent

141. The military is always attempting to <u>retain</u> good service members.

(A) teach
(B) keep
(C) discover
(D) pay

142. Please <u>convey</u> my gratitude to everyone who brought gifts.

(A) release
(B) deny
(C) carry
(D) communicate

143. Fani told her dad that he should <u>approximate</u> the time.

(A) believe

(B) estimate

(C) replicate

(D) change

144. The colonel asked the contractor to submit his <u>proposal</u>.

(A) credentials

(B) plan

(C) refusal

(D) demands

145. Employers are not supposed to have a <u>bias</u> against elderly job applicants.

(A) impression

(B) influence

(C) prejudice

(D) investigation

146. Brandon watched the creature <u>slither</u> away.

(A) slide

(B) wobble

(C) move

(D) lag

147. Although Penny said it was a <u>moot</u> point, Daniel didn't want to argue.

(A) debatable

(B) useful

(C) obvious

(D) indisputable

148. Everything the instructor covered was <u>irrelevant</u> to the test.

(A) applicable

(B) unrelated

(C) pertinent

(D) evidentiary

149. The editor made six <u>amendments</u> to the story before approving it for publication.

(A) changes

(B) retentions

(C) corrections

(D) conditions

150. The candidate handled the insults with <u>equanimity</u>.

(A) nervousness

(B) aplomb

(C) confusion

(D) brashness

151. When the kids weren't fighting, Mom couldn't help but enjoy the <u>accord</u>.

(A) peace

(B) sound

(C) discussion

(D) freedom

152. Your lawyer will <u>advocate</u> for you in court.

(A) discuss

(B) argue

(C) question

(D) cry

153. The training teaches you what to do when <u>disaster</u> strikes.

(A) catastrophe

(B) setback

(C) danger

(D) difficulty

154. "I don't have any money, but maybe we could <u>barter</u>," Rob said.

(A) joke

(B) tease

(C) go

(D) trade

155. The archaeologists used a key to <u>decipher</u> the ancient text.

(A) unlock
(B) decode
(C) obscure
(D) obfuscate

156. Micki is an <u>ardent</u> student of language, and she's always ready to learn something new.

(A) angry
(B) cheerful
(C) enthusiastic
(D) apathetic

157. All the students <u>admired</u> their teacher.

(A) respected
(B) feared
(C) despised
(D) liked

158. All Raven could see was a mile of <u>desolate</u> desert stretching out before him.

(A) apologetic
(B) plain
(C) sandy
(D) deserted

159. Jon is a bit <u>eccentric</u>, but that's never stopped him from fitting in.

(A) strange
(B) fanatical
(C) boorish
(D) creative

160. Most people know the article is <u>satire</u>, but those who don't come up with hilarious responses.

(A) parody
(B) factual
(C) complimentary
(D) odd

161. Three people made the same <u>suggestion</u>.

(A) proposition
(B) hint
(C) definition
(D) alliance

162. Jackson was incredibly <u>conscientious</u>, which made him popular among his superior officers.

(A) inattentive
(B) careful
(C) friendly
(D) dapper

163. There's no <u>ambiguity</u>; the First Amendment protects free speech.

(A) failure
(B) uncertainty
(C) alternative
(D) opacity

164. I tell you this with the <u>caveat</u> that you'll keep it a secret.

(A) threat
(B) apparition
(C) probability
(D) condition

165. There has been a <u>dramatic</u> decrease in homelessness.

(A) significant
(B) moderate
(C) unsettling
(D) dangerous

166. Tana never had reason to doubt JoAnn's <u>integrity</u>.

(A) turpitude
(B) tenacity
(C) honesty
(D) sweetness

167. They haven't been able to buy anything modern since the <u>embargo</u>.

(A) trade ban

(B) disagreement

(C) war

(D) blockade

168. The playground bully <u>mocked</u> the smaller kids every day.

(A) scared

(B) teased

(C) terrorized

(D) punched

169. You must give your <u>testimony</u> so the court can hear your side of the story.

(A) consultation

(B) recording

(C) statement

(D) attorney

170. You'll get used to military <u>jargon</u> by the time you graduate Basic Combat Training.

(A) language

(B) photography

(C) spotlight

(D) exercise

171. The hero was always ensuring that <u>justice</u> was served.

(A) judge

(B) capriciousness

(C) fairness

(D) honesty

172. Kathy and Bonnie walked down the <u>broad</u> staircase together.

(A) narrow

(B) rickety

(C) dangerous

(D) wide

173. As the slowest player, she was often the object of her teammates' <u>scorn</u>.

(A) anger

(B) teasing

(C) contempt

(D) laughter

174. David knew hiring Cheryl would prove <u>advantageous</u> to the company.

(A) thrilling

(B) ideal

(C) powerful

(D) beneficial

175. Heather put her climbing hook into the <u>crevice</u>.

(A) door

(B) narrow

(C) container

(D) crack

176. Jamie was an <u>enigma</u>, and his brother could never figure out why he was friendly one minute and confrontational the next.

(A) mystery

(B) conundrum

(C) bipolar

(D) elusive

177. Only the most <u>gullible</u> people believe that nonsense.

(A) feeble

(B) credulous

(C) confused

(D) difficult

178. "We can bring you as long as you promise not to be a <u>hindrance</u>," Jesse told the girl.

(A) interface

(B) impediment

(C) enigma

(D) traitor

179. Tim was <u>fortunate</u> enough to have a gift for woodworking.

(A) lucky
(B) happy
(C) comforted
(D) strained

180. The general was a <u>formidable</u> man.

(A) meticulous
(B) intimidating
(C) mean
(D) deadly

181. Tina was <u>anxious</u> about the outcome of the trial.

(A) calm
(B) content
(C) transfixed
(D) worried

182. Nothing could <u>deter</u> Sadie from her goal of becoming a psychologist.

(A) discourage
(B) flip
(C) admonish
(D) persuade

183. Jill removed the <u>obstruction</u> so Traci and Donna could get on the stage.

(A) hazard
(B) barrier
(C) cone
(D) danger

184. The puppy ate with <u>zeal</u>.

(A) sluggishness
(B) hunger
(C) lethargy
(D) enthusiasm

185. You must be careful not to <u>alienate</u> your supporters.

(A) evacuate
(B) evict
(C) estrange
(D) confuse

186. The commander told the first sergeant to <u>reprimand</u> the soldiers.

(A) fire
(B) scold
(C) teach
(D) imprison

187. Pili never worried about <u>trivial</u> details.

(A) unimportant
(B) dangerous
(C) large
(D) corresponding

188. Simon could <u>distinguish</u> Spanish from English at an early age.

(A) put out
(B) speak
(C) understand
(D) differentiate

189. Paloma is <u>adept</u> at winning over strangers.

(A) poor
(B) skilled
(C) invigorated
(D) encouraging

190. A <u>strident</u> voice interrupted the rally to demand answers about the candidate's tax returns.

(A) hushed
(B) strained
(C) loud
(D) hoarse

191. Beto could no longer <u>abide</u> the homeowners' association's "No Parking" rules.

(A) tolerate

(B) acknowledge

(C) read

(D) extend

192. The antique vase was <u>authentic</u>.

(A) fake

(B) replicated

(C) disputed

(D) genuine

193. Andrew was prepared to face the <u>consequences</u> of supporting a losing candidate.

(A) concerns

(B) results

(C) punishments

(D) orders

194. Jesse's speech was <u>concise</u>.

(A) lengthy

(B) succinct

(C) expressive

(D) sharp

195. Shanna couldn't shake her <u>trepidation</u> as she walked down the narrow stairs.

(A) disquiet

(B) tremors

(C) trestle

(D) umbrage

196. Krista <u>supplemented</u> her income by taking a job at the local paper.

(A) drained

(B) increased

(C) tracked

(D) used

197. "The <u>onus</u> is on you," Matt said to the prosecutor.

(A) idea

(B) consequences

(C) responsibility

(D) assignation

198. The <u>lavish</u> décor made the boys feel out of place.

(A) modern

(B) frugal

(C) opulent

(D) disgusting

199. I pledge <u>allegiance</u> to the flag.

(A) life

(B) subordination

(C) loyalty

(D) individuality

200. The child had a <u>voracious</u> appetite for sweets.

(A) careful

(B) insatiable

(C) dangerous

(D) satisfactory

Antonyms

201. The word most opposite in meaning to <u>construct</u> is

(A) fabricate.

(B) raise.

(C) destroy.

(D) organize.

202. The word most opposite in meaning to <u>deficiency</u> is

(A) surplus.

(B) fault.

(C) paucity.

(D) shortage.

203. The word most opposite in meaning to vilify is

(A) slander.

(B) traduce.

(C) approve.

(D) serve.

204. The word most opposite in meaning to barren is

(A) infecund.

(B) fruitful.

(C) fallow.

(D) parched.

205. The word most opposite in meaning to fascinate is

(A) tantalize.

(B) bore.

(C) transport.

(D) charm.

206. The word most opposite in meaning to dissect is

(A) slice.

(B) contribute.

(C) combine.

(D) bring.

207. The word most opposite in meaning to quantify is

(A) appraise.

(B) measure.

(C) guess.

(D) rank.

208. The word most opposite in meaning to vacant is

(A) unengaged.

(B) empty.

(C) overflowing.

(D) taken.

209. The word most opposite in meaning to abdicate is

(A) keep.

(B) exercise.

(C) relinquish.

(D) surrender.

210. The word most opposite in meaning to delay is

(A) rescind.

(B) problem.

(C) rush.

(D) stop.

211. The word most opposite in meaning to sanction is

(A) deny.

(B) allow.

(C) confirm.

(D) recommend.

212. The word most opposite in meaning to worthy is

(A) valueless.

(B) admirable.

(C) horrible.

(D) exemplary.

213. The word most opposite in meaning to energetic is

(A) brisk.

(B) lazy.

(C) spirited.

(D) vivacious.

214. The word most opposite in meaning to pinnacle is

(A) obelisk.

(B) apex.

(C) pyramid.

(D) bottom.

215. The word most opposite in meaning to approve is

(A) esteem.

(B) condemn.

(C) respect.

(D) admire.

216. The word most opposite in meaning to confidence is

(A) doubt.

(B) impudence.

(C) morale.

(D) tenacity.

217. The word most opposite in meaning to ungainly is

(A) adroit.

(B) uncouth.

(C) ponderous.

(D) blundering.

218. The word most opposite in meaning to twirl is

(A) twist.

(B) revolve.

(C) gyrate.

(D) straighten.

219. The word most opposite in meaning to strife is

(A) warfare.

(B) animosity.

(C) accord.

(D) dispute.

220. The word most opposite in meaning to revolt is

(A) rebel.

(B) displease.

(C) mutiny.

(D) obey.

221. The word most opposite in meaning to align is

(A) adjust.

(B) disorganize.

(C) range.

(D) order.

222. The word most opposite in meaning to furor is

(A) calm.

(B) outcry.

(C) agitation.

(D) calamity.

223. The word most opposite in meaning to bewilder is

(A) mystify.

(B) enlighten.

(C) muddle.

(D) domesticate.

224. The word most opposite in meaning to detriment is

(A) liability.

(B) prejudice.

(C) handicap.

(D) advantage.

225. The word most opposite in meaning to miniature is

(A) diminutive.

(B) large.

(C) reduced.

(D) miniscule.

226. The word most opposite in meaning to depreciate is

(A) downgrade.

(B) diminish.

(C) abate.

(D) enlarge.

227. The word most opposite in meaning to
clique is

(A) barrage.

(B) cabal.

(C) individual.

(D) crew.

228. The word most opposite in meaning to
dejected is

(A) elated.

(B) crestfallen.

(C) doleful.

(D) abject.

229. The word most opposite in meaning to
cowardice is

(A) weakness.

(B) mettle.

(C) timidity.

(D) diffidence.

230. The word most opposite in meaning to
mend is

(A) rejuvenate.

(B) recondition.

(C) amend.

(D) destroy.

231. The word most opposite in meaning to
peal is

(A) blast.

(B) eeriness.

(C) quiet.

(D) clamor.

232. The word most opposite in meaning to
cognizance is

(A) jurisdiction.

(B) bearing.

(C) ignorance.

(D) thoughtlessness.

233. The word most opposite in meaning to
tact is

(A) coarseness.

(B) rhythm.

(C) felicity.

(D) style.

234. The word most opposite in meaning to
criticize is

(A) approve.

(B) censure.

(C) chide.

(D) blame.

235. The word most opposite in meaning to
germane is

(A) apropos.

(B) pertinent.

(C) irrelevant.

(D) cognate.

236. The word most opposite in meaning to
renowned is

(A) acclaimed.

(B) distinguished.

(C) noted.

(D) common.

237. The word most opposite in meaning to
fluke is

(A) incident.

(B) plan.

(C) fortuitous.

(D) break.

238. The word most opposite in meaning to
incongruous is

(A) consistent.

(B) discordant.

(C) irregular.

(D) incoherent.

239. The word most opposite in meaning to bulky is

(A) airy.

(B) unwieldy.

(C) awkward.

(D) substantial.

240. The word most opposite in meaning to drench is

(A) submerge.

(B) teem.

(C) dehydrate.

(D) cover.

241. The word most opposite in meaning to stubborn is

(A) intractable.

(B) flexible.

(C) adamant.

(D) persistent.

242. The word most opposite in meaning to adolescence is

(A) youth.

(B) juvenility.

(C) boyhood.

(D) adulthood.

243. The word most opposite in meaning to ordinary is

(A) abnormal.

(B) abysmal.

(C) general.

(D) natural.

244. The word most opposite in meaning to lucrative is

(A) fruitful.

(B) lucid.

(C) remunerative.

(D) unprofitable.

245. The word most opposite in meaning to impregnable is

(A) fortified.

(B) questionable.

(C) invincible.

(D) breakable.

246. The word most opposite in meaning to introduction is

(A) induction.

(B) conclusion.

(C) preliminary.

(D) inauguration.

247. The word most opposite in meaning to apathy is

(A) indifference.

(B) lethargy.

(C) interest.

(D) lassitude.

248. The word most opposite in meaning to enduring is

(A) temporary.

(B) permanent.

(C) abiding.

(D) continual.

249. The word most opposite in meaning to ersatz is

(A) counterfeit.

(B) synthetic.

(C) genuine.

(D) bogus.

250. The word most opposite in meaning to ravenous is

(A) satisfied.

(B) greedy.

(C) insatiable.

(D) voracious.

Chapter **2**

Paragraph Comprehension: Understanding What You Read

The Paragraph Comprehension subtest on the ASVAB is an important part of the Armed Forces Qualification Test, or AFQT. That's because the military wants to know whether you can understand what you've read so you can implement it or pass it on to others — both of which are key components of successful military service.

To do well on this subtest, you need to have strong reading comprehension skills. You also have to be able to draw your own conclusions from what you've read. The questions on this part of the ASVAB are random excerpts and passages that cover several topics (this is one more way the military can tell that you're versatile and resilient!). You'll have 22 minutes to answer 11 Paragraph Comprehension questions on the computerized ASVAB or 13 minutes to answer 15 questions on the paper version.

The Questions You'll Work On

The questions on the Paragraph Comprehension subtest ask you to do the following:

>> **Find specific information:** These questions ask you to find details in a passage, such as a date or a name.

>> **Determine the main idea:** These questions want you to pull together all the information from a passage to sum it up in one main idea. Questions that say, "A good title for this passage might be . . ." are just main-idea questions in disguise.

>> **Find a word's meaning in its native habitat:** These questions ask you to figure out what a word means in the context of the passage.

>> **Draw conclusions:** These questions ask you to draw a conclusion based on what you've read.

What to Watch Out For

When you're answering the Paragraph Comprehension questions in this chapter, keep these tips in mind:

>> Skim the passage and read the question. Then go back to the passage to find the answer.

>> Select the correct answer based on the passage rather than your personal knowledge or opinion on the subject.

>> Answer choices that include the word *all, none, always, never,* or some other absolute are rarely correct, so think twice before you settle on one of these answers.

Set 1 (15 Questions)

Questions 251 and 252 are based on the following passage.

All forms of leadership make use of power. The term comes (indirectly) from the Latin adjective potis ("powerful, capable") and verb posse ("to be able to"). Power is about control. To have power is to possess the capacity to control change or to direct it. Power need not be coercive, dictatorial, or punitive. It can be used in a non-coercive manner, for instance to orchestrate, mobilize, direct, and guide members of an institution or organization in the pursuit of a goal or series of objectives. The central issue of power in leadership is not "Will it be used?" but rather "Will it be used wisely and well?"

251. What would be a good title for this passage?

(A) "Famous Powerful Leaders"

(B) "Defining Power"

(C) "Uses of Power"

(D) "Change through Power"

252. According to the passage, the central issue of power in leadership is

(A) whether someone will exercise it.

(B) that dictators use it.

(C) whether it will be used wisely and well.

(D) that you must have a series of objectives in mind.

253. Cultures differ because people live in different conditions, be they ecological, economic, social, or what have you. For example, each culture is ultimately a unique adaptation to the social and environmental conditions in which it evolves.

According to the passage, it is reasonable to assume that

(A) every culture develops its own values.

(B) all cultures share at least one thing in common.

(C) people from most cultures will never see eye-to-eye on economic and social matters.

(D) geography is the primary factor in a culture's development.

254. Most of the fruits of your labors will not be immediate, which will contrast starkly and unfavorably with much of your day-to-day life. With a few clicks, anyone in Western society can research any topic on the Internet, shop for any merchandise, or chat with people anywhere in the world about any subject, however esoteric, at any time of the day or night.

The main idea of this passage is

(A) Western society's reliance on technology.

(B) how easy it is to shop online.

(C) sharing ideas with people in other parts of the world.

(D) the differences between delayed and instant gratification.

255. Humanity is susceptible to many diseases. Some are endemic (always present in a population), and some sweep rapidly through widespread populations as epidemics. Only in the last century or so — when diseases were well-enough understood by science — have large-scale disease-eradication programs been implemented.

According to the passage, endemic diseases are

(A) surprise illnesses that sweep through widespread populations.

(B) easily controllable.

(C) always present in a population.

(D) mostly eradicated by modern science.

256. These days, dog training isn't what it used to be. Owners don't have to feel bad about asking for help, which ends up being better for dog *and* human. Dog-training is a respectable career, and instead of training dogs to jump through hoops and trot among obstacles (which used to be the only type of dog-training available), modern trainers focus on helping people and dogs politely share the same space. Many dog owners take stock of their abilities and realize they're not cut out for the task of training their precious pups, so they hire an expert — no guilty feelings involved.

According to the passage,

(A) in the past, people who hired dog trainers felt guilty.

(B) most people don't want to train their own dogs.

(C) dog-sport enthusiasts and dog trainers have similar goals.

(D) people should feel guilty if they don't train their own dogs.

257. The most powerful statement came toward the end of Davis's acidic opinion. If the president of the United States or a military officer under his command deprived a citizen of the United States of their fundamental rights, "republican government is a failure, and there is an end of liberty regulated by law." Civil liberty and martial law "cannot endure together; the antagonism is irreconcilable; and, in the conflict, one or the other must perish."

According to the passage, what would happen if a government attempted to deprive an American citizen of fundamental rights?

(A) Someone would die.

(B) One side would fail miserably.

(C) Martial law would be inevitable.

(D) The government would fall.

258. Sieges of towns and villages that were strategically valuable to military commanders was exceptionally common. Abyei and Bukavu were two such towns. Kisangani and Goma each overlooked supply routes used by the enemy, and Sierra Leone and Liberia were known to be rich in diamonds, giving invading commanders good reason to lay siege to them.

The main theme of this passage is

(A) the importance of supply routes during war.

(B) why military commanders lay siege to certain areas.

(C) the value of diamonds in Sierra Leone and Liberia.

(D) common forms of extended battle during war.

259. Margaret found a place as nursery governess and felt rich with her small salary. As she said, she was 'fond of luxury', and her chief trouble was poverty. She found it harder to bear than the others because she could remember a time when home was beautiful, life full of ease and pleasure, and want of any kind unknown. She tried not to be envious or discontented, but it was very natural that the young girl should long for pretty things, gay friends, accomplishments, and a happy life.

According to the passage, Margaret struggles with

(A) poverty.

(B) jealousy.

(C) friends.

(D) both A and B.

260. The dry-goods stores were not down among the counting-houses, banks, and wholesale warerooms, where gentlemen most do congregate, but Jo found herself in that part of the city before she did a single errand, loitering along as if waiting for someone, examining engineering instruments in one window and samples of wool in another, with most unfeminine interest, tumbling over barrels, being half-smothered by descending bales, and hustled unceremoniously by busy men who looked as if they wondered 'how the deuce she got there'.

According to the passage, Jo is

(A) out of place.

(B) shopping for bales of hay.

(C) meeting a friend.

(D) late for an appointment.

261. This organization is called the nervous system. The nervous system is the body's communication network. Its function is often compared to the country's telephone system or the Internet. The nervous system allows any part of the body to be in contact with any other part of the body within a fraction of a second.

According to the passage, a person's nervous system

(A) communicates quickly and efficiently.

(B) makes the body work like a machine.

(C) is easily damaged.

(D) takes time to work properly.

262. The water pooled at the low end of the floor, and Celia watched as it dripped from the ceiling. She jumped at a sudden crack of thunder, and as the lights flickered, she wondered whether the roof would hold up much longer. She pulled her cloak tighter and withdrew to the corner, where she fervently hoped she'd make it through the night so she could continue her journey in the morning.

According to the passage, Celia is

(A) hiding in an abandoned shed.

(B) scared of thunder.

(C) cold and lonely.

(D) waiting for a storm to pass.

263. The 1933 Montevideo Convention on the Rights and Duties of States required entities to meet certain requirements to be legally recognized as states. For example, each entity that wanted statehood had to have a clearly defined territory, a permanent population rather than a transient one, a government of its own, and the ability to enter into relations with other states.

According to the passage, what does the Montevideo Convention require for an entity to be considered a state?

(A) A permanent population

(B) A defined territory

(C) A government

(D) All of the above

264. Stress affects everyone differently. Some of the emotional symptoms of stress can include avoiding others, feeling overwhelmed, or having a tough time relaxing. The physical symptoms of stress can include low energy, difficulty sleeping, and aches and pains.

A good title for this passage might be

(A) "Stress Is Different for Everyone."

(B) "Emotional and Physical Symptoms of Stress."

(C) "Why Stress Is Bad for Your Body."

(D) "Eating Disorders and Stress."

265. Nothing could be more simple. Indeed, it was all so simple that Fix and Passepartout felt their hearts beating as if they would crack. They were listening for the whistle agreed upon, when suddenly savage cries resounded in the air, accompanied by reports which certainly did not issue from the car where the duellists were. The reports continued in front and the whole length of the train. Cries of terror proceeded from the interior of the cars.

In this passage, the word *reports* means

(A) screams.

(B) news.

(C) gunshots.

(D) train whistles.

Set 2 (15 Questions)

266. I had remained indoors all day, for the weather had taken a sudden turn to rain, with high autumnal winds, and the Jezail bullet which I had brought back in one of my limbs as a relic of my Afghan campaign throbbed with dull persistence. With my body in one easy-chair and my legs upon another, I had surrounded myself with a cloud of newspapers until at last, saturated with the news of the day, I tossed them all aside and lay listless, watching the huge crest and monogram upon the envelope upon the table and wondering lazily who my friend's noble correspondent could be.

According to the passage, the writer was

(A) exhausted.

(B) wounded during a conflict.

(C) physically weak.

(D) careless.

267. The early motion picture industry appealed primarily to vision. Radio appeals primarily to hearing. Today's motion pictures and television make a combined appeal to vision and hearing. Other senses such as taste and smell play important roles in the food industry and the perfume industry.

This passage's main theme is

(A) how industries appeal to our senses.

(B) why the sense of smell is not involved in television.

(C) senses and the food industry.

(D) early motion pictures.

268. Despite his wealth and social background, Roosevelt struggled with the feeling that he was something of an outsider. He tried out for the football team but was cut because of his slender frame (now he was six feet and one and a half inches tall and weighed 146 pounds). He yearned to be admitted to the Porcellian, the most exclusive social club on campus, as his cousin (and then President) Theodore Roosevelt had been before him, but he was not invited.

This passage is about

(A) Theodore Roosevelt.

(B) Theodore Roosevelt's cousin.

(C) a Harvard graduate.

(D) a famous football player.

269. Cognatic descent is more flexible than unilineal descent because it allows people to track their relationships to the families of each parent. Slightly less than half the world's peoples traditionally use or have used this system; although people in the U.S. typically use the last name of the male parent in naming (which seems to imply unilineal descent), they're actually interested in (and make social and economic use of) the relations of both parents' families, so U.S. residents actually practice cognatic descent.

According to the passage, cognatic descent is the practice of tracing

(A) descent through paternal lines.

(B) descent through maternal lines.

(C) descent through maternal and paternal lines.

(D) genetic anomalies through nonparental descent.

Questions 270 and 271 are based on the following passage.

Unlike the scattered settlements people lived in before the Early Middle Ages, European villages — those in the past and those surviving today — typically feature a cluster of homes and farmland grouped around a church and a cemetery. The village essentially replaced the old, rural settlements because people found it more convenient and practical to live nearer to neighbors.

270. According to the passage, medieval villages included
   (A) castles and dwellings.
   (B) a church and a castle.
   (C) a church and a cemetery.
   (D) a cemetery and a castle.

271. According to the passage, villages were
   (A) mostly symbolic.
   (B) part of a scattered, rural landscape.
   (C) filled with rich farmland.
   (D) a replacement for antiquated living arrangements.

272. International trading such as this required a monetary medium that was stronger and more general than the many feudal currencies. The Byzantine besant played this role up until the twelfth century, but once European trade took off it was no longer satisfactory. The West now reverted to the minting of gold coins that Charlemagne had abandoned.

   The Byzantine besant was a
   (A) merchant.
   (B) form of currency.
   (C) type of fabric.
   (D) trading market.

273. To answer this question we need to consider whether any of the HSE content of bulk silicate Earth could have accreted prior to the Moon-forming event. The Moon is believed to have been formed during the last giant impact on Earth. Because of its large size (at least more massive than one-fourth of Mars), the projectile is expected to have been differentiated.

   According to the passage, the projectile that created our moon was
   (A) made from silicate.
   (B) large enough to break Earth in half.
   (C) undifferentiated.
   (D) larger than 25 percent of the size of Mars.

274. In addition to management-based regulation's use to address foodborne illnesses, workplace accidents, and the dangers of pollution, this form of legal intervention has been increasingly deployed by regulators around the world to address a wide variety of other public policy problems, including financial fraud, terrorist attacks, and pipeline explosions, among others. The growing application of management-based regulation emerges, at least in part, from the growing complexity of the organizational environments within which law is expected to change behavior and achieve socially desirable outcomes.

   The author of this passage would probably agree that management-based regulation is
   (A) necessary to deal with the complexities of the modern workplace.
   (B) one of the best ways to prevent terrorist attacks.
   (C) part of the emergence of new societies.
   (D) designed to regulate industry in general.

275. The traditional view of the juror was as a passive vessel. According to this view, jurors could sit quietly through the trial and remember all that was said and done. However, modern educational theory suggests that people need to be "active" learners – focused on the subject, organizing new material, and asking questions about it so that they understand it.

According to the passage, jurors today need to

(A) absorb the events of a trial.

(B) ask questions to understand.

(C) organize what they've learned.

(D) Both B and C are correct.

276. Amongst the other gods, we sometimes see allusions to their particular power and honours, and to the quarrels that derive from them: Athene, Poseidon, Apollo, Artemis, and Hera take part in the battle at Troy, though Zeus strictly forbids it.

According to the passage,

(A) Zeus forbids other gods from taking part in the battle at Troy.

(B) many mythological Greek gods fought among themselves.

(C) Zeus was the most powerful participant in the battle at Troy.

(D) Athene and Poseidon were the most honorable Greek gods.

277. Insect repellent never repels all the bugs, but you can find many remedies for stings and bites. Besides commercial ones, you can use tobacco or meat tenderizer, which has an enzyme (papain, from the papaya plant) that dissolves protein the insect left in you. But don't get it in your eyes — it'll dissolve your cornea, too.

A good title for this passage might be

(A) "Enzymes from the Papaya Plant."

(B) "Using Tobacco as Insect Repellent."

(C) "Remedies for Bug Bites and Stings."

(D) "Keep Bug Spray Away from Your Eyes."

278. On the birth of a second son, my junior by seven years, my parents gave up entirely their wandering life and fixed themselves in their native country. We possessed a house in Geneva, and a campagne on Belrive, the eastern shore of the lake, at the distance of rather more than a league from the city.

According to the passage, the writer's parents

(A) had three sons.

(B) had houses all over the country.

(C) lived about 20 miles from the city.

(D) used to travel.

Questions 279 and 280 are based on the following passage.

Several telescopes today monitor space for potentially harmful space debris, such as comets and asteroids. These pass by the Earth all the time, and NASA currently considers about a thousand asteroids ranging in size from basketballs to mountains to be potentially hazardous. This means they will probably pass very close to the Earth in the foreseeable future and have a chance of impacting the Earth. If an item about 2 kilometers (1.2 miles) across impacted the Earth at the proper velocity, the explosion would raise so much dust that it would block out the sun, an event that would cripple agriculture to the point that humanity may starve before the dust settled.

279. According to the passage, how many potentially hazardous asteroids is NASA monitoring?

(A) About 1,000

(B) Several thousand

(C) Only a few

(D) The passage doesn't say.

280. According to the passage, a potentially hazardous asteroid could

(A) create superstorms in Earth's atmosphere.

(B) wipe out all human life on Earth.

(C) pass close to Earth in the next year.

(D) block the sun as it passes.

Set 3 (15 Questions)

281. The first wavelength, 750 nanometers, induces the sensation we call "red." The second, 500 nanometers, induces the sensation we call "green." And 400 nanometers induces the sensation we call "violet." The language in the preceding sentences has been carefully chosen in order to make it clear that the "color" is not in the stimulus itself (i.e., a light wave), but is produced by the firing of a certain kind of photoreceptor.

According to the passage, we can see the color violet at a wavelength of

(A) 750 nanometers.

(B) 500 nanometers.

(C) 400 nanometers.

(D) The passage doesn't say.

282. Although lots of animals communicate in all kinds of ways — using scent, bodily postures, and even sounds — human communication by spoken language is particularly fast and conveys more information (and more subtle information) than any other system of communication. Importantly, human language also uses metaphor, in which one word can have several meanings.

According to the passage, animal communication often includes

(A) subtle information.

(B) bodily postures.

(C) metaphors.

(D) all of the above.

283. It is a common custom, in the part of Maryland from which I ran away, to part children from their mothers at a very early age. Frequently, before the child has reached its twelfth month, its mother is taken from it, and hired out on some farm a considerable distance off, and the child is placed under the care of an old woman, too old for field labor. For what this separation is done, I do not know, unless it be to hinder the development of the child's affection toward its mother, and to blunt and destroy the natural affection of the mother for the child. This is the inevitable result.

The author of this passage would probably agree that

(A) children should be separated from their mothers at some point.

(B) children are typically given to a relative after being separated from their mothers.

(C) children often run away to be with their mothers.

(D) separation of mothers and their babies prevents them from developing a bond.

Questions 284 and 285 are based on the following passage.

Companies typically did not like Jim Crow laws. They cost money that ate into the profits. The railroad companies had to add another car even if only one black passenger purchased a ticket for a train. Moreover, if the white cars were full, white passengers could not simply ride with black passengers as the segregation laws prohibited that too. A white man discovered riding in a car reserved for blacks faced the same criminal penalties as did Plessy.

284. Why didn't white people ride in the same train cars as black people, according to the passage?

(A) Both white and black people would be subject to criminal penalties.

(B) Railroads did not allow black passengers.

(C) The tickets cost more money.

(D) White people had no desire to ride in mixed railroad cars.

285. According to the passage, the main reason companies did not want laws that required segregation was that

(A) they caused customers inconvenience.

(B) they required white people to purchase more expensive tickets.

(C) they caused companies to lose money.

(D) they unfairly singled out railroad companies.

Questions 286 and 287 are based on the following passage.

The Hippocratic Oath itself is not a part of typical psychological training or practice, but its tenets are expected to be followed. In sum, the oath states that physicians or healers will not deliberately harm an individual who seeks their help; they will treat anyone who comes seeking their aid; they will not give a deadly drug if the patient requests it; and they keep all information about doctor-patient professional relationships confidential.

286. According to the passage, the Hippocratic Oath applies to

(A) doctors.

(B) psychologists.

(C) healthcare professionals.

(D) all of the above.

287. According to the passage, the Hippocratic Oath requires healthcare providers to

(A) treat anyone who comes to them for help.

(B) prescribe deadly drugs if patients request them.

(C) keep detailed records on patients.

(D) Both A and B are correct.

288. I commenced by inuring my body to hardship. I accompanied the whale-fishers on several expeditions to the North Sea; I voluntarily endured cold, famine, thirst, and want of sleep; I often worked harder than the common sailors during the day and devoted my nights to the study of mathematics, the theory of medicine, and those branches of physical science from which a naval adventurer might derive the greatest practical advantage.

It's reasonable to assume that the person in this passage

(A) was sold into indentured servitude.

(B) wanted to become tougher.

(C) studied physics.

(D) was a common sailor.

289. Some signs of this might include using words in unusual ways (or perhaps making up words), making irrelevant responses to questions, and having no connection between the ideas expressed. At times the connections between thoughts or sentences are arbitrary and difficult to follow. Note that all speech of schizophrenic individuals is not incoherent, just some of it, or certain parts during a discourse. Rules of grammar are often followed, and the words used by schizophrenics are usually not pieced together randomly.

A good title for this passage might be

(A) "Speech Patterns of Schizophrenic Patients."

(B) "Symptoms of Schizophrenia."

(C) "Thought Patterns of Schizophrenic Patients."

(D) "Signs That You May Be Schizophrenic."

290. It was half past six and the hands were quietly moving forwards, it was even later than half past, more like quarter to seven. Had the alarm clock not rung? He could see from the bed that it had been set for four o'clock as it should have been; it certainly must have rung. Yes, but was it possible to quietly sleep through that furniture-rattling noise? True, he had not slept peacefully, but probably all the more deeply because of that.

The alarm clock in the passage

(A) never went off.

(B) most likely went off nearly three hours before the man woke up.

(C) was not very loud.

(D) woke the man from a deep sleep.

291. The beach was a desert of heaps of sea and stones tumbling wildly about, and the sea did what it liked, and what it liked was destruction. It thundered at the town, and thundered at the cliffs, and brought the coast down, madly. The air among the houses was of so strong a piscatory flavour that one might have supposed sick fish went up to be dipped in it, as sick people went down to be dipped in the sea.

According to the passage,

(A) the sea was rough and loud near the shore.

(B) the air smelled good around the shore.

(C) fishermen brought sick fish into the town.

(D) a storm was coming in off the coast.

292. Holmes was certainly not a difficult man to live with. He was quiet in his ways, and his habits were regular. It was rare for him to be up after ten at night, and he had invariably breakfasted and gone out before I rose in the morning. Sometimes he spent his day at the chemical laboratory, sometimes in the dissecting-rooms, and occasionally in long walks, which appeared to take him into the lowest portions of the City.

According to the passage, Holmes

(A) was very physically active.

(B) got up early.

(C) was a chemist.

(D) gained new scientific knowledge.

293. With the small competence he possessed, eked out by such employment as he could pick up, he travelled from town to town through the United States in quest of his enemies. Year passed into year, his black hair turned grizzled, but still he wandered on, a human bloodhound, with his mind wholly set upon the one object upon which he had devoted his life.

The man in the passage is

(A) jobless and homeless.

(B) a private detective.

(C) extremely smart.

(D) searching for his enemies.

294. His nose was prodigiously long, crooked, and inflammatory; his eyes full, brilliant, and acute; his chin and cheeks, although wrinkled with age, were broad, puffy, and double; but of ears of any kind or character there was not a semblance to be discovered upon any portion of his head.

This passage describes

(A) a man with no ears.

(B) an overweight man.

(C) an old man.

(D) all of the above.

295. In Jacob's Island, the warehouses are roofless and empty; the walls are crumbling down; the windows are windows no more; the doors are falling into the streets; the chimneys are blackened, but they yield no smoke. Thirty or forty years ago, before losses and chancery suits came upon it, it was a thriving place; but now it is a desolate island indeed.

How long has it been since Jacob's Island was a thriving place?

(A) 40 or 50 years

(B) 30 or 40 years

(C) 20 or 30 years

(D) The passage does not say.

Set 4 (15 Questions)

296. In front was a quiet sunny landscape, a wheat field ahead on either side of the road, and the Maybury Inn with its swinging sign. I saw the doctor's cart ahead of me. At the bottom of the hill I turned my head to look at the hillside I was leaving. Thick streamers of black smoke shot with threads of red fire were driving up into the still air, and throwing dark shadows upon the green treetops eastward. The smoke already extended far away to the east and west—to the Byfleet pine woods eastward, and to Woking on the west.

What is the person in the passage doing?

(A) Lighting a fire

(B) Fleeing a fire

(C) Extinguishing a fire

(D) None of the above

Questions 297 and 298 are based on the following passage.

I came to typhoid fever—read the symptoms—discovered that I had typhoid fever, must have had it for months without knowing it—wondered what else I had got; turned up St. Vitus's Dance—found, as I expected, that I had that too,—began to get interested in my case, and determined to sift it to the bottom, and so started alphabetically—read up ague, and learnt that I was sickening for it, and that the acute stage would commence in about another fortnight. Bright's disease, I was relieved to find, I had only in a modified form, and, so far as that was concerned, I might live for years. Cholera I had, with severe complications; and diphtheria I seemed to have been born with. I plodded conscientiously through the twenty-six letters, and the only malady I could conclude I had not got was housemaid's knee.

297. This passage describes a person who

    (A) reads a medical book and believes he or she has most of the diseases it describes.

    (B) is a patient in a government hospital.

    (C) has a deadly illness.

    (D) caught an illness while moving across the country.

298. According to the passage, the illness the author does not have is

    (A) cholera.

    (B) the flu.

    (C) housemaid's knee.

    (D) Bright's disease.

299. I was a posthumous child. My father's eyes had closed upon the light of this world six months, when mine opened on it. There is something strange to me, even now, in the reflection that he never saw me; and something stranger yet in the shadowy remembrance that I have of my first childish associations with his white grave-stone in the churchyard, and of the indefinable compassion I used to feel for it lying out alone there in the dark night, when our little parlour was warm and bright with fire and candle, and the doors of our house were—almost cruelly, it seemed to me sometimes—bolted and locked against it.

According to the passage, what happened to the child's father?

    (A) He left the child with his own parents.

    (B) He died before the child was born.

    (C) He was killed shortly after the child was born.

    (D) The passage doesn't say what happened to the child's father.

300. The Pacific Railroad is joined by several branches in Iowa, Kansas, Colorado, and Oregon. On leaving Omaha, it passes along the left bank of the Platte River as far as the junction of its northern branch, follows its southern branch, crosses the Laramie territory and the Wahsatch Mountains, turns the Great Salt Lake, and reaches Salt Lake City, the Mormon capital, plunges into the Tuilla Valley, across the American Desert, Cedar and Humboldt Mountains, the Sierra Nevada, and descends, via Sacramento, to the Pacific—its grade, even on the Rocky Mountains, never exceeding one hundred and twelve feet to the mile.

According to the passage, how many states have branches of the Pacific Railroad?

    (A) Three

    (B) Four

    (C) Five

    (D) Six

301. Today we accord movie star status to many of our leaders. Some of them become cultural icons and cultural role models. For example, the president of the United States is, arguably, the most photographed person in the world.

According to this passage, we view many of our leaders as

    (A) presidents.

    (B) actors.

    (C) celebrities.

    (D) unimportant.

302. Five days after [Rosa] Parks was arrested, she was tried and convicted for disorderly conduct and fined ten dollars and four dollars for court costs. Emboldened by her courage and integrity, a city-wide bus boycott was organized under the leadership of the then 26-year-old Martin Luther King, Jr.

According to the passage, who organized the bus boycott?

(A) Martin Luther King, Jr.

(B) Rosa Parks

(C) City employees

(D) The court system

303. Abraham Lincoln's youthful love of learning freed him from his father's fate as a poor farmer and led him to a successful legal and political career. Although Lincoln had only one year of grade school education, his intellectual curiosity led him to read intensively – the Bible, Shakespeare, the law, and Euclid's geometry.

According to the passage, Abraham Lincoln didn't have to become a poor farmer like his father because

(A) his father taught him to read.

(B) he had a love of learning.

(C) he studied geometry.

(D) he did not enjoy farming.

304. In Saxony the importance of the principle of selection in regard to Merino sheep is so fully recognised, that men follow it as a trade: the sheep are placed on a table and are studied, like a picture by a connoisseur; this is done three times at intervals of months, and the sheep are each time marked and classed, so that the very best may ultimately be selected for breeding.

The main idea of this passage is

(A) how to classify sheep.

(B) the trade of shepherding.

(C) the study of Merino sheep.

(D) the selection of Merino sheep for breeding.

Questions 305 and 306 are based on the following passage.

As Friday, May 24 dawned, Britain's War Cabinet faced an impending calamity. Ten days before, German armored columns had broken out of the Ardennes forest and started an almost unopposed drive across the center of France. French counter-attacks from the south had been turned back with ease, the Belgian army was cut off and surrounded, and German forces were pressing closely against the British Expeditionary Force, which had retreated to a few Channel enclaves.

305. According to the passage, what day did German armored columns break out of the Ardennes forest?

(A) May 24

(B) May 14

(C) May 25

(D) The passage does not say.

306. According to the passage, who were the French attacking?

(A) The British military

(B) The German military

(C) The Belgian military

(D) The passage does not say.

307. The mural he was working on depicted a very neat garden. Men and women in white, doctors and nurses, turned the soil, planted seedlings, sprayed bugs, spread fertilizer. Men and women in purple uniforms pulled up weeds, cut down plants that were old and sickly, raked leaves, carried refuse to trash-burners.

What might be a good title for this passage?

(A) "What to Wear in the Garden"

(B) "How to Paint a Garden"

(C) "The Mural"

(D) "What to Do with Weeds"

308. Buck did not read the newspapers, or he would have known that trouble was brewing, not alone for himself, but for every tide-water dog, strong of muscle and with warm, long hair, from Puget Sound to San Diego. Because men, groping in the Arctic darkness, had found a yellow metal, and because steamship and transportation companies were booming the find, thousands of men were rushing into the Northland. These men wanted dogs, and the dogs they wanted were heavy dogs, with strong muscles by which to toil, and furry coats to protect them from the frost.

What does the passage say is going to cause trouble for Buck and the other local dogs?

(A) Steamship traffic

(B) Adventurers

(C) Gold prospectors

(D) Dog breeders

309. He determined that he would believe nothing which he did not see quite clearly and distinctly to be true. Whatever he could bring himself to doubt, he would doubt, until he saw reason for not doubting it. By applying this method he gradually became convinced that the only existence of which he could be quite certain was his own.

The main idea of this passage is a man's

(A) madness.

(B) skepticism.

(C) innovation.

(D) beliefs.

310. When school hours were over, he was even the companion and playmate of the larger boys and on holiday afternoons would convoy some of the smaller ones home, who happened to have pretty sisters, or good housewives for mothers, noted for the comforts of the cupboard. Indeed, it behooved him to keep on good terms with his pupils.

The person the passage describes is most likely a

(A) teenager.

(B) teacher.

(C) father.

(D) bus driver.

Set 5 (15 Questions)

311. No "early worm," however, tempts him from his grassy nest, for the seeds in the pasture lands and certain tiny insects that live among the grass furnish meals at all hours. He simply delights in the cool, still morning and evening hours and in giving voice to his enjoyment of them.

This passage describes a bird that

(A) eats only in the morning.

(B) sings throughout the day.

(C) is close to starving.

(D) eats bugs throughout the day.

312. Darnley was eighteen years of age: he was handsome, well-made, elegant; he talked in that attractive manner of the young nobles of the French and English courts that Mary no longer heard since her exile in Scotland; she let herself be deceived by these appearances, and did not see that under this brilliant exterior Darnley hid utter insignificance, dubious courage, and a fickle and churlish character.

The author of this passage would probably agree that

(A) Darnley was a manipulative person.

(B) Mary was naïve.

(C) Mary wanted to live in France.

(D) Darnley was a nobleman.

313. At these words, she grew frightfully pale, and, looking about her with a bewildered air, and as if she were about to faint, she leaned against an arm-chair; then, soon, not being able to stand upright, she sat down, threw back her head, and plunged into a mournful reverie.

You can assume that the woman in this passage

(A) cries often.

(B) has just heard bad news.

(C) discovered that she is sick.

(D) became irritated quickly.

314. Wherever the flooring rose slightly towards the edges of the sea of ice, the usual structure appeared again. There were no currents of air in the cave, the candles burning steadily through the whole time of our visit. Excepting for the purpose of detecting disturbance in the air, there is no need of candles, as the two holes in the roof supply sufficient light.

According to this passage, the purpose of the candles was

(A) to provide light.

(B) to detect changes in the air.

(C) to warm the ice cave.

(D) not stated in the paragraph.

315. A few seasons ago I feared the tribe of bluebirds were on the verge of extinction from the enormous number of them that perished from cold and hunger in the South in the winter of '94. For two summers not a blue wing, not a blue warble.

According to this passage, the author is worried that

(A) he will no longer be able to feed the birds in his yard.

(B) bluebirds will go extinct.

(C) many birds died from hunger and illness.

(D) more birds will die in the future.

316. The little Frenchman Martin, the master builder, was another character in his way; a lively, energetic little fellow, whose eyes were everywhere. Not the driving in of a single nail escaped him. Yet, with all his watchfulness, he did more work than any three of his men. The habitual use of salt pork and beans, added to the total absence of vegetable diet during the long winter and summer, had caused scurvy to break out among the men, and poor Martin was suffering very much from it.

According to the passage, what caused Martin's illness?

(A) Scurvy

(B) Lack of rest

(C) Lack of vegetables

(D) Winter weather

317. His choleric temperament had often brought him into trouble from which the magistrates of Roily-le-Tors, like indulgent and prudent friends, had extricated him. Had he not one day thrown the conductor of the diligence from the top of his seat because he came near running over his retriever, Micmac? Had he not broken the ribs of a gamekeeper who abused him for having, gun in hand, passed through a neighbor's property? Had he not even caught by the collar the sub-prefect, who stopped over in the village during an administrative circuit, called by Monsieur Renardet an electioneering circuit, for he was opposed to the government, in accordance with family traditions.

From its use in the passage, you can infer that *choleric* means

(A) funny.

(B) irritable.

(C) cheerful.

(D) shy.

318. Leaders can simply be guilty of making an honest mistake. Or they can be lazy, maladroit, sleazy, or ignoble. They can also be tyrannical megalomaniacs. They can lack cognitive intelligence, emotional intelligence, or practical intelligence. Worse, they can be malignant narcissists who are sadistically aggressive and sociopathic in their relations with all others: friends, foes, family, and followers.

What might be a good title for this paragraph?

(A) "Describing Dictators"

(B) "Ingredients for a Tyrant"

(C) "How to Make a Monster"

(D) "Shortcomings That Identify Bad Leaders"

319. Surprised at two o'clock in the morning by two Austrian divisions, which, concealed by the village of San Gervasio, had reached the right bank of the Adda without their being discovered, the soldiers defending the castle of Trezzo abandoned it and beat a retreat.

What did the soldiers abandon?

(A) A castle

(B) A river

(C) The Austrian Army

(D) San Gervasio

320. Power is about control. To have power is to possess the capacity to control change or to direct it. Power need not be coercive, dictatorial, or punitive. It can be used in a non-coercive manner, for instance to orchestrate, mobilize, direct, and guide members of an institution or organization in the pursuit of a goal or series of objectives.

The author of this passage would probably agree that

(A) powerful people tend to have dictator-like qualities.

(B) power can be used in a positive way.

(C) the sole purpose of power is to have control over something.

(D) power should be used to coerce people into doing things you want them to do.

Questions 321 and 322 are based on the following passage.

Dissociation can be defined where a set of activities, thoughts, or emotions become separated from the rest of the individual's personality and function independently of him or her. The individual may feel detached, unreal, have a sense of déjà vu, or may feel numb in relation to specific events, in this case extreme trauma.

321. What might be a good title for this passage?

    (A) "Functions of Personality"

    (B) "The Personality Disorder of Dissociation"

    (C) "Déjà Vu As a Personality Disorder"

    (D) "Dissociation Defined"

322. According to the passage, what becomes separated from a person's personality in dissociation?

    (A) Emotions

    (B) Activities

    (C) Thoughts

    (D) All of the above

323. And this is Christmas, and the world is supposed to be civilised. They came in from the trenches to-day with blue faces and chattering teeth, and it was all one could do to get them warm and fed. By this evening they were most of them revived enough to enjoy Xmas cards; there were such a nice lot that they were able to choose them to send to Mother and My Young Lady and the Missis and the Children, and have one for themselves.

You can assume that this passage takes place

    (A) in the winter.

    (B) in Russia.

    (C) in a hospital.

    (D) Both A and C are correct.

324. Do not enter a store unless you have some errand. Ask for what you want as explicitly as possible and do not take the time of the attendants by examining fifty things that you do not want. If you do not intend to purchase goods but wish to examine them for future selections, say so. Never try to cheapen goods. If the price is too high for the quality offered, or will not suit your purse, look elsewhere for what will better suit you. Do not stand hesitating at a counter. Make up your mind quickly or leave the store to make your decision, even if you return again. Be careful not to injure goods by handling.

This passage describes

    (A) how to choose products at a store.

    (B) shopping etiquette.

    (C) being kind to attendants.

    (D) why you should avoid bargaining.

325. Henry IV, who insisted that every peasant should have a fowl in his pot, was often referred to as "Good King Henry." He ruled France from 1589 to 1610, and during that time, he was the target of at least one dozen assassination attempts. He became more popular after his death and was remembered for his uncommon concern for his subjects' welfare.

You can infer from the passage that

    (A) Henry IV cared about his subjects.

    (B) Henry IV was killed during his reign.

    (C) Henry IV was popular throughout his reign.

    (D) Henry IV ruled all of Europe.

Set 6 (15 Questions)

326. The man who affects a supercilious disdain for all foreign customs and forms will not convince the natives of his vast superiority. Rather, he will impress them with the belief that he is an ill-bred idiot. The most polite, as well as agreeable travelers are those who will smilingly devour mouse-pie and bird's-nest soup in China, dine contentedly upon horse-steak in Paris, swallow their beef uncooked in Germany, maintain an unwinking gravity over the hottest curry in India, smoke their hookah gratefully in Turkey, mount an elephant in Ceylon, and, in short, conform gracefully to any native custom, however strange it may appear to him.

The main idea of this passage is

(A) situations a man may encounter while traveling.

(B) why it's important to fit in with local cultures while traveling.

(C) whether you should be disdainful of other cultures while traveling.

(D) how to impress natives while traveling.

327. Known collectively as the New Deal, these programs included money and banking regulations, laws setting minimum wages and maximum hours, public works, housing development, social security for retirees, conservation of natural resources, and farm subsidies.

The set of programs listed in the passage were known as

(A) farm subsidies.

(B) general subsidies.

(C) the New Deal.

(D) the Collective Deal.

328. As a rural commune of the Ségou Region of southern-central Mali, Diouna covers approximately 175 square kilometers. Diouna includes a total of 11 villages, and the population comprises about 9,200 people. Diouna is located 49 kilometers east of Ségou, and it serves as what many Americans call the "county seat" of the region, which is essentially the governmental center of a county.

According to the passage,

(A) Diouna is a commune.

(B) Diouna is a city.

(C) Diouna is located inside the city of Ségou.

(D) None of the above are correct.

329. Made from three upright stones that form the shape of an "H" that all support a thick roofing stone, France's Caixa de Rotllan is a historic monument and has been listed as such since 1889. The stones have never been examined by geologists; neither has the building been excavated by archaeologists.

This passage is about

(A) stones in an old building.

(B) the Caixa de Rotllan.

(C) geology and archaeology.

(D) ancient architecture.

330. A position paper is simply an essay that presents an opinion — yours, your boss's, or someone else's — and it's intended for publication in newspapers, trade journals, and other outlets. These papers can enable discussion, or they can propose specific solutions. Many large organizations use position papers to share their official beliefs and recommendations.

According to the passage, position papers

(A) can be published in newspapers.

(B) can outline a company's history.

(C) are intended to change someone's mind.

(D) All of the above are true.

331. Improper pruning causes extensive damage and sometimes, tree death. To prune your trees without causing damage, your knife needs to be sharp. You should use a handsaw for anything you can't cut with a knife or pruning shears. Get a horticultural disinfectant so you don't spread plant diseases. If you prune in the wrong spots, spread disease or prune with dull tools, you'll do more harm than good.

From this passage, you can infer that

(A) all trees need to be pruned.

(B) pruning shears are a necessity.

(C) you could kill trees through improper pruning.

(D) it may be fine to use a dull handsaw.

332. Using Socrates as main interlocutor in the dialogue and presumably as his spokesman, Plato argues that the central problem of politics is to organize the state so as to place control in the hands of individuals who understand that you cannot make people happy by simply making them richer or more powerful than their neighbors. Socrates is convinced that, so long as knowledge is only valued as a means to power and wealth, the helm of the ship of state will be sought after by ambitious individuals who are only motivated by status and profit.

The main theme of this passage is

(A) Plato's beliefs on power and wealth.

(B) Socrates's beliefs on political control.

(C) Plato's ideas on making people happy.

(D) Plato's and Socrates's political leanings.

333. Paradoxically, perhaps, the critical and final "end" task or job of a leader is to make oneself irrelevant or unnecessary. That is, the "end" task of leadership is to make everyone a leader of his or her own job or unit. Leadership is not a sacred totem in itself.

The author of this passage would probably agree that a leader's main job is

(A) to make him- or herself unnecessary.

(B) to shape future leaders.

(C) to command large numbers of people.

(D) Both A and B are correct.

334. Bonhoeffer argued that, whereas earlier forms of leadership were associated with a statesman, a father, or a benefactor, the new leadership of Germany, the *Verführer*, was self-derived, self-defined, self-justifying, and completely and terrifyingly authoritarian. Bonhoeffer went on to claim that this new *Führer Prinzip* (leadership principle) arose from the post-First World War generation in Germany, which was seeking meaning, guidance, direction, and purpose. Both Bonhoeffer and Drucker suggest that the central idea of the *Führer Prinzip* is a bastardization of Friedrich Nietzsche's concept of the *Übermensch*, leader and superman.

According to this passage, the authoritarian form of leadership was

(A) Führer Prinzip.

(B) Übermensch.

(C) Verführer.

(D) Both B and C are correct.

335. Bilberry goats are completely feral, but their herd is led by a dominant nanny. The species looks unlike any other found in the United Kingdom because each goat has a shaggy coat and large horns. These goats are nearing extinction; there are only about 50 of them living in the wild.

According to the passage, what is different about Bilberry goats?

(A) Bilberry goats have shaggy coats.

(B) Bilberry goats have large horns.

(C) Bilberry goat herds are led by a nanny.

(D) Both A and B are correct.

336. When you see one kinglet about, you may be sure there are others not far away, for, except in the nesting season, its habits are distinctly social, its friendliness extending to the humdrum brown creeper, the chickadees, and the nuthatches, in whose company it is often seen; indeed, it is likely to be in almost any flock of the winter birds.

What might be a good title for this passage?

(A) "Winter Birds and Their Habitats"

(B) "Brown Creepers and Chickadees"

(C) "Characteristics of the Kinglet"

(D) "Social Traits of the Kinglet"

337. By some mistake it hasn't rained all day, so we took the opportunity to get on with painting the train. We worked all the morning and afternoon and got a lot done. It looks very smart with huge red crosses on white squares in the middle of each coach and the number of the ward in figures a foot long at each end, this on both sides of the coaches. We have done not quite half the coaches and are praying that it won't rain before it dries. If it does, the result is pitiable.

The speaker in this passage is most likely talking about

(A) the bad weather she has experienced.

(B) an ambulance.

(C) a hospital train.

(D) art and rain.

338. The radio show's producer, who often appeared on-air as "The Beaver," was actually a twenty-something named Bill who sacrificed his personal comfort (and sometimes, his dignity) to make the audience laugh. Bill's voice — and antics — appeared on hundreds of shows throughout the show's history.

According to the passage, "The Beaver" was

(A) a main character of the show.

(B) a radio show producer.

(C) a comedian.

(D) famous.

339. If character is living out what we value, conscience is its inner counterpart, that part of us that makes judgments and evaluations about when, how, and with whom that value should or should not be applied. Conscience is frequently the first step in making a moral decision, the internal uneasiness that prompts us to ask ourselves some hard questions.

According to the passage, conscience

(A) is the gatekeeper of character.

(B) helps us avoid hard questions.

(C) ensures that we don't judge others.

(D) is the opposite of our character.

340. One's chances are increased if the person has one or more of the following characteristics: they are single, they come from a Westernized or industrialized nation, they come from a lower socioeconomic status, they live in an urban area, they had problems while in utero, they were born during the winter, or they had recently experienced some extreme stress.

According to the passage, a person's chances are increased if he or she

(A) is single and wealthy.

(B) is from an industrialized nation and lives in an urban area.

(C) had problems in utero and was born in the summer.

(D) was born during winter and rarely experienced stress.

Set 7 (15 Questions)

341. To capture the distinction, anthropologist Anna Lowenhaupt Tsing (2005) has suggested that we adopt the metaphor of "friction" rather than that of movement in thinking about globalization. Whereas conventional discourse of globalization inflects the notion of mobility (i.e. capital flows freely), the idea of "friction" reminds us that movement of any sort can only occur with engagement.

The main theme of this passage is

(A) Anna Lowenhaupt Tsing.

(B) mobility.

(C) friction.

(D) globalization.

342. The minute particles of two of the substances for many years classed as elements give off electrons; uranium and thorium are radioactive. Electrons are produced by sending an electric discharge through very small traces of different gases, using electrodes of different metals. Electrons are also produced by exposing various metals to the action of ultraviolet light, and by raising the temperature of various metals to incandescence.

According to this passage,

(A) electrons send electric discharges through gas.

(B) ultraviolet light cannot produce electrons.

(C) uranium is radioactive.

(D) incandescent metals react to ultraviolet light.

343. When you buy things made closer to home, you'll cut down your carbon footprint. Local businesses tend to buy from other local businesses, as well, so money stays within the community. Typically, local entrepreneurs are more connected to the community (after all, they live here, too).

The author of this passage would probably agree that

(A) local business owners care about their own communities.

(B) it's better to buy from local businesses.

(C) local businesses will save you money.

(D) both A and B are correct.

344. It was a long house, not very high, yet containing some good-sized bedrooms on the upper story, and rooms below calculated for the entertainment of a much greater company than ever appeared now upon the deserted highroad. It had been an old coaching road, and there were stables at the Seven Thorns which could take in half the horses in the county; but that, of course, was all over now. The greater part of these stables were shut up and falling into decay. So was the large dining room and half of the extensive accommodation downstairs. The great kitchen, and a little room on the other side of the doorway, which was called the parlour, were all that was ever wanted now in the Seven Thorns.

From this passage, you can infer that

(A) the house is the tallest in the community.

(B) fewer people travel the road than did before.

(C) the house is haunted.

(D) the owners didn't care about Seven Thorns.

345. Lillie sat on the floor in front of the grate, her chin on her hands, her eyes fixed on the bright fire. Frank was watching the door, in a very unnatural sort of quietness for a boy, with Tan curled up at his feet; and Jennie was nervously tearing off the corners of her book, since it had grown too dark to read it, thinking that Miss Lane was a very long time in taking off her cloak.

Based on this passage, you can assume that

(A) girls are often destructive.

(B) adults are typically slow.

(C) children are usually nervous.

(D) boys are naturally loud.

346. It looked old-fashioned, but not old, and was in perfect repair. When the sun shone down the beech avenue, which faced to the west, it turned the old bricks of the house into a sort of glorified ruddiness, blended of all the warmest tones—red and russet, and brown and orange, with a touch of black relieving it here and there. The effect in autumn, when all those warm tints which, by the alchemy of nature, bring beauty out of the chilly frost and unlovely decay—was as if all the colors in the rainbow had been poured forth; but all so toned and subdued by infinite gradation that the most violent notes of color were chastened into harmony.

The passage describes the house in what season?

(A) Winter

(B) Spring

(C) Summer

(D) Fall

347. Careful experiments have shown that when one body parts with its energy, the energy is not destroyed but transferred to another body or system of bodies. Just as energy cannot be destroyed, neither can it be created. If one body gains a certain amount of energy, some other body has lost an equivalent amount.

What might be a good title for this passage?

(A) "Experiments in Energy"

(B) "The Transfer of Energy"

(C) "How Particles Gain Energy"

(D) "Energy Cannot Be Created"

348. Even with the best manual in hand, you must not expect to be able to identify every new bird at the first attempt, for some species are either exceedingly shy or obscurely marked, or probably both, while quite a number are so much alike in markings and habits that it is hard to distinguish them from one another.

According to this passage,

(A) you should attempt to identify birds only with a manual.

(B) it can be difficult to identify birds.

(C) a manual will help you identify each bird species.

(D) every bird species is different from the others.

Questions 349 and 350 are based on the following passage.

In 1987 director Oliver Stone created *Wall Street*, a film that critiques the mindset of many high-stake players in the financial world: players who embrace a value system that places profits and wealth, "doing the deal," and winning above all other considerations. In 2010 Stone released *Wall Street: Money Never Sleeps*, which further develops and updates his indictment of self-centered, predatory trading practices that can take the entire world to the brink of a complete economic meltdown.

349. According to the passage, the second film focuses on

(A) high-stake players in the financial world.

(B) Wall Street.

(C) predatory lending practices.

(D) predatory trading practices.

350. According to the films described in this passage, what can happen as a result of the actions of Wall Street's high-stake players?

(A) People put winning above everything else.

(B) The world could face an economic meltdown.

(C) Predatory traders gain more wealth than politicians do.

(D) People embrace a Wall Street mentality.

351. Nancy's father, Irving, was an executive in a company that manufactured voting machines. Her mother, Patricia, was an interior designer who volunteered at the Home for the Blind. After reading a play-wright's autobiography at age 12, Nancy decided she was interested in theater and began to act in local stage productions; today, she's a successful film director, producer and screenwriter.

According to this passage, what caused Nancy to begin acting in local theater?

(A) Reading a playwright's autobiography

(B) Her mother's volunteer work at the Home for the Blind

(C) Growing up in a close-knit community

(D) All of the above are correct.

352. The Mid-Continent Area Power Pool, or MAPP, was one of eight electric reliability councils that fell under the authority of the North American Electric Reliability Corporation, or NERC. NERC and all of its subordinate councils were formed in 1965 after the event known as the "Northeast Blackout of 1965."

According to the passage, you can assume that

(A) MAPP was formed after NERC was.

(B) MAPP was formed in 1965.

(C) NERC and MAPP are the same organization.

(D) NERC is a subordinate agency of MAPP.

353. The Yueshi culture, which flourished between 1900 BCE and 1500 BCE in the Shandong region of China, began in the Late Neolithic Period and lasted through the early Bronze Age. It was replaced by the Erligang culture. More than 340 Yueshi sites have been discovered and excavated in Shandong.

According to the passage, you can infer that

(A) the Late Neolithic Period lasted until 1500 BCE.

(B) the Bronze Age existed by 1500 BCE.

(C) the Yuehsi culture lasted for more than 2,000 years.

(D) the Erligang culture came before the Yueshi culture.

Questions 354 and 355 are based on the following passage.

Roads in Rome were typically created for military use, and they were straight and paved. The Romans had exceptional technical knowledge that allowed them to create useful roadways. Compare that to the Middle Ages, when people used meandering earthen roads to haul goods to market, go to church, or travel to other areas for leisure.

354. According to the passage, roads during the Middle Ages

(A) were winding rather than straight.

(B) were made from bricks or other pavement.

(C) were temporary.

(D) were made for military purposes.

355. After reading this passage, you can assume that

(A) roads were made from brick during the Middle Ages.

(B) marketplaces were permanent during the Middle Ages.

(C) roads were mainly used for military purposes in the Middle Ages.

(D) roads were designed for civilians during the Middle Ages.

Set 8 (15 Questions)

356. Washington's Black Peak, part of the Cascade Range, lies in both the Stephen Mather Wilderness and the North Cascades National Park. It's the 20th-highest peak in Washington, with 8,970 feet in elevation. Its prominence is 3,450 feet, making it the 35th-most prominent peak in the state. This non-volcanic mountain is a mecca for hikers and campers.

According to the passage, Black Peak is

(A) in the Stephen Mather Wilderness.

(B) 3,450 feet in elevation.

(C) 8,970 feet in prominence.

(D) volcanic.

357. Huns, invaders who were particularly feared, managed to advance right into Gaul, where their leader, Attila, a terrifying bogeyman to all Europeans except the Hungarians, was defeated by the Roman Aetius in the battle of the Catalaunian Fields, close to Troyes, and was then forced to withdraw.

Who defeated Attila?

(A) The Catalunians

(B) Gaul

(C) Aetius

(D) Troyes

358. Thiobenzophenone is an organosulfur compound; it is the prototypical thioketone. However, thiobenzophenone doesn't dimerize to form rings and polymers like most other thioketones do; it's actually very stable, despite the fact that it photoxidizes in air and forms sulfur and benzophenone.

From the passage, you can assume that

(A) the compound forms rings.

(B) the compound creates polymers.

(C) many thioketones dimerize.

(D) many thioketones photoxidize.

Questions 359 and 360 are based on the following passage.

Cassiodorus, who lived between 490 and 580, played an important role in medieval European culture. Initially, he worked in politics in Ostrogothic Italy, acting as a mediator between what were then considered barbarians and the Romano-Byzantine people. When Justinian reconquered Italy in 539, Cassiodorus's career came to an abrupt end, forcing him into retirement at the Vivarium monastery in Calabria. From there, Cassiodorus translated several copies of Greek works and made copies of Latin works for educational purposes.

359. According to the passage, Cassadorus

(A) was from a family of average means.

(B) spoke multiple languages.

(C) was killed by Justinian.

(D) was born in Calabria.

360. Cassiodorus died in approximately

(A) 490 BCE.

(B) 490 CE.

(C) 539 CE.

(D) 580 CE.

361. Roads fell into disrepair, along with workshops, warehouses and irrigation systems, and agriculture declined. It was a technological regression in which the use of stone as a major building material diminished and wood made a comeback. The flow of town-dwellers returning to the countryside did not fill the gap left by demographic decline.

The society in this passage experienced

(A) a dearth of people moving to the country.

(B) an increase in town populations.

(C) a decline in agriculture.

(D) Both A and C are correct.

Questions 362 and 363 are based on the following passage.

Do you want to know why Florence Nightingale was the one person out of all the people of England to be asked to go? From her earliest childhood she was always doing what she could to help those who were in trouble. The poor and suffering appealed to her more than to most people. When quite young, she went to visit the poor and sick on her father's estates, carrying to them some little dainties or flowers that they would be sure to like, and helping them to get well. All the animals around her home liked her, because they knew that she would not hurt them; even the shy squirrels would come quite close to her and pick up the nuts she dropped for them.

362. The main theme of this passage is

(A) why Florence Nightingale was asked to go somewhere.

(B) how Florence Nightingale took care of animals.

(C) things Florence Nightingale brought with her to patients' homes.

(D) how Florence Nightingale helped during the war.

363. According to the passage, Florence Nightingale was

(A) a doctor.

(B) sickly.

(C) good with animals.

(D) all of the above.

364. Before 1760 the manufacture of cotton goods was carried on in the homes of the people. A spinner would procure a supply of raw cotton from the dealer and carry it home, where, with the help of his family, he would spin it into threads or yarn and return it to the dealer. The spinning was all done by hand or foot-power on a wheel that required one person to run it, and that would make only one thread at a time.

A good title for this passage might be

(A) "Uses of Cotton Goods Prior to 1760."

(B) "Who Manufactured Cotton Goods Prior to 1760."

(C) "How Cotton Goods Were Manufactured after 1760."

(D) "How Cotton Goods Were Manufactured Prior to 1760."

365. When Columbus landed on the island-fringe of America in 1492, he thought he had found what he had set out to find—the eastern country of India; and he believed it all his life. This idea survived for several generations, partly because of the great wealth of Mexico and Peru. When Europeans were at last convinced that it was not India, they began again to seek a way to the East, and looked on the continent of America merely as an obstacle in their path.

According to the passage, what did Columbus think he had found?

(A) Canada

(B) India

(C) Mexico

(D) Peru

366. The history of a nation is influenced very largely by geographical facts. Its internal relations, whether friendly or hostile, are affected by these. Natural barriers, such as mountains, seas, or great lakes and rivers, are often political frontiers exerting protecting or isolating influence. Its industrial progress depends primarily upon its natural products—minerals, grains, woods, fish, etc., and the facilities which its structure affords for trade, both domestic and foreign. A sea coast, with satisfactory harbors, tends to produce a sea-faring people, and therefore a trading people.

According to the passage,

(A) natural barriers are good.

(B) natural barriers can protect a nation.

(C) natural barriers determine military worth.

(D) natural barriers attract politicians.

367. The New Learning was a phase of a greater movement called the Renaissance, which arose in Italy during the fourteenth century. The Renaissance marked the end of the Middle Ages and the beginning of modern history. It meant rebirth, a new life. People took a new interest in living. The influence of the monk and of the knight was passing, and the man of affairs, with his broader sympathies, his keener vision, his more varied interests, and his love of liberty, was coming into prominence.

The Renaissance could be described as

(A) a suppression.

(B) a conservative movement.

(C) the apex of the Dark Ages.

(D) an awakening.

368. For the first time in my life I was confronted by the phenomenon of audible silence. When we had climbed the first flight of stairs, I added another discovery to my limited knowledge of natural phenomena—that of tangible darkness. A match showed us where the upward road continued. We went to the next floor and then to the next and the next until I had lost count and then there came still another floor, and suddenly we had plenty of light.

The author of this passage would probably agree that

(A) climbing several flights of stairs is difficult.

(B) most people don't understand real silence and darkness.

(C) you should always keep climbing.

(D) perseverance is the key to getting what you want.

369. The U.S. competed at the 1988 Summer Olympics in Seoul, South Korea, with 527 competitors. The teams participated in 230 events spanning 27 different sports, winning 36 gold medals, 31 silver medals, and 27 bronze medals.

According to this passage,

(A) 230 competitors won 527 medals.

(B) 527 competitors won medals.

(C) 527 competitors participated in 27 events.

(D) 527 competitors participated in 230 events.

370. Antimatter comets have never been observed by scientists, and they're unlikely to exist anywhere in the Milky Way Galaxy. In the 1940s, Vladimir Rojansky hypothesized that antimatter comets would generate volatile compounds, and using the Stefan-Boltzmann law, that he could determine their existence by observing comets' temperatures. Because of great technological advancement, which has fostered many new discoveries and theories, scientists today believe that antimatter comets are unlikely to exist at all.

The author of this passage would probably agree that

(A) modern technology can put old theories and hypotheses to rest.

(B) antimatter comets are likely to exist, but scientists haven't yet found them.

(C) modern technology makes it easy to discover, find, and catalog antimatter comets.

(D) modern technology is not as good as physical observation.

Set 9 (15 Questions)

371. Durham University gives Palatinate awards to athletes and former athletes who demonstrate "Ability of a High Standard," "Service to a Club," and "Attitude and Commitment." The highest award is the Full Palatinate, and the second-highest is the Half Palatinate. Honorary Palatinate awards recognize former Durham University students who have moved on to compete in the field of sport.

According to the passage,

(A) the award is only for athletes and former athletes.

(B) there are three categories of Palatinates.

(C) the award is available only to current students.

(D) both A and B are correct.

372. Silent motion pictures were part of an era that lasted between 1894 and 1929. In a silent film, dialogue is transmitted through gestures, title cards, and miming. Technological constraints prevented moviemakers from combining sound with film until the late 1920s, when Audion amplifier tubes and Vitaphone systems became available.

According to the passage, "technological constraints" means

(A) silent movies were possible only because of technology.

(B) the technology to combine movies and sound didn't exist yet.

(C) Vitaphone systems were available but not widely used.

(D) Audion amplifier tubes made miming obsolete.

373. The National Natural Landmarks Program encourages the conservation of pieces of natural history in the U.S., including biological and geological features that are privately and publicly owned. Since its inception in 1962 (May 18, to be exact), the program encourages people to participate voluntarily; they are not legally bound to do so, although the NNL Program is governed by the Historic Sites Act of August 21, 1935. It does not have the protection features of Section 106 of the National Historic Preservation Act of 1966, so either party can terminate the agreement upon notifying the other party.

According to the passage,

(A) the NNLP is part of Section 106 of the National Historic Preservation Act of 1966.

(B) it is possible to terminate your agreement to preserve natural landmarks.

(C) the program applies only to biological features in the U.S. that are publicly or privately owned.

(D) the NNLP is not voluntary.

Questions 374 and 375 are based on the following passage.

As a boy, I travelled the greater part of the United Kingdom, when, reaching twelve, my aptitude for trading in horses (thanks to my father's tuition) began to exhibit itself. My first business transaction consisted of receiving a present of a pony. One day, shortly after the Epping Fair of 1842, I was sent by my parents to the Manor House at Loughton, with some basket-ware. Being some distance from our camp, one of the upper servants very kindly attended to my inward wants, and having packed the silver for the ware, for safety, in a piece of brown paper, in my breeches pocket, I started off for the forest.

374. According to the passage,

(A) the boy decided to sell a horse.

(B) the boy traveled around the United Kingdom.

(C) the boy bought basket-ware at Loughton.

(D) the boy purchased his first horse at the Epping Fair.

375. According to the passage, the boy's first business transaction was

(A) trading horses.

(B) purchasing basket-ware.

(C) receiving a pony as a gift.

(D) in 1841.

376. The interior presented an air of Oriental luxury. A rich carpet covered the floor; cushioned seats invited to repose; and there was not wanting other accessories to remind one of the sybaritic elegance of a Turkish divan. The squalid children were not there, but in their stead appeared a bevy of handsome damsels, with Gitano complexions. The comely girls were attired in robes of the brightest hues, scarlet, pink, and yellow, and from their ears depended large silver rings, which imparted to them a dashing Bohemian mien.

According to the passage,

(A) the scene takes place in Turkey.

(B) beautiful women replaced dirty children.

(C) the women wore bright, attractive clothing.

(D) both B and C are correct.

377. I know popular sympathy leans toward springtime in the country, but for my part, as soon as March has blown itself away, and April comes whirling along the cleared path of the year, I hurry to keep my annual appointment to meet Spring in New York. The trees are budding in the parks, daffodils and tulips are blooming riotously on the street-corners, while hyacinths and lilacs blossom along the curb.

According to the passage,

(A) springtime starts in March in New York.

(B) daffodils and tulips bloom in April in New York.

(C) hyacinths and lilacs bloom in March in New York.

(D) the author prefers to spend spring in the country.

378. Turgenev's art at its highest may well be the despair of artists who have sufficient insight to understand wherein he excels. He is rich in all the gifts, so he penetrates into everything; but it is the perfect harmony existing between his gifts that makes him see everything in proportion. Thus he never caricatures; he is never too forcible, and never too clever. He is a great realist, and his realism carries along with it the natural breath of poetry. His art is highly complex, but its expression is so pellucid, so simple, that we can see only its body, never the mechanism of its body.

The main idea of this passage is

(A) that most artists are amateurs.

(B) the mechanisms that make Turgenev's art possible.

(C) that most artists can create perfect harmony in paintings.

(D) the complexity of Turgenev's art.

379. Even if a team doesn't make it into the end zone to make a touchdown, they can exercise the option of kicking the ball between the goal posts in what's known as a field goal. A field goal earns the team three points, which is three fewer than they'd earn for a touchdown, but any progress is good progress.

According to the passage,

(A) a touchdown is worth fewer points than a field goal is.

(B) a team has to be in the end zone to kick a field goal.

(C) teams can't choose to kick a field goal.

(D) a touchdown is worth six points.

380. The boys who attended Mr. Morton's Select School in the village of Laketon did not profess to know more than boys of the same age and advantages elsewhere; but of one thing they were absolutely certain, and that was that no teacher ever rang his bell to assemble the school or call the boys in from recess until just that particular instant when the fun in the schoolyard was at its highest, and the boys least wanted to come in.

According to the passage,

(A) the boys at Mr. Morton's school knew more than their peers did.

(B) recess always ended when the boys were having the most fun.

(C) teachers never rang the bell to bring the kids in from recess.

(D) the boys never wanted to go to school.

381. The branch of political science that deals with the study and scientific analysis of elections is called *psephology,* and it uses historical voting data, public opinion polls, and campaign finance information to learn about elections. Many psephologists measure the data to make predictions about the outcomes of elections.

A good title for this passage might be

(A) "What Is Psephology?"

(B) "What Does a Psephologist Do?"

(C) "Why Psephology is Important."

(D) "Historical Voting Data and Predictions."

382. Small, perciform marine fish make up the largest order of vertebrates; nearly 41 percent of all bony fish fall into this order. About 160 fish families are perciforms, including the marlin and stout infantfish. These types of fish first appeared and diversified during the Late Cretaceous Period, when cichlids, parrotfish, damselfish, and surgeon fish began to develop.

Based on this passage, you can assume that

(A) perciforms never evolved.

(B) 160 fish families make up about 41 percent of all perciforms.

(C) marlin were fully evolved by the end of the Late Cretaceous Period.

(D) some fish families died out before the end of the Upper Cretaceous Period.

383. Jean Baptiste Greuze was born in 1725 at Tournus, a little manufacturing town in the Department of Saône-et-Loire, in the south of France. From his early boyhood he developed the inclination and taste for art which later made him one of the first of French painters. His first studies were made in Lyons, a great manufacturing center, not very far from his native town. From Lyons he went to Paris, and was so successful that he was enabled to fulfill his ambition of visiting Rome, where he pursued his studies for a considerable period.

According to the passage,

(A) Greuze studied in Rome.

(B) Greuze was from Lyons.

(C) Greuze studied manufacturing.

(D) Greuze disliked art.

384. My experience has convinced me that the question is a useless one. You may train up and control your boys to a certain age; you may make them a present of as good an education as you can afford; you may lay down plans for their future; you may find niches for each one to fill; you may fondly hope that each one in his turn will quietly drop into his niche; that they will live and work together, and in course of time become a help and comfort to you in your declining years. But will they do so?

The author of this passage would probably agree that

(A) all children should have a good education.

(B) parents have a responsibility to plan for their children's futures.

(C) boys often help their parents as they age.

(D) children grow into independent, free-thinking adults.

385. The Joint Improvised-Threat Defeat Organization, or JIDO, is a combat support organization of the U.S. Department of Defense. It supports counter-terrorism and counter-insurgency efforts, employing just over 1,000 people (400 government civilians and military personnel, as well as about 600 contract personnel), on a budget of $450 million per year.

A good title for this passage might be

(A) "Where Do Our Tax Dollars Go?"

(B) "Counter-Terrorism in the U.S."

(C) "JIDO."

(D) "Government Employment."

Set 10 (15 Questions)

386. The day I set out was beautifully clear, and my journey progressed through ever-changing scenery. Before me and on each side were the snow-capped mountains, still white as they had been for six months past, and fringed along their sides by a massive belt of timber, at the foot of which my little pony and old carcase ahead were picking their way, treading lightly lest their weight should precipitate them through the hardened crust of snow.

According to the passage,

(A) it has been cold for several months.

(B) the pony may not make it through the winter.

(C) there were very few trees.

(D) the traveler is waiting for spring.

387. The interview proved a satisfactory one, and Barclay was readily accepted, being vouched for by his friend and companion. It may be said also that his appearance was in his favor, though it would hardly have recommended him for any honest business. When Barclay came out of the office, and again found himself on Broadway, his spirits were perceptibly raised. He was no longer impecunious, but carried with him fifty dollars in counterfeit bills.

Based on the context of the passage, you know that Barclay

(A) was poor.

(B) applied for a job on the railroad.

(C) was friendly.

(D) was miserable.

388. You will need several documents to enroll your child in kindergarten, including proof of age and identity; proof of residence in the district; vaccination and immunization records; and valid tuberculosis test results or a letter from your family's physician stating that your child is low-risk.

According to the passage,

(A) most parents already have what they need to enroll their kids.

(B) you can't enroll your child in school without a driver's license.

(C) different documents are required to enroll an older child in school.

(D) you can bring a letter from your doctor in lieu of tuberculosis test results.

389. Completed in 1937 after more than a decade of hard work, the Appalachian Trail is currently maintained by 31 trail clubs and several partnerships. The National Park Service, the U.S. Forest Service and the Appalachian Trail Conservancy manage the trail, and it's the longest hiking-only trail in the world. Approximately 2 million people hike the Appalachian Trail every year.

According to the passage,

(A) only private organizations maintain the Appalachian Trail.

(B) it took more than 10 years to complete the Appalachian Trail.

(C) millions of people travel the trail each month.

(D) the Appalachian Trail is the only public long-distance hiking trail in the world.

390. I found that nothing paid as well as fine laundry work for ladies. It was a trial to my pride, for I was well brought up and educated, to take in washing for a living, but I would rather do that than see my children suffer. So I stifled my pride and became a laundress. I was fortunate in securing customers, and I have wanted for nothing.

The author of this passage feels that

(A) she makes enough money as a laundress.

(B) she was too educated to be a laundress.

(C) her children are more important than her pride is.

(D) all of the above are correct.

391. It is built of brick, and has an air of quiet elegance which makes it a favorite with ladies and others who like to be spared the noise and bustle which attend other prominent hotels in the city. On the corner just above stands the luxurious home of Jay Gould, the railroad king. A few blocks above is the great Catholic Cathedral, destined one day to rank among the famous churches of the world.

This passage is about

(A) the Catholic Cathedral.

(B) a hotel.

(C) the quietness of the city.

(D) Jay Gould.

392. A number of us had formed the habit of drifting into Dick Little's flat in Chelsea on Sunday evenings for a smoke, a drink and a yarn. That was in Dick's bachelor days and when he was working night and day at "Tims" (St. Timothy's Hospital). There would be Jocelyn Dare, the writer and inveterate hater of publishers, Jack Carruthers, who tolerated everybody except Mr. Lloyd George, sometimes Tom Little, Dick's brother, and about a dozen others, including a lot of men from "Tims."

According to the passage, who is Dick's brother?

(A) Lloyd

(B) Jack

(C) Tom

(D) The passage doesn't say.

393. Many students of elementary biology, as they painfully try to unravel the mystery of molluscan morphology, must have come across small pearls in the tissues of the freshwater mussels (*Unio* or *Anodonta*); but these are said to have less luster and to be more opaque than the sea pearl; so the pearl fisheries of the Welsh and Scotch rivers are falling into disuse.

According to the passage,

(A) students don't usually find pearls when they study mollusks.

(B) pearls from freshwater fisheries have less luster than natural sea pearls.

(C) *Anodonta* mussels are saltwater organisms.

(D) *Unio* mussels produce the best pearls.

394. He was homeless. He had lost his position, that of a butcher's boy, just a little after sunrise. It arose out of a difference of seventy-five cents in the butcher's accounts. Abe had been told under penalty of having "his face shoved in" never to darken the doors of the butcher-shop again.

According to the passage,

(A) the butcher fired Abe for theft.

(B) Abe lived with the butcher.

(C) Abe threatened the butcher.

(D) Abe got a new job immediately.

395. The surface layers of the ocean teem with animal and vegetable life. Every yachtsman must at times have noticed that the sea is thick as a *purée* with jellyfish, or with those little transparent, torpedo-shaped creatures, the *Sagitta*. What he will not have noticed, unless he is a microscopist, is that at almost all times the surface is crowded with minute organisms, foraminifera, radiolaria, diatoms.

According to the passage,

(A) it's typically safe to drink the ocean's surface water.

(B) you need a microscope to find some types of jellyfish.

(C) you can typically see "minute organisms" on the ocean's surface.

(D) there are more than just visible organisms on the surface of the ocean.

Questions 396 and 397 are based on the following passage.

No external rays reach the bottom of the sea, and what light there is must be supplied by the phosphorescent organs of the animals themselves, and must be faint and intermittent. A large percentage of animals taken from the deep sea show phosphorescence when brought on deck; and it may be that this emission of light is much greater at a low temperature, and under a pressure of 1 to 2 tons on the square inch, than it is under the ordinary atmospheric conditions of the surface.

396. According to the passage,

(A) scientists believe that the bottom of the ocean is warmer than its surface.

(B) sunlight doesn't reach the bottom of the ocean.

(C) all animals from the bottom of the sea glow.

(D) you can't observe deep-sea creatures glowing in daylight.

397. According to the passage, many fish that live on the bottom of the ocean

(A) are blind.

(B) are warm-blooded.

(C) produce their own light.

(D) are exceptionally strong.

398. When he first set foot in Virginia, Captain John Smith was only twenty-seven years old; but even then he had made himself somewhat famous in England as a daring traveler in Southern Europe, in Turkey and the East. This extremely vivid and resolute man comes before us for study, not because he was the most conspicuous person in the first successful American colony, but because he was the writer of the first book in American literature.

According to the passage, Captain John Smith

(A) was unknown in England before coming to the Americas.

(B) was in his thirties when he went to Turkey.

(C) wrote the first book of American literature.

(D) was the most famous person in the colonies.

399. With Roger Williams, the mood for composition seems to have come in gusts. His writings are numerous; but they were produced spasmodically and in clusters, amid long spaces of silence. He is known to have written two or three works which were never printed at all, and which are now lost.

According to the passage, Roger Williams

(A) was a famous poet.

(B) was one of the most prolific authors of the 20th century.

(C) published dozens of books.

(D) did not write continuously.

400. The Milwaukee Brewers finished the 1988 season with 87 wins and 75 losses. Paul Molitor, the Brewers' third baseman, had 190 hits that season, as did center fielder Robin Yount; second baseman Jim Gantner had 149 during the 1988 season.

According to the passage,

(A) Molitor and Yount both had 190 hits that season.

(B) Gantner hit more than Molitor did.

(C) Molitor was the Brewers' center fielder.

(D) Yount had 149 base hits during the 1988 season.

Set 11 (15 Questions)

401. The Hubble telescope has helped NASA scientists discover 16 background galaxies around Abell S1063, a distant galaxy that could be home to billions of other worlds. One is about 12.7 billion years old, according to the scientists on the project. Scientists are studying Abell S1063 as part of Frontier Fields, a three-year program that searches for new galaxies.

According to the passage,

(A) Frontier Fields explores the edge of the universe.

(B) scientists have found a 12.7 billion-year-old galaxy.

(C) Frontier Fields is a 16-year-old program.

(D) scientists have discovered only 17 other galaxies.

402. Colombia has six main natural regions, including the Andes mountain range and the Amazon Rainforest region. It's part of the Ring of Fire, which is a region especially prone to earthquakes and volcanic eruptions. As a unitary presidential constitutional republic, which is vastly different from a monarchy, Colombia has a president, a congress and a senate, as well as a Chamber of Representatives.

According to the passage, Colombia is

(A) a democracy.

(B) prone to earthquakes.

(C) governed by a monarch.

(D) primarily located in the rainforest.

403. We men, meanwhile, were cursing ourselves for blockheads, chewing the sharp cud of repentance, and trying in a hundred sheepish, clumsy fashions to make amends. It would have been diverting for an outsider to have watched us; the deference with which we spoke and listened to her, the interest we took in her work, the infinite little politenesses we paid her.

According to the passage, the men

(A) regretted the way they had treated the woman.

(B) verbally apologized to the woman.

(C) continued to be impolite to the woman.

(D) were pleased with the way they had treated the woman.

404. The Smithsonian Institution was established as the United States National Museum in 1846, and today, it's a group of 170 museums and nine research centers. The museum's first animal, plant and mineral specimens, as well as artifacts from the South Pacific Ocean, came from the United States Exploring Expedition, conducted by the U.S. Navy between 1838 and 1842.

The main theme of this passage is

(A) the Smithsonian Institution's collection.

(B) the Smithsonian Institution's beginnings.

(C) the number of the Smithsonian Institution's museums.

(D) why the Smithsonian Institution is the premier research institution in the U.S.

405. Use the northwest entrance at Queen's Park to access the pharmacy building, the northeast entrance to purchase subway tickets in the mezzanine, and the southwest entrance to connect to the Ontario Power building and Mount Sinai Hospital. The southeast entrance is still under construction.

According to the passage, which entrance should you use if you want to purchase a subway ticket?

(A) The southeast entrance

(B) The southwest entrance

(C) The northeast entrance

(D) The northwest entrance

406. *Anxiety* is best defined as an uneasy feeling of fear or apprehension, usually accompanied by increased physiological arousal symptoms such as increased heart rate, increased blood pressure, sweating, pupils dilating, and so forth. Anxiety, which is an emotional reaction, can be seen as an exaggerated fear response to environmental threats.

According to the passage, which of the following is *not* a physical symptom of anxiety?

(A) Sweating

(B) Dilated pupils

(C) Decreased blood pressure

(D) All of the above

407. While dyslexia is often called "reading disorder" because it's characterized by difficulty reading, that's not the only issue it presents. Other problems dyslexia can cause include difficulty with spelling, writing, pronunciation, comprehension and other areas. Experts typically agree that dyslexia involves genetic and environmental factors.

According to the passage, dyslexia does *not* cause problems with which of the following?

(A) Comprehension

(B) Spelling

(C) Pronunciation

(D) None of the above are correct.

408. Of the tobacco and its consequences, I will say nothing but that the practice is at too bad a pass to leave hope that anything that could be said in books would work a cure. If the floors of boarding houses, and the decks of steamboats, and the carpets of the Capitol, do not sicken the Americans into a reform; if the warnings of physicians are of no avail, what remains to be said? I dismiss the nauseous subject.

The author of this passage would probably agree that

(A) people should write more about tobacco.

(B) doctors should find a cure for tobacco addiction.

(C) people should not use tobacco.

(D) only Americans use tobacco.

Questions 409 and 410 are based on the following passage.

It is not happenstance that the intellectual qualities of originally minded organizational leaders overlap with those of artistically inclined personalities, since both types share the qualities of imagination and novelty. In addition, the rapidly changing modern environment, marked as it is by an environment of highly competitive global production, rapid information exchange, and the emergence of new industries catering to cultural desires, rewards leaders who are sensitive to issues of design and to the aesthetic dimensions of products or organizational life.

409. According to the passage,

(A) good leaders are rapidly changing.

(B) good leaders don't need to worry about design issues.

(C) good leaders are highly competitive.

(D) good leaders are both intellectual and artistically inclined.

410. According to the passage, many new industries

(A) need to evolve.

(B) are competitive.

(C) cater to cultural desires.

(D) focus on aesthetics.

411. Education is compulsory. This concluding requirement of the regulations exists in the laws of public instruction of almost all nations. Nevertheless, in its application, the governments pay attention to the social circumstances of the country. In our country parents incur a fine who do not send their children to school, the fine being from one-half to two reals, according to circumstances.

After reading this passage, you can assume that

(A) parents are required to send their children to school.

(B) rich parents pay less for education than poor parents do.

(C) no laws exist to require children to attend school.

(D) few nations have laws about education.

412. He is far too fat to fly — the best he can do is to waddle. But his fat is very useful to him, for it is a kind of greatcoat, and helps to keep him warm while fishing in the bitterly cold waters around the South Pole. There is only one time, in fact, when the penguin becomes lean, and that is when Mother and Father are bringing up their family.

The main idea of this passage is

(A) why penguins can't fly.

(B) penguins' weight.

(C) how penguins raise their young.

(D) why penguins swim.

413. The furniture is very primitive, though better than that of some of the other cells. There are a mattress on the bed of cast iron, a pillow but no bolster, two straw-bottomed chairs, a little white deal table, a jug and a basin which were once enamelled yellow but through which the rusty metal shows. On the bed is a brown rug with the word "Prison" written on it.

What does this passage describe?

(A) A prison

(B) A prison cell

(C) Sleeping arrangements

(D) Primitive décor

Questions 414 and 415 are based on the following passage.

There is a sickness common to all prisoners in Saint Lazare which is known there as "the six o'clock sickness" (le mal de six heures). It attacks all newcomers, and none escape it. It comes on after the walk in the courtyard, when night begins to close in, and the prison settles into silence till the morning. It is an attack of a kind of malarial fever, a shivering fit and a violent headache with a feeling of lassitude and nausea afterwards. When it comes on, the prisoners are given a cachet of quinine from the prison pharmacy.

414. According to the passage, "the six o'clock sickness"

(A) occurs at 6:00 a.m.

(B) is most likely a virus.

(C) is a reaction to being locked in prison.

(D) most likely occurs when inmates eat bad food for dinner.

415. Inmates who have "the six o'clock sickness"

(A) are given drugs to allay the symptoms.

(B) are required to walk in the courtyard.

(C) have malaria.

(D) go to the hospital.

Set 12 (15 Questions)

416. One thing that I think exercises an enormous amount of influence upon the quality of voices is climate. Review the climatic conditions of the various countries, and you cannot help remarking upon the number of natural voices that are met with in Italy and in Australia, in both of which countries the climate is unusually fine.

The author of this passage most likely believes that

(A) Italy produces the best singers.

(B) Australia produces the best singers.

(C) the best singers come from Italy and Australia.

(D) you can't predict which countries will produce the best singers.

417. In the hands of such a nation an international convention is not merely idle and impotent; the convention itself becomes positively dangerous, simply because it can be perverted. It can be used to invest the most barbarous acts with a specious plausibility, and can be turned against the very people whom it was designed to protect.

What is the main theme of this passage?

(A) The dangers of an international convention

(B) The dangers of an international convention in the wrong hands

(C) International conventions are positive things

(D) International conventions almost always protect people

418. I make no apology, and I trust that none is needed, for these speculations. Reports of atrocities can serve no useful purpose unless they move men to reflect no less resolutely than deeply upon what is to be done to deliver Europe from the scourge of their repetition. It may well be that my own reflections will seem cynical to one, depressing to another, arbitrary to a third. They are not the idols of the theatre, and in academic circles they may not be fashionable.

According to the passage,

(A) reporting on atrocities should encourage people to prevent them in the future.

(B) the author is exceedingly cynical.

(C) the author regrets being forced to report on atrocities.

(D) bad circumstances cause a nation to grow.

419. Self-consciousness often does more to mar a good voice than anything else, since it leads to the contraction of the muscles. Have you never noticed how pleasantly some people sing or hum to themselves when they imagine they are not overheard, compared with the indifferent or even unpleasant manner in which they perform publicly?

According to the passage,

(A) people who sing in public must have good voice control.

(B) being self-conscious can make you sing poorly.

(C) many people sing better in private than in public.

(D) both B and C are correct.

420. I believe that it is within the power of an artist to actually lessen, or, at any rate, to temporarily relieve, the cares and worries of which each member of an audience has a share; and I am sure that the easiest way to do so is to sing songs whose meaning, and whose message, is immediately understandable.

The author of this passage would most likely agree that

(A) listening to music can help relieve stress.

(B) audience members have a responsibility to listen to the words of a song.

(C) all songs should have a meaning and message.

(D) songs should never be confusing.

421. Not all anxiety is bad for you! Low levels of anxiety signal to us that we need to get ready for an upcoming event that produces some tension, such as final exams, a wedding, a major presentation, or an audition. Some people call this *positive anxiety*, as it gives you an added energy boost. Anxiety becomes detrimental and crippling when it is too high, thus harming concentration and performance.

A good title for this passage might be

(A) "Positive and Negative Anxiety."

(B) "Energy Boosts from Anxiety."

(C) "Anxiety before Big Events."

(D) "Anxiety Is Good for You."

422. Usually, only a few of these objects are pretty to look at; but each of them has some sort of story to tell. Making the interpretation of his finds is the most important part of the archeologist's job. It is the way he gets at the "sort of history of human activity" which is expected of archeology.

This passage is about

(A) museums.

(B) archaeologists.

(C) interpretation.

(D) artifacts.

423. Martha Slawson sat at her sewing machine, stitching away for dear life. About her, billowed yards upon yards of white cotton cloth, which, in its uncut length, shifted, as she worked, almost imperceptibly piling up a snowy drift in front of her, drawn from the snowy drift behind. This gradual ebb and flow was all that marked any progress in her labor, and her husband, coming in after some hours of absence and finding her, apparently, precisely where he had left her, was moved to ask what manner of garment she was making.

According to the passage, Martha

(A) is an accomplished seamstress.

(B) has a sense of urgency to finish the garment.

(C) is making tremendous progress.

(D) was abandoned by her husband.

424. Toward the end of prehistoric time there was a general settling down with the coming of agriculture, and all sorts of new things began to be made. Archeologists soon got a general notion of what ought to appear with what. Thus, it would upset a French prehistorian digging at the bottom of a very early cave if he found a fine bronze sword, just as much as it would upset him if he found a beer bottle. The people of his very early cave layer simply could not have made bronze swords, which came later, just as do beer bottles. Some accidental disturbance of the layers of his cave must have happened.

According to the passage, why would an archaeologist studying a very early cave be upset at finding a bronze sword?

(A) Archaeologists look for antiquities.

(B) The presence of a sword means the original inhabitants were most likely killed.

(C) The presence of a sword means the site had been disturbed.

(D) A sword is "junk" in archaeology, just as a beer bottle is.

425. As you know, primitive peoples tend to marry and have children rather early in life. So suppose we say that twenty years will make an average generation. At this rate there would be 25,000 generations in a half-million years.

According to the passage, what is an average generation?

(A) The average lifespan of a primitive person

(B) A half-million years

(C) 25 years

(D) 20 years

426. Peking Man had fire. He probably cooked his meat, or used the fire to keep dangerous animals away from his den. In the cave were bones of dangerous animals, members of the wolf, bear, and cat families. Some of the cat bones belonged to beasts larger than tigers. There were also bones of other wild animals: buffalo, camel, deer, elephants, horses, sheep, and even ostriches. Seventy per cent of the animals Peking Man killed were fallow deer. It's much too cold and dry in north China for all these animals to live there today.

After reading this passage, you can assume that

(A) Peking Man was a terrific hunter and gatherer.

(B) temperatures in northern China were warmer during the time when Peking Man lived.

(C) many people contributed to Peking Man's food stores.

(D) Peking Man used most of the animals he killed for food.

427. Drugs that treat and prevent bacterial infections are called antibiotics, and the first — penicillin — was discovered in 1928 by Alexander Fleming. Unfortunately, the overuse of antibiotics has led to the emergence of antibiotic-resistant bacteria (bacteria that antibiotics can't kill). However, medical researchers are always searching for new cures and treatments.

According to the passage, antibiotic-resistant bacteria

(A) is very common.

(B) is uncommon.

(C) can't be killed by antibiotics.

(D) can be killed by antibiotics.

428. The Acheulean core-biface type of tool is worked on two faces so as to give a cutting edge all around. The outline of its front view may be oval, or egg-shaped, or a quite pointed pear shape. The large chip-scars of the Acheulean core-bifaces are shallow and flat. It is suspected that this resulted from the removal of the chips with a wooden club; the deep chip-scars of the earlier Abbevillian core-biface came from beating the tool against a stone anvil. These tools are really the best and also the final products of the core-biface tradition.

According to the passage,

(A) Abbevillian core-biface tools were made by beating stones with a wooden club.

(B) Abbevillian core-biface tools were made by beating stones against a stone anvil.

(C) Acheulean core-biface tools were made in primarily oval shapes.

(D) Acheulean core-biface tools were the earliest ever found.

429. Even under these favorable circumstances there was a "fly in the ointment." On counting noses I made the discovery that the entire ship's company amounted to thirteen (an unlucky number, as every "salt" will testify). A ship's crew of eleven, counting myself, and two passengers, my wife and little daughter. When I called this fact to my wife's attention she laughed at me, saying that was "old sailor's tommyrot" and that we were living in the twentieth century and should have outgrown such silly superstitions.

From the context of the passage, you can determine that "tommyrot" is

(A) nonsense.

(B) unlucky.

(C) a ship's crew.

(D) a truth.

430. A culture lasts, although individual men in the group die off. On the other hand, a culture changes as the different conventions and understandings change. You could almost say that a culture lives in the minds of the men who have it. But people are not born with it; they get it as they grow up. Suppose a day-old Hungarian baby is adopted by a family in Oshkosh, Wisconsin, and the child is not told that he is Hungarian. He will grow up with no more idea of Hungarian culture than anyone else in Oshkosh.

The main theme of this passage is

(A) culture.

(B) adoption.

(C) individuality.

(D) Hungary.

Set 13 (15 Questions)

431. The ruins of Brough Castle in Cumbria still stand today. Built by William Rufus in about 1092, the castle was designed to protect an important route through the Pennine Mountains. The castle was originally destroyed during an 1174 battle, but it was rebuilt; a fire destroyed it again in 1521. After its restoration, another fire in 1666 destroyed it, and its masonry finally began to collapse in about 1800.

According to the passage, Brough Castle

(A) was built in the 10th century.

(B) is a tourist attraction.

(C) was destroyed by a battle in 1521.

(D) was destroyed twice by fire.

432. This transition was rather unpleasant; for when the children who had all along been kept at home in a secluded, pure, refined, yet strict manner, were thrown among a rude mass of young creatures, they were compelled unexpectedly to suffer everything from the vulgar, bad, and even base, since they lacked both weapons and skill to protect themselves.

The author of this passage would probably agree that children

(A) can adapt to anything.

(B) can learn only from their environments.

(C) shouldn't be sent out of the house without weapons.

(D) need to be prepared for transitions.

433. Dogs that suffer from degenerative myelopathy, arthritis, or paralysis can often use custom or adjustable wheelchairs designed to help pets with mobility problems. Typically, the wheelchair's frame is attached to wheels that replace the rear legs' functions, and a harness holds the whole contraption in place.

According to the passage,

(A) dogs that have mobility problems can use wheelchairs.

(B) harnesses replace the function of a dog's legs.

(C) paralysis is not preventable in some dogs.

(D) degenerative myelopathy is a form of blindness.

434. The emperor, as the ally of Russia, declared war against Turkey on the 10th of February, 1788. Operations were carried on by the Austrians around Belgrade and on the Danube. The Russians, bent on extending their power on the Black Sea, invested Oczakow at the mouth and on the right bank of the Dnieper, Kinburn on the left side having already been ceded to them by the treaty of Kainardji. The czarina also decided to renew in the Mediterranean the diversion of 1770, again sending ships from the Baltic.

According to the passage, the Russians wanted to

(A) partner with the emperor.

(B) fight against Turkey.

(C) extend their power.

(D) invade Kinburn.

435. Magnolia is one of the best-known trees in the eastern part of the state. No other tree excels it in the combined beauty of leaves and flowers. Occurring naturally in rich moist soil on the borders of river swamps and nearby uplands in the Coastal Plain to the valley of the Brazos River, it has been widely cultivated for its ornamental value.

According to the passage, magnolia trees are cultivated because they are

(A) beautiful.

(B) easy to grow.

(C) found only on riverbanks.

(D) exceptionally tall.

436. The Texas Forestry Association is a statewide, nonprofit agency concerned primarily with the educational phase of forest conservation. Organized in 1914, the Association was largely responsible for the passage of the law which created the Department of Forestry at the Agricultural and Mechanical College of Texas, and from which the Texas Forest Service emerged.

According to the passage, the Texas Forestry Association is now concerned with

(A) creating laws.

(B) working with universities.

(C) becoming part of Texas A&M.

(D) education on forest conservation.

437. When you think of the practice of law, you might picture a courtroom, a judge, and a pair of lawyers arguing on behalf of their clients — but the reality is that there's much more to it than that. Attorneys study laws and regulations, looking for loopholes that help their clients; they also question witnesses before trials, stick to legal rules, and maintain current knowledge of precedents and case law. For the most part, a trial lawyer needs experience in court to claim professional expertise. Would you trust an attorney who'd never been to court? Natural talent is one thing, but experience is what separates good lawyers from great lawyers.

According to the passage,

(A) experience in court helps attorneys claim professional expertise.

(B) witnesses are exceptionally important but don't persuade juries.

(C) legal rules are the main component of a trial.

(D) legal officials are always familiar with rules of evidence.

438. Using the self-cleaning feature on your oven may be dangerous. Temperatures reach as high as 1,000 degrees F during the self-cleaning process, which means food particles, chemicals and debris are being charred. The resulting fumes can cause respiratory problems for people and pets, the buildup of carbon monoxide, or other dangerous health hazards.

According to this passage, what is one of the possible negative effects of using an oven's self-cleaning feature?

(A) High temperatures

(B) Respiratory problems

(C) Smoke alarms going off

(D) Burned food

439. Neither of them much over eighteen years of age, they had, during their short career in the Navy, each made his mark in no uncertain fashion. In his chosen branch of the service, Ned Strong was admired by the officers and adored by the men. His advance had been rapid, and some of his more enthusiastic friends were already hinting at a commission in sight for him in the time to come. As for the merry, light-hearted Herc Taylor, that befreckled youth had as many friends among officers and men as Ned, and was one of the youngest bos'un's mates in the Navy.

According to the passage, Ned Strong was

(A) younger than Herc Taylor.

(B) quickly promoted in rank.

(C) handsome.

(D) more enthusiastic than most sailors.

440. We found to our surprise that we were not the first human beings who had sought a shelter in this desolate spot. A few ruined walls here and there showed that it had once been the seat of a rude settlement; and in the little knoll which we cleared away to cover in our storehouse of valuables, we found the mortal remains of their former inhabitants.

What did the people in the passage find?

(A) Valuables

(B) A storehouse

(C) Cooking utensils

(D) Skeletons

441. When the Continental war was going on, the news from the field of battle was generally eight or nine days old. But this, of course, was nothing to the time which elapsed in the case of India, for events which had happened there in February were given to the public as news in August! Then, indeed, to send a boy to the East was to part with him in reality. There was a long voyage round the Cape, prolonged indefinitely by wind and weather, to encounter. It would be a year from his setting out before the news of his arrival could reach his relations in England.

According to the passage, how long did it take for battlefield news to travel to the public?

(A) Six months

(B) More than a week

(C) One year

(D) The passage doesn't say

442. Used for detecting the obstruction of a light beam, an electric eye is a type of photodetector in wide use. One of the electric eye's primary uses is in the safety systems of garage doors. They're also used as highway vehicle counters, alarm systems and more.

According to the passage, the electric eye is

(A) a photodetector.

(B) used as a vehicle counter.

(C) foolproof.

(D) Both A and B are correct.

443. Olfactory receptors — also known as odorant receptors — are responsible for detecting smell. They start a cascade of chemical reactions in our bodies that create a nerve impulse; the nerve impulse travels to our brains, and from there, we're able to detect smells. While many scientists haven't been able to study them extensively (they're extremely small), Linda B. Buck and Richard Axel won the Nobel Prize in Physiology or Medicine for their work on olfactory receptors in 2004.

According to the passage, olfactory receptors

(A) are nerve impulses.

(B) are catalysts.

(C) were discovered in 2004.

(D) start chemical reactions.

444. Of all the writers of fiction, Jane Austen is most thoroughly English. She never went abroad, and though her native good sense and shrewd gift of observation saved her from becoming insular, yet she cannot be conceived as writing of any but the sweet villages and the provincial towns of her native country. Even the Brontës, deeply secluded as their lives were, crossed the German Ocean, and saw something of Continental life from their school at Brussels.

According to the passage, Jane Austen

(A) was only moderately observant.

(B) never left England.

(C) wrote about exotic locations.

(D) traveled with the Brontës.

445. In the present stage of educational development, there are today millions of young men and women who find in the public library the only open door through which they catch glimpses of opportunity beyond their own immediate domain. With all the limitations involved, this is a hopeful circumstance, for instances are plentiful where "the chance encounter with a book has marked the awakening of a life."

A good title for this passage might be

(A) "The Importance of Books."

(B) "Public Libraries Are a Necessity."

(C) "Young People Learning through Books."

(D) "Work Opportunities in Libraries."

Set 14 (11 Questions)

446. Your AFQT scores are ranked by percentile. Your own percentile shows the percentage of people taking the test who scored at or below the same score. For example, if you get an AFQT score of 93, it means you performed as well as (or better than) 93 percent of the people tested from the original reference group.

According to the passage, an AFQT score of 93

(A) is the lowest passing score.

(B) means you performed better than only 7 percent of the original reference group.

(C) means you performed as well as or better than 93 percent of the original reference group.

(D) is the highest possible score.

447. He lived simply, but had apparently enough money to allow his daughters the privileges of gentlewomen, and they went to all the dances and balls in the neighborhood, and paid frequent visits to their brothers' houses for weeks at a time.

From this passage, it's safe to assume that

(A) the man was actually very wealthy.

(B) the daughters bought several dresses.

(C) people with less money could not afford to go to dances and balls.

(D) the man had four sons.

448. Some might argue that Gordie Howe was the best hockey player in the history of the sport. He spent his first 25 seasons with the Detroit Red Wings and earned the nickname "Mr. Hockey." He held several hockey scoring records until Wayne Gretzky broke them in the 1980s, but nobody has been able to touch his records for most games and seasons played.

According to the passage,

(A) Gordie Howe was nicknamed "Mr. Hockey."

(B) Wayne Gretzky broke Howe's record for most games played.

(C) Gordie Howe played only 25 seasons of hockey.

(D) Gordie Howe was the best hockey player of all time.

449. The Detroit Red Wings have a rich history dating back to 1926. Founded as the Detroit Cougars, the team's name changed to the Falcons between 1930 and 1932. Finally, in 1932, the team adopted its current name, under which it plays at Joe Louis Arena in Detroit.

According to the passage, the team became the Detroit Red Wings in

(A) 1926.

(B) 1930.

(C) 1932.

(D) 2016.

450. The South Lyon Hotel, tucked away on the corner of Lafayette and Whipple, burned on June 22. The hotel, which was built in August of 1867, has been through at least two previous fires. Nearby residents tried to stop the blaze, but ultimately, the entire second floor of the building was consumed by flames; the first floor suffered significant water damage.

According to the passage, the South Lyon Hotel

(A) had at least two floors.

(B) was not damaged.

(C) was built by local residents.

(D) had to be demolished.

451. Why is it important to explore and understand the Solar System? Because the third planet from the Sun is our home: Earth is the only place yet discovered where living organisms and intelligent life exist, or have ever existed.

According to the passage, Earth is

(A) one of three places for living organisms.

(B) the largest planet in the Solar System.

(C) not finished growing.

(D) the third planet from the Sun.

452. In the last 50 years, spacecraft have flown past or orbited all of the major planets, landed on the Moon, Mars, Titan and an asteroid, and brought back samples of Moon rock, the solar wind, asteroid and comet dust. This era of robotic and human exploration has revolutionized scientists' knowledge of our corner of the Galaxy, and further astounding revelations are expected in the decades to come.

According to the passage, spacecraft have landed on

(A) Titan.

(B) an asteroid.

(C) Mars.

(D) All of the above are correct.

453. Biologically, humanity needs to know itself if it's going to make good decisions about everything from medicine to genetically engineering food crops; that knowledge comes from anthropology. And culturally, knowledge of our past can help us understand what we are today, for better and worse; that knowledge, today, also comes from the field of anthropology.

A good title for this passage might be

(A) "Uses of Anthropology."

(B) "Genetically Engineered Food Crops."

(C) "Cultural Knowledge in Studies."

(D) "Biological Uses of Anthropology."

454. Paying students to collect objects and curios any time they traveled abroad, Wurm assembled an impressive collection of artifacts, skeletons, fossils, rocks, ancient statuary, and other bric-a-brac. Working under the impression that the world was just a few thousand years old, Wurm organized the objects in his museum — not according to age, but by how much they resembled one another.

According to the passage, Wurm

(A) classified his collection by similarities.

(B) primarily collected fossils.

(C) traveled widely.

(D) must have been very wealthy.

455. The three-day festival called Kivgiq, hosted by Inupiat natives of North Alaska, centered on dances performed by members of many communities across Arctic Canada and Alaska. As I watched, I learned that the feast and the dances were much more than just a big party: They were reminders of an ancient code, an ancient way of life that was important to get right because it kept people alive.

Based on the passage, it's safe to assume that Kivgiq is

(A) held in Canada.

(B) a dance performed by professionals.

(C) held on the same dates every year.

(D) an important cultural tradition.

456. Probably the strangest primate is the aye-aye of Madagascar. About the size of a cat with enormous, hairless ears, the aye-aye climbs through trees by moonlight listening for larvae beneath tree bark. When it hears a squirming treat, it uses a thin, elongated finger to scoop the meal out of the bark.

Based on the passage, it's safe to assume that the aye-aye

(A) is a type of cat.

(B) swings from its tail.

(C) eats larvae.

(D) uses its feet to catch food.

Set 15 (11 Questions)

457. Training your dog takes weeks (or more), and you'll have to put a lot of energy into it. You must train more than one behavior, and each usually takes several steps. Also, repetition is important; you can't expect your dog to remember each behavior without practicing it repeatedly. For these reasons, many people put it off — or worse, give up entirely.

According to the passage, dog training

(A) takes time and money.

(B) takes time and energy.

(C) is not rewarding.

(D) is rewarding only for those who procrastinate.

458. All living things ingest the element carbon in the form of its isotope carbon 14 (14C), which floats freely in the atmosphere and is present in all foods. When a life form stops ingesting 14C (when it, you know, dies), no new 14C enters the body, and the 14C in the body begins to radioactively decay into 14N (nitrogen isotope 14). Importantly, 14C decays into 14N at a known and pretty stable rate: After about 5,600 years, only half of the original 14C remains because the rest has decayed into 14N.

According to the passage, scientists can observe radioactive decay to determine

(A) free-floating 14C.

(B) when a living organism died.

(C) how quickly 14C turns into 14N.

(D) when atmospheric conditions changed.

459. You can't expect to see results immediately, which is a big change (and usually, not a welcome one) from the way most of us live in the U.S. Just look at the Internet; anyone who has it can research, shop, and contact distant places at any time. Want to watch a movie? Rent one online or drive to the convenience store, where you can pay a few dollars to borrow the newest releases for a couple of days. In the Western world, in addition to these conveniences, most people have cell phones that keep them connected to everyone who matters. A fast-food establishment is probably close to your home, so if you're not up to cooking, you can still eat.

The main theme of this passage is

(A) cheaters never win.

(B) the differences between delayed and instant gratification.

(C) things are too easy for most Westerners.

(D) few people are accustomed to working for what they want.

460. All of the celestial objects, including the Sun, moved across the sky from east to west (with the occasional exception of a comet or a shooting star). However, since no one experienced any of the sensations that would be expected if Earth was continually spinning, it seemed logical to believe that it was the heavens which were in motion around Earth.

According to the passage, people didn't believe Earth spun because

(A) the Sun moved across the sky from west to east.

(B) shooting stars rarely appeared.

(C) nobody could feel it spinning.

(D) the Sun moved from east to west.

461. Most people find that sitting and lying down are great behaviors to teach their dogs, and they're great replacements for undesirable behaviors. If your dog follows your command "Sit," she won't bark at strangers when you're on a walk; she won't jump on guests or beg at the dining room table. If you can train your dog to come when you call her, you'll be able to let her roam without a leash (supervised, but off-leash), and that's a great way to provide mental stimulation for your four-legged family member.

According to this passage,

(A) most dogs need to learn to sit and watch.

(B) all dogs deserve time off their leashes.

(C) dogs who bark at people or other dogs are bad dogs.

(D) training your dog can mitigate bad behaviors.

462. The encyclopedia was a favorite among scholars during the Middle Ages. The earliest encyclopedias — inspired by the Greeks — included information on past culture and enabled the current culture to move forward. Even today, Europeans rely on encyclopedias for lessons from the past, both in formal and informal instruction, and the youngest students are able to find information cataloged in these wonderful inheritances from the past.

According to the passage, the encyclopedia

(A) is a modern invention.

(B) was used during the Middle Ages.

(C) was invented during the Middle Ages.

(D) is relatively unknown as a teaching tool.

Questions 463 and 464 are based on the following passage.

A symptom is something that the individual himself or herself experiences. It is internal. For example, feeling depressed, anxious, or confused are symptoms the self perceives as distressing. A cluster of signs and symptoms is called a syndrome. Psychiatrists and clinical psychologists use recognizable syndromes as the primary basis for classifying and diagnosing mental disorders.

463. According to the passage, a syndrome is

(A) a cluster of signs and symptoms.

(B) a personal experience.

(C) depression and anxiety.

(D) something recognizable.

464. Based on this passage, you can assume that

(A) psychiatrists spend several years in school.

(B) just one sign or symptom is a syndrome.

(C) psychiatrists use more than one method to diagnose mental disorders.

(D) psychiatrists primarily treat severely mentally disordered people.

465. A moment's reflection reveals that much human behavior occurs in group settings: the family, school, club, church, military unit, and so forth. These group settings automatically imply interactions with other people. The way in which we interact with others such as our friends, parents, siblings, and coworkers affects our moods and much of what we do.

According to the passage,

(A) nobody can affect the way we feel.

(B) some people are friendlier than others are.

(C) interactions shape our moods and actions.

(D) most people don't like to interact with others.

466. The basic geometrical method they used was called parallax. This involved measurement of the apparent shift in position of an object when viewed from two different locations. To illustrate this, hold one finger upright in front of your nose and close first one eye and then the other. The finger seems to shift position against the background, although it is, of course, stationary. When the finger is moved closer, the shift appears larger, and vice versa.

A good title for this passage might be

(A) "How to Illustrate Parallax."

(B) "Teaching Measurements."

(C) "The Shifting Finger Method."

(D) "Measuring in Geometry."

467. Tom appeared on the sidewalk with a bucket of whitewash and a long-handled brush. He surveyed the fence, and all gladness left him and a deep melancholy settled down upon his spirit. Thirty yards of board fence nine feet high. Life to him seemed hollow, and existence but a burden. Sighing, he dipped his brush and passed it along the topmost plank; repeated the operation; did it again; compared the insignificant whitewashed streak with the far-reaching continent of unwhitewashed fence, and sat down on a tree-box discouraged.

Based on the passage, you can assume that

(A) Tom is an adult.

(B) Tom suffers from depression.

(C) Tom doesn't want to whitewash the fence.

(D) none of the above are correct.

Set 16 (11 Questions)

468. Huckleberry was cordially hated and dreaded by all the mothers of the town, because he was idle and lawless and vulgar and bad—and because all their children admired him so, and delighted in his forbidden society, and wished they dared to be like him. Tom was like the rest of the respectable boys, in that he envied Huckleberry his gaudy outcast condition, and was under strict orders not to play with him. So he played with him every time he got a chance.

According to the passage, mothers didn't want their children playing with Huckleberry because

(A) their children were a lot like him.

(B) he was a bad influence.

(C) Tom played with him.

(D) he was gaudy.

469. Circles of big stones like Stonehenge were rebuilt so that the sun's position with respect to the stones would indicate the day of longest sunlight and the day of shortest sunlight. Between these days there was an optimum time to harvest the crops before fall, when plants dried up and leaves fell from the trees. The winter solstice, when the days began to get longer was cause for celebration. In the next season, there was an optimum time to plant seeds so they could spring up from the ground as new growth. So farming gave rise to the concept of a year.

According to the passage,

(A) Stonehenge was rebuilt during the winter.

(B) people celebrated the winter solstice.

(C) farming was central in medieval society.

(D) crops needed to be dried in the fall.

First, the scientist makes observations about the relationships among variables (such as air temperature and its effect on water). She then forms a hypothesis, or a statement about what effects she believes those variables will have on one another. (For example, she may hypothesize that exposure to cold air will cause water to freeze.) To test her hypothesis, she performs experiments to see whether her predictions are correct.

470. According to the passage, the first thing a scientist does is

(A) make observations.

(B) form a hypothesis.

(C) test a hypothesis.

(D) prove a hypothesis was correct.

471. According to the passage,

(A) the last step a scientist takes is experimentation.

(B) scientists call guessing a "hypothesis."

(C) experiments can support or disprove a hypothesis.

(D) cold air causes water to freeze.

472. History, as the saying goes, is written by the winners, which is another way of saying that each story has (at least) two sides. The use of propaganda, the convenient omission of inconvenient facts from state records, and the wholesale creation of "facts" are nothing new; these occurred in every ancient civilization, from Sumer to the Incan empire.

According to the passage, you can assume that

(A) not all written records of history are completely true.

(B) most historical records are false.

(C) propaganda is a relatively new form of deception.

(D) ancient civilizations had no written records of history.

473. Linguistic anthropology studies human language, the animal kingdom's most uniquely powerful — and at the same time subtle — system of communication between individuals. Language is basically a system of information transmission and reception; humans communicate these messages by sound (speech), by gesture (body language), and in other visual ways such as writing.

According to the passage, language includes

(A) speech.

(B) gestures.

(C) writing.

(D) all of the above.

474. The first red giant phase ends abruptly when there is no longer enough hydrogen available to continue the fusion process that leads to the creation of helium. As the core temperature soars to 100 million degrees Celsius, the intense heat and pressure initiate nuclear reactions that use helium as fuel. In this process, three helium atoms are fused to create one carbon atom.

According to the passage, what is a direct result of a hydrogen deficiency?

(A) Helium is used as fuel.

(B) The red giant phase ends.

(C) Helium atoms fuse together to create carbon atoms.

(D) Both A and C are correct.

475. Dark surfaces, such as those covered with vegetation and soil, have a low albedo (reflectivity). They heat up more quickly than lighter, more reflective surfaces, such as ice sheets. Ice and snow reflect some 80% of the solar energy they receive, compared with 20% for an area of grassland and 10% for a dry, black soil.

According to the passage, which surface heats the fastest?

(A) Ice

(B) Snow

(C) Dry, black soil

(D) Grassland

476. The craft pranced and reared, and plunged like an animal. As each wave came, and she rose for it, she seemed like a horse making at a fence outrageously high. The manner of her scramble over these walls of water is a mystic thing, and, moreover, at the top of them were ordinarily these problems in white water, the foam racing down from the summit of each wave, requiring a new leap, and a leap from the air. Then, after scornfully bumping a crest, she would slide, and race, and splash down a long incline, and arrive bobbing and nodding in front of the next menace.

The main subject of this passage is

(A) a storm.

(B) a watercraft.

(C) the ocean.

(D) a horse.

477. Outstanding leaders abhor deception and misrepresentation. They recognize the value of honest communication as an essential expression of respect for others and for themselves. They do not regard honesty as just the best policy — a tool for achieving one's goals — but as a commitment prior to all policy-making, as a fundamental requirement of sound communal life.

According to the passage, what do outstanding leaders value the most?

(A) Deception

(B) Misrepresentation

(C) Communication

(D) Honesty

478. Cold currents moving from high latitudes towards the equator tend to cool nearby coastal areas. Since cool air is relatively dense and stays near the surface, fog is quite common but clouds and rain are rare. As a result, places such as southern California, northern Chile and south western Africa experience desert conditions.

According to the passage, northern Chile experiences desert conditions because

(A) it's located on the coast.

(B) fog is very common.

(C) cold currents move toward the equator.

(D) it has the same temperature as southern California.

Set 17 (11 Questions)

479. Most of Earth's seas experience two high and two low tides each day. There is also a less noticeable tide in its solid crust, which causes a variation in height of about half a meter. The tides are caused by the combined effects of the gravitational pull of the moon and the sun. Clearly, the pull of lunar gravity is greatest where Earth's surface is nearest the moon. On the opposite side of Earth, the pull of lunar gravity is weakest. The overall result is that there are equal-sized oceanic bulges on opposite sides of the planet.

According to the passage, tides are caused by

(A) gravitational pull.

(B) the moon and the sun.

(C) lunar gravity alone.

(D) oceanic bulges.

480. Such global warming is generally attributed to an increase in greenhouse gases, particularly carbon dioxide and methane. Most of these gases have been added to the atmosphere by human activity, notably the clearing of forests by slash and burn farming, changes in agricultural land use, increased use of fossil fuels and rampant urbanization/industrialization. Since about 1860, levels of atmospheric carbon dioxide have increased by more than 30% and methane levels have more than doubled.

According to the passage, what is *not* a cause of global warming?

(A) Increased use of fossil fuels

(B) Sustainable farming

(C) Urbanization

(D) Clearing of forests

481. The haka is a traditional Maori dance often performed by groups of men for various reasons. Few haka are performed by women. Originally, haka were performed by soldiers to intimidate the opposition while demonstrating courage and strength; today, the haka is used to welcome distinguished guests, celebrate milestones, and pay respect at funerals. Each haka has its own lyrics, meaning and movements, but typically, the dance is characterized by vigorous movements and strong rhythm.

Which of the following is true about the haka?

(A) The haka originated as a means of fighting.

(B) Women perform as many haka as men do.

(C) Haka are used to say goodbye to guests.

(D) The haka was originally a pre-war dance.

482. For example, around 10,000 years ago people in the Danube River valley of southeastern Europe were highly mobile foragers who left only short-lived campsites for archaeologists to discover, but by about 7,000 years ago, they were a rather sedentary people, living in riverside villages that you would normally associate with farming people. However, the folk of these villages, including the fascinating site of Lepenski Vir, weren't farmers; they continued to hunt and gather.

Based on the passage, it's safe to assume that

(A) something changed drastically within that 3,000-year period.

(B) the foragers died out and made way for permanent civilizations.

(C) a catastrophe struck at Lepenski Vir.

(D) the people within the civilization at Lepenski Vir became lazy.

483. In order to draw an ellipse, place two drawing pins some distance apart and loop a piece of string around them. Place a pencil inside the string, draw the string tight and move the pencil around the pins. Now move one of the pins and repeat the process. Note how the shape of the ellipse has changed.

The main theme of this passage is

(A) pencils and pins.

(B) how to draw an ellipse.

(C) changing the shape of an ellipse.

(D) strings, pencils, and pins.

484. When stress and turmoil cause those around them to lose their moral bearings and to succumb to questionable values or policies, great leaders stay on course. In challenging circumstances, this trait of great leaders sometimes causes consternation among followers. When others are ready to capitulate or bend, such leaders can appear stubborn and inflexible. In their most challenging moments, leaders like Lincoln, Churchill, Rosa Parks, or Martin Luther King, Jr. sometimes looked behind and saw their most committed followers losing heart or fleeing.

According to the passage, great leaders

(A) continue to follow their moral compasses.

(B) have lost thousands of followers.

(C) are rarely flexible.

(D) only come along once in a generation.

485. The term "Green Beret" refers to the U.S. Army Special Forces because they wear — you guessed it — green berets. The Green Berets specialize in unconventional warfare, special reconnaissance, and a handful of other tasks that require the Army to choose members carefully.

According to the passage, the Army's Special Forces

(A) wear green berets.

(B) focus on peacekeeping efforts.

(C) specialize in unconventional warfare.

(D) Both A and C are correct.

486. Charlemagne decreed rules affecting the major fields of government, rules that applied to the entire territory of the empire. They affected everywhere and everybody: the large rural estates, teaching, legislation, the various divisions of the kingdom, and the emperor's own envoys, the *missi dominici*. These rules were known as the *capitularies*. In similar fashion, Charlemagne strove to unify the currency of his empire by establishing a monetary system based on a silver coin, the denier.

According to the passage, Charlemagne

(A) wrote laws and created a financial system.

(B) made rules that royalty was exempt from following.

(C) created capitularies that the emperor's envoys enforced.

(D) was stamped on a new coin.

487. It is only really by enlightened people that this book can be read; the ordinary man is not made for such knowledge; philosophy will never be his lot. Those who say that there are truths which must be hidden from the people, need not be alarmed; the people do not read; they work six days of the week, and on the seventh go to the inn. In a word, philosophical works are made only for philosophers, and every honest man must try to be a philosopher, without pluming himself on being one.

The author of this passage most likely believes that

(A) few people should strive to become philosophers.

(B) enlightened people are better than others.

(C) common people cannot read.

(D) philosophy is too complex for ordinary people.

Questions 488 and 489 are based on the following passage.

Some believe it originated in a random manner, possibly in a chemical "soup" enriched by early atmospheric gases such as methane and carbon dioxide, with energy supplied by lightning or solar ultraviolet light. Others suggest the raw materials, or life itself, were delivered by comets and meteorites – a theory known as "panspermia." Yet another possibility is that the first life forms lived deep beneath Earth's surface, where the temperature was far above 100°C, with sulfur in the rocks as their source of nutrition. Warm environments around deep sea volcanic vents, known as black smokers, are another alternative.

488. According to the passage,

(A) temperatures above 100°C cause life forms to feed on sulfur.

(B) ultraviolet light is a source of energy for methane and carbon dioxide.

(C) there are multiple theories about how life began on Earth.

(D) black smokers are fueled by carbon dioxide and methane.

489. According to the passage, early atmospheric gases included

(A) sulfur and methane.

(B) methane and carbon dioxide.

(C) volcanic ash and carbon.

(D) carbon dioxide and black smokers.

Set 18 (11 Questions)

490. Within a short time, he had obtained visual evidence to support the theories of Copernicus and Kepler. Galileo became the first person in history to see the phases of Venus caused by its movement around the Sun. He also observed mountains and craters on the Moon, and saw the planets as disks, rather than points of light.

According to the passage, who first observed the phases of Venus?

(A) Galileo

(B) Copernicus

(C) Kepler

(D) The passage doesn't say.

491. Rock strata that were once horizontal may even be bent back or turned upside down, so that the older rocks are now on top of younger rocks. Beneath the crater floor is a lens-shaped body of breccia — rock that has been broken and pulverized by the shock wave. The incoming object itself is melted or partly vaporized.

According to the passage, breccia is

(A) bent rock strata.

(B) horizontal rock strata.

(C) broken rock.

(D) vaporized.

492. Add two inches of water to the saucepan and place your double-boiler inside it. Put 3 cups of wax shavings into the double-boiler and turn on the burner to melt the wax. Insert a thermometer every minute or so to find out when the wax reaches 150°F. At 150°F, remove the double-boiler from the saucepan and pour the wax into your molds. Wait for the candles to cool before lighting them.

According to this passage, you can assume that

(A) wax shavings melt quickly.

(B) you should remove the wax from the heat when it reaches 150°F.

(C) making candles requires expertise.

(D) saucepans are best for melting wax.

493. Just as deep honesty does not mean total transparency, deep selflessness does not require total self-abnegation. A deeply selfless leader may exhibit forms of self-regard, or even self-indulgence. This can include a needed retreat from others in order to gather strength, or private behaviors that may assault conventional sensibilities.

From the context of the passage, you can assume that

(A) great leaders can be self-indulgent.

(B) selfless leaders always put themselves last.

(C) a good leader doesn't take vacations.

(D) private behaviors need to be approved by followers.

494. The lathe faceplate is an accessory that belongs with a wood or metal turning lathe. It's usually made from cast iron in a circular shape, and it fixes to the end of the lathe spindle. So how do you use it? Clamp the piece you're working on to the faceplate using T-nuts in the slots.

A good title for this passage might be

(A) "Using T-Nuts."

(B) "Lathe Faceplates."

(C) "Accessories for Lathes."

(D) "Cast Iron Lathe Plates."

495. From a philosophical and ethical point of view, moral courage is not an "extra" or a "supererogatory" virtue, but rather a critical human quality that serves as a necessary precondition for all other forms of human conduct. Moral courage is about our willingness to act on an idea, a belief, or a value. Moral courage is the readiness to endure danger for the sake of principle.

The author of this passage would probably agree that

(A) everyone has similar morals.

(B) most people have moral courage.

(C) principle isn't as important as courage.

(D) moral courage is an essential human quality.

496. After attending the rigorous Vincentian Catholic High School in Albany, Burke went on to Holy Cross. A brief stint in the navy was followed by the Harvard Business School. He joined J&J in 1953 as brand manager for Band–Aids and quickly rose through the ranks. By 1976 he was named CEO.

According to the passage, during what year did Burke join J&J?

(A) 1950

(B) 1953

(C) 1970

(D) 1976

Questions 497 and 498 are based on the following passage.

In the hard scrabble world of Lincoln's youth, manhood entailed more than just reaching a certain age. It meant strength, endurance, and physical contests of all kinds. At six foot, four inches tall with a well-muscled physique, thanks to years of heavy farm work, Lincoln could hold his own against boys and men alike. In 1832, as a militia volunteer in the Black Hawk Wars, Lincoln was elected captain not only because of his affability and popularity, but also because he was the company's champion wrestler.

497. According to the passage, Lincoln was

(A) popular.

(B) a wrestler.

(C) muscular.

(D) all of the above.

498. Based on the context of the passage, you can assume that

(A) Lincoln was a good fighter.

(B) Lincoln was drafted into the militia.

(C) Lincoln fought on the farm.

(D) boys had to complete physical tests to become men.

499. More refractory elements condense in the warm, inner regions of the nebula, while icy grains condense in the cold outer regions. Individual grains collide and stick together, growing into centimeter-sized particles. These swirl around at different rates within the flared disk, partly due to turbulence and partly as the result of differences in the drag exerted by the gas.

According to the passage,

(A) cold grains and refractory elements mix to create gas.

(B) you can find refractory elements in the inner regions of the nebula.

(C) ice typically develops into one-centimeter grains.

(D) turbulence and gas create drag.

500. Rosa Parks' courageous decision to act by not acting, by not getting up, and her subsequent arrest and conviction on charges of disorderly conduct proved to be the "tipping point" for race relations and for the beginning of the Civil Rights Movement in America. According to activist and author Eldridge Cleaver, because of Rosa Parks, "somewhere in the universe, a gear in the machinery shifted."

According to the passage, what was the "tipping point"?

(A) Rosa Parks' conviction

(B) Rosa Parks' arrest

(C) Rosa Parks' decision to act by not acting

(D) All of the above

Chapter **3**

Mathematics Knowledge: Making Sure the Answers Add Up

The ASVAB's Mathematics Knowledge subtest is a big deal. It forms a large part of your AFQT score, so you need to do well on it to pass muster. This subtest covers a big range of mathematical concepts, including arithmetic, algebra, and geometry, so it's a good idea to dust off the corners of your brain where you stashed all this knowledge during high school. You're going to find questions that include fractions, square roots, inequalities, factoring, graphing, and much more on the test. You'll have 20 minutes to answer 16 Mathematics Knowledge questions on the computerized ASVAB or 24 minutes to answer 25 questions on the paper version. Calculators are not allowed.

The Questions You'll Work On

The Mathematics Knowledge subtest includes the following:

>> **Basic mathematics:** These questions include ratios, scientific notation, and arithmetic (such as addition, subtraction, multiplication, and division).

>> **Fractions:** These questions ask you to work with parts of a whole by multiplying, dividing, adding, subtracting, and converting fractions.

>> **Algebra:** These questions require you to solve equations and inequalities, factor, solve for variables, and work with exponents. You'll even find a few quadratic equations.

>> **Geometry:** These questions ask you to define the properties of figures, find angles and relationships between points, and measure specific distances.

What to Watch Out For

When you work on the Mathematics Knowledge questions, keep these tips in mind:

» The order of operations is important, so remember the acronym PEMDAS for Parentheses, Exponents, Multiplication and Division, and Addition and Subtraction.

» Read the problem thoroughly before trying to calculate an answer.

» Write out the full problem before you start your calculations. That way, you can spot opportunities to cross-cancel fractions.

» Reduce fractions to their lowest terms.

» Keep an eye on units of measurement, and make sure you're using the same ones across the board.

» You get unlimited scratch paper when you take the ASVAB, so use it to work out solutions and draw diagrams whenever possible. Visualizing a problem often makes solving it easier.

Fractions

501. Solve: $\frac{4}{8}+\frac{1}{9}$

 (A) $\frac{11}{18}$

 (B) $\frac{3}{17}$

 (C) $\frac{5}{17}$

 (D) $\frac{5}{18}$

502. Solve: $\frac{2}{5}-\frac{1}{4}$

 (A) $\frac{7}{20}$

 (B) $\frac{3}{20}$

 (C) $\frac{1}{3}$

 (D) 3

503. Solve: $1\frac{7}{8}\times\frac{5}{6}$

 (A) $1\frac{9}{16}$

 (B) $\frac{26}{16}$

 (C) $1\frac{3}{4}$

 (D) $3\frac{13}{16}$

504. Simplify: $\frac{x^2}{x^2+x-12}\cdot\frac{x^2-9}{2x^6}$

 (A) $\frac{x}{x^3+2x+2}$

 (B) $\frac{x^3}{3}x$

 (C) $3\frac{x^2}{2x}$

 (D) $\frac{x+3}{2x^5+8x^4}$

505. Reduce to lowest terms: $\frac{9x^3y}{3xy^5}$

 (A) $\frac{9x}{3xy^3}$

 (B) $3x^2y^4$

 (C) $\frac{3x^2}{y^4}$

 (D) $\frac{3x^2y^4}{9}$

506. Simplify: $\frac{1+\sqrt{7}}{2-\sqrt{7}}$

 (A) $3\sqrt{-1}$

 (B) $3\sqrt{1}$

 (C) $3-\sqrt{7}$

 (D) $-3-\sqrt{7}$

507. Solve: $32^{\frac{1}{5}}$

(A) 2

(B) 3

(C) 5

(D) 6

508. Which fractions are not equivalent?

(A) $\frac{3}{7}, \frac{6}{14}$

(B) $\frac{3}{10}, \frac{9}{30}$

(C) $\frac{9}{3}, \frac{36}{9}$

(D) $\frac{12}{6}, \frac{48}{24}$

509. Solve: $\frac{1}{3} + \frac{1}{4} + \frac{1}{4}$

(A) $\frac{1}{11}$

(B) $\frac{3}{11}$

(C) $\frac{5}{6}$

(D) $\frac{3}{12}$

510. Simplify: $\frac{3y^2}{x+1} \div \frac{y}{2}$

(A) $\frac{3y^2}{x+3}$

(B) $\frac{6y}{x+1}$

(C) $\frac{4y^2}{x+1}$

(D) $\frac{y^2}{x+3}$

Percentages

511. Find 25 percent of 200.

(A) 50

(B) 25

(C) 15

(D) 12.5

512. 250 is 40% of what number?

(A) 650

(B) 625

(C) 6,250

(D) 6,500

513. 8 is what percent of 20?

(A) 35

(B) 16

(C) 20

(D) 40

514. 15 is what percent of 375?

(A) 45

(B) 5

(C) 6

(D) 4

515. 450 is 75% of what number?

(A) 650

(B) 550

(C) 600

(D) 675

516. What is 33% of 120?

(A) 39

(B) 40.6

(C) 39.6

(D) 38.9

517. What is 55% of 150?

(A) 75

(B) 83.5

(C) 80

(D) 82.5

518. Find 8.6% of 310.

(A) 26.66

(B) 25.8

(C) 25.68

(D) 28.56

519. What percent of 56 is 14?

(A) 30

(B) 28

(C) 25

(D) 22.5

520. Find 12.5% of 989. Convert the answer into a fraction.

(A) 123.375

(B) $123\frac{5}{8}$

(C) $865\frac{7}{8}$

(D) 865.375

Ratios

521. Express the ratio of ducks to geese: There are 16 ducks and 9 geese in a park.

(A) $\frac{9}{16}$

(B) $\frac{16}{9}$

(C) $16:9$

(D) Both B and C

522. Express the ratio of women to men as a fraction and simplify: There are 15 women and 20 men in the group.

(A) $\frac{75}{100}$

(B) $\frac{3}{4}$

(C) $\frac{45}{60}$

(D) $\frac{15}{20}$

523. The ratio of a to b to c to d to e is 5 to 4 to 3 to 2 to 1. If $a = 60$, what is the value of c?

(A) 24

(B) 36

(C) 63

(D) 61

524. There are 27 males and 38 females in Group A, and there are 42 females and 26 males in Group B. Express these relationships as a pair of ratios of males to females.

(A) $27:38,\ 26:42$

(B) $38:27,\ 26:42$

(C) $27:26,\ 38:42$

(D) $27:38,\ 42:26$

525. Use a height-to-width ratio to express the fact that a horse is 7 feet, 6 inches tall and 10 feet long.

(A) $7.6:10$

(B) $7.5:120$

(C) $75:120$

(D) $90:120$

526. Solve for x if $a = 150$ and $b = 7$:

$a:x$

$b:70$

$c:y$

$d:z$

(A) 1,200

(B) 10,500

(C) 1,500

(D) Not enough information provided

527. Convert 297.85 centimeters to feet.

(A) 10 feet

(B) 9 feet

(C) 8 feet

(D) 11 feet

528. Convert 12.8 meters to centimeters.

(A) 12,800 cm

(B) 1,280 cm

(C) 1,300 cm

(D) 1,250 cm

529. One of 20 dogs at the shelter has three legs, two ears, and one tail. Express the ratio of dogs that have three legs to the remaining dogs as a fraction.

(A) $\frac{1}{20}$

(B) $\frac{19}{20}$

(C) $\frac{1x}{20}$

(D) $\frac{1}{19}$

530. The ratio of 1.5 to 32 equals the ratio of $\frac{1}{5}$ to x. Solve for x.

(A) 0.4

(B) 0.45

(C) 0.39

(D) 0.43

Scientific Notation

531. Express 7,000 in scientific notation.

(A) 7×10^2

(B) $7^{10 \times 2}$

(C) 7×10^3

(D) 7^3

532. Express 0.59784 in scientific notation.

(A) 5.9784×10^{-1}

(B) 5.9784×10^{-2}

(C) 5.9784×10^1

(D) 0.59784×10^{-1}

533. Express 6,000,000 in scientific notation.

(A) 6×10^{-6}

(B) 6×10^6

(C) 60×10^6

(D) 6.0×10^5

534. Multiply 4.1357×10^{-15} and 5.4×10^2.

(A) 2.233278×10^{-12}

(B) 2.233278×10^{-13}

(C) 22.33278×10^{-12}

(D) 2.233278×10^{-14}

535. What number does 854.345×10^{-3} represent?

(A) 854,345

(B) 8,543,450

(C) 0.0854345

(D) 0.854345

Square Roots

536. Solve: $\sqrt{49}$

(A) 9

(B) 6

(C) 7

(D) 8

537. Simplify: $\sqrt{12a^4b^3c^2}$

(A) $2a^2bc\sqrt{3b}$

(B) $2a^2c\sqrt{3b^3c}$

(C) $2a^2bc^2\sqrt{3}$

(D) $2\sqrt{3a^2}b^{\frac{3}{2}}c$

538. Solve $\sqrt{-75x}$ when $x = -3$.

(A) 15^2

(B) 25

(C) 1.5

(D) 15

539. Simplify: $5\sqrt[3]{x^5y^2} \times \sqrt[3]{8x^2y^4}$

(A) $10x^4y^2\sqrt[3]{x}$

(B) $10x^2y^2\sqrt[3]{2x^2}$

(C) $10x^2y^2\sqrt[3]{x}$

(D) $10x^2y^3\sqrt[3]{x}$

540. Solve: $\sqrt[3]{343}$

(A) 114

(B) 7

(C) 12

(D) 8

Algebra

541. Solve for a: $2a + 27 = 33$

(A) 3

(B) 4

(C) 5

(D) 6

542. Solve for x:

$$\begin{bmatrix} 3 & 2 \\ 5 & 4 \\ 7 & 3 \end{bmatrix} + \begin{bmatrix} 6 & 1 \\ 5 & x \\ 3 & 6 \end{bmatrix} = \begin{bmatrix} 9 & 3 \\ 10 & 8 \\ 10 & 9 \end{bmatrix}$$

(A) 4

(B) 3

(C) −1

(D) 12

543. Solve for x: $-32 = x + 3$

(A) 35

(B) −35

(C) 29

(D) −29

544. Solve for x: $29 + \dfrac{3x}{1} = 65$

(A) 3

(B) 14

(C) 21

(D) 12

545. Solve for a: $ra = 11a + 7$

(A) $a = \dfrac{7}{r + 11}$

(B) $a = \dfrac{7}{11}$

(C) $a = \dfrac{7}{r - 11}$

(D) Not enough data

546. What is $y + 3x - 6 = 0$ in slope-intercept form?

(A) $y = 3x + 6$

(B) $y = -3x + 6$

(C) $y = -3x - 6$

(D) $6y = -3x$

547. Solve for x: $17x = 85$

(A) 5

(B) 17

(C) 6

(D) 8

548. Convert into a mathematical expression:

The fourth root of 239 equals the log with respect to the base a of the product of x and y.

(A) $\sqrt{4} \times 239 = \log_a(xy)$

(B) $\sqrt[4]{239} = \log_a(xy)$

(C) $\sqrt[4]{239} = \log^a xy$

(D) $\sqrt[4]{239} = \log_{239a}(xy)$

549. Solve for x: $4x + 6 = -30$

(A) −8

(B) 4

(C) −9

(D) 9

550. Solve for y: $6(y + 7) = 3y$

(A) 14

(B) 13

(C) −14

(D) 17

551. Solve for x: $x + 10 = 19 - 2x$

(A) 3

(B) −2

(C) −3

(D) 4

552. Solve for x: $17x + -2 = 117 + 3x$

(A) 9

(B) 8

(C) 8.5

(D) 11

553. Solve for x: $134(x + 12) = 402x$

(A) 4

(B) 6

(C) −6

(D) 22

554. Simplify: $\left(3x^7y^5\right)^2$

(A) $9x^7y^5$

(B) $9x^{14}y^5$

(C) $9x^7y^{10}$

(D) $9x^{14}y^{10}$

555. Express in standard form:
$7x^3 + 4y^5 - 2y^2 - 8y + 9y^4 + 32$

(A) $9y^4 - 8y + 7x^3 + 4y^5 - 2y^2 + 32$

(B) $4y^5 + 9y^4 + 7x^3 - 2y^2 - 8y + 32$

(C) $32 + 9y^4 - 8y + 7x^3 + 4y^5 - 2y^2$

(D) $4y^5 + 9y^4 + 7x^3 + 2y^2 + 8y + 32$

556. Simplify: $x^4 4x^2 + 4x - 12$

(A) $4x^8 + 4x - 12$

(B) $8x^6 - 12$

(C) $16x + 4x - 12$

(D) $4x^6 + 4x - 12$

557. Solve for x: $\frac{x}{7} = 42$

(A) 294

(B) 295

(C) 290

(D) 6

558. Rewrite in slope–intercept form:
$x + y + 9 - 4x + 2y = 0$

(A) $y = x + 3$

(B) $3y = 3x + 9$

(C) $y = \frac{3x}{9} - 9$

(D) $y = x - 3$

559. Solve: $|5c + 9| < 3$

(A) $-\frac{12}{5} < c < -\frac{6}{5}$

(B) $\frac{12}{5} < c < \frac{6}{5}$

(C) $-\frac{12}{5} < -\frac{6}{5}$

(D) $c < -\frac{6}{5} < -\frac{12}{5}$

560. Factor: $36x^2 - 49y^2$

(A) $(6x + 7y)(6x - 7y)$

(B) $\left(6x(6x)\right)\left(7y(7y)\right)$

(C) $(6x + 6x)(7y - 7y)$

(D) $\left(6x^3\right)\left(7y^3\right)$

561. Solve for x: $-10x + -23 = 23 + -8x$

(A) −22

(B) 23

(C) −23

(D) −24

562. Factor: $64x^3 - 27y^3$

(A) $(4x - 3y)\left(4x^2 - 12xy + 3y^2\right)$

(B) $(4x - 3y)\left(4x^2 + 12xy + 3y^2\right)$

(C) $(4x - 3y)\left(16x^2 + 12xy + 9y^2\right)$

(D) $(4x - 3y)\left(16x^2 - 12xy + 9y^2\right)$

563. Simplify: $\frac{5x^2 - 5}{6x + 24} \times \frac{x + 4}{x - 1}$

(A) $\frac{5}{6}x + \frac{5}{6}$

(B) $\frac{5}{6}x$

(C) $\frac{5}{6}x + \frac{5}{6}$

(D) $\frac{5}{6}x^2 + \frac{5}{6}$

564. Solve: $-4x + 6 \geq 10$

(A) $x \geq -1$

(B) $x \geq 1$

(C) $x \leq -1$

(D) $4x \leq 1$

565. Identify: $x + 3 \leq 2$

(A)

(B)

(C)

(D)

566. Solve for x: $\frac{47}{94}x + 17 = 8.5$

(A) 24

(B) 17

(C) −17

(D) −19

567. Find the equation for a straight line with a slope of 4 that passes through the point $(-2, -12)$.

(A) $y = 4x - 4$

(B) $y = -4x - 4$

(C) $y = 4x + 4$

(D) $-12 = mx - 4x$

568. Simplify: $\left(\left(x^5\right)^7\right)^9$

(A) x^{21}

(B) x^{22}

(C) x^{31}

(D) x^{315}

569. If $a = 2$ and $b = 5$, solve: $5a + 2b = c$

(A) 100

(B) 110

(C) 120

(D) 95

570. Solve for x: $\frac{3}{2}x + 4 = 13$

(A) 11

(B) 9

(C) 18

(D) 6

571. Reduce to the lowest terms: $\frac{x^2 - 6x - 7}{x^2 - 10x + 21}$

(A) $\frac{x+1}{x-2}$

(B) $\frac{x-3}{x+1}$

(C) $\frac{x+1}{x-3}$

(D) $\frac{x+7}{x-3}$

572. $(a+b)+c =$

(A) $a+(b+c)$

(B) $a(b+c)$

(C) $ab + ac$

(D) $a^2 b^2$

573. Solve for x: $4x + 8y = 6x$

(A) $4y$

(B) $6y$

(C) 4

(D) 5

574. Solve for x: $5x + 7 = 5(x-2) - 3(3x-3)$

(A) $\frac{8}{9}$

(B) $-\frac{9}{8}$

(C) $-\frac{8}{9}$

(D) $-1\frac{1}{9}$

575. Which of the following is true if $a = b$?

(A) $a + c = b + c$

(B) $a - c = b - c$

(C) $ac = bc$

(D) All of the above

576. Solve for a: $475.5a + 38 = 1,464.5$

(A) 4

(B) 3

(C) 2

(D) −2

577. Simplify: $(x+7)(3x+9)$

(A) $3x^3 + 30x^2 + 63$

(B) $3x^2 + 60x + 33$

(C) $3x^2 + 30x + 63$

(D) $3x^2 + 35x + 33$

578. Solve: $(1+4i) - (-16+9i)$

(A) $9 \pm 5i$

(B) $17 \pm 5i$

(C) $4 - 9i$

(D) $17 - 5i$

579. If $x = 7$ and $y = 9$ solve for z: $z = 4x - 3y$

    (A) −1

    (B) 0

    (C) 1

    (D) 2

580. Solve for x: $(9 \times 1)(10 - 8)(-6 + 8) = x^2$

    (A) 6

    (B) 6 or −6

    (C) 36 or −36

    (D) 36

581. Solve for c: $12c + 18c = 90$

    (A) 30

    (B) 3

    (C) −3

    (D) 60

582. Factor: $12x^3 (6x^2) - x - 2$

    (A) $72 - x^5 - 2$

    (B) $72x^5 - x - 2$

    (C) $72x^6 - 2$

    (D) $72x^5 - 2 + x$

583. Solve: $(1 + i)(1 - i)$

    (A) $2i$

    (B) $2i^2$

    (C) i^2

    (D) 2

584. Solve: $\ln\left(4^{2x}\right)$

    (A) $2x \ln(2)$

    (B) $4x \ln(2)$

    (C) $\log_2 4 \ln^2$

    (D) $\ln\left(2^2\right)$

585. $x^2\left(x^3\right) =$

    (A) x^5

    (B) x^6

    (C) x^{-1}

    (D) $5x$

586. Solve for x: $\frac{3}{4} \div x = \frac{3}{8}$

    (A) 3

    (B) 2

    (C) $\frac{1}{4}$

    (D) $\frac{3}{4}$

587. If $a = b$ and $c \neq 0$, then

    (A) $\frac{ab}{c} = \frac{1}{2}cb$

    (B) $\frac{a}{c} = \frac{b}{c}$

    (C) both A and B are correct.

    (D) none of the above.

588. Solve for x: $5x - 2 - 3x = 3(x - 1) - 8$

    (A) 9

    (B) −9

    (C) 11

    (D) 12

589. Solve the system:
$$\begin{cases} x + y = 5 \\ x - y = 3 \end{cases}$$

    (A) $x = 5$ and $y = 1$

    (B) $x = 4$ and $y = 1$

    (C) $x = 4$ and $y = 2$

    (D) $x = 5$ and $y = 2$

590. Solve for y: $1{,}200y + 4y = 7{,}224$

    (A) 7

    (B) 6

    (C) 10

    (D) 9

591. Solve: $\log_4 64 = x$

    (A) 4

    (B) 3

    (C) −4

    (D) 7

592. Find the equation of the line that passes through $(-2, 4)$ and $(1, 2)$.

(A) $y = -\frac{2}{3}x + \frac{8}{3}$

(B) $y = \frac{2}{3}x + \frac{8}{3}$

(C) $y = -\frac{2}{3}x - \frac{8}{3}$

(D) $y = \frac{2}{3}x - \frac{8}{3}$

593. Given $|a + bi|$ in the complex plane, which of the following is *not* true?

(A) $|a + bi| = 1 + |a + bi| - 1$

(B) $|a + bi| = \sqrt{a^2 + b^2}$

(C) $|a + bi| = |a + bi^2|$

(D) $|a + bi^2| = |a + bi^2|$

594. Simplify: $2(a - 3) + 4b - 2(a - b - 3) + 5$

(A) $-4a + 6b + 5$

(B) $6b + 17$

(C) $4a + 6b + 5$

(D) $6b + 5$

595. Find the equation for a line with a slope of 50 and a y-intercept of 32.

(A) $y = 32x + 50$

(B) $y = 50x + 32$

(C) $y = \frac{1}{50}x + 32$

(D) $y = 32x + 50$

596. Choose the appropriate graph for $3(4x - 7) \leq 15$.

(A) $-5\ -4\ -3\ -2\ -1\ 0\ 1\ 2\ 3\ 4\ 5$

(B) $-5\ -4\ -3\ -2\ -1\ 0\ 1\ 2\ 3\ 4\ 5$

(C) $-5\ -4\ -3\ -2\ -1\ 0\ 1\ 2\ 3\ 4\ 5$

(D) $-5\ -4\ -3\ -2\ -1\ 0\ 1\ 2\ 3\ 4\ 5$

597. If $a = -15$ and $b = -13$, then $a(a - b) =$

(A) 30

(B) -420

(C) 420

(D) -30

598. Solve for y if $a = 3$, $b = 7$, and $x = 4$:
$4a + 10b - 6x = y$

(A) 58

(B) 57

(C) 51

(D) 60

599. Solve: $|2x + 3| = 4x - 3$

(A) $\{3, 3\}$

(B) $\{3, 0\}$

(C) $\{3, 12\}$

(D) $\{-3, 3\}$

600. Identify the group of prime numbers.

(A) 2, 3, 5

(B) 7, 9, 11

(C) 2, 4, 6

(D) 6, 7, 9

601. Solve for x: $2x + 6 = 10$

(A) 5

(B) 4

(C) 0.5

(D) 2

602. What is the greatest common factor of 10 and 100?

(A) 10

(B) 1

(C) 100

(D) 50

603. Solve for p: $5p + 14 = 29 + 2p$

(A) 2

(B) 3

(C) -5

(D) 5

604. If $x = 3$, solve for y: $y = x^2 + 4x - x^4$

(A) 100

(B) -60

(C) 60

(D) 160

605. Solve for x: $5x - 6 = 3x - 8$

  (A) 0

  (B) −1

  (C) −2

  (D) 1

606. Solve for a: $-20 = -4a - 6a$

  (A) −2

  (B) 3

  (C) 2

  (D) 1

607. Solve for x: $(5(5x)) + 7 = 25x + 7$

  (A) 4

  (B) 1

  (C) 3

  (D) All of the above

608. Solve: $6x = 3!$

  (A) 1

  (B) −1

  (C) 0

  (D) 6

609. Simplify: $(xxx)(x^7)$

  (A) $3x^7$

  (B) $3x^9$

  (C) x^{10}

  (D) x^{21}

610. Solve for x: $6^3 + 4^3 + x = 282$

  (A) 2

  (B) $2x$

  (C) $2x^3$

  (D) 4

611. Simplify: $\sqrt{100x^3 y^4 z^2}$

  (A) $10x^{\frac{3}{2}} yz$

  (B) $10x^{\frac{3}{2}} y^2 z$

  (C) $10x^{\frac{2}{3}} y^2 z$

  (D) $10x^{\frac{3}{2}} y^3 z^2$

612. Solve for x: $8x \geq 6$

  (A) $\frac{1}{2}$

  (B) 1

  (C) $\frac{3}{4}$

  (D) $1\frac{1}{2}$

613. Solve: $\begin{cases} x + y = 1 \\ x + 3y = 9 \end{cases}$

  (A) $(3, 4)$

  (B) $(4, 3)$

  (C) $(-3, 4)$

  (D) $(-3, -4)$

614. Solve for x: $x + 9 + 3 = 20$

  (A) 12

  (B) 9

  (C) 8

  (D) 6

615. Simplify: $6x^3 + 5x^3 + 4x^3 + x + 7$

  (A) $15x^3 + x + 7$

  (B) $15x^9 + x + 7$

  (C) $16x^3 + 7$

  (D) $15x^6 + x + 7$

616. Simplify: $38x^{17} - 24x^{17} + 3$

  (A) $62x^{17} + 3$

  (B) $62x^{34} + 3$

  (C) $14x^{34} + 3$

  (D) $14x^{17} + 3$

617. If $a = 7$, $b = 3$, and $c = 1$, solve for x: $ax^2 + bx + c = 0$

  (A) $x = \dfrac{-3 \pm \sqrt{-19}}{14}$

  (B) $x = \dfrac{-7 \pm \sqrt{-3}}{14}$

  (C) $x = \dfrac{-3 \pm \sqrt{-25}}{14}$

  (D) $x = \dfrac{-3 \pm \sqrt{19}}{14}$

618. Find the equation for a line with a slope of 4 when $x = -1$ and $y = -6$.

(A) $y = 4x - 2$

(B) $y = -6x$

(C) $y = 4x + 2$

(D) $y = 6x - 2$

619. Find the equation of the line that passes through the points $(2, 4)$ and $(4, 8)$.

(A) $y = 2x + 4$

(B) $y = 2x$

(C) $y = 4x + 8$

(D) $4 = 2x + 8$

620. Factor: $x^2 - 5x + 6$

(A) $(x - 6)(x + 1)$

(B) $3(x - 2)(x - 3)$

(C) $x(x - 2) - 3(x - 3)$

(D) $(x - 2)(x - 3)$

621. Solve for x: $\left(\frac{1}{2}\right)^{2x+1} = 1$

(A) $\frac{1}{2}$

(B) $-\frac{1}{2}$

(C) Both A and B are correct.

(D) Neither A nor B is correct.

622. Solve for x: $26x + 35 = 68$

(A) $\frac{33}{26}$

(B) $\frac{34}{27}$

(C) $\frac{26}{33}$

(D) $1\frac{3}{2}$

623. Factor: $3x - 6$

(A) $3(x - 2)$

(B) $3(x - 3)$

(C) $2(x - 2)$

(D) $2(x - 3)$

624. Find y: $27x^3 + 35x^3 + 42x^2 = 85y$

(A) $\frac{62x + 42x}{85}$

(B) $\frac{62x^3 + 42x^2}{85y}$

(C) $\frac{85x^3 + 42x^2}{62}$

(D) $\frac{62x^3 + 42x^2}{85}$

625. Solve for x: $y = 2\log_3 x + \log_3 5$

(A) $\pm\sqrt{\frac{3^y}{5}}$

(B) $\pm\sqrt{\frac{3^y}{5}}$

(C) $\pm\sqrt{\frac{3^y}{5}}$

(D) $\pm\sqrt{\frac{3^y}{5}}$

626. Solve for x: $6x + 10 = 46$

(A) 36

(B) 6

(C) 8

(D) 16

627. Solve for x: $5x + 13 = |10x + 3|$

(A) 2 or $-\frac{16}{15}$

(B) 2

(C) $-\frac{16}{15}$

(D) -2 or $\frac{15}{16}$

628. Solve for x when $2x - 4 < 10$ and $x + 17 < 20$.

(A) $x \le 1$

(B) $x < -3$

(C) $x > 7$

(D) $x < 3$

629. Express x as greater than or equal to 3 in interval notation.

(A) $(3, \pm\infty)$

(B) $[3, +\infty)$

(C) $(3, -\infty)$

(D) $(3, +\infty]$

630. Solve for b: $3b + b = 28$

    (A) 7

    (B) $\frac{1}{2}$

    (C) 7.5

    (D) 4

631. Solve for x: $5x = 25$

    (A) 5^5

    (B) 3

    (C) 2

    (D) 5

632. If $4x - 2 = 3x + 4$, find $6x$.

    (A) 6

    (B) 36

    (C) 2

    (D) 24

633. Simplify: $48x + 27y = 75y$

    (A) $x = 2y$

    (B) $x = y$

    (C) $2x = y^2$

    (D) $x - y = y^2$

634. Simplify: $18a^2 + 2a^2 + b$

    (A) $20a + b$

    (B) $16a + b$

    (C) $20a^4 + b$

    (D) $20a^2 + b$

635. Solve for x: $48 + \frac{1}{3}x = 49$

    (A) $\frac{1}{2}$

    (B) $\frac{2}{3}$

    (C) 3

    (D) 6

636. Solve for x: $2(5x + 1) = 11x$

    (A) 2

    (B) 1

    (C) 3

    (D) 0

637. Solve for c: $0.5c + 12c = 37.5$

    (A) 3.5

    (B) 3

    (C) 2.5

    (D) 2

638. Simplify: $\sqrt{45x^2}$

    (A) $3\sqrt{5x^2}$

    (B) $3\sqrt{5x}$

    (C) $3x\sqrt{5}$

    (D) $5x\sqrt{3}$

639. Express a quantity with a coefficient of 3, a base of x, and an exponent of 5.

    (A) $x3^5$

    (B) $\frac{1}{3}x^5$

    (C) $3x^5$

    (D) $\frac{3^5}{x}$

640. Solve for a if $b = 2$: $8a + 9b = ab + 36$

    (A) 3

    (B) 2

    (C) 4

    (D) 6

Quadratic Equations

641. Solve for x: $\left(5\left(x^2\right) + 7\right) = -35 - 5x^2$

    (A) $\sqrt{-\frac{21}{5}}$

    (B) $\pm\sqrt{\frac{21}{5}}$

    (C) $\pm i\sqrt{\frac{21}{5}}$

    (D) $\pm\sqrt{-\frac{35}{5}}$

642. Express as a quadratic equation: $2x^2 - 8x - 4 = 3x - x^2$

    (A) $x^2 - 11x - 4 = 0$

    (B) $3x^2 - 11x - 4 = 0$

    (C) $3x^2 - 5x - 4 = 0$

    (D) $3x^2 - 11x - 3 = 0$

643. Solve for x: $x^2 - 8x + 15 = 0$

(A) $x = -3$, $x = 5$

(B) $x = -3$, $x = -5$

(C) $x = 3$, $x = -5$

(D) $x = 3$, $x = 5$

644. Solve for x by factoring: $3x^2 - 9x - 162 = 0$

(A) $x = -6$, $x = -9$

(B) $x = -6$, $x = 9$

(C) $x = -9$, $x = 6$

(D) $x = 6$, $x = 9$

645. Solve for x: $x^2 - 3x = 0$

(A) $x = 0$, $x = 3$

(B) $x = 3$, $x = 3$

(C) $x \pm 3$

(D) $x = 0$, $x = -3$

646. Solve for x: $x^2 = -3x + 2$

(A) $x = \dfrac{-3 + \sqrt{17}}{2}$, $x = \dfrac{-3 - \sqrt{17}}{2}$

(B) $x = \dfrac{-3 + \sqrt{17}}{2}$, $x = -\dfrac{3 + \sqrt{17}}{2}$

(C) $x = \dfrac{-3 + \sqrt{15}}{2}$, $x = \dfrac{-3 - \sqrt{15}}{2}$

(D) Not enough data

647. Solve: $(x-3)(x-4) = 0$

(A) $x = -4$, $x = 3$

(B) $x = -4$, $x = 5$

(C) $x = 2$, $x = 4$

(D) $x = 3$, $x = 4$

648. Solve: $x^2 + 5x + 6 = 0$

(A) $x = -2$, $x = -3$

(B) $x = -3$, $x = -4$

(C) $x = 3$, $x = -3$

(D) $x = -2$, $x = 3$

649. Solve for x: $2x^2 - 3x + 1 = 0$

(A) $x = 1$, $x = \dfrac{3}{2}$

(B) $x = 1$

(C) $x = 1$, $x = \dfrac{1}{2}$

(D) $x = \dfrac{1}{2}$, $x = \dfrac{1}{3}$

650. Solve: $4x^2 - 19x + 12 = 0$

(A) $x = 3$, $x = \dfrac{1}{4}$

(B) $x = \dfrac{1}{4}$, $x = \dfrac{1}{3}$

(C) $x = \dfrac{1}{2}$, $x = \dfrac{3}{4}$

(D) $x = 4$, $x = \dfrac{3}{4}$

Geometry

651. According to the figure, the intersection of line a is a

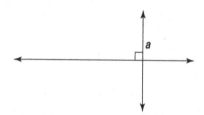

(A) parallel line.

(B) right angle.

(C) transversal.

(D) complementary angle.

652. Find the perimeter of the right triangle:

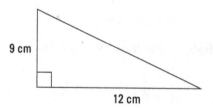

(A) 35 cm

(B) 36 cm

(C) 21 cm

(D) 15 cm

653. In the figure below, which angles are complementary?

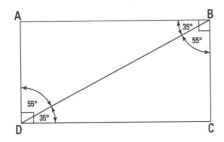

    (A) ∠DCB, ∠ACD

    (B) ∠ADC, ∠ABC

    (C) ∠ABC, ∠ABD

    (D) ∠ADB, ∠CDB

654. Find the area:

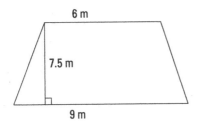

    (A) 56.25 m³

    (B) 56.75 m²

    (C) 56.5 m²

    (D) 56.25 m²

655. According to the figure, the angles formed by ray *DB* intersecting ∠*ADC* are

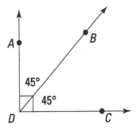

    (A) supplementary

    (B) right

    (C) complementary

    (D) parallel

656. The polygon depicted here is a/an _____ polygon.

    (A) hexagonal

    (B) convex

    (C) perpendicular

    (D) equilateral

657. Find the area:

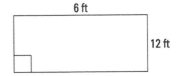

    (A) 72 sq. ft

    (B) 60 sq. ft

    (C) 18 sq. ft

    (D) None of the above

658. What is the formula to find the volume of a cube?

(A) $V = \pi r^2$

(B) $V = \left(\frac{4}{3}\right)\pi r^3$

(C) $V = 6s^2$

(D) $V = s^3$

659. Identify the Pythagorean theorem.

(A) $a^2 + b^2 + c^2 = s$

(B) $2a + b^2 = c^2$

(C) $a^2 + b^2 = c^2$

(D) $a^2 + b = c$

660. Find the length of b:

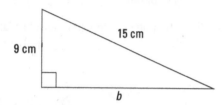

(A) 24 cm

(B) 12 cm

(C) 6 cm

(D) 33 cm

661. What is the measure of angle x if L1 and L2 are parallel lines?

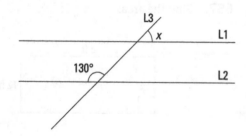

(A) 30°

(B) −40°

(C) 40°

(D) 50°

662. Find the area of sector c:

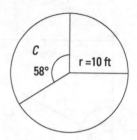

(A) 30.3 ft²

(B) 50.5 ft²

(C) 51 ft²

(D) 50.6 ft²

663. Find the area of this square:

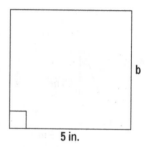

(A) 125 sq. in.

(B) 25 sq. in.

(C) 10 sq. in.

(D) 15 sq. in.

664. Find the measure of the interior angle x:

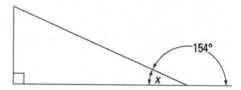

(A) 206°

(B) 16°

(C) 26°

(D) 36°

665. Find angle *b*:

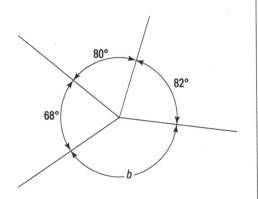

(A) 120°

(B) 125°

(C) 104°

(D) 130°

666. Find the perimeter of this square:

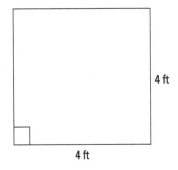

4 ft

4 ft

(A) 16 ft

(B) 16 ft^2

(C) 12 ft

(D) 8 ft

667. Find the surface area:

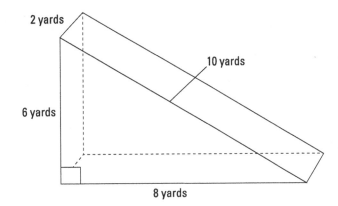

2 yards

10 yards

6 yards

8 yards

(A) 48 square yards

(B) 72 square yards

(C) 90 square yards

(D) 96 square yards

668. Find the measure of ∠C:

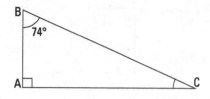

    (A) 106°

    (B) 16°

    (C) 36°

    (D) 30°

669. Which of the following statements is true of a line?

    (A) It has only one dimension.

    (B) It stops at two points.

    (C) It has a finite length.

    (D) It has width.

670. Find the total area:

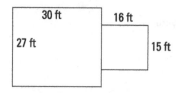

    (A) 1,050 ft²

    (B) 176 ft²

    (C) 352 ft²

    (D) 1,100 ft²

671. Find the perimeter:

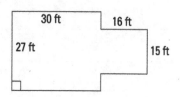

    (A) 88 ft

    (B) 161 ft

    (C) 145 ft

    (D) 146 ft

672. Find the area of the polygon if the apothem a is 10:

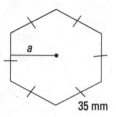

    (A) 1,100 mm²

    (B) 1,000 mm²

    (C) 1,050 mm²

    (D) 350 mm²

673. Find x:

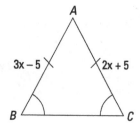

    (A) 10

    (B) 5

    (C) 4

    (D) 8

674. Find the measure of ∠B:

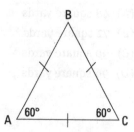

    (A) 120°

    (B) 60°

    (C) 180°

    (D) 90°

675. Find the measure of ∠C:

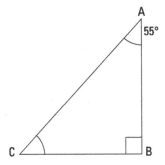

(A) 35°

(B) 45°

(C) 55°

(D) 40°

676. Find x, y, and z:

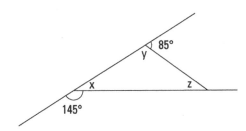

(A) $x = 35°$, $y = 95°$, $z = 40°$

(B) $x = 35°$, $y = 95°$, $z = 50°$

(C) $x = 45°$, $y = 95°$, $z = 45°$

(D) $x = 40°$, $y = 90°$, $z = 60°$

677. Find y:

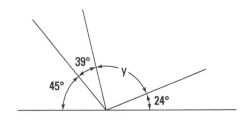

(A) 72°

(B) 70°

(C) 64°

(D) 80°

678. Label angle a:

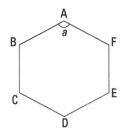

(A) ∠BAF

(B) ∠CBA

(C) ∠FBA

(D) ∠ABF

679. Identify the type of angle depicted:

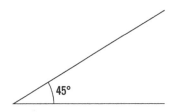

(A) Obtuse

(B) Straight

(C) Acute

(D) Right

680. Find the perimeter:

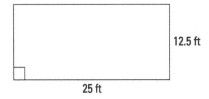

(A) 60 ft

(B) 100 ft

(C) 37.5 ft

(D) 75 ft

681. Find the measure of ∠R in △DRJ:

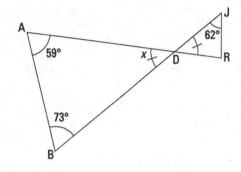

(A) 70°

(B) 78°

(C) 64°

(D) 112°

682. Find x:

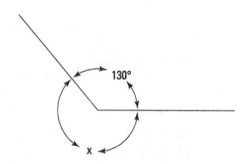

(A) 220°

(B) 230°

(C) 50°

(D) 170°

683. Identify the complementary angles:

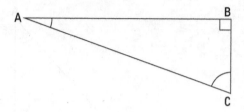

(A) ∠A, ∠B

(B) ∠B, ∠C

(C) ∠A, ∠C

(D) ∠A, ∠B, ∠C

684. Find the area:

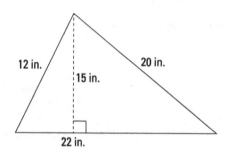

(A) 165 sq. in.

(B) 150 sq. in.

(C) 330 sq. in.

(D) 68 sq. in.

685. Find the area:

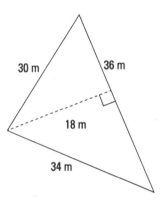

(A) 348 m

(B) 324 m²

(C) 348 m²

(D) 648 m²

686. The formula for finding the radius of a circle is

(A) $r = \dfrac{2\pi}{2C}$

(B) $r = \dfrac{2C}{\pi}$

(C) $r = 2\pi C$

(D) $r = \dfrac{C}{2\pi}$

687. Find the area of the circle:

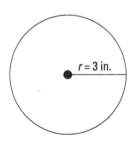

(A) 28.26 in.²

(B) 30 in.²

(C) 25.8 in.²

(D) 24 in.²

688. Find the radius of the circle:

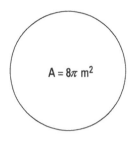

$A = 8\pi$ m²

(A) $\sqrt{7}$

(B) $\sqrt{8}$

(C) $\sqrt{9}$

(D) $\sqrt{9.5}$

689. Identify the standard formula to find the perimeter of a rectangle:

(A) $P = 2(l + w)$

(B) $P = s_1 + s_2 + s_3$

(C) $P = 2b + 2s$

(D) $P = s_1 + s_2 + s_3 + s_4$

690. Find the area of the circle:

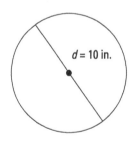

$d = 10$ in.

(A) 75 in.²

(B) 78.5 in.²

(C) 75.8 in.²

(D) 78 in.²

691. Find the radius:

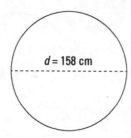

$d = 158$ cm

(A) 79 cm

(B) 52.7 cm

(C) 49.6 cm

(D) 78 cm

692. Find the circumference of the circle:

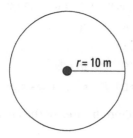

$r = 10$ m

(A) 58.8 meters

(B) 60 meters

(C) 62 meters

(D) 62.8 meters

693. Find the perimeter:

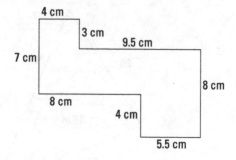

4 cm

3 cm

9.5 cm

7 cm

8 cm

4 cm

8 cm

5.5 cm

(A) 47.5 cm

(B) 49 cm

(C) 41 cm

(D) 56 cm

694. Find the circumference of the circle:

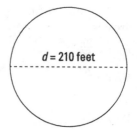

$d = 210$ feet

(A) 215π

(B) 650π

(C) 210π

(D) 205π

695. Find the radius of the circle:

$A = 210$ sq. ft

(A) $r = \sqrt{\dfrac{210}{\pi}}$

(B) $r = -\sqrt{\dfrac{210}{\pi}}$

(C) $r = \sqrt{\dfrac{21}{\pi}}$

(D) $r = \sqrt{\dfrac{290}{\pi}}$

696. Find the perimeter:

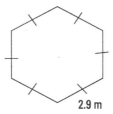

2.9 m

(A) 17.4 m

(B) 14.5 m

(C) 20.3 m

(D) 23.2 m

697. Find the volume of the cube:

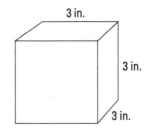

3 in.

3 in.

3 in.

(A) 72 cubic inches

(B) 9 cubic inches

(C) 27 cubic inches

(D) 81 cubic inches

698. Find the area:

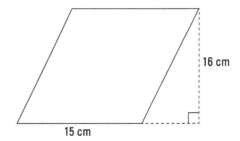

16 cm

15 cm

(A) 262 cm²

(B) 245 cm²

(C) 62 cm²

(D) 240 cm²

699. Find the volume of the cube:

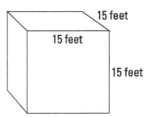

15 feet

15 feet

15 feet

(A) 3,375 cubic feet

(B) 3,300 cubic feet

(C) 2,500 cubic feet

(D) 3,500 cubic feet

700. Find the volume of the right square pyramid:

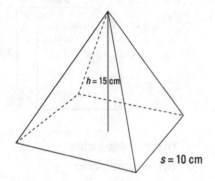

(A) 450 cm³

(B) 500 cm³

(C) 1,500 cm³

(D) 150 cm³

701. Find the volume:

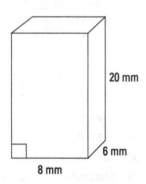

(A) 960 mm³

(B) 480 mm³

(C) 120 mm³

(D) 840 mm³

702. Identify the triangle:

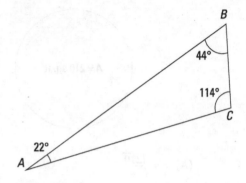

(A) Equilateral

(B) Scalene

(C) Isosceles

(D) Right

703. The interior angles of a quadrilateral add up to

(A) 180°.

(B) 90°.

(C) 360°.

(D) 270°.

704. Find the volume:

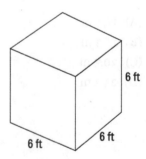

(A) 212 cubic feet

(B) 216 cubic feet

(C) 360 cubic feet

(D) 300 cubic feet

705. Find the volume:

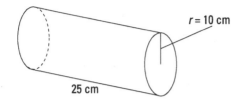

$r = 10$ cm

25 cm

(A) 314 cm³

(B) 7,850 cm³

(C) 785 cm³

(D) 8,850 cm³

706. The formula to find the circumference of a circle is

(A) $C = \pi r^2$

(B) $C = \frac{1}{2}\pi r$

(C) $C = 2\pi r$

(D) $C = \pi r^3$

707. Find the circumference:

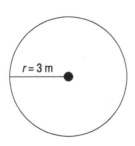

$r = 3$ m

(A) 18.84 meters

(B) 21 meters

(C) 17.75 meters

(D) 18.12 meters

708. Find the volume:

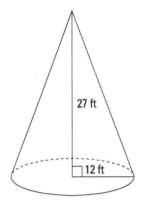

27 ft

12 ft

(A) 4,069.44 ft³

(B) 4,960.39 ft³

(C) 1,620 ft³

(D) 4,169.25 ft³

709. Find the volume:

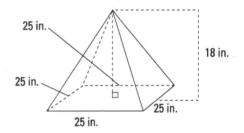

25 in.

18 in.

25 in.

25 in.

25 in.

(A) 3,700 cubic inches

(B) 5,000 cubic inches

(C) 250 cubic inches

(D) 3,750 cubic inches

710. Find the diameter:

$A = 144\pi$

(A) 12 units

(B) 24 units

(C) 30 units

(D) 25 units

711. Find the area:

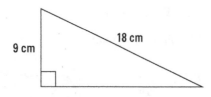

18 cm

9 cm

(A) $\frac{81\sqrt{3}}{2}$ cm²

(B) $\frac{9\sqrt{3}}{2}$ cm²

(C) $\frac{81\sqrt{\pi}}{2}$ cm²

(D) $\frac{81\sqrt{2}}{3}$ cm²

712. Identify the figure:

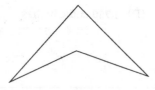

(A) Pentagon

(B) Quadrilateral

(C) Four-sided triangle

(D) Hexagon

713. Identify the lines that appear to be parallel:

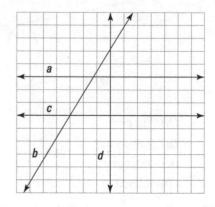

(A) Lines a and c

(B) Lines c and b

(C) Lines a and d

(D) None of the lines are parallel.

714. Find the area of the shaded region:

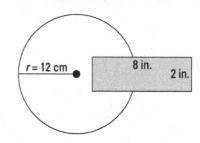

$r = 12$ cm

8 in.

2 in.

(A) $2\pi r$

(B) $\sqrt[3]{16}$

(C) 20 in.²

(D) 16 in.²

715. Find the area:

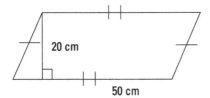

(A) 100 cm²

(B) 1,000 cm²

(C) 500 cm²

(D) 890 cm²

716. Find the measure of angle *d:*

(A) 160°

(B) 45°

(C) 35°

(D) 40°

717. Angle *b* is a(n)

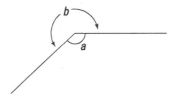

(A) acute angle.

(B) straight angle.

(C) obtuse angle.

(D) reflex angle.

718. Identify the points:

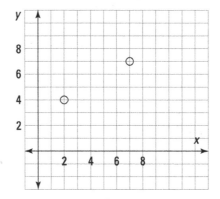

(A) (4, 2), (7, 7)

(B) (2, 4), (7, 7)

(C) (4, 2), (6, 8)

(D) (2, 4), (8, 6)

719. Find the measure of the angle in the shaded portion:

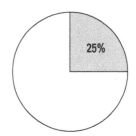

(A) 90°

(B) 270°

(C) 180°

(D) 45°

720. Find the area of the kite:

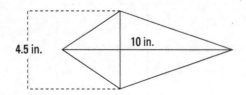

(A) 45 in.²

(B) 27.5 in.²

(C) 22 in.²

(D) 22.5 in.²

721. Find the measure of the angle:

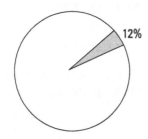

(A) 43°

(B) 18°

(C) 43.2°

(D) 44°

722. Find the perimeter:

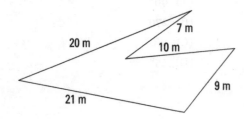

(A) 67 m

(B) 38 m

(C) 68 m

(D) 75 m

723. Find the area:

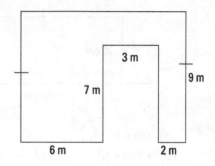

(A) 81 m²

(B) 47 m²

(C) 75 m²

(D) 78 m²

724. Find the value of a:

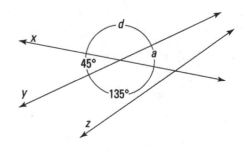

(A) 90°

(B) 112°

(C) 45°

(D) Not enough data.

725. Lines *x* and *y* are parallel lines. Which angles are congruent angles?

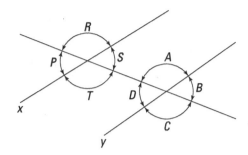

(A) $\angle P, \angle B$

(B) $\angle S, \angle D$

(C) $\angle R, \angle D$

(D) Both A and B

726. Find the area:

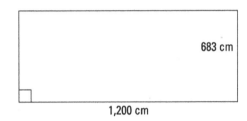

683 cm

1,200 cm

(A) 8,199 m²

(B) 819,600 m²

(C) 8,196 m²

(D) 81.96 m²

727. These angles are

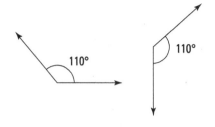

110°   110°

(A) congruent.

(B) obtuse.

(C) complementary.

(D) congruent and obtuse.

728. Classify this angle:

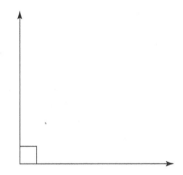

(A) Right

(B) Acute

(C) Straight

(D) Reflex

729. Find the surface area:

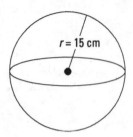

(A) 2,800 cm²

(B) 2,820 cm²

(C) 2,826 cm²

(D) 2,152 cm²

730. Identify the interior angles:

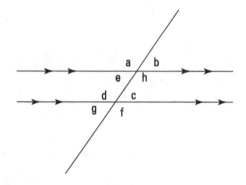

(A) c, d, e, f

(B) c, d, e, h

(C) f, g, a, b

(D) a, b, f, g

731. Find the measure of angle x:

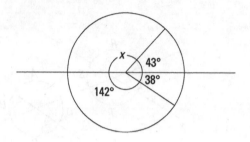

(A) 112°

(B) 52°

(C) 137°

(D) 189°

732. Find the volume:

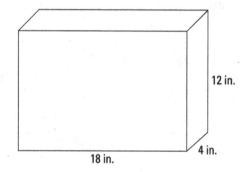

(A) 898 in.³

(B) 815 in.³

(C) 964 in.³

(D) 864 in.³

733. Find the measure of angle *a*:

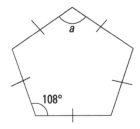

108°

(A) 118°

(B) 108°

(C) 45°

(D) 120°

734. Find the surface area of the cylinder:

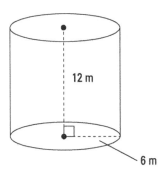

12 m

6 m

(A) 216 m²

(B) 678.24 m²

(C) 216.85 m²

(D) 678.14 m²

735. The interior angles in a triangle add up to

(A) 90°

(B) 120°

(C) 150°

(D) 180°

736. Find the measure of ∠CDE:

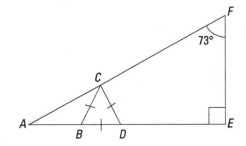

(A) 140°

(B) 120°

(C) 130°

(D) 180°

737. Identify this triangle:

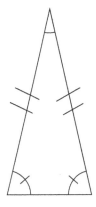

(A) Isosceles

(B) Obtuse

(C) Right

(D) Equilateral

738. Find the measure of angle *a*:

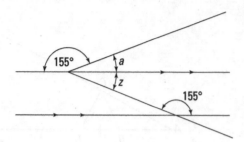

(A) 15°

(B) 145°

(C) 35°

(D) 25°

739. Find the hypotenuse:

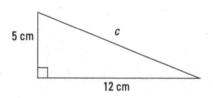

(A) 12 cm

(B) 15 cm

(C) 13 cm

(D) 16.9 cm

740. Find the area of the base:

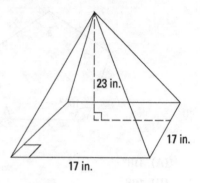

(A) 290 in.²

(B) 289 in.²

(C) 340 in.²

(D) 329 in.²

741. Find the measure of angle *C* in the parallelogram:

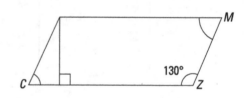

(A) 60°

(B) 55°

(C) 54°

(D) 50°

742. Find the area if $CO = 10$ and $MB = 12$:

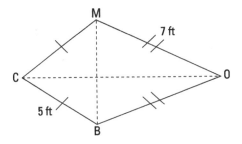

(A) 70 ft²

(B) 24 ft²

(C) 35 ft²

(D) 60 ft²

743. Find the area of the shaded region of the square:

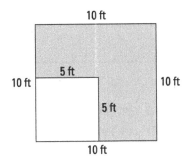

(A) 25 ft²

(B) 90 ft²

(C) 75 ft²

(D) 80 ft²

744. Find the circumference of the circle:

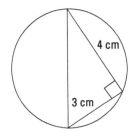

(A) 5 cm

(B) 15.1 cm

(C) 16 cm

(D) 15.7 cm

745. Find the measure of angle A:

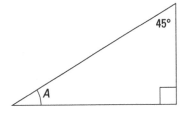

(A) 45°

(B) 60°

(C) 75°

(D) 90°

746. Find the measure of angle T:

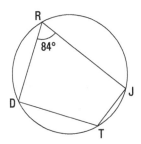

(A) 84°

(B) 96°

(C) 92°

(D) 87°

747. Find the area:

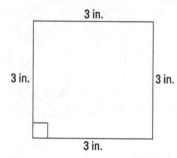

(A) 9 in.²

(B) 12 in.²

(C) 30 in.²

(D) 11 in.²

748. Find the measure of each arc in the circle, assuming that each sector is equal:

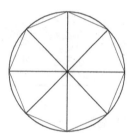

(A) 40°

(B) 36°

(C) 45°

(D) 42.5°

749. Find x:

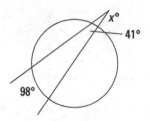

(A) 41°

(B) 28.5°

(C) 57°

(D) 28°

750. Find the area:

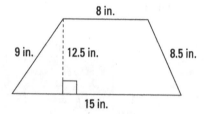

(A) 143.75 in.²

(B) 145.5 in.²

(C) 147.75 in.²

(D) 148 in.²

Chapter 4

Arithmetic Reasoning: Solving Word Problems with Math

The Arithmetic Reasoning subtest on the ASVAB measures your ability to pull information from word problems and solve mathematical concepts in real-world situations. Like the Mathematics Knowledge subtest, it formulates a big part of your AFQT score, and it's also used to help determine which jobs you'll be most suited for when you're in the military.

This subtest requires you to read a word problem, figure out what mathematical concept it's asking you to use, and arrive at the correct answer. It includes questions that involve fact-finding, algebra, and geometry. You'll have to use your reasoning skills to cut through unnecessary information, choose which type of math to use, and find the right answers. You have 39 minutes to work through 16 Arithmetic Reasoning questions on the computerized ASVAB or 36 minutes to complete 30 questions on the paper ASVAB. Calculators are not allowed.

The Questions You'll Work On

You'll find three types of questions on the Arithmetic Reasoning subtest:

>> **Algebra:** The algebra questions on this subtest deal with unknown variables. It's your job to figure out what the question is asking before you calculate the answer.

>> **Geometry:** These questions ask you to solve for circumference, area, volume, and similar values. They also include distance and several other geometry concepts.

>> **Fact-finding:** Fact-finding questions ask you to read through a word problem and find specific facts; they include fractions, percentages, ratios, and other concepts that don't fall into the algebra and geometry categories.

What to Watch Out For

As you work your way through the Arithmetic Reasoning questions in this chapter, keep these tips in mind:

» Read the questions thoroughly and make sure you understand what they're asking — otherwise, you could end up working out the wrong problem.

» Ensure that you're using the correct units of measurement for each problem, and if you need to, convert them.

» Pay attention to whether your answer is realistic in the problem's context.

» Use estimates when you can because they can help you identify the right answer while allowing you to skip tricky calculations.

» Don't forget to solve for additional information when it's necessary; the ASVAB is about attention to detail, and two-step problems are common.

Algebra

751. A football team at its own 10-yard line loses 10 yards, and then it gains 15 more. What is the team's net progress after these two plays?

(A) 5 yards

(B) 10 yards

(C) 15 yards

(D) 20 yards

752. Cheryl bought a caramel latte for herself and one for each member of her 10-person team. Each latte cost $4.50, so how much did Cheryl save after receiving a 10 percent loyalty discount?

(A) $4.75

(B) $44.55

(C) $4.95

(D) $45

753. Angela is 6 years older than Christina. Six years ago, Angela was twice Christina's age. How old are they now?

(A) Christina: 14; Angela: 21

(B) Christina: 18; Angela: 24

(C) Christina: 6; Angela: 12

(D) Christina: 12; Angela: 18

754. David paid $17.50 for a toy after receiving a $15 military discount. What was the toy's original price?

(A) $35

(B) $20

(C) $32

(D) $32.50

755. Perry sold a house for $192,500. She makes a 3 percent commission on the house's total sale price. What was Perry's commission?

(A) $5,725

(B) $5,500

(C) $5,770

(D) $5,775

756. Kim has a pocket full of change that includes pennies, nickels, and dimes. She has three more nickels than dimes and four times as many pennies as nickels. How many of each coin does Kim have if the total value is 65 cents?

(A) 2 dimes, 5 nickels, and 20 pennies

(B) 4 dimes, 3 nickels, and 16 pennies

(C) 4 dimes, 6 nickels, and 1 penny

(D) 5 dimes, 2 nickels and 1 penny

757. The sum of two numbers is 20. One number is 34. What is the remaining number?

(A) −14

(B) 14

(C) 12

(D) 23

758. Amy has 6 times as many dimes as she has quarters in her piggy bank. She has a total of 21 coins, and they total $2.55. How many dimes and quarters does she have?

(A) 10 dimes, 11 quarters

(B) 18 dimes, 3 quarters

(C) 19 dimes, 2 quarters

(D) 17 dimes, 5 quarters

759. Half a number plus 12 is 35. What is the number?

(A) 45

(B) 46

(C) 58

(D) 23

760. Danielle leaves San Antonio at 5:00 p.m., driving 35 miles per hour. Her sister Abigail leaves San Antonio at 6:00 p.m., traveling in the same direction on the same road, driving at 40 miles per hour. How long will it be (from the time Danielle left) before their cars are side-by-side on the expressway?

(A) 8 hours

(B) 6.5 hours

(C) 6.8 hours

(D) 7.2 hours

761. Matthew has a 12-coin collection that includes only nickels and dimes. If the total amount of money in Matthew's collection is $1.10, how many of each coin does he have?

(A) 6 nickels, 8 dimes

(B) 3 nickels, 9 dimes

(C) 2 nickels, 10 dimes

(D) 4 nickels, 9 dimes

762. Dan bought a fishing pole from David Edwin's Fishing Emporium for $15.95. Dan spent some money on bait and twice as much on tackle. His total bill was $36.95. How much did he spend on bait and tackle?

(A) $14 on bait; $7 on tackle

(B) $7 on bait; $14 on tackle

(C) $16 on tackle; $5 on bait

(D) $18 on bait, $3 on tackle

763. Luke has 4.5 hours to play soccer and read. The time he spends playing soccer is twice the amount of time he spends reading. How long will Luke play soccer?

(A) 3 hours

(B) 3.5 hours

(C) 2.75 hours

(D) 15 minutes

764. Two pilots, Justin and Bradley, leave MacDill Air Force Base in KC-135 aircraft at 12:00 p.m. and 12:30 p.m., respectively. Justin flies his aircraft at 464 miles per hour, and Bradley flies his at the aircraft's maximum flying speed, which is 580 miles per hour. How long will it take Bradley to catch up to Justin?

(A) 2.5 hours

(B) 2.75 hours

(C) 2 hours

(D) 3 hours

765. A truck begins driving from a warehouse in Tampa and heads toward Jacksonville driving 40 miles per hour. Two hours later, a truck leaves the same warehouse with a delivery for Jacksonville but travels at 60 miles per hour. How long will the first truck have been on the road by the time the second truck overtakes it?

(A) 2 hours

(B) 4 hours

(C) 6 hours

(D) The second truck will never overtake the first.

766. How long will it take Ayla to bicycle 6 miles if she's pedaling at 8 miles per hour?

(A) 1 hour

(B) 1 hour, 10 minutes

(C) 45 minutes

(D) 55 minutes

767. Fani has 18 awards to give to her troops during an award ceremony. One-third of the awards are Army Commendation Medals. One-half of the awards are Army Achievement Medals. The remaining awards are Certificates of Achievement. How many Certificates of Achievement will Fani give to her troops?

(A) 3

(B) 4

(C) 5

(D) 6

768. Marie and Darl are filling a swimming pool. It will take Marie 6 hours to fill the pool alone, and it will take Darl 5 hours to fill it alone. How quickly can they fill it together?

(A) 2.5 hours

(B) 2.7 hours

(C) 3 hours

(D) 1.5 hours

769. Jesse, Tina, and David have $80 among them. Tina has twice as much as Jesse does, and David has $5 less than Tina does. How much does David have?

(A) $29

(B) $18

(C) $17

(D) $34

770. Express as an equation: The product of two numbers is 75, and one of them is 15 more than the other.

(A) $75 = x(15x)$

(B) $75 = x(x+15)$

(C) $y = 75 - x(x+15)$

(D) Both A and B are correct

771. The sum of two consecutive odd numbers is 60. What is the higher odd number?

(A) 27

(B) 33

(C) 17

(D) 31

772. Patrick has $50, which is $8 more than twice what Noah has. How much money does Noah have?

(A) $38

(B) $23

(C) $21

(D) $42

773. Express as an equation: Four times a number is six more than one-third of the number.

(A) $4\frac{1}{3}x + 6$

(B) $4x = 6\frac{1}{3}$

(C) $4x + \frac{1}{3}x = 6$

(D) $4x = 6 + \frac{1}{3}x$

774. Pili has $346, which is $36 more than twice what Beto has. How much does Beto have?

(A) $145

(B) $168

(C) $155

(D) $157

775. Andrew and Kara charge Evan 20 percent of their total rent per month to live in their condo. Together, they pay a total of $1,875 in rent. Andrew and Kara pay equal amounts, so how much is Andrew paying?

(A) $750

(B) $800

(C) $815

(D) $805

776. Divana has x green marbles in a bag. The pink marbles total nine more than twice the number of green marbles in the same bag. Which equation shows how many pink marbles Divana has?

(A) $y = 3x + 3^2$

(B) $y = 2x - 9$

(C) $y = 9x + 2$

(D) $y = 2x + 9$

777. Janice spent $135 at the casino. Her twin sister Judi spent half of what Janice spent, but Judi also paid $23 for the taxi ride home. How much more money did Janice spend than Judi?

(A) $34.00

(B) $29.50

(C) $44.50

(D) $38.00

778. Pat has taken his grandson Gavin to an amusement park. When they get in line for the biggest roller coaster, there are 48 other people waiting. There are now eight fewer females than males in line, so how many females are there?

(A) 22

(B) 21

(C) 29

(D) 30

779. Charra and Glenn have teamed up to create a website for a client. Charra bills $110 per hour, and Glenn bills $95 per hour. How long would it take Charra to build the website alone if the total cost to the client were $4,750?

(A) 45.43 hours

(B) 38.7 hours

(C) 42.12 hours

(D) 43.18 hours

780. A group of 1,008 people includes five times more men than children and three times more women than children. How many more men than women are in the group?

(A) 224

(B) 336

(C) 560

(D) 218

781. Express as an equation: Ten is the product of four and an unknown number.

(A) $10 = 4 + x$

(B) $4 + 10 = x$

(C) $10 = 4x$

(D) $10x = 4 + x$

782. Two consecutive numbers have a sum of 109. What are the numbers?

(A) 64 and 65

(B) 54 and 55

(C) 53 and 54

(D) 52 and 56

783. Four consecutive numbers have a sum of 54. What is the greatest number in the sequence?

(A) 15

(B) 16

(C) 13

(D) 12

784. Steve and Stan made 14 pies. Fran made twice as many pies as Steve and Stan made. How many did Fran make?

(A) 27

(B) 14

(C) 28

(D) 29

785. Jim and his girlfriend, Stacy, spent $400,000. If Jim spent $48,000 plus three times what Stacy spent, how much did he spend?

(A) $315,000

(B) $88,000

(C) $310,000

(D) $312,000

786. Bryan bought his dog, Roscoe, three times as many red balls as yellow balls, some yellow balls, and half as many orange balls as yellow balls. Altogether, Roscoe has 36 balls. How many red balls does Roscoe have?

(A) 12

(B) 24

(C) 8

(D) 18

787. Divide $106 among Sadie, Chandler, and Faith so Sadie has $4 plus three times the amount Faith has and Chandler has twice as much as Faith does. How much does Sadie have?

(A) $34

(B) $21

(C) $55

(D) $51

788. Mike, Dani, and Nicklaus have to split $33.75 so that Mike has twice as much as Dani and Nicklaus has $2.50 more than Mike does. How much does Nicklaus have?

(A) $15.75

(B) $12.50

(C) $6.25

(D) $15

789. Express as an equation: Janae had 47 books. She gave some of them to Ellis, so she has 29 left.

(A) $47 - x = 29$

(B) $47x = 29$

(C) $47 - 29x = 12$

(D) $x - 29 = 47$

790. Three consecutive odd numbers have a sum of 21. What are the three numbers?

(A) 1, 3, and 5

(B) 7, 9, and 11

(C) 3, 5, and 7

(D) 5, 7, and 9

791. Jill, Traci, and Donna made $141 at the community yard sale. Jill made $11 more than Traci made, and Donna made twice what Jill made. How much did Traci and Donna make combined?

(A) $130

(B) $65

(C) $103

(D) $114

792. Queiana and Charles are choosing teams for dodgeball. There are b boys in the class, which is two more than twice the number of girls in the class. How many girls are in the class?

(A) $x = \dfrac{b-2}{2}$

(B) $x = b - 2$

(C) $x = \dfrac{b-x}{2}$

(D) $x = \dfrac{2-b}{4}$

793. Private Joe Snuffy spent $42 on new combat boots. This was $14 less than twice what he spent on tan T-shirts for his uniform. How much were the tan T-shirts?

(A) $38

(B) $28

(C) $27

(D) $56

794. Luz filled up her 10-gallon gas tank with regular unleaded fuel for $30. Tony used premium fuel, which costs 25 percent more per gallon, to fill his 10-gallon gas tank. Assuming both of their gas tanks were empty, how much did Tony spend?

(A) $37.75

(B) $3.75

(C) $37.50

(D) $30

795. Express in an equation: The quotient of y and 5 is x.

(A) $x = y + 5$

(B) $x = 5y$

(C) $x = \frac{y}{5}$

(D) Both A and C are correct.

796. Two dogs, Jack and Cujo, escaped from the yard. Cujo left at 10 a.m. and ran down the street at 5 miles per hour. Jack left six minutes later and ran down the same street in the same direction at 10 miles per hour. What time did Jack catch up with Cujo?

(A) 10:12 a.m.

(B) 10:18 a.m.

(C) 10:19 a.m.

(D) 10:20 a.m.

797. How long will it take Toby to run 26.2 miles if he averages exactly 5 miles per hour?

(A) 5.24 hours

(B) 6 hours

(C) 5.18 hours

(D) 4.94 hours

798. Express the length mathematically: The length of a field, x, is 35 yards more than its width, y.

(A) $35y = x$

(B) $x = \frac{35}{y}$

(C) $x = \frac{y}{35}$

(D) $x = y + 35$

799. Two journalists are racing to a political rally that's 420 miles away. They both leave at 12:15, but Channel 7's reporter is driving 70 miles per hour while Channel 4's reporter is driving 60 miles per hour. How much sooner, in minutes, will Channel 4's reporter arrive to get the scoop?

(A) 60 minutes

(B) 75 minutes

(C) 48 minutes

(D) 23 minutes

800. Express mathematically: The product of x and y is greater than or equal to the quotient of b and c.

(A) $xy \geq bc$

(B) $\frac{x}{y} \geq bc$

(C) $xy \geq \frac{b}{c}$

(D) $xc \geq \frac{y}{b}$

801. Safir has six times as much money as Abbas does, but if Safir earns $6 and Abbas earns $8, Safir will have three times as much money as Abbas. How much does Safir have after both men earn the additional money?

(A) $14

(B) $42

(C) $44

(D) $36

802. The sum of two numbers is 638. One of the numbers is 164 more than the other. What are the two numbers?

(A) 212 and 426

(B) 164 and 474

(C) 164 and 401

(D) 167 and 471

803. Ron and Lillian worked for a month. Ron made three-quarters of what Lillian made, plus $164. How much did Ron make if, together, they made $4,600?

(A) $2,100

(B) $2,065.15

(C) $2,650.15

(D) $1,965

804. The sum of two consecutive numbers is 51. What are the numbers?

(A) 25 and 26

(B) 23 and 24

(C) 26 and 27

(D) 27 and 28

805. Renee picks strawberries at a rate of 110 per hour. Jeniece picks strawberries at a rate of 108 per hour. How many strawberries can the women pick together in three hours?

(A) 664

(B) 687

(C) 654

(D) 655

806. Chris has twice as many military awards as Omar does, and Michael has 3 fewer than twice as many as Omar. Together, they have 32 awards. How many military awards does Michael have?

(A) 9

(B) 11

(C) 12

(D) 8

807. Bill brewed a small pot of coffee for his guests. Sam drank one-third of the coffee, Bernie drank a quarter of it, and Bill had one full cup. How many cups of coffee were in the pot?

(A) 3 cups

(B) 2.8 cups

(C) 2.4 cups

(D) 2 cups

808. Bonnie and Kathleen went shopping. Kathleen spent half her money on a bee-keeping suit, one-third of her money on a ukulele, and one-tenth of her money to take Bonnie to lunch. If Kathleen came home with $12, how much money did she have to begin with?

(A) $175

(B) $177.50

(C) $180

(D) $182.50

809. A number halved, plus one third of the number, plus three equals the number. What is the number?

(A) 18

(B) 27

(C) 24

(D) 14

810. Eight plus three-fifths of a number is equal to the number. What is the number?

(A) 28

(B) 23

(C) 20

(D) 25

811. Sgt. 1st Class Stith has been asked to make his famous caramel sauce for his unit's family fun day. However, when he was pouring the sugar, half of it spilled on the floor, a quarter of it spilled on the counter, and one-sixth of it spilled into the sink. Just three tablespoons remained in the container. How much sugar was originally in the container?

(A) 36 tablespoons

(B) 38 tablespoons

(C) 19 tablespoons

(D) None of the above

812. Jules has two times the toys Robbie has, and together they have 39 toys. How would you express that in an equation?

(A) $\frac{2}{3}x = 39$

(B) $x + 3x = 39$

(C) $3x = 39$

(D) $\frac{39}{2}x = 3$

813. A boat travels downstream for three hours with a current of 4 miles per hour. It returns the same distance, only against the curent, in four hours. How far did the boat travel one way?

(A) 96 miles

(B) 92 miles

(C) 89 miles

(D) 28 miles

814. A boat travels for three hours with a current of 3 miles per hour. It returns the same distance, but it travels against the current for four hours. What is the boat's speed in calm water?

(A) 25 mph

(B) 21 mph

(C) 24 mph

(D) 18 mph

815. The sum of four consecutive odd numbers is 328. What is the greatest number in the sequence of four consecutive odd numbers that add up to 328?

(A) 91

(B) 83

(C) 85

(D) 89

816. Charlie bought a 10-pound mixture of two candies for a total of $80. If one of the candies was salted caramel, which costs $5 per pound, and the other was chocolate, which costs $10 per pound, how much of the 10-pound mixture was chocolate?

(A) 5.5 pounds

(B) 5 pounds

(C) 6 pounds

(D) 4 pounds

817. A group of 400 students takes a class trip to Washington, D.C. One-fourth of them tour the Capitol while the remaining three-fourths go to the National Mall. Of the students who visit the National Mall, there are four times as many boys as girls. How many boys go to the National Mall?

(A) 230

(B) 80

(C) 240

(D) 125

818. Divide $564 among three people so the second will have twice as much as the first has and the third will have four dollars more than the second has. How much does the third person have?

(A) $230

(B) $112

(C) $224

(D) $228

819. If Jakson can spend $5 on apples, how many apples can he buy when they're priced at $0.20 each?

(A) 10

(B) 25

(C) 23

(D) 15

820. How much will it cost Quintin to buy hardwood flooring for a room that measures 12 feet by 15 feet if hardwood flooring costs $8 per square foot?

(A) $1,100

(B) $1,840

(C) $1,650

(D) $1,440

821. Heather ran laps around a hexagonal track, and each side of the track measured 880 feet. How many laps would she need to run to reach a total of 73,920 feet?

(A) 12.5

(B) 12

(C) 14

(D) 11.75

822. Julian has an international calling plan on his phone that costs a flat $15-per-month fee, plus $0.21 per minute (or any portion thereof). How many minutes did he use if his bill was $71.70?

(A) 270

(B) 250

(C) 310

(D) 307

823. Omar had 28 paperclips, and Fred gave him n more. After Fred gave Omar n paperclips, Omar had 412. Express this as an equation.

(A) $n - 412 = 28$

(B) $\dfrac{28}{n} = 412$

(C) $28 - n = 412$

(D) $28 + n = 412$

824. Rose sells custom-printed vinyl banners for $2.32 per square foot. What was the size of the banner, in square feet, that Gabriela bought from Rose if she spent $118.32?

(A) 48 square feet

(B) 49.25 square feet

(C) 51 square feet

(D) 52 square feet

825. A road runs parallel to a set of train tracks. A car and a train start moving in opposite directions from the same point at the same time. The car travels at 45 miles per hour, while the train travels at 60 miles per hour. How long will it be until the car and the train are 100 miles apart?

(A) 51 minutes

(B) 57 minutes

(C) 43 minutes

(D) None of the above

826. Nathan is raising money to benefit a children's hospital. He wants to raise $1,500, but the donation sheet only provides space for 25 donors. On average, how much would each donor have to pitch in if Nathan reaches his goal while using only one donation sheet?

(A) $59.50

(B) $65

(C) $65.25

(D) $60

827. Ryan spends $235 on four shirts, four pair of pants, and one tie. If each pair of pants costs $30 and each shirt costs $25, how much is one tie?

(A) $13.50

(B) $15.00

(C) $16.00

(D) $18.00

828. All the kids in Hall Elementary are going on a field trip. For safety reasons, there needs to be one teacher to supervise every 24 students. If 288 students went on the field trip, how many teachers were there?

(A) 24

(B) 20

(C) 16

(D) 12

829. Benjamin works 15 hours per week to be eligible for a work-study program. In order to keep up his grades, Benjamin needs to study at least 12 more hours per week than he works. What is the minimum number of hours Benjamin needs to study to keep up his grades?

(A) 15 hours

(B) 28.5 hours

(C) 27 hours

(D) 30 hours

830. Mariam and Adam start driving in opposite directions at the same time, from the same point. Mariam is driving at 38 miles per hour, while Adam is driving at 22 miles per hour. How long will it take Mariam and Adam to drive until they're 50 miles apart?

(A) 55 minutes

(B) 45 minutes

(C) 1 hour, 5 minutes

(D) 50 minutes

831. Tysha went to the bookstore and purchased $626.15 worth of books. Paperback books cost $15.95 each, and hardcover books cost $27.95 each. She purchased a total of 37 books, so how many of them were paperbacks?

(A) 34

(B) 30

(C) 12

(D) 28

832. Olivia must mix a 20 percent concentrate with a mixture that has a 60 percent concentration to get 80 gallons of a mixture with a concentration of 30 percent. How many gallons of the 20 percent concentrate does the scientist need?

(A) 24 gallons

(B) 48 gallons

(C) 70 gallons

(D) 60 gallons

833. Create an equation that expresses the fact that Neil made 17 loaves of bread and each loaf weighs z ounces. All of the loaves together weigh 340 ounces.

(A) $17z = 340$

(B) $340z = 17$

(C) $\frac{17}{z} = 340$

(D) $\frac{z}{17} = 340$

834. Robert is 9 years older than Sylvia is. In 7 years, the sum of their ages will equal 93. How old is Robert today?

(A) 35

(B) 40

(C) 44

(D) 16

835. Deb bought boxes of candy bars to sell for a fundraiser. She paid $15 per box. She sold all but 20 boxes for $30 each, and she made a profit of $150 total. How many boxes of candy did Deb sell for the fundraiser?

(A) 49 boxes

(B) 30 boxes

(C) 31 boxes

(D) 50 boxes

836. Connor is conducting an experiment in biology class in which the number of bacteria in a petri dish quadruples every 8 hours. If Connor begins the experiment with 200 bacteria, how many bacteria will there be in 12 hours?

(A) 1,800

(B) 1,600

(C) 2,400

(D) 1,950

837. Dorothy needs to exercise her horses for 12 hours per week. She needs to groom the horses at least 10 more hours per week than she spends exercising them. What is the minimum number of hours Dorothy must spend grooming the horses each week?

(A) 22 hours

(B) 23 hours

(C) 18 hours

(D) 10 hours

838. How many legs do four dogs, three chickens, and six cats have?

(A) 46

(B) 47

(C) 48

(D) 44

839. Rossalyn spent $2.50 per balloon on decorative balloons. She sells them in her party supply store for $5 each. At the end of one week, she made a profit of $1,225 because she sold all but 10 of them. How many decorative balloons did Rossalyn sell?

(A) 510

(B) 505

(C) 500

(D) 495

840. Kathy took four geometry tests and scored 78, 83, 89, and 92. Her final exam is worth two test grades. What grade does Kathy need on the final exam to get an A (which is 90 or better) in geometry?

(A) 95

(B) 97.5

(C) 98

(D) 99

841. In history class, tests are worth 40 percent of the grade. Projects are worth 15 percent, homework is worth 25 percent, and quizzes are worth 20 percent.

Jazmine and Jeneva are competing for the best final grade. Jazmine has scored:

- 92 percent on tests
- 100 percent on projects
- 89 percent on homework
- 80 percent on quizzes

Jeneva has scored:

- 88 percent on tests
- 78 percent on projects
- 85 percent on homework
- 92 percent on quizzes

By how many percentage points did Jazmine beat Jeneva?

(A) 3.2

(B) 3.8

(C) 3.5

(D) 4.1

842. Alejandra has $112. She spent $34.20 on a new shirt, but she returned home and decided she didn't want it. She sold it to Tatiana at a 5 percent loss. How much money does Alejandra have after selling the shirt to Tatiana?

(A) $76.09

(B) $78.20

(C) $112.50

(D) $110.29

843. Bonnie has a change jar containing $53 in one-dollar bills as well as 15 coins totaling $2.70. If the coins are quarters and dimes, how many dimes does she have?

(A) 10

(B) 9

(C) 8

(D) 7

844. Bobby's parents sent him to the bakery with $200 so he could purchase a combination of single-layer and double-layer cakes, but he must leave with six cakes. Single-layer cakes cost $25, and double-layer cakes cost $50. How many double-layer cakes should he buy to use the whole $200?

(A) 3

(B) 2

(C) 1

(D) 4

845. Jillian's dance studio offers exercise mats in small, medium, and large. Small mats cost $20, medium mats cost twice as much as small mats do, and large mats cost $60. The studio has 10 yellow mats (3 small, 5 medium, and 2 large), 15 red mats (10 small, 2 medium, and 3 large), and 20 blue mats (13 small, 3 medium, and 4 large). What is the total resale value of all the mats?

(A) $1,460

(B) $1,500

(C) $1,370

(D) $1,470

846. Jessika bought a used car that cost $10,500. If her car's value depreciates at a rate of 10 percent per year, approximately how much will it be worth in one year?

(A) $7,500

(B) $9,450

(C) $10,000

(D) $6,500

847. Leonard bought a car for $20,000. After one year, the value was $15,000. Assuming the same rate of decrease, find the approximate value of the car after one more year.

(A) $8,400

(B) $9,200

(C) $10,300

(D) $11,250

848. Captain Mike leaves the dock at 10:00 a.m. and travels down the calm river in his boat at 55 miles per hour. How far will he have traveled by 5:00 p.m.?

(A) 330 miles

(B) 275 miles

(C) 380 miles

(D) 385 miles

849. Matt, an attorney, invested the $35,000 profit he made from criminal defense cases. If the interest compounds monthly and he earns 5 percent interest on his investment, how much will he have earned in interest at the end of one year?

(A) $36,790.67

(B) $1,358.45

(C) $1,790.67

(D) $37,408.45

850. Bill forgets his 8-ounce glass of lemonade by the pool. If the lemonade evaporates at a rate of 50 percent every six hours, how much of the lemonade will be left after 18 hours?

(A) 1.25 ounces

(B) 1 ounce

(C) 2 ounces

(D) 2.25 ounces

851. Melanie's age is one-third of the age of her mother, Jeanne. In 12 years, Melanie will be half Jeanne's age. How old is Jeanne right now?

(A) 32

(B) 34

(C) 36

(D) 40

852. Starla and Phoenix each buy a membership to the hands-on museum for $7. For the next year, they can visit the museum for just $1. How much will they pay, together, if they each visit the museum 31 times in the next year?

(A) $75

(B) $62

(C) $76

(D) $79

853. Emmanuel saved nearly enough money to buy a $150 software program for his computer. He has 11 $10 bills, two fewer $1 bills, 17 quarters, eight dimes, and three nickels. How much more money does he need to save?

(A) $25.80

(B) $30.20

(C) $26.00

(D) $21.50

854. Cheese sells for $8 per pound, and turkey sells for $12 per pound. How many pounds of turkey should you buy to go home with a 19-pound combination of cheese and turkey that costs $200?

(A) 12 pounds

(B) 14 pounds

(C) 8 pounds

(D) 7 pounds

855. Express as an equation: The reciprocal of a number is equal to the sum of two times the number and its opposite.

(A) $\frac{1}{x} = 2x - x$

(B) $\frac{2}{x} = x + -x$

(C) $\frac{1}{x} = 2x + -x$

(D) Both A and C are correct.

856. Corporal Perry is shoveling sand into sandbags at a rate of 12 per hour. Gunny Peters comes to help, and he can shovel sand into sandbags at a rate of 16 per hour. How long would it take both Marines to fill 56 sandbags?

(A) 1 hour, 50 minutes

(B) 2 hours, 6 minutes

(C) 2 hours, 30 minutes

(D) 2 hours

857. A machine fills a full set of crayon molds with wax in 6 hours. The old model of the same machine takes 8 hours to fill a full set of crayon molds. Together, how much time would it take both machines to fill a full set of crayon molds?

(A) $3\frac{1}{7}$ hours

(B) $3\frac{3}{7}$ hours

(C) $3\frac{3}{8}$ hours

(D) $3\frac{9}{7}$ hours

858. Express "The quantity of a number increased by nine is divided by three times itself, and the quotient equals y."

(A) $x + 9 + 3x = y$

(B) $\frac{x+y}{3x} = 9$

(C) $\frac{x+9}{3x} = y$

(D) $\frac{x+9}{3y} = x$

859. An Army team and a Navy team are running a relay race with participants stationed 500 meters apart. The first runner from each team starts from the same point at the same time. The Army runner runs at 8.6 miles per hour, and the Navy runner runs 0.3 miles per hour slower than the Army runner does. How much sooner will the Army runner reach her team's second participant than the Navy runner will?

(A) 2.5 seconds

(B) 3 seconds

(C) 2.1 seconds

(D) 2.7 seconds

860. If the product of a number and −3 is reduced by 4, the resulting number is 14 more than the opposite of that number. What is the number?

(A) 18

(B) 23

(C) −7

(D) −9

861. Shane is buying an unknown number of pounds of apples, which cost $4.50 per pound. He'll ultimately spend $27 on apples. How many pounds of apples will Shane buy?

(A) 5

(B) 5.5

(C) 6

(D) 6.5

862. A computer depreciates in value by 20 percent each year. In two years, how much will a computer purchased for $1,500 be worth?

(A) $980

(B) $1,200

(C) $600

(D) $960

863. The sum of twice a number and the number is 90. What is the number?

(A) 33

(B) 90

(C) 25

(D) 30

864. Nichole needs to study English, chemistry, physics, and history, but she has only two hours to do so. She must study chemistry and physics twice as long as she studies English and history. How much total time can Nichole dedicate to chemistry and physics?

(A) 1 hour, 10 minutes

(B) 1 hour, 20 minutes

(C) 1 hour, 30 minutes

(D) 1 hour, 40 minutes

865. John Q. Private received his first paycheck from the military for $1,900. The amount reflected his earnings after 20 percent was taken out in taxes and other deductions. What was his gross (before deductions) pay?

(A) $1,975

(B) $2,300

(C) $2,375

(D) $2,500

866. The price of a piano has increased by 15 percent. It was originally on sale for $1,820. What's the new price?

(A) $2,093

(B) $2,090

(C) $3,000

(D) $1,547

867. In chemistry class, you and your lab partner must mix a 15 percent concentrate with a 45 percent concentrate to get 100 milliliters of a mixture that has a concentration of 27 percent. How much of the 45 percent concentrate do you need?

(A) 0.5 milliliters

(B) 40 milliliters

(C) 35 milliliters

(D) 37.5 milliliters

868. Rod works for $20 per hour. A total of 30 percent of his salary is deducted for taxes and insurance, but he's trying to save $1,000 for a new TV. How many hours must Rod work to take home $1,000 if he saves everything he earns (aside from what comes out for taxes and insurance)?

(A) About 71.5 hours

(B) About 80 hours

(C) About 60 hours

(D) About 65.5 hours

869. With the wind behind it (a tailwind), a plane travels 1,120 miles in seven hours. Against the wind (a headwind), the plane covers the same distance in eight hours. At what speed is the wind blowing?

(A) 8 mph

(B) 12 mph

(C) 10 mph

(D) 14 mph

870. Two military recruiters drove for a half hour. The first recruiter drove twice as far as the second recruiter did, and together, they drove 90 miles. How many miles did the first recruiter drive?

(A) 30 miles

(B) 40 miles

(C) 50 miles

(D) 60 miles

871. 490 airmen are going on a field training exercise. There are $\frac{4}{3}$ as many male airmen as there are female airmen. How many male airmen are there?

(A) 280

(B) 290

(C) 210

(D) 200

872. April's algebra teacher told her to find the greatest number in a sequence of four even numbers that add up to 220. If April gives the correct answer, what will she say?

(A) 52

(B) 58

(C) 46

(D) 48

873. Misty has 21 coins in her purse. Some of them are nickels, and some are dimes. She has a total of $1.70 in change, so how many of the coins are dimes?

(A) 13

(B) 14

(C) 15

(D) 16

874. A station wagon and a motorcycle start at the same place. The station wagon is traveling at 40 miles per hour, while the motorcycle is traveling at 75 miles per hour in the opposite direction. How long will it be until the station wagon and the motorcycle are 250 miles apart?

(A) 2 hours

(B) 2.17 hours

(C) 2.5 hours

(D) 3.2 hours

875. Three-fifths of a number is less than five less than the same number. Choose the graph that represents this expression.

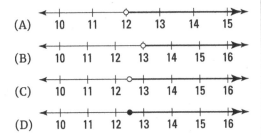

(A) 10 11 12 13 14 15

(B) 10 11 12 13 14 15 16

(C) 10 11 12 13 14 15 16

(D) 10 11 12 13 14 15 16

Geometry

876. A circle's radius is 6 centimeters. What is the circle's circumference?

(A) 10 cm

(B) 8π cm

(C) 12π cm

(D) 6 cm

877. A circle's area is 81π square centimeters. How long is the circle's diameter?

(A) 9 cm

(B) 14 cm

(C) 16 cm

(D) 18 cm

878. Krystal called Woody's Fences Inc. to order a new fence for her 13,950-square-foot garden. She ordered 486 feet of fencing. She wants the fence to be white on the side of the garden that faces the street, which is narrower than the side that doesn't face the street; the rest will be green. How much white fencing will Woody's Fences Inc. need to send with the workers?

(A) 90 feet

(B) 93 feet

(C) 96 feet

(D) 99 feet

879. A square has an area of 25 square meters. How long is each of its sides?

(A) 12.5 meters

(B) 0.5 meters

(C) 15 meters

(D) 5 meters

880. How much sheet metal is necessary to create a cylinder-shaped water tank that is 300 feet long and has a diameter of 80 feet?

(A) 85,408 sq. ft

(B) 85,408 cu. ft

(C) 84,016 sq. ft

(D) 82,971 sq. ft

881. A small field's perimeter is 32 meters. Its width is three times its length. What is the field's width?

(A) 12 m

(B) 14 m

(C) 16 m

(D) 32 m

882. The radius of a circle is 8 centimeters. What is the circumference of the circle?

(A) 40.22 cm

(B) 27.38 cm

(C) 50.24 cm

(D) 55.78 cm

883. A silver, 8-gauge wire 54 centimeters long is bent into a rectangle with a width that is twice its length. What is the rectangle's area?

(A) 36 cm²

(B) 108 cm²

(C) 154 cm²

(D) 162 cm²

884. Rob's grandmother wants to have a circular swimming pool installed in her backyard. She also wants a concrete surface of uniform width built around it. The biggest pool and concrete combination she can afford has a pool with a diameter of 28 feet and a concrete surface with an area of 60π square feet. How wide is the concrete surface?

(A) 1.5 feet

(B) 4 feet

(C) 2 feet

(D) 3.5 feet

885. A square has an area of 49 square centimeters. How long is each side?

(A) 5 cm

(B) 4.9 cm

(C) 7 cm

(D) 8 cm

886. A cubic swimming pool's edge length is 9 feet. What is the cube's volume?

(A) 700 cubic feet

(B) 629 cubic feet

(C) 81 cubic feet

(D) 729 cubic feet

887. A circle's area is 379.94 square millimeters. What is the circle's diameter?

(A) 11 millimeters

(B) 22 millimeters

(C) 33 millimeters

(D) 39 millimeters

888. A triangle's height is twice its base, which measures 2 inches across. What is the triangle's area?

(A) 5 in.²

(B) 4 in.²

(C) 3 in.²

(D) 2.5 in.²

889. The sum of the legs of a right triangle is 49 inches. The hypotenuse is 41 inches. How long is the shortest side?

(A) 8 inches

(B) 7 inches

(C) 9 inches

(D) 11 inches

890. A rectangular picture frame has an interior perimeter of 38 inches. One interior side of the frame is 11 inches long. How long is the other interior side of the picture frame?

(A) 12 in.

(B) 16 in.

(C) 27 in.

(D) 8 in.

891. The least angle of a triangle is 65 degrees less than the greatest angle. The third angle is 10 degrees greater than the least angle. What is the measure of the greatest angle?

(A) 100°

(B) 90°

(C) 110°

(D) Not enough information to solve

892. One side of a square is doubled in length, and the adjacent side is tripled. The area of the resulting rectangle is 125 square centimeters greater than the area of the original square. How long is the rectangle's longest side?

(A) 12 cm

(B) 12.5 cm

(C) 14 cm

(D) 15 cm

893. Emil's mom, Bertha, wants him to build a rectangular garden in her backyard by walling off an area with planks. She wants it to cover an area of 162 square feet with an 18-foot border on at least one side. If the garden is 18 feet long, what is its width?

(A) 9 feet

(B) 9.5 feet

(C) 10 feet

(D) 18.5 feet

894. A triangle with an area of 100 square meters has a height that measures half as much as its base. What's the triangle's height?

(A) 10 meters

(B) 12 meters

(C) 15 meters

(D) 20 meters

895. Mason's Manholes Inc. needs to install a manhole cover over an open, circular pipe that has a diameter of 18 inches. If the manhole cover must have a $\frac{1}{2}$-inch overlap all around, what is the manhole cover's surface area?

(A) 287.93 square inches

(B) 275.25 square inches

(C) 283.39 square inches

(D) 299.39 square inches

896. Sergeant First Class Aziz ordered his troops to fill four rectangular boxes with sand to hold down the flight line. If each box is 2.5 feet wide, 1 foot high, and 2 feet long, how many cubic feet of sand will the soldiers put into the boxes altogether?

(A) 20 cu. ft

(B) 22 cu. ft

(C) 5 cu. ft

(D) 18.5 cu. ft

897. An exterminator starts each day with a full canister of pesticide. If his 12-inch-tall cylindrical canister has a diameter of 10 inches, how many cubic inches of pesticide does it contain at the beginning of the exterminator's shift?

(A) 1,200 in.³

(B) 1,143 in.³

(C) 1,011 in.³

(D) 942 in.³

898. A can of soda has a diameter of 10 cm and a height of 15 cm. What is the volume of the soda in the can if 1 cm of space is left at the top of the can?

(A) 999 cm³

(B) 1,350 cm³

(C) 1,099 cm³

(D) 1,031 cm³

899. A triangle's longest side is four times the length of its shortest side, and its third side is 12 centimeters longer than the shortest side. The triangle's perimeter is 162 cm, so how long is its shortest side?

(A) 24 cm

(B) 25 cm

(C) 37 cm

(D) 40 cm

900. If one side of a square is increased by 6 cm and an adjacent side is decreased by 2 cm, a rectangle with a perimeter of 28 cm is formed. What is the area of the rectangle?

(A) 19 cm²

(B) 25 cm²

(C) 31 cm²

(D) 33 cm²

901. The smallest angle of a triangle has a measure that is 18 degrees less than the measure of the second angle, and the measure of the second angle is 33 degrees less than the measure of the greatest angle. What is the greatest angle's measurement?

(A) 91°

(B) 88°

(C) 55°

(D) 37°

902. Find the measure of $\angle C$ in a triangle with $\angle A$ measuring 38° and $\angle B$ measuring 47°.

(A) 88°

(B) 90°

(C) 91°

(D) 95°

903. Specialists Vasquez and Wolley were told to sweep the company's motor pool. Vasquez started at 10 a.m. and swept a 50-foot by 50-foot portion of the motor pool, and Wolley began at 10:45 a.m. and swept the remainder of the motor pool, which was just as wide but 15 feet shorter than what Vasquez swept. What is the motor pool's total area?

(A) 4,250 square feet

(B) 4,475 square feet

(C) 5,000 square feet

(D) 3,850 square feet

904. Deedee needs to sweep her porch, which is 8 feet long and 12 feet wide. How many square feet will she have swept when she's finished with the entire porch?

(A) 96 ft²

(B) 102 ft²

(C) 98 ft³

(D) None of the above

905. Carson and Jolie are stacking 2-inch by 2-inch blocks together. How many blocks do they need to stack to create a wall that is one foot tall and one foot wide?

(A) 12

(B) 20

(C) 28

(D) 36

906. A kite has one diagonal length of 21.5 cm and another diagonal length of 15 cm. What is the kite's area?

(A) 158 cm²

(B) 161.25 cm²

(C) 165 cm²

(D) 167.5 cm²

907. The lengths of two adjacent sides of a kite are 24.5 inches and 30.4 inches. What is the kite's perimeter?

(A) 108.9 in.

(B) 109.8 in.

(C) 111 in.

(D) 117.2 in.

908. A rectangle is six times as long as it is wide. If you increase its length by two inches and decrease its width by one inch, the area will be 190 square inches. What is the area of the original rectangle?

(A) 184 square inches

(B) 192 square inches

(C) 210 square inches

(D) 216 square inches

909. A square garden with an area of 169 square meters needs to be surrounded by a walkway that's 2 meters across. What is the walkway's area?

(A) 56 m²

(B) 110 m²

(C) 120 m²

(D) 128 m²

910. Find the difference between the circumference of a circle with a radius of 5 centimeters and the circumference of a circle with a diameter of 12 centimeters.

(A) 7.75 cm

(B) 6.28 cm

(C) 4.1 cm

(D) 2 cm

911. In a triangle measured in centimeters, the lengths of the sides are all consecutive integers. The perimeter is eight more than twice the shortest side. What is the triangle's perimeter?

(A) 15 cm

(B) 16.5 cm

(C) 18 cm

(D) 20.5 cm

912. The area of a trapezoid is 52 square inches. The bases are 11 inches and 15 inches. What is the trapezoid's height?

(A) 4 in.

(B) 5 in.

(C) 8 in.

(D) 9 in.

913. Find the area of an acute triangle with a base of 12 cm and a height of 4 cm.

(A) 24 cm²

(B) 27 cm²

(C) 16 cm²

(D) 48 cm²

914. Ms. Ruiz is searching for a triangular mat for her art classroom. She needs one that measures 18 square feet and has a base of 3 feet so it can fit in a certain corner that measures 90°. Find the height of the mat Ms. Ruiz needs to buy.

(A) 15 feet

(B) 12 feet

(C) 9 feet

(D) 6 feet

915. Find the area of a trapezoid with a base of 8 feet, a base of 12 feet, and a height of 7 feet.

(A) 120 square feet

(B) 130 square feet

(C) 140 square feet

(D) 150 square feet

916. In a quadrilateral, two angles are equal. The third angle is equal to the sum of the two equal angles, and the fourth angle is twice the sum of the third angle. The sum of all the internal angles is 360°. What is the measure of the fourth angle in the quadrilateral?

(A) 210°

(B) 180°

(C) 160°

(D) 170°

917. Find the exact circumference of a circle if its radius is 12 feet.

(A) 12π ft

(B) 16π ft

(C) 6π ft

(D) 24π ft

918. What is the volume of a right cylinder that's 8 cm high and has a radius of 4 cm?

(A) 118 cm³

(B) 156π cm³

(C) 128π cm³

(D) 135π cm³

919. A horse is tied to a post at the 90° inside corner of a 12-foot by 12-foot fence. The rope tying the horse in place is 6 feet long. Approximately how much area can the horse graze on if he stays tied to the post?

(A) 18 square feet

(B) 20.65 square feet

(C) 25.37 square feet

(D) 28.26 square feet

920. Find the surface area of a cube with edges measuring 18 centimeters each.

(A) 1,850 cm²

(B) 1,944 cm²

(C) 2,112 cm²

(D) 2,242 cm²

921. Vicki is 5 feet, 6 inches tall and casts a shadow that's 11 feet long. She wants to figure out how tall her office building is, so she measures its shadow, which is 60.5 feet long. How tall is Vicki's office building?

(A) 28.5 feet

(B) 30 feet

(C) 30.25 feet

(D) 31.75 feet

922. Marina needs to design a large billboard shaped like a parallelogram for a major advertising campaign. When she orders the paint, the customer service representative asks how many square feet the billboard is. If the billboard is 18 feet long and 11 feet high, what is Marina's answer?

(A) 150 sq. ft

(B) 170 sq. ft

(C) 198 sq. ft

(D) 207 sq. ft

923. A parallelogram-shaped vegetable garden has an area of 224 square feet and a base of 16 feet. What is its height?

(A) 14 feet

(B) 15 feet

(C) 16 feet

(D) 18 feet

924. An obtuse triangle has a base of 7 inches and a height of 12 inches. What is the triangle's area?

(A) 19 in.²

(B) 38 in.²

(C) 42 in.²

(D) 84 in.²

925. If the first angle in a triangle measures the sum of five and two times the second angle, and the second angle measures twice the third angle, what is the measure of the third angle?

(A) 35°

(B) 37°

(C) 43°

(D) 45°

926. Cherina wants to put a round hot tub on her patio. Her patio measures 18 feet by 11 feet. What is the greatest circumference the hot tub can have without overlapping the edges of the patio?

(A) 32.25 feet

(B) 34.54 feet

(C) 36.82 feet

(D) 38.8 feet

927. A right triangle is 15 inches high; its base is two times its height plus four inches. What is the triangle's area?

(A) 240 in.²

(B) 255 in.²

(C) 270 in.²

(D) 281 in.²

928. A quadrilateral inscribed in a circle has a 107° angle and a 98° angle. What is the smallest angle in the quadrilateral?

(A) 70°

(B) 73°

(C) 77°

(D) 82°

929. With two concentric circles, the larger has a radius of 10 meters and the smaller has a radius of 5 meters. What is the area of the larger circle minus the area of the smaller circle?

(A) 78.5 m²

(B) 112.75 m²

(C) 153 m²

(D) 235.5 m²

930. Find the area of a rectangle that has two sides measuring six yards each and two sides measuring three yards each.

(A) 12 square yards

(B) 14 square yards

(C) 16 square yards

(D) 18 square yards

931. The angles depicted here are

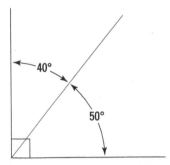

(A) supplementary.

(B) complementary.

(C) congruent.

(D) None of the above are correct.

932. Mandy is folding a note in class to give to Peter. She needs to smuggle it past her teacher, who can usually see notes that have an area of 5 square inches or greater. If Mandy folds the note into a triangle so it has a base of 2 inches and a height of 3 inches, what will its area be?

(A) 1.6 in.²

(B) 3 in.²

(C) 4.8 in.²

(D) 6 in.²

933. Find the surface area of a cube with edges that measure 8 inches each.

(A) 384 in.²

(B) 394 in.²

(C) 404 in.²

(D) 2,304 in.²

934. Nathan is wrapping a rectangular gift box for Andrea. In order to buy the right amount of wrapping paper, he takes the box's dimensions; it's 8 inches wide, 12 inches long, and 6 inches high. What is the gift box's surface area?

(A) 384 in.²

(B) 400 in. ²

(C) 432 in. ²

(D) 454 in. ²

935. Find the approximate volume of a sphere that has a diameter of 10 inches.

(A) 501 in.³

(B) 523.33 in.³

(C) 542.66 in.³

(D) None of the above

936. A parallelogram's area is 24 square inches, and its base is 4 inches. What is the parallelogram's height?

(A) 4.4 in.

(B) 8 in.

(C) 6 in.

(D) 20 in.

937. What is the measurement of an inscribed angle made of chords $\overline{AB}$ and $\overline{BC}$, where the intercepted arc is 100°?

(A) 50°

(B) 53°

(C) 200°

(D) 150°

938. Nola, an interior decorator, needs to fill a square pyramid with colored sand. The pyramid has a base measuring 17 square inches, and the pyramid is 51 inches tall. How much colored sand can the pyramid hold?

(A) 175 cu. in.

(B) 867 cu. in.

(C) 68 cu. in.

(D) 289 cu. in.

939. Find $\angle D$ in a quadrilateral where $\angle A$ measures 220°, $\angle B$ measures 34°, and $\angle C$ measures 83°.

(A) 50°

(B) 34°

(C) 23°

(D) 18°

940. Tim has to lay sod on a customer's lawn. After measuring, he finds that the customer's lawn has two parallel sides (one is 80 feet long, and the other is 120 feet long) that are connected by a straight, 90-foot perpendicular border. The remaining border connects the other ends of the two parallel sides. What is the area of the customer's lawn?

(A) 9,000 square feet

(B) 8,500 square feet

(C) 8,125 square feet

(D) 7,990 square feet

941. If a circle is intercepted by two secants forming $\angle ACE$ with intercepted arcs $\overset{\frown}{BD}$ and $\overset{\frown}{AE}$, what is $m\angle ACE$ if $m\overset{\frown}{BD} = 20°$ and $m\overset{\frown}{AE} = 80°$?

(A) 30°

(B) 40°

(C) 60°

(D) 100°

942. A 48-square-foot rectangle with a length of 8 feet and a height of 6 feet is increased by 13 feet on each side. What is the new rectangle's area?

(A) 624 ft²

(B) 399 ft²

(C) 247 ft²

(D) 209 ft²

943. Josie's four bedroom walls are each 10 feet long and 8 feet high. The door is 2 feet wide and 7 feet high. One quart of paint covers approximately 90 square feet. How much paint does Josie need to cover the whole room (minus the space for the door)?

(A) 1.75 quarts

(B) 3.4 quarts

(C) 4.1 quarts

(D) 5 quarts

944. Find the exact circumference of a circle if its radius is 4.43 meters.

(A) 7.5π

(B) 8.43π

(C) 8.86π

(D) 9.17π

945. Mr. Gray is hand-carving round, wooden coasters for his woodworking business. He wants to carve coasters for cups that have a radius of 2 inches, so he decides to carve the coasters each with a radius of 3 inches. What is the approximate area of each coaster?

(A) 28.26 in.²

(B) 31.33 in.²

(C) 34.2 in.²

(D) 37.28 in.²

946. If you walk around an entire city block that measures 1,234 feet on each side, how far have you walked?

(A) 5,280 feet

(B) 5,103 feet

(C) 4,936 feet

(D) 4,572 feet

947. A small town is installing new sidewalks, but the city's budget only allows them to lay 1,200 square feet of concrete each month. If the sidewalks are all 3 feet wide, by what length will the sidewalk grow each month?

(A) 350 feet

(B) 300 feet

(C) 420 feet

(D) 400 feet

948. A round puddle with a diameter of 8 inches evaporates in the hot sun. For each half hour of evaporation, its diameter shrinks by an inch. After an hour and a half, what is the puddle's approximate area?

(A) 17.5 in.²

(B) 19.6 in.²

(C) 21.3 in.²

(D) 24.04 in.²

949. In a triangle, the angle with the least measure is one-third of the measure of the second angle, which is 5 degrees less than the measure of the greatest angle. What is the measure of the largest angle in the triangle?

(A) 75°

(B) 77°

(C) 79°

(D) 80°

950. Identify the formula to find the area of a triangle:

(A) $A = \frac{1}{2}bh$

(B) $A = \frac{bh}{2}$

(C) $A = 2lw$

(D) Both A and B are correct.

951. Davy was riding his scooter. When he hit the top of the ramp, he jumped, turned, and landed facing the opposite direction. What was the angle of Davy's turn?

(A) 90°

(B) 180°

(C) 270°

(D) 360°

952. Mrs. Scott baked a cherry pie in a pan that measured 9 inches across. She baked an apple pie in a pan that measured 11 inches across. What is the difference in area between the two pies?

(A) 31.4 square inches

(B) 32 square inches

(C) 33.57 square inches

(D) 35.75 square inches

953. Jesse wants to turn his backyard into a laser tag field. If his backyard is shaped this way, how much space does he have?

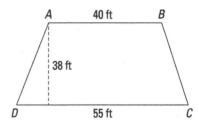

(A) 3,610 square feet

(B) 2,950 square feet

(C) 2,275 square feet

(D) 1,805 square feet

954. What is the area of a square whose perimeter is 10 meters?

(A) 6 m²

(B) 6.25 m²

(C) 6.5 m²

(D) 6.75 m²

955. Chris pointed the minute hand on a clock at the number 9. How many degrees will the minute hand travel before it reaches 12?

(A) 45°

(B) 90°

(C) 120°

(D) 180°

956. The measure of one supplementary angle, $\angle A$, is twice the measure of its counterpart, $\angle B$. What is the measure of $\angle A$?

(A) 60°

(B) 90°

(C) 120°

(D) 150°

957. Two artists drew congruent angles. The first drew a 49° angle. What is the measure of the angle the second artist drew?

(A) 41°

(B) 49°

(C) 91°

(D) 131°

958. If two lines, Line A and Line B, are perpendicular, and Line B has a slope of 5, what is Line A's slope?

(A) −0.2

(B) 0.2

(C) 0.5

(D) 1

959. How much will it cost to put hardwood floors in a room that's 13 feet long and 18 feet wide if hardwood flooring costs $60 per square yard?

(A) $1,500

(B) $1,560

(C) $1,620

(D) $4,680

960. A square with an area of 16 cm² is inside a square with sides measuring 9 cm each. What is the remaining area if you remove the smaller square?

(A) 50 cm²

(B) 53.75 cm²

(C) 65 cm²

(D) 81 cm²

Fact-Finding

961. If Sergeant Jones rides his bicycle 5 miles every day, how many miles will he ride in one week?

(A) 35 miles

(B) 40 miles

(C) 45 miles

(D) 50 miles

962. There are 100 vehicles in the barracks parking lot. Sixty of the vehicles are sports cars, 30 of the vehicles are pickup trucks, and the remaining vehicles are motorcycles. When the soldiers are released from duty, everyone gets in his or her vehicle and leaves. What is the probability of a sports car leaving second, after a motorcycle or truck has left?

(A) $\frac{1}{10}$

(B) $\frac{29}{33}$

(C) $\frac{20}{33}$

(D) $\frac{20}{34}$

963. A bakery made 16 wedding cakes and 24 birthday cakes. What is the ratio of wedding cakes to birthday cakes?

(A) 16 : 24

(B) 16/24

(C) 16 to 24

(D) All of the above are correct.

964. A recipe to make 10 cakes requires 24 cups of flour and four tablespoons of baking powder. If the baker needs to make only three cakes, how many cups of flour will he need?

(A) 6.25 cups
(B) 6.8 cups
(C) 7.2 cups
(D) 7.5 cups

965. Notting Hill Road and Van Dorn Street intersect. On the northwest side, the streets intersect at a 131° angle. What is the measure of the angle on the southwest corner of Notting Hill and Van Dorn?

(A) 311°
(B) 221°
(C) 59°
(D) 49°

966. Gordon spent $1\frac{1}{4}$ hours preparing dinner. He spent $\frac{1}{4}$ of his time actually cooking. How many hours did Gordon spend cooking?

(A) $\frac{5}{16}$ hours
(B) $\frac{1}{4}$ hours
(C) $\frac{9}{16}$ hours
(D) $\frac{15}{16}$ hours

967. How many passwords using six digits are possible if the first two digits must be a letter from A to Z and the last four digits must be numerals from 0 to 9?

(A) 6.25 million
(B) 6.54 million
(C) 6.76 million
(D) 6.91 million

968. Amira gets $11 per week in allowance. She spent $\frac{3}{4}$ of this week's allowance on new school supplies. Of the money she spent on new school supplies, she spent $\frac{5}{6}$ of it on pens. How much money did she spend on pens?

(A) $6.50
(B) $6.75
(C) $6.88
(D) $6.97

969. A hockey player won 74% of the games he played over the course of his career. If he played 1,200 games, how many games did he win?

(A) 812
(B) 853
(C) 888
(D) 902

970. Potatoes sold for $0.75 per pound last week. This week, they sell for $0.81 per pound. By what percentage did the price of potatoes increase?

(A) 7%
(B) 8%
(C) 9%
(D) 10%

971. With a ratio of 16 horses to 9 dogs, how many dogs would there be if there were 192 horses?

(A) 101
(B) 108
(C) 132
(D) None of the above

972. A retailer sells clothes at a markup of 40%. If a pair of jeans costs the retailer $25, how much will the retailer charge customers?

(A) $27.50
(B) $30.00
(C) $33.75
(D) $35.00

973. A traveling shoe salesman sells shoes at $79.75 per pair. He sells them at a 45% markup over the wholesale price he pays, so how much does the traveling shoe salesman spend on each pair of shoes?

(A) $50

(B) $55

(C) $60

(D) $62.50

974. A TV that normally sells for $415 is on sale for 15% off. What is the TV's sale price?

(A) $298

(B) $315.85

(C) $352.75

(D) $373.50

975. The school cafeteria is on a tight budget. When Mrs. Stevens bakes rolls for all the students, she needs 11 pounds of flour. The least expensive option would be

(A) 6 pounds of white flour at $1.49 each and 4 pounds of wheat flour at $1.59 each

(B) 10 pounds of white flour at $1.49 each and two 8-ounce bags of wheat flour at $0.90 each

(C) Eight 8-ounce bags of white flour at $0.75 each and seven pounds of white flour at $1.69 each

(D) 11 pounds of wheat flour at $1.79 each

976. Nuan is a sales clerk at a candy store. A bin of candy bars contains three dozen bars when it's full, and Nuan's boss tells her to reorder them when the bin is $\frac{1}{6}$ full. How many candy bars are in the bin when it's time for Nuan to place an order?

(A) 4

(B) 5

(C) 6

(D) 7

977. The wake-up alarm on Sachi's smartphone goes off every five minutes until he gets up for work. If the alarm begins going off at 6:25 a.m. and continues chiming every five minutes until Sachi gets up with the last alarm at 8:15 a.m., how many times will his alarm have sounded?

(A) 21

(B) 22

(C) 23

(D) 24

978. Robbie's parents hid his birthday presents in the closet and put a combination lock on the door. The lock has a two-digit combination; on the first reel, the numbers 0 through 9 appear. On the second reel, the letters A through Z appear. How many possible combinations will Robbie have to go through to get an early peek at his birthday presents?

(A) 212

(B) 224

(C) 240

(D) 260

979. If one foot is 30.48 centimeters, how many centimeters are there in 32 inches?

(A) 70.73 cm

(B) 81.28 cm

(C) 84.44 cm

(D) 105.3 cm

980. One-ninth of the books sold at a bookstore are audiobooks; $\frac{5}{8}$ of the rest of the books are used, and the remainder of the books are new. If the bookstore has 81 new books, how many more used books are there than audiobooks?

(A) 54

(B) 60

(C) 108

(D) Not enough data to answer the question

981. Javier and Gloria drove to the beach at 65 miles per hour. They stopped at a hotel after traveling for 8 hours. The next day, they drove 4 more hours at 70 miles per hour before reaching the beach. How far is the beach from Javier and Gloria's home?

(A) 750 miles

(B) 800 miles

(C) 850 miles

(D) 860 miles

982. The ratio of females to males in Marine boot camp is $4:5$. In one cycle of boot camp, there are 360 recruits. How many females are there?

(A) 145

(B) 150

(C) 155

(D) 160

983. Oroka bought his girlfriend a diamond ring for $1,199. The jeweler offered him insurance for 15% of the ring's value per month. How much will it cost Oroka to insure the ring for a year, assuming its value doesn't depreciate?

(A) $215.82

(B) $658.33

(C) $1,750.50

(D) $2,158.20

984. One-twelfth of Micah's CDs are rap music. One-third of the collection is classic rock, and Micah has 175 CDs of alternative music. How many classic rock CDs does Micah have?

(A) 100

(B) 125

(C) 148

(D) 150

985. A rectangular chicken coop is $1\frac{3}{4}$ times as long as it is wide, and its perimeter is 192.5 feet. Use the perimeter formula, $P = 2l + 2w$, to find out how wide the chicken coop is.

(A) 28 feet

(B) 31.75 feet

(C) 35 feet

(D) 37.5 feet

986. If every cup contains 8 ounces of liquid, how much liquid can you hold in 42 cups?

(A) 310

(B) 317

(C) 332

(D) 336

987. It costs $3,120 per year for weekly house-keeping services. At the same rate, how much does weekly housekeeping cost for 12 weeks?

(A) $680

(B) $700

(C) $720

(D) $740

988. Diana is training to run her first marathon, and after a month, she can run 15 miles at a pace of $7\frac{1}{2}$ miles per hour. At that pace, about how long will it take her to run 26 miles?

(A) 3.15 hours

(B) 3.23 hours

(C) 3.33 hours

(D) 3.5 hours

989. A bag of rice holds 36 cups, and each serving is $\frac{1}{2}$ cup. How many servings are in the bag?

(A) 72

(B) 74

(C) 76

(D) 78

990. A restaurant offers dinner specials in which you get to choose one item from each of three different categories:

Beverages: Soda or tea

Entrées: Burger, hot dog, or lasagna

Desserts: Ice cream or frozen yogurt

How many different meals are possible?

(A) 7

(B) 9

(C) 10

(D) 12

991. Pascual's thesis is seventy-two pages long. His printer can print eight pages per minute. If he starts printing at 7:00 p.m., what time will his printer wrap up the job?

(A) 7:05 p.m.

(B) 7:07 p.m.

(C) 7:09 p.m.

(D) 7:10 p.m.

992. A laptop is marked down 25% so that its sale price is $487.50. What was its original price?

(A) $650

(B) $675

(C) $700

(D) $725

993. Connor Crete's Paving Co. poured a 20-foot by 30-foot driveway in front of a house. The driveway reduced the front-yard lawn area by 25%. About how large was the front yard before Connor Crete's Paving Co. poured the driveway?

(A) 2,400 square feet

(B) 2,450 square feet

(C) 2,500 square feet

(D) 2,750 square feet

994. The fastest recorded giant tortoise speed in the world is 5 miles per hour. Usually, giant tortoises move at an average of 0.17 miles per hour. How long would it take a giant tortoise moving at average speed to move a distance of 0.34 miles?

(A) 0.20 hours

(B) 1.5 hours

(C) 0.17 hours

(D) 2 hours

995. Ninety-six guests attended Kim and Gerry's wedding. Twelve people sat at each table. How many tables did the wedding planner have to set up?

(A) 7

(B) 8

(C) 9

(D) 10

996. The population of South Lyon, Michigan, is 11,327. If the next census shows a growth of approximately 5%, what will South Lyon's population be?

(A) 11,543

(B) 11,599

(C) 11,801

(D) 11,893

997. Mount Everest, the highest mountain in the world, is 8,848 meters. Alaska's Denali, also known as Mount McKinley, is just under 70 percent of Mount Everest's height. How tall is Denali, rounded to the nearest ten meters?

(A) 5,988 meters

(B) 6,190 meters

(C) 6,220 meters

(D) 7,540 meters

998. A lawn sprinkler puts out 12 gallons of water per minute. The hose puts out 14 gallons of water per minute. How much more water does the hose put out over the course of 35 minutes?

(A) 70 gallons

(B) 35 gallons

(C) 20 gallons

(D) 10 gallons

999. There are 16 marbles in a jar. Three marbles are red, six are blue, five are purple, and two are orange. If you reach in once, what is the probability that you will pull out a blue marble?

(A) $\frac{1}{2}$

(B) $\frac{3}{8}$

(C) $\frac{6}{9}$

(D) $\frac{1}{16}$

1,000. Your Internet connection can transmit 50 megabits of data per second. How much data can it transmit in 11 seconds?

(A) 500 megabits

(B) 520 megabits

(C) 535 megabits

(D) 550 megabits

1,001. If $\frac{3}{4}$ of the student body at a school of 500 children is involved in volleyball, basketball, music, or another extracurricular activity, how many children are not involved in extracurricular activities?

(A) 375

(B) 300

(C) 210

(D) 125

2

The Answers

IN THIS PART . . .

Check your answers to the questions in Part 1.

Review the answer explanations to understand why the right answer is correct and the others are incorrect.

If you discover that you haven't done so well in a certain category, don't worry. The *For Dummies* series offers plenty of excellent resources that provide more instruction and review. Here are a few that I recommend (all published by Wiley):

- *Vocabulary For Dummies* by Laura E. Rozakis
- *Basic Math & Pre-Algebra For Dummies* by Mark Zegarelli
- *Algebra I For Dummies* by Mary Jane Sterling
- *Geometry For Dummies* by Mark Ryan
- *Math Word Problems For Dummies* by Mary Jane Sterling

If you want to brush up on the other topics on the ASVAB, check out the latest edition of *ASVAB For Dummies* by Rod Powers and Angie Papple Johnston (Wiley).

Chapter 5
Answers

Word Knowledge

1. **A. agreement.**

Accord is a noun that means to have a concurrence of opinion.

"About 90 percent of voters were in accord with the candidate's plan."

2. **A. set up.**

Establish is a verb that means to set up, found, or create.

"Will you help me establish a new chapter of the club in Oakland?"

3. **C. get.**

Obtain is a verb that means to come into possession of.

"You'll do much better if you obtain a copy of the answer key."

4. **D. bold.**

Brazen is an adjective that means excessively bold or brash.

"Steve's brazen attempt to ruffle his opponent's feathers didn't work."

5. **B. useless.**

Vain is an adjective that means fruitless, unproductive, or futile.

"Kim tried in vain to stop them, but the papers flew out the window."

Vain is also an adjective that means excessively proud or conceited (for example, "He's so vain that he can't walk past a mirror without stopping to look at himself").

Don't confuse vain with vein, which is a tube in your circulatory system that carries blood.

6. A. strength.

Fortitude is a noun that means strength or guts in the face of adversity.

"She had the intestinal fortitude to join the military."

Strength is a better answer than Choice (B), *bravado*, because bravado refers to a bold manner or a show of bold actions intended to impress or intimidate; you can be bold or show off without being strong in the face of adversity.

7. B. believable.

Plausible is an adjective that means believable; it describes something that has the appearance of truth or reason.

"The prosecutor outlined a plausible scenario so the jury would convict the defendant."

8. D. convince.

Persuade is a verb that means to convince someone to do something by advising or urging.

"I tried to persuade my recruiter to let me skip the ASVAB."

9. C. conversation.

Dialogue is a noun that means a conversation between people.

"Let's start a dialogue on improving customer service."

10. B. excused.

Exempt means free from, excused from, or not subject to an obligation to which others or other things are subject.

"I'm exempt from getting my flu shot at work because I already got one at the pharmacy."

11. A. support.

Buttress is a verb that means to support or hold up. It's also a noun that refers to something that offers support (*flying buttresses* are the curved supports you see on the outer walls of a lot of gothic cathedrals).

"After the first wall collapsed, the builder rebuilt it with a buttress."

12. **A. strange.**

> *Bizarre* is an adjective that means conspicuously unconventional or unusual.
>
> "Seasoning your chicken with curry and maple syrup creates a bizarre taste."

13. **D. responsible.**

> *Liable* is an adjective that means subject to legal action, held legally responsible, or subject to be affected by something.
>
> "The hotel owners were liable for the guest's fall down the stairs because they failed to repair the railing."
>
> *Libel* is a false, harmful statement that appears in writing; if that had been the word in the question, Choice (B) would be the correct answer. *Slander* is a false, harmful spoken statement.

14. **C. hopeful.**

> *Optimistic* is an adjective that means expecting the best.
>
> "I'm optimistic that you'll do well on the Word Knowledge subtest because you're using this book."

15. **B. change.**

> *Affect* is a verb that means to have an effect upon something.
>
> "Don't let her love of country music affect your friendship."

16. **C. maze.**

> *Labyrinth* is a noun that means a complex system of pathways or tunnels in which it's easy to get lost — like a maze.
>
> "The mouse made its way through the labyrinth and found the cheese six times today."

17. **B. obvious.**

> *Blatant* is an adjective that means completely lacking in subtlety; it describes something that's done openly and unashamedly.
>
> "That's a blatant lie!"

18. **A. movement.**

Maneuver is a noun that means a deliberate, coordinated movement to reach a particular goal; typically, a maneuver requires some level of skill.

"The pilots have been practicing that maneuver for months."

19. **A. tell.**

Disclose is a verb that means to reveal or make public.

"Owners are required to disclose problems with their homes when potential buyers ask."

20. **D. isolate.**

Quarantine is a verb that means to place into isolation (such as for medical reasons).

"If you get sick, we'll have to quarantine you."

21. **D. skilled.**

Adept is an adjective that means extremely skilled.

"Danielle is adept at preventing mistakes from slipping through."

22. **C. retreat.**

Recede is a verb that means to pull back, move backward, or retreat.

"We watched the fog recede as the sun came up."

23. **A. changeable.**

Volatile is an adjective that means subject to rapid or unexpected change.

"The situation is becoming more volatile as more people arrive on the scene."

24. **D. brave.**

Intrepid is an adjective that means brave in the face of danger.

"The intrepid soldiers of the 82nd Airborne Division have no qualms about strapping on a parachute and jumping from a perfectly good airplane."

25. **B. anger.**

> *Wrath* is a noun that means vengeful anger or punishment.
>
> "Sarah, afraid of incurring her sister's wrath, hid the stained shirt."

26. **B. grow.**

> *Proliferate* is a verb that means to grow rapidly.
>
> "Stories of the mishap proliferated until the whole school knew about it."

27. **C. abandon.**

> *Vacate* is a verb that means to abandon, empty, or move out of something.
>
> "We all need to vacate the building when the alarm sounds."

28. **A. pitiful.**

> *Pathetic* is an adjective that means causing or evoking pity, sympathetic sadness, or sorrow.
>
> "The rain-soaked kitten looked so pathetic that I tried to dry her with my jacket."

29. **D. sanctuary.**

> *Refuge* is a noun that means a safe place, shelter, or sanctuary.
>
> "The wildlife needed a safe place to go, so the county created a refuge within the park."

30. **B. scrub.**

> *Scour* is a verb that means to polish or clean a surface by washing, rubbing, or scrubbing with an abrasive cloth.
>
> "The drill sergeant made us scour the floor before we could go to chow."
>
> *Scour* can also mean to thoroughly search something, such as when someone says, "She scoured the crime scene for evidence."

31. **C. dislike.**

> *Aversion* is a noun that refers to a feeling of intense dislike.
>
> "She had an aversion to broccoli, but she adored cauliflower."

32. A. conflict.

Strife is a noun that means bitter conflict, a lack of agreement or harmony, or violent dissension.

"There's strife within the community over the proposed base closure."

33. C. sustain.

Nourish is a verb that means to sustain, provide with nourishment, or supply.

"Adding fertilizer to the soil helps nourish your plants."

34. A. step on.

Tread is a verb that means to put down your foot; you can also use it as a noun when you're describing the grooved surface of a tire.

"Tread softly, or you'll wake the guard dog."

35. D. comfort.

Console is a verb that means to give moral or emotional strength to another person or an animal.

"Parents can sometimes console a crying baby by singing."

36. B. repartee.

Banter is a noun that means teasing, joking repartee.

"When you aren't cleaning or training, you'll have plenty of time for witty banter."

37. A. believable.

Credible is an adjective that means believable, plausible, or likely to be true.

"Can you provide a credible source for your claims?"

38. B. deteriorate.

Erode is a verb that means to wear down, deteriorate, or decay.

"The stream, which had been running through the mountains for years, caused the rock to erode."

39. B. create.

Generate is a verb that means to bring into existence or to supply.

"We need to generate awareness on this topic."

40. D. way.

Mode is a noun that refers to how something is done or how it happens.

"Which mode of learning works best for you?"

41. D. prevent.

Foil is a verb that means to hinder or prevent someone's efforts, plans, or desires.

"If you make noise, you'll foil my plan to sneak out."

42. A. enclosed space.

Chamber is a noun that means an enclosed space; it can also mean a legislative, administrative, or judicial assembly.

"He closed the door to the chamber so he could have privacy."

43. D. helper.

Aide is a noun that refers to someone who acts as an assistant or helper.

"He didn't write the speech. His aide did."

Don't let Choice (A) throw you off — *abet* means to aid or help, but the word in the question is *aide*. The *e* on the end changes the meaning.

44. A. confuse.

Although *stump* is a noun meaning the base of a tree left after it's been chopped down, it's also a verb that means to confuse, perplex, or confound someone.

"Difficult Arithmetic Reasoning questions always stump me."

45. B. assert.

Insist is a verb that means to assert one's position strongly or to be emphatic or resolute in a refusal to compromise.

"I insist that you stop working, sit down, and relax."

Choice (D) is a close choice, but it's not the best answer. To *demand* is to make a request while insisting on immediate attention or obedience, as if the person making the demand had a right to it.

46. **A. uninteresting.**

> *Bland* is an adjective that means uninteresting or lacking stimulating characteristics; it can also refer to flavorless, tasteless food.
>
> "The beginning of the movie was so bland that I almost didn't watch the rest of it."

47. **B. lookout.**

> *Sentinel* is a noun that refers to a person who keeps watch.
>
> "Give the sentinel the password, and he'll let you in."

48. **D. cancel.**

> *Repeal* is a verb that means to cancel officially.
>
> "The president wanted to repeal the law because he believed it was unconstitutional."

49. **D. work.**

> *Labor* is a noun that means any piece of work that is undertaken or attempted, such as a project or task.
>
> "When you build a house, you should be paid fairly for your labor."

50. **A. anomaly.**

> *Aberration* is a noun that means a departure from what's normal or expected.
>
> "We found an aberration in the results, but we don't need to worry about it."

51. **D. charming.**

> *Winsome* is an adjective that means attractive or appealing in appearance or character.
>
> "His talent and winsome smile made him a great choice for the lead role."

52. **A. first.**

> *Initial* is an adjective that means existing or occurring at the beginning of something.
>
> "My initial thought was that the house was locked, but then I realized the door was open."

53. C. fanatical.

Rabid is an adjective that describes extreme or fanatical belief or support of something.

"The rabid zealots couldn't stand the idea of others not sharing their belief system."

54. A. movable.

Mobile is an adjective that means able to move freely or easily.

"The team set up a mobile command center that they can use anywhere."

55. D. request.

Solicit is a verb that means to ask for or try to obtain something.

"Volunteers knocked on every door in the neighborhood to solicit donations."

56. B. misconception.

Fallacy is a noun that means mistaken belief.

"The notion that everything on the Internet is true is a fallacy."

Although Choice (A) could be true, it's not the best choice because *misnomer* refers to a wrong or inaccurate name or designation, not a belief.

57. C. outer surface.

External is an adjective that refers to the outer surface of an object.

"Power-wash the external part of your home to increase its curb appeal."

58. B. vehement.

Vociferous is an adjective that describes a person or speech that is vehement or makes a loud, confused noise.

"The vociferous crowd wouldn't stop shouting, even after the controversial comedian left the stage."

59. A. change.

Convert is a verb that refers to something that causes a change in form, character, or function.

"It's easy to convert this rain poncho into a shelter."

60. **D. think.**

Consider is a verb that means to think carefully about something.

"The lieutenant had to consider all his options before making a decision."

61. **C. fast.**

Prompt is an adjective that means immediate or done without delay.

"I appreciate your prompt reply because we have only two more hours to take action."

62. **A. depravity.**

Turpitude is a noun that means depravity, moral corruption, or wickedness.

"You can be barred from U.S. citizenship for moral turpitude."

63. **C. substitute.**

Makeshift is an adjective that refers to something that serves as a temporary substitute for something better.

"The soldiers put together a makeshift fighting position, which we call a 'hasty' in the military."

64. **B. is composed of.**

Comprise is a verb that means to consist of or to be made up of.

"This book comprises 1,001 practice questions."

65. **D. bogus.**

Spurious is an adjective that means false or fake.

"The reporter had to sort through both authentic and spurious claims to find the truth."

66. **C. area.**

Expanse is a noun that means an area of something (usually land or sea) that presents a continuous surface.

"The humpback whale can travel anywhere within the expanse of ocean between Alaska and Hawaii."

67. **A. menacing.**

Fearsome is an adjective that means menacing, frightening, or scary.

"Kids with active imaginations may believe there are fearsome monsters in their bedroom closets."

68. **B. pretentious.**

Sophomoric is an adjective that means pretentious or juvenile.

"His antics were sophomoric and, frankly, quite irritating."

69. **D. infuriate.**

Exasperate is a verb that means to irritate intensely or to infuriate.

"The rest of the group was exasperated by Liliana's lack of commitment to the project."

70. **B. shortage.**

Scarcity is a noun that describes the state of being in short supply of something or experiencing a shortage of something.

"A scarcity of food on the savannah caused the lion to move his pride closer to the city."

71. **A. withstand.**

Resist is a verb that means to withstand the action or effect of something.

"The reinforced walls can resist high winds."

72. **A. fake.**

Ersatz is an adjective that means fake or unreal. You can also use it to describe a product that's made or used as an inferior substitute for something else.

"These ersatz paintings could pass for works by the masters."

73. **D. be a warning.**

Portend is a verb that refers to someone or something acting as sign or warning that something big or calamitous is about to happen.

"A common misconception is that green clouds always portend a tornado."

74. **C. understandable.**

Lucid is an adjective that means easy to understand.

"The author gives a lucid account of early American history."

75. **B. excluded.**

Ostracized is a verb that means excluded from a group by general consent.

"When Patrick and D.J. decided not to follow in their father's footsteps, the family ostracized them."

Although Choice (C), *parted*, is similar, it's not the best answer because being separated or parted refers to the result of being ostracized.

76. **A. tempt.**

Allure is a verb that means to attract, charm, or tempt.

"Flowers evolved with bright colors to allure bees to fertilize them."

77. **B. joyful.**

Gleeful is an adjective that means triumphantly joyful, happy, or delighted.

"The children's gleeful laughter made all the adults smile."

78. **A. sedate.**

Tranquilize is a verb that means to have a calming or sedative effect on.

"Wildlife officials will have to tranquilize the bear if they see it in a neighborhood."

79. **C. resist.**

Oppose is a verb that means to actively resist or refuse to comply with a person or a system.

"Half the community was ready to oppose the school's reopening."

80. **A. customs.**

Mores is a noun that refers to the characteristic customs and conventions of a community. It's pronounced like *morays* (the eels).

"Some things that are normal in other countries are against social mores in the U.S."

81. **D. become chafed.**

Chap is a verb that means to become chafed, cracked, rough, or sore, most often through exposure to cold weather.

"If you don't use lip balm, your lips will chap."

82. **B. bossy.**

Overbearing is an adjective that means unpleasantly or arrogantly bossy or domineering.

"The older twin was overbearing, while the younger was meek and quiet."

83. **B. fairness.**

Equity is a noun that describes the quality of being fair and impartial.

"Fighting for pay equity is a cornerstone of the candidate's campaign."

84. **A. understated.**

Subtle is an adjective that describes a change or distinction that's delicate and understated.

"The subtle fragrance of flowers drifted through the open window."

85. **C. economic.**

Pecuniary is an adjective that means of or relating to money.

"He was held liable for pecuniary damages when the jury found him guilty."

86. **B. impermanent.**

Temporary is an adjective that means lasting for a limited period of time.

"The benefits of energy drinks are temporary; they wear off after a few hours."

87. **D. perceptive.**

Insightful is an adjective that means being perceptive; it also means having or showing an accurate, deep understanding.

"The professor gave an insightful presentation that left the entire class in awe."

88. **A. without depth.**

Superficial is an adjective that means occurring or existing at or on the surface.

"He suffered superficial burns, but he'll be okay."

89. **C. deliver.**

Render is a verb that means to provide, give, furnish, or deliver. In business, people may ask for payment for "services rendered."

"The jury won't be gone long before they render a verdict."

90. **B. unchanging.**

Constant is an adjective that means occurring continuously over time. It's also a noun that means a situation or state of affairs that doesn't change.

"The constant noise became irritating."

91. **A. delegation.**

Commission is a noun that refers to a group of people who have been officially charged with a particular responsibility.

"The commission's main responsibility is to gather information on ASVAB test results."

92. **C. endeavor.**

Venture is a noun that means a risky or daring undertaking or endeavor.

"Bravo Company ventured into the city after dark to find hidden caches of weapons."

93. **D. vary.**

Range is a verb that means to vary or extend between certain limits.

"The students' ages range between 15 and 18 years."

94. **A. plan.**

Scheme is a noun that means a systematic plan or arrangement.

"The pair came up with a scheme to rob the bank."

95. C. request.

Plea is a noun that means an urgent, emotional request.

"The king heard the crowd's collective plea for mercy."

96. B. post

Stake is a noun that refers to a post with a point at one end. Don't get *stake* confused with *steak* — the former holds up your tent when you're on field exercises, and the latter is what you dream about while you're in Basic Combat Training.

"Use a mallet rather than a claw hammer to pound in the stakes."

97. B. characteristic.

Attribute is a noun that refers to a characteristic inherent in someone or something.

"The dog's friendliness is his best attribute."

98. C. impressive.

Awesome is an adjective that means extremely impressive. It's typically used for something that inspires great admiration, apprehension, or fear.

"The awesome collection on display at the museum leaves visitors speechless."

99. D. annoy.

Provoke is a verb that means to deliberately annoy someone or make someone angry.

"Don't provoke your siblings by calling them names."

100. B. quote.

Cite is a verb that means to quote something as evidence.

"Cite your sources in the bibliography."

Pay attention to the way things are spelled on the ASVAB; if you were rushing, you may have chosen Choice (D) — but that would be the answer only if the question asked you to define *site*.

101. A. lectured

Addressed is a verb that means to speak to a person or a group, usually in a formal way.

102. **D. examine**

Analyze is a verb that means to examine critically.

103. **C. racket**

Cacophony is a noun that refers to a harsh, discordant mixture of sounds.

104. **B. contain**

Include is a verb that means to contain or to place in a category, or to make part of a whole set.

105. **A. idea**

Concept is a noun that means a general notion or idea.

106. **B. answer**

Solution is a noun that means the state of being solved; it also means an explanation or answer.

107. **D. thread**

Strand is a noun that means a thread or threadlike part of something.

108. **A. logical**

Coherent is an adjective that means logical, consistent, or orderly.

109. **B. choice**

Selection is a noun that means choice; it also means an aggregate of things displayed for someone to choose from.

110. **D. commentary**

Narrative is a noun that means a commentary, story, or account of events.

111. **A. pertinent**

Relevant is an adjective that means pertinent or bearing on a certain matter.

112. D. assembly

Rally is a noun that means a get-together or assembly.

113. A. separate

Divide is a verb that means to separate into parts, groups, or sections.

114. B. speed

Velocity is a noun that means the speed of something in a given direction.

115. D. distinguish

Differentiate is a verb that means to mark differently or distinguish.

116. B. current

Draft is a noun that means a current of air in any enclosed space; it can also refer to a drawing or text. Remember that these questions on the ASVAB are also about context — the only answer that makes sense in this context is Choice (B).

117. C. important

Significant is an adjective that means important or of consequence.

118. A. stress

Emphasis is a noun that means special stress or importance put on something.

119. D. mistake

Error is a noun that means a mistake or the state or condition of being wrong.

120. A. passage

Excerpt is a noun that means a part or passage taken from a book, speech, or other text.

121. C. mix

Combine is a verb that means to mix, unite, or join things.

122. **B. skillful**

Resourceful is an adjective that means able to deal with events skillfully and promptly.

123. **D. itemize**

Enumerate is a verb that means to mention something separately, as if in counting; it also means to itemize.

124. **A. foundational**

Underlying is an adjective that means fundamental, basic, or foundational.

125. **B. data**

Statistics is a noun that means numerical facts or data.

126. **C. conform**

Assimilate is a verb that means to conform or adjust to the customs of a group, nation, or other entity.

127. **C. essential**

Crucial is an adjective that means essential or critical.

128. **A. materialization**

Emergence is a noun that describes the act or process of emerging, materializing, or developing.

129. **B. beginning**

Genesis is a noun that means beginning or origin.

130. **D. uncomplicated**

Simple is an adjective that means plain or uncomplicated.

131. **C. advice**

Counsel is a noun that means advice, opinion, or instruction. Don't confuse *counsel* with *council*, which is a noun that means an assembly of people who get together for consultation, deliberation, or advice.

132. **C. authenticate**

Corroborate is a verb that means to make more certain, confirm, or authenticate.

133. **A. obtain**

Achieve is a verb that means to get or obtain through effort.

134. **B. compensate**

Reimburse is a verb that means to refund, pay back, or compensate.

135. **C. environment**

Milieu is a noun that means environment or surroundings, particularly of a social or cultural nature.

136. **D. nondiscriminatory**

Egalitarian is an adjective that means characterized by belief in the equality of all people, especially in politics and economics.

137. **A. thin**

Narrow is an adjective that means thin, not broad or wide.

138. **A. insufficient**

Meager is an adjective that means insufficient; it also means deficient in quantity or quality.

139. **C. unfavorable**

Adverse is an adjective that means unfavorable or opposing one's interests.

140. **D. equivalent**

Tantamount is an adjective that means equivalent.

141. **B. keep**

> *Retain* is a verb that means to keep possession of, to continue to use, or to continue to hold or have.

> Make sure you're paying attention to detail on the ASVAB. Even one letter in a word can change an answer; if you saw *retrain* instead of *retain*, you'd pick Choice (A).

142. **D. communicate**

> *Convey* is a verb that means to communicate or make known. It also means to carry, bring, or transport something, but that definition doesn't work in this context.

143. **B. estimate**

> *Approximate* is a verb that means to estimate. *Approximate* can also be an adjective that means nearly exact but not perfectly accurate or correct.

144. **B. plan**

> *Proposal* is a noun that means a plan or scheme that someone has put together.

145. **C. prejudice**

> *Bias* is a noun that means a prejudice or hostile feelings about a social group. It also means a particular inclination, feeling, or opinion, especially if it's preconceived or unreasoned.

146. **A. slide**

> *Slither* is a verb that means to slide down or along a surface or to walk or move with a sliding motion.

> You'll encounter questions on the ASVAB that have choices that seem a bit confusing. In this instance, Choice (C), *move*, seems like a pretty good fit — but it's your job to find the most correct answer. The word *slither* does refer to a movement, but it's a very specific type of movement.

147. **A. debatable**

> *Moot* is an adjective that means open to discussion or debate.

148. B. unrelated

Irrelevant is an adjective that means not relevant, not applicable, or not pertinent.

149. A. changes

Amendment is a noun that means an alteration that's made by correction, addition, or deletion.

Choice (C), *corrections,* comes very close to being the correct answer, but the sentence simply says the editor made amendments to the story; it doesn't specify whether the changes were corrections, additions, or deletions.

On the ASVAB, you'll have to choose the most correct answer (which means you won't always find an exact definition among your choices). In this case, the one that's most correct is Choice (A).

150. B. aplomb

Equanimity is a noun that refers to aplomb, imperturbable self-possession, or poise.

151. A. peace

Accord is a noun that means proper relationship or harmony.

152. B. argue

Advocate is a verb that means to support or urge by argument.

153. A. catastrophe

Disaster is a noun that describes a sudden event that causes great damage or loss of life.

154. D. trade

Barter is a verb that means to exchange goods or services for other goods or services without using money, or essentially, to trade.

155. B. decode

Decipher is a verb that means to decode or discover the meaning of something that's difficult to understand.

156. C. enthusiastic

Ardent is an adjective that means enthusiastic or passionate.

157. A. respected

Admire is a verb that means to regard a person, quality, or thing with respect or approval.

158. D. deserted

Desolate is an adjective that means deserted of people, bleak, or dismal.

159. A. strange

Eccentric is an adjective that means unconventional, abnormal, or strange.

160. A. parody

Satire is a noun that refers to the use of irony, exaggeration, humor, or ridicule to criticize something.

161. A. proposition

Suggestion is a noun that means an idea, proposition, or plan that's put forward for consideration.

162. B. careful

Conscientious is an adjective that means careful, hard-working, and attentive.

163. B. uncertainty

Ambiguity is a noun that means uncertainty or inexactness of meaning.

164. D. condition

Caveat is a noun that means a warning of specific conditions, limitations, or stipulations.

165. A. significant

Dramatic is an adjective that means sudden, striking, or significant.

166. **C. honesty**

Integrity is a noun that refers to honesty and the quality of having strong moral principles.

167. **A. trade ban**

Embargo is a noun that means an official ban on trade or commercial activity with a particular country.

168. **B. teased**

Mock is a verb that means to tease or laugh at in a mean manner.

169. **C. statement**

Testimony is a noun that means a written or spoken statement.

170. **A. language**

Jargon is a noun that refers to special words and expressions used by a certain group of people that can be difficult for others to understand.

171. **C. fairness**

Justice is a noun that means fair behavior or treatment.

172. **D. wide**

Broad is an adjective that means wide.

173. **C. contempt**

Scorn is a noun that means contempt. It also describes the feeling or belief that someone or something is worthless or despicable.

174. **D. beneficial**

Advantageous is an adjective that means beneficial.

175. **D. crack**

Crevice is a noun that means a narrow opening or fissure.

176. **A. mystery**

Enigma is a noun that means a person or thing that is mysterious, difficult to understand, or puzzling.

177. **B. credulous**

Gullible is an adjective that means credulous or easily persuaded to believe something.

178. **B. impediment**

Hindrance is a noun that refers to a thing that provides resistance, delay, or obstruction to something or someone.

179. **A. lucky**

Fortunate is an adjective that means favored, lucky, or prosperous.

180. **B. intimidating**

Formidable is an adjective that means intimidating or inspiring fear or respect though impressive size, power, or intensity.

181. **D. worried**

Anxious is an adjective that means experiencing worry, nervousness, or unease.

182. **A. discourage**

Deter is a verb that means to discourage someone from doing something, usually by instilling doubt or fear.

183. **B. barrier**

Obstruction is a noun that means an obstacle, barrier, or blockage.

184. **D. enthusiasm**

Zeal is a noun that means great energy or enthusiasm.

185. **C. estrange**

Alienate is a verb that means to cause someone to feel estranged or isolated.

186. B. scold

Reprimand is a verb that means to rebuke or scold.

187. A. unimportant

Trivial is an adjective that means of little value or importance.

188. D. differentiate

Distinguish is a verb that means to recognize something as different.

189. B. skilled

Adept is an adjective that means very skilled or proficient at something.

190. C. loud

Strident is an adjective that means loud, harsh, and raucous.

191. A. tolerate

Abide is a verb that means to tolerate, obey, or observe.

192. D. genuine

Authentic is an adjective that means genuine or of undisputed origin.

193. B. results

Consequence is a noun that means a result or effect of a certain action or condition.

194. B. succinct

Concise is an adjective that means succinct, or brief but comprehensive.

195. A. disquiet

Trepidation is a noun that means a feeling of disquiet, fear, or agitation about something that might happen.

196. B. increased

Supplemented is a verb that means to add an extra amount to something.

197. **C. responsibility**

Onus is a noun that means responsibility or duty.

198. **C. opulent**

Lavish is an adjective that means sumptuously rich, opulent, or luxurious.

199. **C. loyalty**

Allegiance is a noun that means loyalty or commitment to a group or cause.

200. **B. insatiable**

Voracious is an adjective that means wanting or devouring great quantities of food.

201. **C. destroy.**

Construct is a verb that means to build.

202. **A. surplus.**

Deficiency is a noun that means a lack or shortage.

203. **C. approve.**

Vilify is a verb that means to speak or write about in a disparaging, abusive way.

204. **B. fruitful.**

Barren is an adjective that means infertile, fruitless, or unproductive.

205. **B. bore.**

Fascinate is a verb that means to draw attention and interest.

206. **C. combine.**

Dissect is a verb that means to cut up or take apart.

207. C. guess.

Quantify is a verb that means to express or measure the precise quantity of something.

208. C. overflowing.

Vacant is an adjective that means empty, unoccupied, or unfilled.

209. A. keep.

Abdicate is a verb that means to fail to fulfill or undertake a duty or responsibility.

210. C. rush.

Delay is a verb that means to make someone or something late or slow; it also means to postpone or defer an action.

211. A. deny.

Sanction is a verb that means to give official permission or approval for an action.

212. A. valueless.

Worthy is an adjective that means deserving of effort, attention, or respect.

213. B. lazy.

Energetic is an adjective that means showing or involving great activity.

214. D. bottom.

Pinnacle is a noun that refers to a high, pointed piece of rock, a peak, or a crest.

215. B. condemn.

Approve is a verb that means to agree that something is satisfactory, good, or worthy.

216. A. doubt.

Confidence is a noun that means belief in oneself or something else.

217. A. adroit.

Ungainly is an adjective that means awkward or clumsy. (And just for the record, *adroit* is an adjective that means clever or skillful with hands or mind.)

218. D. straighten.

Twirl is a verb that means to turn around circularly or spin.

219. C. accord.

Strife is a noun that means struggle or battle.

220. D. obey.

Revolt is a verb that means to rise in rebellion.

221. B. disorganize.

Align is a verb that means to place or arrange things in a straight line.

222. A. calm.

Furor is a noun that means excitement, anger, or disturbance.

223. B. enlighten.

Bewilder is a verb that means to confuse or baffle.

224. D. advantage.

Detriment is a noun that means disadvantage.

225. B. large.

Miniature is an adjective that means tiny.

226. D. enlarge.

Depreciate is a verb that means to lose value or diminish in value over time.

227. C. individual.

Clique is a noun that refers to a small group of people who have shared interests or other common features.

228. A. elated.

Dejected is an adjective that means sad, depressed, or dispirited.

229. B. mettle.

Cowardice is a noun that means lack of bravery, courageous behavior, or valor.

230. D. destroy.

Mend is a verb that means to correct, improve, or fix.

231. C. quiet.

Peal is a noun that means chime, clanging, or ringing.

232. C. ignorance.

Cognizance is a noun that means knowledge, comprehension, or awareness.

233. A. coarseness.

Tact is a noun that means sensitivity in dealing with others or difficult issues.

234. A. approve.

Criticize is a verb that means to disapprove or judge as bad.

235. C. irrelevant.

Germane is an adjective that means appropriate or relevant.

236. D. common.

Renowned is an adjective that means famous, distinguished, or illustrious.

237.   B. plan.

Fluke is a noun that means chance occurrence.

238.   A. consistent.

Incongruous is an adjective that means not in harmony or out of place.

239.   A. airy.

Bulky is an adjective that means taking up a lot of space, large, or unwieldy.

240.   C. dehydrate.

Drench is a verb that means to wet thoroughly.

241.   B. flexible.

Stubborn is an adjective that means unyielding, difficult to move, or willful.

242.   D. adulthood.

Adolescence is a noun that refers to the period during which a young person develops from a child into an adult.

243.   A. abnormal.

Ordinary is an adjective that means common, regular, or average.

244.   D. unprofitable.

Lucrative is an adjective that means producing a great deal of profit.

245.   D. breakable.

Impregnable is an adjective that means unyielding.

246.   B. conclusion.

Introduction is a noun that refers to a beginning, establishment, or initiation; it's the act of introducing something.

247. C. interest.

Apathy is a noun that means lack of interest, concern, or enthusiasm.

248. A. temporary.

Enduring is an adjective that means continuing or long-lasting.

249. C. genuine.

Ersatz is an adjective that means artificial, synthetic, or fake.

250. A. satisfied.

Ravenous is an adjective that means very hungry or voracious.

ANSWERS
201–300

Paragraph Comprehension

251. B. "Defining Power"

Because the passage deals with the concept of power — what it means, ways it can be used, and the goals of exercising power — "Defining Power" would be a good title.

The passage doesn't have anything to do with famous powerful leaders, and it addresses more than just the uses of power, so Choices (A) and (C) are incorrect. The passage doesn't refer to effecting change with power, either, so Choice (D) can't be right.

Many of the questions on the ASVAB require you to choose the answer that's *most correct*, as this one does.

252. C. whether it will be used wisely and well.

Although some of the other answers are mentioned in the passage, the passage explicitly says, "The central issue of power in leadership is not 'Will it be used?' but rather 'Will it be used wisely and well?'"

253. A. every culture develops its own values.

Although many cultures do share at least one thing in common, be careful with ASVAB answer choices that say "all," such as Choice (B). There's nothing in this passage that supports the statement that all cultures share some commonality. Choice (C) is also unrelated to the passage; it asks you to jump to a conclusion on your own. Choice (D) isn't mentioned in the passage, either, and it's an all-or-nothing answer, which you should always be wary of on the ASVAB. That leaves Choice (A) as the best interpretation of this passage.

CHAPTER 5 Answers   187

254. D. the differences between delayed and instant gratification.

The first sentence of the passage describes its main idea: "Most of the fruits of your labors will not be immediate, which will contrast starkly and unfavorably with much of your day-to-day life." The passage continues to discuss how much instant gratification people in Western society experience, but it does so to contrast it with the delayed gratification of working toward a goal.

255. C. always present in a population.

In the second sentence, the passage says, "Some are endemic (always present in a population)."

The passage doesn't say that endemic diseases are surprise illnesses, Choice (A); that would be more appropriate if the question asked you to define epidemic diseases. Although some endemic diseases are easily controllable, and many have been eradicated, nothing in the passage suggests that either Choice (B) or Choice (D) is correct.

256. A. in the past, people who hired dog trainers felt guilty.

The first and last sentences in the passage tell you that Choice (A) is correct. The biggest tipoffs are the phrases *these days* and *used to be*. The last sentence says, "No guilty feelings involved," and the rest of the information in the passage supports the idea that hiring dog trainers for basic obedience is relatively new.

257. B. One side would fail miserably.

The passage says that civil liberty and martial law "cannot endure together" and that "in the conflict, one or the other must perish." It doesn't say anything about people dying — just the ideas of martial law and civil liberty.

There's nothing in the passage that supports Choices (C) and (D), which say that martial law would be inevitable and that the government would fall.

258. B. why military commanders lay siege to certain areas.

Although the passage touches on the information in Choices (A) and (D), it's really describing the reasons certain areas are besieged; they're strategically valuable, they overlook supply routes, or they're sources of minerals or diamonds.

Nothing in the passage discusses Choice (A), (C), or (D).

259. D. both A and B.

> The passage says that Margaret's "chief trouble was poverty" and that she "tried not to be envious or discontented."

260. A. out of place.

> The passage begins by telling readers that the dry-goods stores weren't in the same part of the city as Jo was in, and it closes by indicating that men wondered how she got there.
>
> Although the passage mentions bales of hay, it doesn't say that Jo was shopping for them. It doesn't say that Jo was meeting a friend or late for an appointment, either, which makes Choice (A) the only correct choice.

261. A. communicates quickly and efficiently.

> The passage describes the similarities between the nervous system and a country's telephone system or the Internet. It also says that the nervous system "allows any part of the body to be in contact with any other part of the body within a fraction of a second," which makes Choice (A) the correct choice. Although it's not directly stated in the passage, it's the only one that's clearly implied.

262. D. waiting for a storm to pass.

> Although Celia may be scared of thunder as well as cold and lonely, the passage describes her waiting for the storm to pass so she can continue her journey. There's nothing in the passage that says she's hiding in an abandoned shed, so Choice (A) isn't the correct choice, either.

263. D. All of the above

> The passage lists what an entity needed to be legally recognized as a state under the 1933 Montevideo Convention on the Rights and Duties of States, which included the following:

- A defined territory
- A permanent population
- A government
- A capacity to enter into relations with other states

264. B. "Emotional and Physical Symptoms of Stress."

The passage describes some of the emotional and physical symptoms of stress, making Choice (B) the correct choice.

Although it's true that stress is different for everyone, the passage doesn't support Choice (A) because that title doesn't reflect the passage as a whole. The paragraph doesn't mention why stress is bad for your body, Choice (C), or anything about eating disorders, Choice (D), so neither of those is correct, either.

265. C. gunshots.

The passage gives you several clues that tell you *reports* means gunshots. First, it says "reports which certainly did not issue from the car where the duellists were." That means shots could be expected from the car carrying people dueling with guns, but gunshots coming from elsewhere were unexpected. The passage also says, "The reports continued in front and the whole length of the train. Cries of terror proceeded from the interior of the cars."

266. B. wounded during a conflict.

The paragraph says, "The Jezail bullet which I had brought back in one of my limbs as a relic of my Afghan campaign throbbed with dull persistence," which means he was wounded during a conflict.

The passage doesn't say that he's exhausted, physically weak, or careless, making Choice (B) the only correct choice.

267. A. how industries appeal to our senses.

The passage describes several industries — movies, television, food, and perfume — that appeal to human senses.

Choice (B) is incorrect because the passage doesn't say anything about why smell and TV don't go hand-in-hand, and Choice (C) is incorrect because the passage discusses more than just the food industry.

You might've picked Choice (D) if you didn't read past the first sentence. When you're taking the ASVAB, make sure you read the passages so you understand them. You can always go back to skim the passage if the answer doesn't jump out at you right away.

268. B. Theodore Roosevelt's cousin.

The passage is about Franklin Delano Roosevelt, Theodore Roosevelt's fifth cousin. It says, "as his cousin (and then President) Theodore Roosevelt had been before him."

Although these events did happen at Harvard University, nothing in the passage says that. The passage also says that Roosevelt was cut from the football team because he was too thin, so Choice (D) is likely wrong.

269.   **C. descent through maternal and paternal lines.**

The passage says that cognatic descent "allows people to track their relationships to the families of each parent," which means it shows connections through the paternal (father's) side and through the maternal (mother's) side.

270.   **C. a church and a cemetery.**

The passage says that medieval villages survive throughout Europe and that they featured "a cluster of homes and farmland grouped around a church and a cemetery."

271.   **D. a replacement for antiquated living arrangements.**

The passage begins by saying, "Unlike the scattered settlements people lived in before the Early Middle Ages," which tells you that you're about to read contrasting information. It also says, "The village essentially replaced the old, rural settlements," which makes Choice (D) the correct answer.

272.   **B. form of currency.**

The passage doesn't explicitly say that the Byzantine besant was a form of currency, but you can infer that it was because the passage tells you it was no longer satisfactory after European trade took off. The passage also tells you that "the West now reverted to the minting of gold coins that Charlemagne had abandoned."

273.   **D. larger than 25 percent of the size of Mars.**

The last sentence in the passage gives you the answer: "Because of its large size (at least more massive than one-fourth of Mars), the projectile is expected to have been differentiated."

274.   **A. necessary to deal with the complexities of the modern workplace.**

The author says that management-based regulation is coming "from the growing complexity of the organizational environments," which refers to modern workplaces.

Although management-based regulation has been used to address public policy problems, such as terrorist attacks, the passage doesn't say that it's one of the best solutions. The passage doesn't say anything about new societies or the regulation of industries in general, either, which leaves Choice (A) as the correct choice.

275. **D. Both B and C are correct.**

The passage says that modern theory suggests jurors should be "active" learners, which includes asking questions to ensure they understand and organizing new material.

276. **A. Zeus forbids other gods from taking part in the battle at Troy.**

The passage lists a number of mythological Greek gods and says that they all participated in the battle at Troy, despite the fact that Zeus forbade it.

277. **C. "Remedies for Bug Bites and Stings."**

The passage describes a couple of remedies for bug bites and stings, which include tobacco and meat tenderizer, and says that you can find commercially available remedies as well.

278. **D. used to travel.**

Because the passage says, "my parents gave up entirely their wandering life and fixed themselves in their native country," you can assume that they used to travel.

279. **A. About 1,000**

The passage says, "NASA currently considers about a thousand asteroids ranging in size from basketballs to mountains to be *potentially hazardous*."

280. **B. wipe out all human life on Earth.**

The last sentence in the passage describes the impact and its resulting dust as "an event that would cripple agriculture to the point that humanity may starve before the dust settled."

281. **C. 400 nanometers.**

The passage describes the different wavelengths at which people see — or sense — colors. It says that we see red at 750 nanometers, green at 500 nanometers, and violet at 400 nanometers.

Tip: It's a good idea to read the question before you read the passage while you're taking the Paragraph Comprehension subtest. That way, you'll know what you're looking for. The passages and questions will appear on the same screen when you take the CAT–ASVAB, and they'll be right in front of you if you're taking the paper version.

282. B. bodily postures.

The passage compares human communication to communication between other species, but it clearly says that human language conveys more (and more subtle) information. Therefore, Choice (A) applies only to humans. Choice (C) also applies only to human language.

Choice (B), bodily postures, is the only choice that broadly applies to animal communication.

283. D. separation of mothers and their babies prevents them from developing a bond.

The passage describes the custom of removing infants from their mothers. It says it inevitably results in the hindrance of the "development of the child's affection toward its mother" and blunts and destroys "the natural affection of the mother for the child."

284. A. Both were subject to criminal penalties.

The passage says, "A white man discovered riding in a car reserved for blacks faced the same criminal penalties as did Plessy." (This passage is about the 1896 Supreme Court case *Plessy v. Ferguson*, in which the justices upheld the "separate but equal" doctrine.) Both black and white people faced criminal penalties for mingling in places that were supposed to remain segregated under the law.

285. C. they caused companies to lose money.

The second sentence in the passage states why companies didn't like Jim Crow laws: "They cost money that ate into the profits."

Although segregation laws certainly caused customers inconvenience, nothing in the passage says that's the reason companies didn't like the laws. The passage mentions railroad companies, but there's nothing that says Jim Crow laws targeted railroad companies or that white people had to buy more expensive tickets.

286. D. all of the above.

The passage tells you that the Hippocratic Oath isn't an explicit part of psychological training, but it says that it applies to physicians and healers. Therefore, Choice (D) is the correct choice.

287. **A. treat anyone who comes to them for help.**

The Hippocratic Oath lists several things healthcare providers must do, and the passage says "they will treat anyone who comes seeking their aid."

The passage specifically says, "They will not give a deadly drug if the patient requests it," which makes Choice (B) incorrect. It also says that healthcare providers will keep information about doctor–patient relationships confidential, but it doesn't say that providers are required to keep detailed records on their patients.

288. **B. wanted to become tougher.**

The passage starts with "I commenced by inuring my body to hardship." Because the person in the passage wants to become used to hardship, including cold, famine, thirst, and a lack of sleep, it's reasonable to assume that he or she wanted to become tougher.

The passage doesn't support Choice (A). The person studied "physical science" (not physics), which makes Choice (C) incorrect. The passage also draws a contrast between the speaker and "common sailors," so Choice (D) can't be correct, either.

289. **A. "Speech Patterns of Schizophrenic Patients."**

The passage describes the occasional speech patterns of people with schizophrenia. It's not as broadly focused as Choice (B), and it doesn't even touch on Choice (C). Choice (D) is incorrect because the passage isn't a self-diagnostic tool; it just outlines some of the speech patterns people with schizophrenia have.

290. **B. most likely went off nearly three hours before the man woke up.**

The passage says that the man set his alarm clock for 4:00, but he didn't wake up until 6:45. "It certainly must have rung," the man reasons.

According to the passage, the alarm clock was quite loud and makes a "furniture-rattling noise," so Choice (C) can't be correct. Neither can Choice (D), because the man was questioning whether he could've slept nearly three hours after the alarm was supposed to have sounded.

291. **A. the sea was rough and loud near the shore.**

Choice (B) isn't correct — *piscatory* means of, relating to, or dependent on fish or fishing, and sick fish do not smell good. Choice (C) doesn't appear anywhere in the passage. Although the passage says the sea was rough and loud, it doesn't say that was because of a storm; the passage simply describes a rocky beach, which means Choice (D) is also incorrect.

292. **B. got up early.**

The passage says, "It was rare for him to be up after ten at night, and he had invariably breakfasted and gone out before I rose in the morning." It's safe to assume that he got up early. The passage doesn't support any of the other answers.

293. **D. searching for his enemies.**

The passage says, "He travelled from town to town through the United States in quest of his enemies."

Choice (A) is incorrect because the man "eked out by such employment as he could pick up." Choice (B) is incorrect because nothing in the passage supports the idea that he was acting as a private detective. And Choice (C) is incorrect because the passage says "with the small competence he possessed," which means he wasn't very competent.

294. **D. all of the above.**

The passage describes a man with no ears ("but of ears of any kind or character there was not a semblance to be discovered upon any portion of his head"). It also says the man was old and overweight ("his chin and cheeks, although wrinkled with age, were broad, puffy, and double").

295. **B. 30 or 40 years**

The passage says, "Thirty or forty years ago, before losses and chancery suits came upon it, it was a thriving place; but now it is a desolate island indeed."

Many of the questions you encounter on the ASVAB require you to find facts. In many cases, it's a good idea to skim the paragraph, look at the answer choices, and choose the right one so you can move on quickly.

296. **B. Fleeing a fire.**

"I turned my head to look at the hillside I was leaving" suggests that the person was fleeing, and "Thick streamers of black smoke shot with threads of red fire were driving up into the still air" suggests a fire.

Nothing in the passage says that the person is lighting the fire or that he or she is putting it out.

297. A. reads a medical book and believes he or she has most of the diseases it describes.

The passage says, "I plodded conscientiously through the twenty-six letters, and the only malady I could conclude I had not got was house-maid's knee." The speaker believes he or she has everything from ague to St. Vitus's Dance, based on the symptoms in the book.

298. C. housemaid's knee.

The passage describes a list of illnesses, but the last sentence says, "The only malady I could conclude I had not got was housemaid's knee."

Make sure you pay attention to detail when you take the ASVAB — this question asks what illness the author does *not* have.

299. B. He died before the child was born.

The passage says, "My father's eyes had closed upon the light of this world six months, when mine opened on it." Nothing in the passage supports Choice (A) or Choice (C), and Choice (D) is incorrect because the passage does say what happened to the child's father.

300. B. Four

You'll run into several "fact-finding" paragraph comprehension questions on the ASVAB, so if you can, read the question and then skim the paragraph for the answer. This passage lists four states as having branches of the Pacific Railroad: Iowa, Kansas, Colorado, and Oregon.

301. C. celebrities.

The passage says, "Today we accord movie star status to many of our leaders." It goes on to describe leaders as cultural icons and role models and points out that the U.S. president is one of the most photographed people in the world. That means it's reasonable to say that we view many of our leaders as celebrities, Choice (C).

302. A. Martin Luther King, Jr.

The passage says that Martin Luther King, Jr., organized a city-wide bus boycott when he was 26 years old, just after Rosa Parks was arrested and fined.

303. B. he had a love of learning.

The passage says, "Abraham Lincoln's youthful love of learning freed him from his father's fate as a poor farmer."

Although the passage says he read quite a bit, it doesn't say that his father taught him; that makes Choice (A) incorrect. Lincoln did study Euclidean geometry, but the passage doesn't attribute his successful career to his skills with angles and theorems, so Choice (C) is wrong. The passage doesn't say that Lincoln didn't enjoy farming, so Choice (D) is incorrect as well.

304. **D. the selection of Merino sheep for breeding.**

The passage says that selection of Merino sheep is actually a trade for some people in Saxony, and it describes the process of selection these men use.

305. **B. May 14**

The passage describes the events of Friday, May 24, but it also says, "Ten days before, German armored columns had broken out of the Ardennes forest and started an almost unopposed drive across the center of France."

Make sure you're paying attention to detail when you take the ASVAB. Some questions are designed to help the military determine whether you're capable of following instructions!

306. **B. The German military**

The passage describes how "German armored columns had broken out of the Ardennes forest and started an almost unopposed drive across the center of France." It immediately goes on to say, "French counter-attacks from the south had been turned back with ease," which means that the French military was attempting to attack the German military.

307. **C. "The Mural"**

This passage describes a mural that a man is painting. Although it does tell you what the people in the mural are wearing and what the people in the mural are doing with the weeds, the passage doesn't say what you should wear in a garden or what to do with weeds, which makes Choices (A) and (D) incorrect. The passage doesn't contain instructions on how to paint a garden, which makes Choice (B) incorrect, too.

308. **C. Gold prospectors**

The passage says that "men, groping in the Arctic darkness, had found a yellow metal" and that "thousands of men were rushing into the Northland." It goes on to say that the men rushing into the Northland wanted strong, sturdy dogs with plenty of fur.

309. **B. skepticism.**

Skepticism is the theme throughout the passage. It's about a man who wouldn't believe anything he didn't see to be true and who doubted many things until he had proof.

310. **B. teacher.**

The passage begins with "when school hours were over," which is the first clue about the person's identity. The last sentence says, "Indeed, it behooved him to keep on good terms with his pupils." Teachers have students, and *pupils* is synonymous with students, which makes Choice (B) the correct answer.

311. **D. eats bugs throughout the day.**

The passage says that seeds and "tiny insects that live among the grass furnish meals at all hours," which makes Choice (D) the correct one.

Although the passage does say the bird sings in the mornings and evenings, it doesn't say it sings all day; that makes Choice (B) incorrect. Nothing in the passage says the bird is close to starving, Choice (C), or that the bird eats only in the morning, Choice (A).

312. **A. Darnley was a manipulative person.**

The passage says, "Under this brilliant exterior Darnely hid utter insignificance, dubious courage, and a fickle and churlish character." The key in this sentence is the word *hid*, which implies that Darnley didn't want Mary to know what he was really like.

313. **B. has just heard bad news.**

The passage says, "At these words she grew frightfully pale," and it continues to describe the actions of a person who's visibly distraught. Because it says "at these words," you can assume that she has just heard bad news.

314. **B. to detect changes in the air.**

The passage says, "Excepting for the purpose of detecting disturbance in the air, there is no need of candles as the two holes in the roof supply sufficient light."

That means the candles weren't used to provide light, Choice (A), nor were they used to warm the ice cave, Choice (C).

315. B. bluebirds will go extinct.

The passage says, "I feared the tribe of bluebirds were on the verge of extinction," which makes Choice (B) the correct answer.

316. C. Lack of vegetables

The passage says that Martin's men had scurvy, which was caused by "the habitual use of salt pork and beans, added to the total absence of vegetable diet." Choice (A) is wrong because scurvy is the name of the disease, not the cause of it.

317. B. irritable.

If you didn't already know what *choleric* meant (it means bad-tempered or irritable), you could infer its meaning from the clues in the passage. The passage describes throwing a conductor from his seat, breaking someone's ribs, and catching someone by the collar over incidents that don't warrant such severe responses.

318. D. "Shortcomings That Identify Bad Leaders"

This passage lists a number of reasons some people are poor leaders. It's not just about dictators or tyrannical leaders, which makes Choices (A) and (B) incorrect. Choice (C) is also incorrect because although some of the leaders the passage describes would certainly resemble monsters, the first sentence says, "Leaders can simply be guilty of making an honest mistake."

319. A. A castle

The passage says, "The soldiers defending the castle of Trezzo abandoned it and beat a retreat," which makes Choice (A) correct. The Adda River and the village of San Gervasio are points used by the Austrian Army. Although the soldiers who fled Trezzo were running from the Austrian Army, they abandoned their posts at the castle.

320. B. power can be used in a positive way.

The passage says, "Power need not be coercive, dictatorial, or punitive. It can be used in a non-coercive manner."

321. **D. "Dissociation Defined"**

The first sentence in the passage says, "Dissociation can be defined . . ." which lays out the theme. The passage isn't about all the functions of personality, Choice (A), nor does it say that dissociation is a personality disorder, Choice (B). Finally, although a sense of déjà vu is mentioned as a symptom, the passage doesn't describe it as a personality disorder, Choice (C).

322. **D. All of the above**

Many questions in the Paragraph Comprehension subtest of the ASVAB require you to go on a fact-finding mission. It's often helpful to skim the paragraph, read the question, and return to the paragraph to find the answers.

323. **A. in the winter.**

This passage does take place during the winter, Choice (A), which you can tell because it mentions Christmas and "blue faces and chattering teeth." Nothing in the passage supports Choice (B) or (C), so Choice (D) is also incorrect.

324. **B. shopping etiquette.**

The passage contains a list of things you should and shouldn't do while you're shopping.

325. **A. Henry IV cared about his subjects.**

The passage says that Henry IV "was remembered for his uncommon concern for his subjects' welfare." Although it does mention 12 assassination attempts, the passage doesn't support Choice (B), nor does it suggest that he was popular throughout his reign or that he ruled all of Europe.

326. **D. how to impress natives while traveling.**

The passage describes several situations that give travelers an opportunity to impress the natives by conforming to their customs. It also says that someone who is disdainful of foreign customs "will not convince the natives of his vast superiority"; rather, he'll do nothing but show the locals that "he is an ill-bred idiot."

327. **C. the New Deal.**

The passage says, "Known collectively as the New Deal" and subsequently lists the programs that fell under it.

328. **A. Diouna is a commune.**

The first sentence says, "As a rural commune" in describing Diouna. Then the passage describes its size and population. The passage never says that Diouna is a city, Choice (B), or that it's located inside the city of Ségou, Choice (C), but it does say that it's part of the Ségou Region.

329. **B. the Caixa de Rotllan.**

The passage describes the Caixa de Rotllan, a historic monument in France. Although it mentions the stones, as well as geology, archaeology, and architecture, the overall passage is about the building.

330. **A. can be published in newspapers.**

The only statement the passage supports is Choice (A), which says that position papers can be published in newspapers.

Although a position paper could outline a company's history and could be used to change someone's mind, that's not what the passage says. When you take the ASVAB, remember that the military wants you to pay attention to what they're asking; don't answer any more than what the question asks.

331. **C. you could kill your trees through improper pruning.**

The first sentence in the passage says that improper pruning can cause "extensive damage and sometimes, tree death."

332. **B. Socrates's beliefs on political control.**

In the passage, Plato suggests that "the central problem of politics is to organize the state so as to place control in the hands of individuals." However, the passage also says, "Using Socrates as the main interlocutor in the dialogue and presumably as his spokesman," which means that you're reading about the ideas of Socrates rather than Plato. Although both men may have believed the same things, the passage's main theme is the expression of Socrates's beliefs.

333. **D. Both A and B are correct.**

The passage says that the "end" task of a leader is to make him- or herself "irrelevant or unnecessary" by making "everyone a leader of his or her own job or unit."

The passage doesn't say anything about commanding large numbers of people; however, good leaders often do work their way through the ranks (especially in the military) and end up being in charge of larger groups.

334. **C. Verführer.**

There are quite a few foreign terms in this passage, so keeping them straight can be tough. The first sentence refers to "other forms of leadership" and says that the "new leadership of Germany, the *Verführer*, was self-derived self-defined, self-justifying, and completely and terrifyingly authoritarian."

335. **D. Both A and B are correct.**

The passage says that Bilberry goats look "unlike any other found in the United Kingdom because each goat has a shaggy coat and large horns."

336. **D. "Social Traits of the Kinglet"**

The passage describes the social traits of kinglets, saying that they are friendly toward other birds and typically join other species' flocks.

337. **C. a hospital train.**

The passage doesn't directly say that it's about painting a hospital train, but it does mention "huge red crosses on white squares" and "the number of the ward in figures a foot long at each end." Together, these two clues tell you that the speaker in the passage is describing painting a hospital train.

338. **B. a radio show producer.**

The passage says, "The radio show's producer, who often appeared on-air as 'The Beaver,'" which tells you that Choice (B) is correct. Nothing in the passage says that "The Beaver" was a main character or that he was famous. Choice (C) may be true, but the passage doesn't explicitly state it; because "radio show producer" is explicitly stated, Choice (B) is the most correct answer.

339. **A. is the gatekeeper of character.**

The passage says that conscience is character's "inner counterpart" —
not its opposite — and that it's the "part of us that makes judgments
and evaluations about when, how, and with whom that value should or
should not be applied."

340. **B. is from an industrialized nation and lives in an urban area.**

The passage lists several characteristics that increase a person's chances
for an unknown experience. One is being from an industrialized nation,
and another is living in an urban area. Choice (B) is the only answer that
has two characteristics that appear in the list given in the passage. (If
you're curious, this passage comes from a book chapter on
schizophrenia.)

341. **D. globalization.**

The passage describes a distinction between globalization and something
else. It mentions mobility and friction as well as an anthropologist, but
the main theme is globalization. The passage uses friction as a metaphor
for globalization, but it's not the dominant idea the passage describes.

342. **C. uranium is radioactive.**

The passage says, "Uranium and thorium are radioactive." Nothing in
the passage supports Choice (A), (B), or (D).

343. **D. both A and B are correct.**

The passage supports Choice (A) by saying, "Typically, local entrepreneurs are more connected to the community (after all, they live here,
too)." It also supports Choice (B) because it highlights several reasons
people should work with local businesses. However, nothing in the passage supports Choice (C), which leaves Choice (D) as the correct answer.

344. **B. fewer people travel the road than did before.**

The passage implies that few people travel the road anymore because it
says the rooms were created "for the entertainment of a much greater
company than ever appeared now upon the deserted highroad." It also
says that the road "had been an old coaching road," and that "that, of
course, was all over now."

345. **D. boys are naturally loud.**

The question asks you about the passage, regardless of whether you think boys are louder than girls in the real world. The passage says, "Frank was watching the door, in a very unnatural sort of quietness for a boy," which suggests boys are naturally loud.

346. **D. Fall**

The passage says, "The effect in autumn, when all those warm tints which, by the alchemy of nature, bring beauty out of the chilly frost and unlovely decay—was as if all the colors in the rainbow had been poured forth," which means that it's describing a house during the fall.

347. **B. "The Transfer of Energy"**

The main theme of this passage is the transfer of energy, Choice (B). Although it does mention experiments, the passage isn't really about specific experiments; that makes Choice (A) incorrect. The passage also mentions the way particles gain energy, Choice (C), and the fact that energy cannot be created, Choice (D). However, the best title for this passage is "The Transfer of Energy" because it covers the main idea.

348. **B. it can be difficult to identify birds.**

The passage says that you shouldn't expect to identify every new bird on your first try, because some are "shy or obscurely marked, or probably both." It also says that some birds look so similar to others (and have such similar habits) that it's tough to tell them apart.

349. **D. predatory trading practices.**

Halfway through the passage, the author mentions the second film. It says that Stone indicts "self-centered, predatory trading practices that can take the entire world to the brink of a complete economic melt-down." Choice (B) isn't the best answer because it's too broad.

350. **B. The world could face an economic meltdown.**

According to the passage, the "high-stake players" who engage in "self-centered, predatory trading practices" could take the world "to the brink of a complete economic meltdown."

351. **A. Reading a playwright's autobiography**

The passage does touch on Nancy's mother's volunteer work, Choice (B), but it doesn't say that was why Nancy chose to act in local theater. The passage doesn't say anything about the community Nancy grew up in, Choice (C), and Choice (D) is clearly incorrect.

Watch for ASVAB questions that deal in absolutes. *All* or *none* is a tall order, so be sure that you've evaluated each choice carefully before settling on an answer like that.

352. **B. MAPP was formed in 1965.**

The passage says, "NERC and all of its subordinate councils were formed in 1965" after it tells you that MAPP was one of eight councils that fell under NERC.

Acronyms may be confusing, but you'll learn to love them in the military. You'll eat in the DFAC (dining facility), and you'll probably drive your POV (privately owned vehicle) around your post or base . . . and that's just the beginning.

353. **B. the Bronze Age existed by 1500 BCE.**

The passage says that the Yueshi culture "flourished between 1900 BCE and 1500 BCE in the Shandong region of China, began in the Late Neolithic Period and lasted through the early Bronze Age." That tells you that the Bronze Age certainly existed by 1500 BCE. The passage doesn't support any of the other answers.

354. **A. were winding rather than straight.**

The passage discusses two types of roads: The first were built for the Romans, and the second were built for the people of the Middle Ages. The second type of roads — those built during the Middle Ages — were "meandering earthen roads."

355. **D. roads were designed for civilians during the Middle Ages.**

The passage contrasts two types of roads: those built by the Romans, which were paved and straight, and those built for the men and women of the Middle Ages, which wouldn't be very suitable for military purposes. Therefore, Choice (D) is the correct answer.

356. **A. in the Stephen Mather Wilderness.**

The first sentence tells you that Black Peak is located in the Stephen Mather Wilderness and the North Cascades National Park, which makes Choice (A) correct.

The figures are flipped in Choices (B) and (C); the actual elevation is 8,970 feet, and the prominence is 3,450 feet. The passage also says that Black Peak is non-volcanic, which makes Choice (D) incorrect.

357. **C. Aetius**

The passage says that Attila, the leader of the Huns, was defeated by Aetius and forced to withdraw.

358. **C. many thioketones dimerize.**

The passage says, "However, thiobenzophenone doesn't dimerize to form rings and polymers like most other thioketones do." That means it's safe to assume that many thioketones dimerize.

359. **B. spoke multiple languages.**

Although the passage doesn't directly say that Cassiodorus spoke multiple languages, it does say that after his retirement, "Cassiodorus translated several copies of Greek works and made copies of Latin works for educational purposes."

360. **D. 580 CE.**

BCE means "before the Common Era," and CE refers to the "Common Era." BCE is the same era as BC (Before Christ), and CE is the same era as AD (*Anno Domini*).

When you see a time period in which the first year is lower than the last, as in 490–580 (which is a 90-year period), you know that the time is CE. If the first year is higher than the last, as in 580–490 (which is a 110-year period, as the Common Era begins in year 1), the time is BCE. The abbreviation *ca.* means *circa*, which you can translate to "around."

Looking at the dates, you can see that Cassiodorus died in approximately 580 CE, which makes Choice (D) correct.

361. **C. a decline in agriculture.**

The passage says, "Roads fell into disrepair, along with workshops, warehouses and irrigation systems, and agriculture declined," which makes Choice (C) correct.

Many people moved to the country, which makes Choice (A) the wrong pick; towns lost those people, which makes Choice (B) incorrect as well.

362. **A. why Florence Nightingale was asked to go somewhere.**

The passage describes what made Florence Nightingale the person chosen to go assist the injured during war, such as her commitment to helping others and the way people and animals trusted her.

Make sure you pay attention to detail on the ASVAB. Choice (D) is almost correct, but it says "*how* Florence Nightingale helped during the war," not *why* she helped during the war.

363. **C. good with animals.**

The passage doesn't support any of the answer choices except Choice (C). It doesn't say she was a doctor, Choice (A), or that she was sickly, Choice (B). It does say, "All the animals around her home liked her, because they knew that she would not hurt them."

364. **D. "How Cotton Goods Were Manufactured Prior to 1760."**

The passage explains how, before 1760, a spinner would obtain raw cotton and turn it into yarn or thread, so Choice (D) is the best answer for the question.

This passage doesn't say what cotton goods were used for before 1760, which makes Choice (A) incorrect. Although it mentions who manufactured cotton goods, that's not what the passage is about; that makes Choice (B) incorrect. Choice (C) is incorrect because of the word *after*. The passage is about the period of time before 1760.

365. **B. India**

The passage says that Columbus set out to find India, but instead, he found the Americas.

366. **B. natural barriers can protect a nation.**

The passage says, "Natural barriers [. . .] are often political frontiers exerting protecting or isolating influence."

367. **D. an awakening.**

The word *awakening* means an act or moment of becoming suddenly aware of something, and according to the passage, that's exactly what happened during the Renaissance. The passage says, "It meant rebirth, a new life" and "The man of affairs, with his broader sympathies, his keener vision, his more varied interests, and his love of liberty, was coming into prominence." Both of those quotes describe an awakening.

368. **B. most people don't understand real silence and darkness.**

The author describes the silence he experienced as "audible" and the darkness he experienced as "tangible." Those are strong words to describe silence and darkness, which suggests that most people don't understand the depth of either.

369. **D. 527 competitors participated in 230 events.**

The passage says that 527 competitors participated in 230 events, which were part of 27 different sports.

370. **A. modern technology can put old theories and hypotheses to rest.**

The last sentence in the passage says, "Because of great technological advancement, which has fostered many new discoveries and theories, scientists today believe that antimatter comets are unlikely to exist at all."

Nothing in the passage suggests Choice (B) is correct. In fact, the passage says just the opposite. The passage doesn't support Choice (C), either, because it says that technological advancements have made scientists doubt the existence of antimatter comets. Choice (D) is incorrect because the passage highlights how modern technology has helped scientists.

371. **D. both A and B are correct.**

The passage says, "Durham University gives Palatinate awards to athletes and former athletes," which shows you that Choice (A) is correct. It also goes on to describe three awards: the Full Palatinate, the Half Palatinate, and the Honorary Palatinate, which makes Choice (B) correct.

Choice (C) is incorrect because the passage says that the "Honorary Palatinate awards recognize former Durham University students who have moved on to compete in the field of sport."

372. **B. the technology to combine movies and sound didn't exist yet.**

The passage says that technological constraints prevented the combination of sound and film "until the late 1920s, when Audion amplifier tubes and Vitaphone systems became available," which means that the invention of these items made it possible.

373. **B. it is possible to terminate your agreement to preserve natural landmarks.**

The last sentence in the passage says, "Either party can terminate the agreement upon notifying the other party," which makes Choice (B) the correct answer.

Choice (A) is incorrect because the passage contrasts the NNLP with Section 106 of the National Historic Preservation Act of 1966. Choice (C) is incorrect because the program applies to both biological and geological features, and Choice (D) is incorrect because the passage says, "The program encourages people to participate voluntarily."

374. **B. the boy traveled around the United Kingdom.**

The passage says, "As a boy, I travelled the greater part of the United Kingdom," which tells you that Choice (B) is correct. Nothing in the passage says the boy is going to sell a horse, that he bought basket-ware at Loughton (he brought it to Loughton, according to the passage), or that he purchased his first horse at the Epping Fair. Nothing in the passage supports Choice (A), (C), or (D).

375. **C. receiving a pony as a gift.**

The passage says, "My first business transaction consisted of receiving a present of a pony."

376. **D. both B and C are correct.**

The passage says, "The squalid children were not there, but in their stead appeared a bevy of handsome damsels," which tells you that the beautiful women replaced the dirty children who had been there before. The passage also describes the women's clothing as bright and attractive when it says that they were "attired in robes of the brightest hues, scarlet, pink, and yellow."

Choice (A) is incorrect because although the passage says the setting had the "sybaritic elegance of a Turkish divan," it doesn't say anything about being in Turkey.

377. **B. daffodils and tulips bloom in April in New York.**

The passage says that when "April comes whirling along the cleared path of the year [. . .] daffodils and tulips are blooming riotously on the street-corners."

378. **D. the complexity of Turgenev's art.**

The passage says, "His art is highly complex," but there's more to it than that. The entire piece describes harmony and how Turgenev "is never too forcible, and never too clever." It also says that Turgenev's art is so complex "that we can see only its body, never the mechanism of its body."

When you're taking the ASVAB, it's often a good idea to skim a passage, read the question, and then find the answer within the passage through closer reading.

379. D. a touchdown is worth six points.

The passage says, "A field goal earns the team three points, which is three fewer than they'd earn for a touchdown." That means a touchdown is worth six points. (*Note:* After a touchdown, the team gets a chance to score an extra point.)

That's the opposite of Choice (A), and Choice (B) is incorrect because the passage says, "Even if a team doesn't make it into the end zone to make a touchdown, they can exercise the option of kicking the ball between the goal posts in what's known as a field goal." Choice (C) is incorrect because the passage says teams can "exercise the option," which means they have a choice.

380. B. recess always ended when the boys were having the most fun.

The passage says the teachers never rang the bell to call the boys in from recess "until just that particular instant when the fun in the schoolyard was at its highest, and the boys least wanted to come in."

381. A. "What Is Psephology?"

The passage defines *psephology* and mentions its uses, so Choice (A) is the most correct answer.

Choices (B), (C), and (D) are mentioned in the passage, but none of them encompass the main theme.

382. B. 160 fish families make up about 41 percent of all perciforms.

The passage says that "nearly 41 percent of all bony fish fall into this order. About 160 fish families are perciforms."

Choice (A) is incorrect because the passage says that perciforms began to appear and diversify during the Late Cretaceous Period. Choice (B) is incorrect because the passage doesn't say marlin have finished evolving. Choice (D) is incorrect because the question says, "Based on this passage." Although it may be true that entire fish families became extinct before the end of the Upper Cretaceous Period, there's nothing to support that statement in the passage. That's why it's so important that you pay attention to detail when you're taking the ASVAB.

383. A. Greuze studied in Rome.

The passage says Greuze "was enabled to fulfill his ambition of visiting Rome, where he pursued his studies for a considerable period."

Although Lyons is mentioned in the passage, Choice (B) is incorrect. It says that Greuze studied in Lyons, "not very far from his native town." Choice (C) is incorrect because the passage says, "His first studies were made in Lyons, a great manufacturing center"; it doesn't say that he studied manufacturing. The passage also says that "he developed the inclination and taste for art which later made him one of the first of French painters." That sentence also makes Choice (D) incorrect.

384. **D. children grow into independent, free-thinking adults.**

The author of the passage describes several things parents do to try to influence the adults their children will become, but his final question, "But will they do so?" shows that he realizes kids don't always follow the paths their parents want them to follow.

385. **C. "JIDO."**

The passage describes the Joint Improvised-Threat Defeat Organization, which is also known by the acronym JIDO. Therefore, the best title for this passage is Choice (C), "JIDO."

386. **A. it has been cold for several months.**

The passage says, "Before me and on each side were the snow-capped mountains, still white as they had been for six months past," which makes Choice (A) the best answer.

Nothing in the passage supports Choice (B), and the passage says the exact opposite of Choice (C): "fringed along their sides by a massive belt of timber." The passage doesn't say that the traveler minds the weather or that he's waiting for spring, either, which makes Choice (D) incorrect.

387. **A. was poor.**

The passage says, "He was no longer impecunious, but carried with him fifty dollars in counterfeit bills." Taking that sentence apart shows you that *impecunious* means Barclay didn't have much (or any) money, but now, he has $50 in counterfeit bills.

388. **D. you can bring a letter from your doctor in lieu of tuberculosis test results.**

The passage says that you can bring "valid tuberculosis test results or a letter from your family's physician stating that your child is low-risk." The word *or* suggests you can bring the letter instead of actual test results.

Nothing in the passage supports Choice (A), (B), or (C).

389. B. it took more than 10 years to complete the Appalachian Trail.

The passage says that the Appalachian Trail was "completed in 1937 after more than a decade of hard work," which means that it took more than 10 years.

The passage lists the organizations that manage the trail, but it doesn't say whether they're public or private (and in case you didn't know, the National Park Service and the U.S. Forest Service are both public). That makes Choice (A) incorrect. The passage also says, "Approximately 2 million people hike the Appalachian Trail every year." Make sure you're paying attention to detail; the passage says millions of people hike the trail each *year*, not each month. Choice (D) is incorrect because the passage says that the Appalachian Trail is "the longest hiking-only trail in the world," not the only long-distance hiking trail.

390. D. all of the above are correct.

The passage describes a woman who didn't want to take on laundry work because she was "well brought up and educated," Choice (B). It also says, "I would rather do that than see my children suffer," which makes Choice (C) correct. Choice (A) is also correct, because the passage says, "I have wanted for nothing."

391. B. a hotel.

The passage describes a hotel. First, the passage explains that the building is made of brick and has "an air of quiet elegance," and it compares the building to "other prominent hotels." The other locations mentioned in the passage — Jay Gould's house and the Catholic Cathedral — are in the passage only to describe the hotel's location.

392. C. Tom

The passage says, "sometimes Tom Little, Dick's brother," which means Choice (C) is correct.

If you weren't sure which was the correct answer, notice that the first sentence of the passage says, "A number of us had formed the habit of drifting into Dick Little's flat in Chelsea," which tells you that both men have the same last name.

393. B. pearls from freshwater fisheries have less luster than natural sea pearls.

The passage says that *Unio* and *Anodonta* are two freshwater varieties of mussel but that they produce pearls with less luster (and that are more opaque) than sea pearls. Because of this, the fisheries in the Welsh and Scotch rivers are "falling into disuse."

394. **A. the butcher fired Abe for theft.**

The passage describes the fact that the butcher accused Abe of stealing $0.75 and continues to say that the butcher threatened Abe (not the other way around, as Choice (C) suggests).

Nothing in the passage says that Abe lived with the butcher, Choice (B), or that he got another job, Choice (D).

395. **D. there are more than just visible organisms on the surface of the ocean.**

The passage says that many people notice jellyfish on the ocean's surface but most don't notice the minute organisms, such as foraminifera, radiolara, and diatoms.

396. **B. sunlight doesn't reach the bottom of the ocean.**

The first sentence in the passage says, "No external rays reach the bottom of the sea." That means sunlight can't reach those depths. The little light that researchers *do* find comes from the animals that live there.

397. **C. produce their own light.**

The passage mentions phosphorescence, which refers to light being emitted without combustion or heat — but even if you didn't know that, you could figure it out by reading the whole passage. The passage says, "What light there is must be supplied by the phosphorescent organs of the animals themselves" and "It may be that this emission of light is much greater at a low temperature." Both quotes are clues that the fish that live on the bottom of the ocean produce their own light.

398. **C. wrote the first book of American literature.**

The last sentence in the passage says that Captain John Smith "was the writer of the first book in American literature."

399. **D. did not write continuously.**

The passage says that Roger Williams's writings "were produced spasmodically and in clusters, amid long spaces of silence." That means he wasn't continuously writing.

Nothing in the passage supports Choice (A) or (B), and the passage doesn't say that Williams published dozens of books, Choice (C), only that "his writings are numerous."

400.
A. Molitor and Yount both had 190 hits that season.

The passage says, "Paul Molitor, the Brewers' third baseman, had 190 hits that season, as did center-fielder Robin Yount." The key is the phrase *as did*; that tells you that Yount did the same thing that Molitor did.

Choice (B) is incorrect because Gantner had fewer base hits than Molitor did; the passage says Gantner had 149, while Molitor had 190. Choice (C) is incorrect because the passage says Molitor was the Brewers' third baseman. Choice (D) is incorrect because Yount had 190 hits (Gantner was the one with 149 hits).

401.
B. Scientists have found a 12.7 billion-year-old galaxy.

The passage refers to the 16 background galaxies by saying, "One is about 12.7 billion years old, according to the scientists on the project."

Nothing in the passage supports Choice (A), and Choice (C) is incorrect because the passage tells you that Frontier Fields is a three-year program. Choice (D) is also incorrect; although the passage mentions 17 galaxies (one is Abell S1063, and there are 16 background galaxies), nothing in the passage says that these are the only galaxies scientists have discovered.

402.
B. prone to earthquakes.

The passage says that Colombia is "part of the Ring of Fire, which is a region especially prone to earthquakes and volcanic eruptions."

The passage doesn't say that Colombia is a democracy, Choice (A), or that it's governed by a king or queen, Choice (C). Although part of Colombia is located in the Amazon Rainforest region, nothing in the passage tells you that most of the country is located there.

403.
A. regretted the way they had treated the woman.

The passage says the men "were cursing ourselves for blockheads, chewing the sharp cud of repentance, and trying in a hundred sheepish, clumsy fashions to make amends," which means they were sorry for the way they had previously treated the woman.

The passage doesn't say that they verbally apologized to her, that they continued to be impolite, or that they were happy with the way they had treated her; in fact, it says they became very polite toward her.

404.
B. the Smithsonian Institution's beginnings.

The passage describes the Smithsonian Institution's earliest days and the specimens that filled the United States National Museum in 1846.

405.
C. The northeast entrance

The passage says to use "the northeast entrance to purchase subway tickets in the mezzanine."

406.
C. Decreased blood pressure

The question asks which is *not* a physical symptom of anxiety; make sure you're paying attention to detail when you're taking the real ASVAB. Decreased blood pressure isn't mentioned in the passage, so Choice (C) is correct.

407.
D. None of the above are correct.

The question asks you which of the answers isn't a problem with dyslexia. The passage says that difficulty with each of the choices — comprehension, spelling, and pronunciation — can be caused by dyslexia, which means Choice (D) is the only correct answer.

408.
C. people should not use tobacco.

You can assume the author of this passage believes people should not use tobacco, because he describes it with words such as "sicken" and "nauseous." Nothing in the passage supports the other answers.

409.
D. good leaders are both intellectual and artistically inclined.

The passage says, "the intellectual qualities of originally minded organizational leaders overlap with those of artistically inclined personalities" and that the modern environment "rewards leaders who are sensitive to issues of design and to the aesthetic dimensions of products or organizational life." That makes Choice (D) the most correct answer.

410.
C. cater to cultural desires.

The passage says "the emergence of new industries catering to cultural desires" is what rewards certain types of leaders.

411.
A. parents are required to send their children to school.

The passage says, "Education is compulsory," which means it's required. It also says, "In our country parents incur a fine who do not send their children to school." (*Note:* The *real* is the currency of Brazil.)

412. B. penguins' weight.

The passage describes penguins as "fat," but it also discusses when they become thin. That makes Choice (B), penguins' weight, the correct answer.

The passage mentions the other answers, but the main theme stays true to penguins' weight.

413. B. A prison cell

The passage says that the furniture is primitive but "better than that of some of the other cells." It also says, "On the bed is a brown rug with the word 'Prison' written on it," so you can surmise that the whole passage is about one prison cell.

414. C. is a reaction to being in prison.

The passage doesn't directly say it, but there are clues that "the six o'clock sickness" is a reaction that new inmates have as a result of being locked in prison. The passage says, "It attacks all newcomers, and none escape it" and that it comes on "when night begins to close in, and the prison settles into silence till the morning."

Choice (A) is incorrect because the "illness" occurs in the evening. Choice (B) is incorrect because the passage implies that it's psychological, not viral. Choice (D) is incorrect because the passage doesn't say anything about inmates eating bad food for dinner.

415. A. are given drugs to allay the symptoms.

The passage says, "When it comes on, the prisoners are given a cachet of quinine from the prison pharmacy."

Although the passage mentions walking in the courtyard, it says that "the six o'clock sickness" comes on after the inmates have walked and when night begins to settle in. That makes Choice (B) incorrect. Choice (C) is incorrect because the passage says, "It is an attack of a kind of malarial fever, a shivering fit and a violent headache with a feeling of lassitude and nausea afterwards." That means it has the same physical symptoms, not that it *is* malaria. The passage doesn't say that inmates go to the hospital; it says that they're treated with quinine from the prison pharmacy, which means Choice (D) is incorrect.

416. C. the best singers come from Italy and Australia.

Although it may not be true, the author of this passage clearly believes that the climate in Italy and Australia contribute to those countries' ability to produce the world's best singers.

417. B. The dangers of an international convention in the wrong hands

The passage says, "In the hands of such a nation an international convention is not merely idle and impotent; [it] becomes positively dangerous." That means in the wrong hands, an international convention won't function the way it was designed to function.

418. A. reporting on atrocities should encourage people to prevent them in the future.

The passage says, "Reports of atrocities can serve no useful purpose unless they move men to reflect no less resolutely than deeply upon what is to be done to deliver Europe from the scourge of their repetition." That sentence means that the author believes people should learn from the past and take preventive measures so history (at least the worst parts of it) does not repeat itself.

419. D. both B and C are correct.

The passage says, "Self-consciousness often does more to mar a good voice than anything else." It also says that people sing pleasantly when they believe nobody is listening, but when they're performing publicly, their singing is "indifferent or even unpleasant."

420. A. listening to music can help relieve stress.

The author of this passage says, "I believe that it is within the power of an artist to actually lessen, or, at any rate, to temporarily relieve, the cares and worries of which each member of an audience has a share."

Nothing in the passage says audience members have a responsibility to listen to a song's words, Choice (B), or that all songs should have a meaning and message, Choice (C). The passage doesn't say that songs should never be confusing, either, Choice (D).

421. A. "Positive and Negative Anxiety."

The passage discusses positive and negative types of anxiety, describing the benefits and drawbacks of certain amounts.

Although the passage does mention that some types of anxiety give you an "energy boost" and that many people experience anxiety before big events, the titles in Choices (B) and (C) don't cover the main idea of the passage. Choice (D) is incorrect because that would imply that the passage presents only the benefits of anxiety (and suggests that all anxiety is good for you).

422. **D. artifacts.**

The passage discusses the actual objects archaeologists study, which are artifacts.

423. **B. has a sense of urgency to finish the garment.**

The passage says Martha "sat at her sewing machine, stitching away for dear life." Because she's been working on the same thing for several hours ("her husband, coming in after some hours of absence and finding her, apparently, precisely where he had left her"), you can infer that she has a sense of urgency to finish her task.

424. **C. The presence of a sword means the site had been disturbed.**

The passage says, "Some accidental disturbance of the layers of his cave must have happened." The passage compares finding a beer bottle and a sword as if they're similarly out of place; the archaeologist wouldn't be happy to find either.

425. **D. 20 years**

The passage says, "Suppose we say that twenty years will make an average generation."

426. **B. temperatures in northern China were warmer during the time when Peking Man lived.**

The passage says, "It's much too cold and dry in north China for all these animals to live there today," which means you can assume that temperatures were warmer during Peking Man's time.

The passage doesn't say that Peking Man killed all the animals himself, and it doesn't mention vegetation, Choice (A). It doesn't say that anyone contributed to Peking Man's food stores, Choice (C). Finally, the passage doesn't say what Peking Man actually did with the animals whose remains were found in his cave, Choice (D).

427. **C. can't be killed by antibiotics.**

The passage says, "Unfortunately, the overuse of antibiotics has led to the emergence of antibiotic-resistant bacteria (bacteria that antibiotics can't kill)."

428. **B. Abbevillian core-biface tools were made by beating stones against a stone anvil.**

The passage says, "The deep chip-scars of the earlier Abbevillian core-biface came from beating the tool against a stone anvil."

429. A. nonsense.

The passage says that the author mentioned the "unlucky number" of passengers and says, "When I called this fact to my wife's attention she laughed at me." The author's wife said that they "were living in the twentieth century and should have outgrown such silly superstitions."

430. A. culture.

The passage discusses how culture is passed down through generations and notes that people learn it as they grow.

431. D. was destroyed twice by fire.

The passage mentions two times that Brough Castle was destroyed by fire: once in 1521 and again in 1666.

The year 1092 is part of the 11th century, which makes Choice (A) incorrect. Even if you didn't know that, though, you'd find the correct answer by carefully reading through all your choices. Although Brough Castle is a tourist destination, you wouldn't know that by reading the passage; that makes Choice (B) incorrect. Choice (C) is also incorrect, because the battle that destroyed the castle took place in 1174.

432. D. need to be prepared for transitions.

The passage says that "thrown among a rude mass of young creatures, [the children] were compelled unexpectedly to suffer everything from the vulgar, bad, and even base, since they lacked both weapons and skill to protect themselves," which makes Choice (D) correct.

Choice (A) is incorrect because the passage doesn't say children can adapt to anything. Choice (B) is also incorrect because the passage doesn't say kids learn only from their environments. Choice (C) is wrong because the passage doesn't say that children in general should be sent out with weapons.

433. A. dogs that have mobility problems can use wheelchairs.

The passage describes wheelchairs that are "designed to help pets with mobility problems."

434. C. extend their power.

The passage says, "The Russians, bent on extending their power on the Black Sea," which tells you that Choice (C) is correct.

435. **A. beautiful.**

The passage says that the magnolia tree "has been widely cultivated for its ornamental value." It also says, "No other tree excels it in the combined beauty of leaves and flowers."

Nothing in the passage supports Choice (B), (C), or (D).

436. **D. education on forest conservation.**

The passage says, "The Texas Forestry Association is a statewide, non-profit agency concerned primarily with the educational phase of forest conservation."

437. **A. experience in court helps attorneys claim professional expertise.**

The passage says, "For the most part, a trial lawyer needs experience in court to claim professional expertise."

Nothing in the passage says that witnesses are important or that they don't persuade juries, Choice (B), or that legal rules are the main component in a trial, Choice (C). Finally, Choice (D) is incorrect because the passage doesn't say that officials are always familiar with the rules of evidence.

When you take the ASVAB, be careful about choosing answers that say "never" or "always." Most correct answers don't deal in absolutes!

438. **B. Respiratory problems**

The passage says, "The resulting fumes can cause respiratory problems for people and pets, the buildup of carbon monoxide, or other dangerous health hazards."

439. **B. quickly promoted in rank.**

The passage says, "His advance had been rapid, and some of his more enthusiastic friends were already hinting at a commission in sight for him in the time to come," which means he's been quickly promoted.

Nothing in the passage says that Ned Strong was younger than his friend, Herc Taylor, Choice (A), or that he was handsome, Choice (C). The passage says that Ned's friends were enthusiastic but not that he was, Choice (D).

440. **D. Skeletons**

The passage says, "We found the mortal remains of their former inhabitants," which means that they found human remains.

441. B. More than a week

The passage says, "When the Continental war was going on, the news from the field of battle was generally eight or nine days old."

When you're taking the ASVAB, try to skim the passages and read the question before you start hunting for answers. You have 22 minutes to answer 11 questions on the CAT-ASVAB, or you have 13 minutes to answer 15 questions on the paper version of the test. Pace yourself and adjust your answering speed based on how much time is left on the clock. (Most people have plenty of time to answer all the questions.)

442. D. Both A and B are correct.

The passage describes an electric eye by saying it's "a type of photodetector in wide use." Additionally, the passage says, "They're also used as highway vehicle counters, alarm systems and more."

443. D. Start chemical reactions.

The passage says that olfactory receptors "start a cascade of chemical reactions in our bodies that create a nerve impulse," which makes Choice (D) the correct answer.

444. B. never left England.

The first sentence in the passage tells you that Jane Austen is "most thoroughly English." The second sentence says, "She never went abroad," which means she never left England.

Choice (A) is incorrect because the passage says she had a "shrewd gift of observation." Choice (C) is also incorrect because the passage tells you, "She cannot be conceived as writing of any but the sweet villages and the provincial towns of her native country," and her native country was England. Choice (D) is incorrect because the passage compares Jane Austen's experiences with those of the Brontës; it doesn't say that they traveled together.

445. B. "Public Libraries Are a Necessity."

The passage says that millions of youth "find in the public library the only open door through which they catch glimpses of opportunity beyond their own immediate domain." It also says, "Instances are plentiful where 'the chance encounter with a book has marked the awakening of a life,'" which means Choice (B) is correct.

Choice (A) is partly correct — you can't have a library without books. On the ASVAB, you'll have to choose between answers that are possibly correct to find the one that's *most* correct, and in this case, the passage's main theme is why public libraries are necessary.

446. **C. means you performed as well as or better than 93 percent of the original reference group.**

The passage says, "For example, if you get an AFQT score of 93, it means you performed as well as (or better than) 93 percent of the people tested from the original reference group."

447. **C. people with less money could not afford to go to dances and balls.**

The passage says that the man "had apparently enough money to allow his daughters the privileges of gentlewomen" despite living simply, which tells you that people with less money couldn't afford the "privileges of gentlewomen" listed (which includes going to dances and balls, as well as visiting their brothers "for weeks at a time").

448. **A. Gordie Howe was nicknamed "Mr. Hockey."**

The passage says Howe "earned the nickname 'Mr. Hockey.'" That means Choice (A) is correct.

Choice (B) is incorrect because although Gretzky broke many of Howe's records, the passage says, "Nobody has been able to touch his records for most games and seasons played." Choice (C) is incorrect because the passage says, "He spent his *first* 25 seasons with the Detroit Red Wings." That tells you he continued to play after leaving the Red Wings. Choice (D) is also incorrect. The first sentence reads, "Some might argue that Gordie Howe was the best hockey player in the history of the sport." It doesn't say that he was *certainly* the best player of all time.

449. **C. 1932.**

The passage lists the team's name changes as taking place in 1926 (when they were the Detroit Cougars), 1930 (when they became the Detroit Falcons), and 1932 ("the team adopted its current name").

Many of the Paragraph Comprehension questions on the ASVAB ask you to hunt for facts, which is yet another reason to skim the passage, read the question, and go back into the passage to find the answer.

450. A. had at least two floors.

The passage says, "The entire second floor of the building was consumed by flames; the first floor suffered significant water damage." That doesn't tell you exactly how many floors the hotel had, but it does let you know that it had at least two.

451. D. The third planet from the Sun.

The passage says, "The third planet from the Sun is our home," which makes Choice (D) the correct answer.

452. D. All of the above are correct.

The passage says that spacecraft have "landed on the Moon, Mars, Titan and an asteroid."

453. A. "Uses of Anthropology."

The passage describes two uses for anthropology: biology and culture.

Choice (B) is incorrect because although the passage mentions genetically engineering food crops, that's not its main theme. The same goes for Choice (C) — the passage mentions cultural knowledge, but it's not the main theme. Choice (D) is also incorrect because the passage is about more than biological uses of anthropology.

454. A. classified his collection by similarities.

The passage says, "Wurm organized the objects in his museum — not according to age, but by how much they resembled one another," which makes Choice (A) the correct answer.

455. D. an important cultural tradition.

The passage tells you that the feast and dances of Kivgiq are "reminders of an ancient code, an ancient way of life that was important to get right because it kept people alive."

456. C. eats larvae.

The passage says that the aye-aye "climbs through trees by moonlight listening for larvae beneath tree bark" and that when it hears them, "it uses a thin, elongated finger to scoop the meal out of the bark."

457. B. takes time and energy.

The passage says, "Training your dog takes weeks (or more), and you'll have to put a lot of energy into it," which makes Choice (B) the only correct answer.

458. B. when a living organism died.

The passage explains how scientists observe radioactive decay to find out how long it has been since a living organism died. The passage says, "When a life form stops ingesting 14C (when it, you know, dies), no new 14C enters the body, and the 14C in the body begins to radioactively decay into 14N."

Choice (A) is incorrect because although 14C "floats freely in the atmosphere," that's not what scientists determine by looking at radioactive decay. Choice (C) is incorrect because the passage says, "After about 5,600 years, only half of the original 14C remains because the rest has decayed into 14N," which is something scientists already know. Choice (D) is also incorrect because nothing in the passage says scientists are trying to determine when atmospheric conditions changed.

459. B. the differences between delayed and instant gratification.

The passage starts with, "You can't expect to see results immediately, which is a big change (and usually not a welcome one) from the way most of us live in the U.S." That sentence outlines the passage's main theme, and the passage continues to describe how most people in Western society are used to instant gratification.

460. C. nobody could feel it spinning.

The passage says, "Since no one experienced any of the sensations that would be expected if Earth was continually spinning, it seemed logical to believe that it was the heavens which were in motion around Earth." That makes Choice (C) the only correct answer.

461. D. training your dog can mitigate bad behaviors.

The passage outlines a number of activities dogs can be taught to perform that will replace "undesirable behaviors," such as barking at strangers, jumping on guests, or begging at the dining room table.

462. B. was used during the Middle Ages.

The passage says, "The encyclopedia was a favorite among scholars during the Middle Ages."

463. **A. a cluster of signs and symptoms.**

The passage says, "A cluster of signs and symptoms is called a syndrome."

464. **C. psychiatrists use more than one method to diagnose mental disorders.**

The passage says, "Psychiatrists and clinical psychologists use recognizable syndromes as the primary basis for classifying and diagnosing mental disorders." The key word there is *primary*; that tells you that this isn't the only method psychiatrists and psychologists use to diagnose their patients.

465. **C. interactions shape our moods and actions.**

The last sentence in the passage says, "The way in which we interact with others such as our friends, parents, siblings, and coworkers affects our moods and much of what we do."

Nothing in the passage supports Choice (A), (B), or (D).

466. **A. "How to Illustrate Parallax."**

The passage describes how to illustrate the geometric method called *parallax:* by closing one eye while keeping the other open.

467. **C. Tom doesn't want to whitewash the fence.**

The passage says, "He surveyed the fence, and all gladness left him and a deep melancholy settled down upon his spirit." It continues to describe the size of the fence and says that Tom "compared the insignificant whitewashed streak with the far-reaching continent of unwhitewashed fence, and sat down on a tree-box discouraged." This comparison suggests that he's dreading the work.

468. **B. he was a bad influence.**

The passage says, "Huckleberry was cordially hated and dreaded by all the mothers of the town, because he was idle and lawless and vulgar and bad."

469. **B. people celebrated the winter solstice.**

The passage says, "The winter solstice, when the days began to get longer was cause for celebration."

470. **A. make observations.**

> The passage says, "First, the scientist makes observations," which means Choice (A) is the correct answer.

> (Scientists don't form and test a hypothesis until after they've made observations. Furthermore, hypotheses are refuted or supported, never proven.)

471. **C. experiments can support or disprove a hypothesis.**

> The passage says, "To test her hypothesis, she performs experiments to see whether her predictions are correct." That means the scientist's predictions may — or may not — be correct; the experiments will help tell either way.

> You may have heard a hypothesis referred to as an "educated guess," but remember, Paragraph Comprehension questions on the ASVAB ask you only about the passage you've just read (not your own experience). Nothing in the passage says that scientists call guessing a "hypothesis."

472. **A. not all written records of history are completely true.**

> The passage says, "The use of propaganda, the convenient omission of inconvenient facts from state records, and the wholesale creation of 'facts' are nothing new." That tells you that not all written records are completely true.

473. **D. all of the above.**

> The passage says that language is a system of information transmission that humans use through "sound (speech), by gesture (body language), and in other visual ways such as writing."

474. **D. Both A and C are correct.**

> The passage says that once hydrogen is depleted, the first red giant phase ends abruptly. That means Choice (B) is incorrect, because the question asks about the result of hydrogen deficiency.

> Choices (A) and (C) are correct — which makes Choice (D) the right answer — because the passage says that "the intense heat and pressure initiate nuclear reactions that use helium as fuel. In this process, three helium atoms are fused to create one carbon atom."

475. **C. Dry, black soil**

> The passage says that dark surfaces have a low reflectivity and "heat up more quickly than lighter, more reflective surfaces, such as ice sheets." Because dark surfaces heat more quickly and reflect the least, Choice (C) is correct.

476. B. a watercraft.

The subject of this passage is the "craft" mentioned in the first sentence. The passage, referring to the watercraft as "she," describes the way it moves in the waves of the ocean.

477. D. Honesty

The passage says that outstanding leaders "recognize the value of honest communication as an essential expression of respect for others and for themselves." It continues to say that honesty isn't "just the best policy"; it's a commitment that all leaders should make.

478. C. cold currents move toward the equator.

The passage says, "Cold currents moving from high latitudes towards the equator tend to cool nearby coastal areas." Although this doesn't fully explain the answer, the rest of the passage does. It says, "Clouds and rain are rare. As a result, places such as southern California, northern Chile and south western Africa experience desert conditions."

Choice (B) is incorrect because although the passage says fog is very common, that's not the reason northern Chile experiences desert conditions.

479. A. gravitational pull.

The passage says, "The tides are caused by the combined effects of the gravitational pull of the moon and the sun," which makes Choice (A) the correct answer.

Choice (B) is incorrect because the passage says the tides are caused by gravitational pull of the moon and the sun — not by the moon and the sun themselves. Choice (C) is incorrect because the passage tells you the sun has a role to play in the tides, as well, and Choice (D) is incorrect because oceanic bulges aren't the cause of the tides; they're the result.

480. B. Sustainable farming

The passage lists several causes of global warming, including the increased use of fossil fuels, Choice (A); urbanization, Choice (C); and the clearing of forests, Choice (D). The only answer the passage doesn't mention is sustainable farming, Choice (B).

Make sure you're paying attention to detail on the ASVAB. This question asks you which practice is *not* a cause of global warming, and you'll see plenty of questions like it when you take the test at MEPS.

481. **D. The haka was originally a pre-war dance.**

The passage says, "Originally, haka were performed by soldiers to intimidate the opposition while demonstrating courage and strength."

482. **A. something changed drastically within that 3,000-year period.**

The passage explains that the people in the Danube River valley were "highly mobile foragers who left only short-lived campsites for archaeologists to discover" about 10,000 years ago; it then says, "by about 7,000 years ago, they were a rather sedentary people, living in riverside villages that you would normally associate with farming people." The passage doesn't tell you what happened, only that something changed during that time, which makes Choice (A) the correct answer.

483. **B. how to draw an ellipse.**

The passage describes how you can draw an ellipse, which makes Choice (B) the correct answer.

Although the passage does mention pencils, pins, and strings — Choices (A) and (D) — as well as how to change the shape of an ellipse, Choice (C), the main theme of the passage is simply how to draw one.

484. **A. continue to follow their moral compasses.**

The passage says that stress can cause followers to "lose their moral bearings and to succumb to questionable values or policies," while "great leaders stay on course."

Although Choice (B) may be true, that's not what the passage says; the passage only mentions losing "their most committed followers," not thousands. Choice (C) is incorrect because the passage says, "When others are ready to capitulate or bend, such leaders can appear stubborn and inflexible." That doesn't mean that great leaders are rarely flexible; it means that their commitment to the goal remains strong. Nothing in the passage supports Choice (D).

485. **D. Both A and C are correct.**

The passage says that the Army's Special Forces wear green berets and specialize in unconventional warfare. Nothing in the passage supports Choice (B).

When you're taking the ASVAB, make sure you read all your answer choices. If you'd stopped at Choice (A) on this question, you would've gotten the answer wrong.

486. **A. wrote laws and created a financial system.**

The passage says, "Charlemagne decreed rules affecting the major fields of government" that "affected everywhere and everybody." It also says that he established "a monetary system based on a silver coin, the denier."

487. **D. philosophy is too complex for ordinary people.**

The passage says, "The ordinary man is not made for such knowledge," which means he believes that philosophy is too complex for "the ordinary man" to understand.

The rest of the passage supports Choice (D), as well, when it says, "Those who say that there are truths which must be hidden from the people, need not be alarmed; the people do not read; they work six days of the week, and on the seventh go to the inn."

488. **C. there are multiple theories about how life began on Earth.**

The passage describes four theories about how life began on Earth.

489. **B. methane and carbon dioxide.**

The first sentence in the passage says "possibly in a chemical 'soup' enriched by early atmospheric gases such as methane and carbon dioxide," which makes Choice (B) the correct answer.

490. **A. Galileo**

The passage says that "Galileo became the first person in history to see the phases of Venus."

491. **C. broken rock.**

The passage says, "Beneath the crater floor is a lens-shaped body of breccia — rock that has been broken and pulverized by the shock wave." That means Choice (C) is the correct answer.

492. **B. you should remove the wax from the heat when it reaches 150°F.**

The passage describes the process of melting wax over a burner before it says, "At 150°F, remove the double-boiler from the saucepan and pour the wax into your molds." That means you can assume that you should remove the wax from its heat source at that time, making Choice (B) the correct answer.

493. **A. great leaders can be self-indulgent.**

The passage says that deep selflessness does not require total self-abnegation (*abnegation* is self-denial). Even if you didn't know that, you could assume that Choice (A) is correct because the passage says, "A deeply selfless leader may exhibit forms of self-regard, or even self-indulgence."

494. **B. "Lathe Faceplates."**

The passage describes what a lathe faceplate is and explains how to use one, which makes Choice (B) the correct answer. The other answers are too specific to describe the passage's main idea.

495. **D. moral courage is an essential human quality.**

The passage says that moral courage is "a critical human quality that serves as a necessary precondition for all other forms of human conduct."

496. **B. 1953**

The passage says, "He joined J&J in 1953," making Choice (B) the right answer.

Sometimes ASVAB questions really send you on fact-finding missions. When that happens, skim the passage to find the information you need; you'll save time that you may need to spend on more difficult questions.

497. **D. all of the above.**

The passage says that Lincoln had "a well-muscled physique," which makes Choice (C) correct. It continues to say that Lincoln was affable (friendly and good-natured) and popular and that "he was the company's champion wrestler." That means all the answer choices are correct, making Choice (D) the right answer.

498. **A. Lincoln was a good fighter.**

The passage describes Lincoln as a strong and well-muscled man, and it says, "Lincoln could hold his own against boys and men alike." It also says that "he was the company's champion wrestler."

499. B. you can find refractory elements in the inner regions of the nebula.

> The passage begins with "More refractory elements condense in the warm, inner regions of the nebula," which makes Choice (B) the correct one.
>
> Choice (A) is incorrect because the passage doesn't say the two elements mix to create gas. Choice (C) is also incorrect because the passage isn't discussing ice. Choice (D) is incorrect because the passage describes turbulence and drag as two distinct reasons the particles swirl around the disk at different rates.

500. D. All of the above

> The passage says, "Rosa Parks' courageous decision to act by not acting, by not getting up, and her subsequent arrest and conviction on charges of disorderly conduct proved to be the 'tipping point' for race relations." The key word in that sentence is *and*; that tells you that all three of those events worked together and were the "tipping point."

Mathematics Knowledge

501. A. $\frac{11}{18}$

> To add fractions, simplify and rewrite one or both fractions to ensure that the denominator is the same. Add the numerators and write the answer over the denominator. Don't forget to keep the value of the fraction the same; you may need to multiply the numerator over one or both denominators.
>
> You can reduce the first fraction before you look for common denominators:
>
> $$\frac{4}{8} = \frac{1}{2}$$
>
> Follow the steps to add fractions by finding the lowest common denominator. In this case, it's 18:
>
> $$\frac{1 \times 9}{2 \times 9} = \frac{9}{18}$$
> $$\frac{1 \times 2}{2 \times 9} = \frac{2}{18}$$
>
> Now add the fractions in their new forms:
>
> $$\frac{9}{18} + \frac{2}{18} = \frac{11}{18}$$

502. B. $\frac{3}{20}$

To subtract fractions, simplify and find the lowest common denominator. In this case, the lowest common denominator is 20. Make the denominators the same, remembering to keep the value of the fraction the same:

$$\frac{2\times 4}{5\times 4}=\frac{8}{20}$$
$$\frac{1\times 5}{4\times 5}=\frac{5}{20}$$

When you have the appropriate fractions, subtract the numerators, remembering that the denominator must stay the same:

$$\frac{8}{20}-\frac{5}{20}=\frac{3}{20}$$

503. A. $1\frac{9}{16}$

Before working with mixed fractions, convert them into improper fractions:

$$1\frac{7}{8}=\frac{15}{8}$$

To multiply fractions, multiply the first numerator by the second; then multiply the first denominator by the second. Cross-cancel before you multiply to save time and eliminate the need to reduce the fraction:

$$\frac{15}{8}\times\frac{5}{6}=\frac{\overset{5}{\cancel{15}}}{8}\times\frac{5}{\underset{2}{\cancel{6}}}=\frac{25}{16}$$

Convert the fraction back into a mixed number:

$$1\frac{9}{16}$$

504. D. $\frac{x+3}{2x^5+8x^4}$

Before multiplying complex fractions, factor the numerator and the denominator:

$$\frac{x^2}{x^2+x-12}\cdot\frac{x^2-9}{2x^6}=\frac{x^2}{(x+4)(x-3)}\cdot\frac{(x-3)(x+3)}{2x^6}$$

You can cancel out $(x-3)$ because it appears in the numerator and the denominator. After you cancel, you have simpler fractions to work with:

$$\frac{1}{x+4}\cdot\frac{x+3}{2x^4}$$

Perform multiplication and simplify:

$$\frac{x+3}{2x^5 + 8x^4}$$

505. **C.** $\dfrac{3x^2}{y^4}$

To reduce a fraction to its lowest terms, it's often helpful to expand the numerator and denominator so you can keep track of the exponents:

$$\frac{9 \cdot x \cdot x \cdot x \cdot y}{3 \cdot x \cdot y \cdot y \cdot y \cdot y \cdot y}$$

Reduce by a common constant factor of 3 (divide the 9 and the 3 by 3) and cancel out the variables that correspond in the numerator and denominator:

$$\frac{9 \cdot \cancel{x} \cdot x \cdot x \cdot \cancel{y}}{3 \cdot \cancel{x} \cdot \cancel{y} \cdot y \cdot y \cdot y \cdot y}$$

You can remove one x from the top and one from the bottom; you can also remove one y from the top and one from the bottom:

$$\frac{3x^2}{1y^4} = \frac{3x^2}{y^4}$$

506. **D.** $-3 - \sqrt{7}$

Get rid of the radicals in the denominator and simplify the expression. First, you need to multiply the top and bottom by the conjugate of the denominator; the *conjugate* is the same expression with the opposite sign between the terms, so the conjugate of $2 - \sqrt{7}$ is $2 + \sqrt{7}$:

$$\frac{1+\sqrt{7}}{2-\sqrt{7}} = \left(\frac{1+\sqrt{7}}{2-\sqrt{7}}\right)\left(\frac{2+\sqrt{7}}{2+\sqrt{7}}\right)$$

Multiply and then simplify the expression:

$$\frac{2+3\sqrt{7}+7}{4-7} = \frac{9+3\sqrt{7}}{-3}$$

Factor the expression (remember, you need 3 times the square root of 7) to simplify:

$$\frac{3\left(3+\sqrt{7}\right)}{-3} = \frac{\left(3+\sqrt{7}\right)}{-1} = -3 - \sqrt{7}$$

507. A. 2

This type of question is really asking you, "What number did we raise to the 5th power to reach 32?" To solve it quickly, use algebra, letting n equal the number raised to the 5th power:

$$32 = n^5$$

On the ASVAB, it's often easy to "plug and play" with the answers. Because you know how to solve the expression, and because you probably know that $2^5 = 32$, you could determine this answer without much work.

508. C. $\frac{9}{3}, \frac{36}{9}$

By finding the lowest common denominator in each set of fractions, you can tell which fractions are equal. In Choice (C), the lowest common denominator is 9. Keep the value of the fractions the same:

$$\frac{9}{3} = \frac{27}{9}, \ \frac{36}{9}$$

The two fractions in Choice (C) aren't equal; all of the other fractions *are* equal.

509. C. $\frac{5}{6}$

When you're adding fractions, you need to find a common denominator. The lowest common denominator for 3 and 4 is 12. Convert all the fractions while keeping their values the same:

$$\frac{1}{3} = \frac{4}{12}$$

$$\frac{1}{4} = \frac{3}{12}$$

$$\frac{1}{4} = \frac{3}{12}$$

Add your new fractions, and remember that the denominator stays the same; you only need to add the numerators:

$$\frac{4}{12} + \frac{3}{12} + \frac{3}{12} = \frac{10}{12}$$

Simplify the fraction:

$$\frac{10}{12} = \frac{5}{6}$$

510. B. $\frac{6y}{x+1}$

To divide fractions, you need to flip the fraction you want to divide by; then use the standard multiplication rules to work out the problem and simplify it as much as possible:

$$\frac{3y^2}{x+1} \div \frac{y}{2} = \frac{3y^2}{x+1} \cdot \frac{2}{y}$$
$$= \frac{(3y^2)(2)}{(x+1)(y)}$$
$$= \frac{6y^2}{(x+1)(y)}$$
$$= \frac{6y}{x+1}$$

511. A. 50

Calculating percentages is simple. Convert the percent to a decimal:

$$25\% = 0.25$$

Then multiply the given number (in this case, it's 200) by the decimal:

$$200 \times 0.25 = 50$$

If you're already familiar with percentage and fraction conversions, you may have recognized that $25\% = \frac{1}{4}$. In that case, you could've arrived at the answer by dividing 200 by 4.

Remember, you'll only be allowed scratch paper and a pencil when you're taking the ASVAB.

512. B. 625

To determine a whole number when you know a part and a percent, you can use a proportion; let x equal the whole. The proportion looks like this:

$$\frac{\text{part}}{\text{whole}} = \frac{\text{percent}}{100}$$

Plug in the numbers you know:

$$\frac{250}{x} = \frac{40}{100}$$

Cancel out the zeros in the fraction to make the problem a bit easier:

$$\frac{250}{x} = \frac{4\cancel{0}}{10\cancel{0}}$$
$$4x = 2,500$$

(Remember, though, you can't cancel out zeros on the other side of the equals sign.)

Divide both sides by 4 to isolate x:

$$\frac{4x}{4} = \frac{2,500}{4}$$
$$x = 625$$

You can check your work by putting the variable in the original equation and making sure the fractions are equal:

$$\frac{4(625)}{4} = \frac{2,500}{4}$$

513. D. 40

To find a part of a whole when you only know the numbers, you can look at the problem as if it's a fraction. Let x equal the percent you're trying to find:

$$\frac{8}{20} = \frac{x}{100}$$

Cross-multiply:

$$20x = 800$$

Divide each side by 20 to solve for x:

$$\frac{20x}{20} = \frac{800}{20}$$
$$x = 40$$

You don't have to follow an algebraic route to get the correct answer, though. If you phrase the question, "What is 8 out of 20?" you can visualize that in mathematical terms:

$$\frac{8}{20}$$

Perform division to get the answer, and then convert the decimal into a percent:

$$8 \div 20 = 0.4 = 40\%$$

514. D. 4

Use the standard proportion, filling in what you already know:

$$\frac{15}{375} = \frac{x}{100}$$

Reduce the fraction to make the numbers easier to work with:

$$\frac{\overset{5}{\cancel{15}}}{\underset{125}{\cancel{375}}} = \frac{x}{100} \qquad \frac{\overset{3}{\cancel{15}}}{\underset{75}{\cancel{375}}} = \frac{x}{100} \qquad \frac{\overset{1}{\cancel{15}}}{\underset{25}{\cancel{375}}} = \frac{x}{100}$$

$$125x = 500 \quad \text{or} \quad 75x = 300 \quad \text{or} \quad 25x = 100$$

$$x = 4 \qquad\qquad x = 4 \qquad\qquad x = 4$$

Even if the fraction isn't in its lowest terms, the numbers will be less complicated.

Remember that on the ASVAB, one answer may be wildly out of place — like Choice (A) is here — and you can rule that one out right away.

515. C. 600

Set up a proportion, letting x represent the unknown number:

$$\frac{450}{x} = \frac{75}{100}$$

Reduce the fraction so the problem is easier to work with:

$$\frac{450}{x} = \frac{\overset{3}{\cancel{75}}}{\underset{4}{\cancel{100}}}$$

$$3x = 1,800$$

$$x = 600$$

516. C. 39.6

Convert 33% into the decimal 0.33. Multiply 120 by 0.33 to arrive at the answer, which is 39.6.

517. D. 82.5

You can convert 55% into a decimal (0.55) and multiply it by 150 to arrive at the answer, which is 82.5, or you can use a proportion where x equals the number you need to find:

$$\frac{x}{150} = \frac{55}{100}$$

Cross-multiply:

$$100x = 8,250$$

Divide each side by 100 to isolate x:

$$\frac{100x}{100} = \frac{8,250}{100}$$

$$8,250 \div 100 = 82.5$$

$$x = 82.5$$

You can't use a calculator on the ASVAB, so figure out which method of finding percentages is easiest for you *before* you take the test.

ANSWERS
501–600

CHAPTER 5 Answers   237

518.   **A. 26.66**

Let x equal the part of 310 you need to find:

$$\frac{x}{310} = \frac{8.6}{100}$$

Cross-multiply and isolate the variable by dividing both sides by 100:

$$\frac{(310)(8.6)}{100x} = \frac{2,666}{100}$$
$$x = 26.66$$

Another method is to multiply 310 by 0.086 (that's the percent converted into a decimal):

$$310 \times 0.086 = 26.66$$

519.   **C. 25**

Let x represent the unknown quantity in a proportion:

$$\frac{\text{part}}{\text{whole}} = \frac{\text{percent}}{100}$$
$$\frac{14}{56} = \frac{x}{100}$$

Factor a 7 out of the fraction, and then factor out the 2 to simplify:

$$\frac{\overset{2}{\cancel{14}}}{\underset{8}{\cancel{56}}} = \frac{x}{100}$$
$$\frac{\overset{1}{\cancel{2}}}{\underset{4}{\cancel{8}}} = \frac{x}{100}$$
$$4x = 100$$
$$x = 25$$

520.   **B. $123\frac{5}{8}$**

Multiply 989 by 0.125:

$$989 \times 0.125 = 123.625$$

To convert that into a fraction, take the 0.625 and put it over 1,000; then reduce:

$$= 123\frac{625}{1,000}$$
$$= 123\frac{625 \div 125}{1,000 \div 125}$$
$$= 123\frac{5}{8}$$

You can automatically rule out Choices (A) and (D) because you paid attention to detail (right?) when the question clearly told you to convert the answer into a fraction.

521. **D. Both B and C**

You can express this ratio in one of three ways:

$$\frac{16}{9}$$

$16:9$

16 to 9

Note that because the question asks for the ratio of ducks to geese, the elements of the ratio are expressed with ducks first. If the question had asked for the ratio of geese to ducks, you'd switch the order of elements in the ratio.

522. **B. $\frac{3}{4}$**

To express the ratio as a fraction, you'd write:

$$\frac{15}{20}$$

Using what you know of fractions, simplify $\frac{15}{20}$ to $\frac{3}{4}$.

Although Choices (A), (C), and (D) express the same ratio in different numbers, they're incorrect because the question asks you to simplify the fraction. Many of the questions on the ASVAB require you to pay attention to detail, so make sure you read before you answer!

523. **B. 36**

One way to solve this problem is to use your scratch paper to scribble out a ratio table. Your ratio table should look like something this:

a	5
b	4
c	3
d	2
e	1

Based on your ratio table, you know that

$a:5$

$b:4$

$c:3$

$d:2$

$e:1$

Note that the ratio table shows you that $a:c=5:3$. Write these ratios as fractions and set up a proportion, replacing the variable a with 60 — the value the problem gives you:

$$\frac{a}{c}=\frac{5}{3}$$
$$\frac{60}{c}=\frac{5}{3}$$
$$5c=180$$
$$c=36$$

You don't need to figure out the rest of the values. It would take up your valuable time, and you have only 20 minutes to answer 16 questions on the computerized ASVAB.

524. **A. 27:38, 26:42**

Order matters when you're writing ratios. The first ratio is Group A, where the number of males is mentioned first. The correct ratio for Group A is $27:38$.

The second ratio represents Group B, in which females are mentioned first. You have to reverse the order to follow the directions. The ratio for Group B is $26:42$.

525. **D. 90:120**

You can automatically rule out Choice (A), because 7 feet, 6 inches is 7.5 feet, not 7.6 feet. Choice (B) is incorrect because the measurements aren't in the same units; the height is in feet, whereas the length is in inches. Choice (C) is incorrect because 7 feet, 6 inches translates to 90 inches. That leaves only one possible correct answer, Choice (D).

526. **C. 1,500**

Based on the ratios you have, you can determine the value of x without worrying about the other variables. You know that

$$\frac{a}{x}=\frac{b}{70}$$
$$\frac{150}{x}=\frac{7}{70}$$

Cross-multiply:

$$7x = 10,500$$

Divide both sides by 7 to isolate x:

$$\frac{7x}{7} = \frac{10,500}{7}$$
$$x = 1,500$$

Note: You can also use mental math when solving ratio problems. Look at $\frac{150}{x} = \frac{7}{70}$ and consider the fraction on the right. Think, "What times 7 gives me 70?" The answer is 10, so to get x, multiply 150 (on the left) by 10 to get 1,500.

527.   A. 10 feet

One hundred centimeters equals 1 meter, so start by converting those (unless you know that 1 centimeter equals 0.0328084 feet; in that case, you're all set to become a military astrophysicist). You can express the ratio this way, with x representing the number of unknown meters:

$$\frac{100}{1} = \frac{297.85}{x}$$

Cross-multiply:

$$100x = 297.85$$

Divide both sides by 100 to isolate x:

$$\frac{100x}{100} = \frac{297.85}{100}$$
$$x = 2.9785$$

Now you'll have to rely on your knowledge of feet versus meters (and it's good to have, because the military measures everything in meters rather than feet).

One meter is approximately 3.28 feet, so for a tricky problem like this one, it's best to round that number to 3.3. Before you convert 2.9785 meters into feet by multiplying, round that number up to 3:

$$2.9785 \times 3.28 \approx 3.0 \times 3.3$$
$$\approx 9.9$$
$$\approx 10$$

Here's another way: If you're fortunate enough to remember that 2.54 centimeters equals 1 inch, use your rounding skills to make the problem easier.

Round 297.85 up to 300 and 2.54 down to 2.5; then divide 300 by 2.5:

$$300 \div 2.5 = 120$$

Divide that answer by 12 (remember, there are 12 inches in a foot):

$$120 \div 12 = 10$$

528.   B. 1,280 cm

Because 1 meter equals 100 centimeters, you can do this problem the quick way (multiply 12.8 by 100, which equals 1,280) or the not-so-quick way, which looks like this:

$$\frac{1}{100} = \frac{12.8}{x}$$

Cross-multiply to find the value of x:

$$x = 1,280$$

529.   A. $\frac{1}{20}$

A ratio is a statement that shows how two numbers compare. In this case, there are a total of 20 dogs. One of them has three legs. Therefore, one out of 20 dogs has three legs, which you can express as $\frac{1}{20}$.

(For the record, you can also express this ratio by writing $1:20$ or 1 to 20.)

530.   D. 0.43

It's easiest to solve problems when you're working with like terms. Convert $\frac{1}{5}$ into 0.2 so you're not working with fractions.

Write an equation to find x:

$$\frac{1.5}{32} = \frac{0.2}{x}$$

Cross-multiply:

$$1.5x = 0.64$$

Divide both sides of the equation to isolate x:

$$\frac{1.5x}{1.5} = \frac{0.64}{1.5}$$
$$x = 0.43$$

531.   C. 7×10^3

Scientific notation is a simple way to deal with long numbers. The best way to find a number's scientific notation is to put a decimal point after the first digit and count the number of places from the decimal point to the end of the number.

In this case, you put a decimal point after the 7 and before the three zeros: 7.000. Because there are three zeros to the right of your new decimal placement, the exponent needs to be 3.

532.
A. 5.9784×10^{-1}

Because the original number is less than 1, you need to move the decimal point to the right in order to place it to the right of the first digit. You move the decimal point one place, making the exponent −1.

533.
B. 6×10^6

You need to put a decimal point after the numeral 6, leaving six zeros following the decimal. You express 6,000,000 in scientific notation by writing 6×10^6.

534.
A. 2.233278×10^{-12}

Multiply the numeric parts of the problem:

$$4.1357 \times 5.4 = 22.33278$$

Multiply the powers of ten by adding the exponents:

$$10^{-15} \times 10^2 = 10^{-15+2}$$
$$= 10^{-13}$$

Write the answer as the product of the two numbers:

$$22.33278 \times 10^{-13}$$

The first number isn't between 1 and 10, which means you need to move the decimal point one place to the left and add 1 to the exponent to arrive at 2.233278×10^{-12}.

535.
D. 0.854345

The exponent is −3, which tells you that you need to move the decimal point three places to the left (a positive exponent tells you to move the decimal to the right).

536.
C. 7

$\sqrt{n}$ is the number that gives n when it's multiplied by itself. In this case, 7 multiplied by 7 is 49; that means the square root of 49 is 7 (or −7, because −7 multiplied by −7 is also 49).

537.

A. $2a^2bc\sqrt{3b}$

To simplify, apply the exponent rule, which is $\sqrt{a \cdot b} = \sqrt{a} \cdot \sqrt{b}$:

$$\sqrt{12}\sqrt{a^4}\sqrt{b^3}\sqrt{c^2}$$
$$= 2\sqrt{3}\sqrt{a^4}\sqrt{b^3}\sqrt{c^2}$$
$$= 2\sqrt{3}a^2b^{\frac{3}{2}}c$$
$$= 2a^2bc\sqrt{3b}$$

538.

D. 15

First evaluate the expression inside the square root symbol by filling in the value of x:

$$-75(-3) = 225$$

Find $\sqrt{225}$ by determining that $15 \times 15 = 225$.

539.

C. $10x^2y^2\sqrt[3]{x}$

Both radicals are cube roots, so multiply the radicands. Because $\sqrt[x]{a} \times \sqrt[x]{b} = \sqrt[x]{ab}$, you get

$$5\sqrt[3]{x^5y^2 \cdot 8x^2y^4}$$

Factor and simplify, and look for perfect cubes to make it easier:

$$5\sqrt[3]{8 \cdot x^5 \cdot x^2 \cdot y^2 \cdot y^4}$$
$$5\sqrt[3]{8 \cdot x^{5+2} \cdot y^{2+4}}$$
$$5\sqrt[3]{8 \cdot x^7 \cdot y^6}$$
$$5\sqrt[3]{(2)^3 \cdot x(x^2)^3 \cdot (y^2)^3}$$

Rewrite the numbers and variables as the product of radicals so you continue to work with like terms:

$$5\sqrt[3]{(2)^3} \cdot \sqrt[3]{(x^2)^3} \cdot \sqrt[3]{(y^2)^3} \cdot \sqrt[3]{x} = 5 \cdot 2 \cdot x^2 \cdot y^2 \cdot \sqrt[3]{x}$$

Solve what you can and simplify:

$$10x^2y^2\sqrt[3]{x}$$

540. B. 7

To solve this problem, you need to find the cube root of 343. You can express the problem this way:

$$x \cdot x \cdot x = 343$$
$$7 \cdot 7 \cdot 7 = 343$$

If you're not quite sure how to work out a problem but you can get the answer by trying out your options, give it a shot! For this question, you can ignore Choice (A) (just a glance tells you that $114 \times 114 \times 114$ is far greater than 343).

541. A. 3

Isolate a:

$$2a + 27 = 33$$
$$2a + 27 - 27 = 33 - 27$$
$$2a = 6$$
$$\frac{2a}{2} = \frac{6}{2}$$
$$a = 3$$

With simple algebra problems, plugging in the answer choices is often faster than working through all the math. (You'll still want to understand the math, though, because you'll find plenty of more complicated problems on the test.)

542. A. 4

Adding matrices only requires you to add corresponding elements. Look at the first number in the matrix on the left and then the first number in the center matrix (they're 3 and 6, respectively); $3 + 6 = 9$, which is the first number in the matrix on the right.

To solve for x, express your equation as a simple addition problem, and then solve:

$$4 + x = 8$$
$$x + 4 - 4 = 8 - 4$$
$$x = 4$$

543. B. –35

Isolate x:

$$-32 = x + 3$$
$$x + 3 = -32$$
$$x = -32 - 3$$
$$x = -35$$

Check your work by inserting –35 in the original equation:

$$-35 + 3 = -32$$

544. D. 12

Remember that $\frac{3x}{1} = 3x$, so you can simplify the problem before you isolate x:

$$29 + 3x = 65$$
$$3x + 29 - 29 = 65 - 29$$
$$3x = 36$$
$$\frac{3x}{3} = \frac{36}{3}$$
$$x = 12$$

545. C. $a = \dfrac{7}{r - 11}$

Put all the variables on the same side of the equation by subtracting 11a from both sides:

$$ar = 11a + 7$$
$$ar - 11a = 11a - 11a + 7$$
$$ar - 11a = 7$$

Factor out a and divide both sides by $r - 11$:

$$a(r - 11) = 7$$
$$\frac{a(r - 11)}{r - 11} = \frac{7}{r - 11}$$
$$a = \frac{7}{r - 11}$$

546. B. $y = -3x + 6$

The formula for slope-intercept form is $y = mx + b$, with m representing the slope and b representing the y-intercept. Isolate y:

$$y + 3x - 6 = 0$$
$$y + 3x - 6 - 3x = 0 - 3x$$
$$y - 6 = -3x$$
$$y - 6 + 6 = -3x + 6$$
$$y = -3x + 6$$

547. **A. 5**

Isolate x by dividing both sides by 17:

$$17x = 85$$
$$\frac{17x}{17} = \frac{85}{17}$$
$$x = 5$$

548. **B.** $\sqrt[4]{239} = \log_a (xy)$

When you're searching for roots, the number above the radical is called the *index*. The problem asks you to find the fourth root of 239, which is expressed as $\sqrt[4]{239}$. Next, insert the equals symbol, and express "log to the base of a" as $\log_a$. The value you want to find is the product of x and y, which refers to multiplication and belongs in parentheses beside the base. Therefore, your expression needs to look like this:

$$\sqrt[4]{239} = \log_a (xy)$$

549. **C. –9**

Isolate x:

$$4x + 6 = -30$$
$$4x + 6 - 6 = -30 - 6$$
$$4x = -36$$
$$\frac{4x}{4} = \frac{-36}{4}$$
$$x = -9$$

550. **C. –14**

Use the distributive property to simplify the equation:

$$6(y + 7) = 3y$$
$$(6)(y) + (6)(7) = 3y$$
$$6y + 42 = 3y$$

Put the variables on the same side of the equation and solve:

$$6y + 42 = 3y$$
$$6y + 42 - 3y = 3y - 3y$$
$$3y + 42 - 42 = 0 - 42$$
$$3y = -42$$
$$\frac{3y}{3} = \frac{-42}{3}$$
$$y = -14$$

551. A. 3

The goal with this type of problem — in which there's a variable on both sides of the equation — is to put the variables on the same side. Start by using the addition property of equality, which tells you that adding the same number to each side of an equation gives you an equivalent equation.

$$x + 10 = 19 - 2x$$
$$x + 10 + 2x = 19$$
$$x + 2x = 19 - 10$$

Combine like terms:

$$3x = 9$$

Isolate x by dividing both sides by 3:

$$\frac{3x}{3} = \frac{9}{3}$$
$$x = 3$$

552. C. 8.5

Use the addition property of equality to put both variables on the same side. Then combine like terms and isolate x:

$$17x + -2 = 117 + 3x$$
$$17x = 117 + 3x + 2$$
$$17x = 119 + 3x$$
$$17x - 3x = 119$$
$$14x = 119$$
$$\frac{14x}{14} = \frac{119}{14}$$
$$x = 8.5$$

553. B. 6

Simplify both sides of the equation by distributing:

$$134(x + 12) = 402x$$
$$(134)(x) + (134)(12) = 402x$$
$$134x + 1,608 = 402x$$

Subtract 134x from both sides, and then isolate x to solve:

$$134x + 1,608 - 134x = 402x - 134x$$
$$1,608 = 268x$$
$$\frac{1,608}{268} = \frac{268x}{268}$$
$$6 = x$$

You don't *always* have to work through all the math. If you're not confident in your ability to do the calculations correctly, start plugging in answer choices until you hit the right one.

554.   **D. $9x^{14}y^{10}$**

To simplify expressions that contain exponents, raise everything in the parentheses by the exponent outside the parentheses. Technically, you'll apply the exponent rule, which says $(ab)^n = a^n b^n$. In this case,

$$\left(3x^7 y^5\right)^2 = 3^2 \left(x^7\right)^2 \left(y^5\right)^2$$
$$= 9\left(x^{7(2)}\right)\left(y^{5(2)}\right)$$
$$= 9x^{14} y^{10}$$

555.   **B. $4y^5 + 9y^4 + 7x^3 - 2y^2 - 8y + 32$**

Writing a polynomial in standard form requires you to organize the expression with the highest exponent first and subsequent exponents in descending order. Remember, the constant (the number with no variable) always goes last. The given expression is

$$7x^3 + 4y^5 - 2y^2 - 8y + 9y^4 + 32$$

Rank the terms in descending order by exponent:

$$4y^5 + 9y^4 + 7x^3 - 2y^2 - 8y + 32$$

556.   **D. $4x^6 + 4x - 12$**

Simplify by adding like terms, including exponents:

$$x^4 x^2 = x^{4+2} = x^6$$

Combine all the terms:

$$4x^6 + 4x - 12$$

On the ASVAB, ruling out answers that are clearly wrong can pay off — especially if you have to resort to guessing. You can tell that Choice (C) is wrong because there are two like terms that aren't combined: $16x$ and $4x$. If you're guessing, you now have 1 in 3 odds of getting the right answer.

557. **A. 294**

Because this equation has only a variable in the numerator a fraction, multiply both sides of the equation by 7:

$$\frac{x}{7} = 42$$

$$\frac{x}{7}(7) = 42(7)$$

$$x = 294$$

558. **D. $y = x - 3$**

The formula for slope-intercept form is $y = mx + b$, so combine like terms and isolate y:

$$x + y + 9 - 4x + 2y = 0$$
$$-3x + 3y + 9 = 0$$
$$3y + 9 = 0 + 3x$$
$$3y + 9 = 3x$$
$$3y + 9 - 9 = 3x - 9$$
$$3y = 3x - 9$$

Simplify the equation by dividing each term by 3:

$$3y = 3x - 9$$
$$\frac{3y}{3} = \frac{3x}{3} - \frac{9}{3}$$
$$y = x - 3$$

559. **A. $-\frac{12}{5} < c < -\frac{6}{5}$**

Remember that $|f(c)| < a \rightarrow f(c) < a$ and $f(c) > -a$, which translates to

$$5c + 9 < 3 \qquad \text{and} \qquad 5c + 9 > -3$$

Subtract 9 from both sides of the first inequality, and then subtract 9 from both sides of the second inequality, solving both for c:

$$5c + 9 < 3 \qquad \text{and} \qquad 5c + 9 > 3$$
$$5c + 9 - 9 < 3 - 9 \qquad\qquad 5c + 9 - 9 > -3 - 9$$
$$5c < -6 \qquad\qquad\qquad 5c > -12$$
$$\frac{5c}{5} < -\frac{6}{5} \qquad\qquad\qquad \frac{5c}{5} > \frac{-12}{5}$$
$$c < -\frac{6}{5} \qquad\qquad\qquad c > -\frac{12}{5}$$

You can now combine the ranges to arrive at the answer:

$$-\frac{12}{5} < c < -\frac{6}{5}$$

560. **A. (6x + 7x)(6x − 7y)**

When you factor, keep in mind that $ax^2 - by^2 = \left(\sqrt{ax} + \sqrt{by}\right)\left(\sqrt{ax} - \sqrt{by}\right)$.

That tells you when you have squares, the roots of those squares (which are given in the problem) can be factored out. In this problem,

$$36x^2 - 49y^2 = (6x + 7y)(6x - 7y)$$

561. **C. −23**

Put the variables on the same side of the equation:

$$-10x + -23 = 23 + -8x$$
$$-10x + -23 + 8x = 23$$
$$-2x - 23 + 23 = 23 + 23$$
$$-2x = 46$$

Isolate x by dividing both sides of the equation by −2:

$$\frac{-2x}{-2} = \frac{46}{-2}$$
$$x = -23$$

562. **C. (4x − 3y)(16x² + 12xy + 9y²)**

Factor using the algebraic property $a^3 - b^3 = (a - b)\left(a^2 + ab + b^2\right)$:

$$64x^3 - 27y^3 = (4x - 3y)\left(16x^2 + 12xy + 9y^2\right)$$

The idea is to find the cube roots and then refine the expression:

$$a = \sqrt[3]{64x^3} = 4x$$
$$b = \sqrt[3]{27y^3} = 3y$$

Plug in 4x for all a's and 3y for all b's in the formula.

If you're not sure how to factor cubed exponents, you may not want to spend much time trying to solve problems such as this one. (You have 20 minutes to answer 16 questions, so you can spend an average of just over a minute on each.)

563. **A.** $\frac{5}{6}x + \frac{5}{6}$

Multiply the fractions:

$$\frac{\left(5x^2 - 5\right)(x + 4)}{(6x + 24)(x - 1)}$$

Factor the binomials:

$$\frac{5(x+1)(x-1)(x+4)}{6(x+4)(x-1)}$$

Cancel out the common factors:

$$\frac{5(x+1)\cancel{(x-1)}\cancel{(x+4)}}{6\cancel{(x+4)}\cancel{(x-1)}}$$

Finally, use the distributive property to multiply $\frac{5}{6}$ through the remaining binomial $(x+1)$:

$$\frac{5}{6}x+\frac{5}{6}$$

564. C. $x \le -1$

Solve the inequality by subtracting 6 from both sides; then reverse the inequality when you divide both sides by -4 to isolate x:

$$-4x+6-6 \ge 10-6$$
$$-4x \ge 4$$
$$\frac{-4x}{-4} \le \frac{4}{-4}$$
$$x \le -1$$

565. D.

Solve the inequality first:

$$x+3 \le 2$$
$$x+3-3 \le 2-3$$
$$x \le -1$$

To graph this inequality, draw a shaded circle at -1 and shade the line pointing to the left to show all numbers less than or equal to 1 on the number line.

566. C. -17

Reduce the fraction on the left:

$$\frac{47}{94}x+17 = 8.5$$
$$\frac{1}{2}x+17 = 8.5$$

Subtract 17 from both sides:

$$\frac{1}{2}x + 17 - 17 = 8.5 - 17$$

$$\frac{1}{2}x = -8.5$$

Multiply both sides by 2 to isolate x:

$$2\left(\frac{1}{2}x\right) = 2(-8.5)$$

$$x = -17$$

567. A. $y = 4x - 4$

Use slope-intercept form, $y = mx + b$, where m represents slope and b represents the y-intercept. You know that $m = 4$, $x = -2$, and $y = -12$. Insert all the values you know and solve for b:

$$y = mx + b$$
$$-12 = (4)(-2) + b$$
$$-12 = -8 + b$$
$$-12 + 8 = -8 + b + 8$$
$$-4 = b$$

Now you know the values you need to create the line equation, so use $y = mx + b$:

$$y = 4x - 4$$

568. D. x^{315}

Apply the exponent rule, which says $\left(a^b\right)^c = a^{b \cdot c}$. Multiply the exponents, beginning with the innermost parentheses:

$$\left(x^5\right)^7 = x^{5(7)} = x^{35}$$

Move on to the outer exponent:

$$\left(x^{35}\right)^9 = x^{35(9)} = x^{315}$$

569. B. 110

Replace the variables with the given numbers and solve for c:

$$5(2) + 2(50) = c$$
$$10 + 100 = c$$
$$c = 110$$

570. D. 6

Isolate the x term by subtracting 4 from both sides:

$$\frac{3}{2}x + 4 - 4 = 13 - 4$$

$$\frac{3}{2}x = 9$$

To isolate x, multiply both sides by $\frac{2}{3}$, the *multiplicative inverse* of $\frac{3}{2}$ (the number you can multiply your fraction by to get 1). Then simplify:

$$\frac{2}{3} \cdot \frac{3}{2}x = 9 \cdot \frac{2}{3}$$

$$x = \frac{9}{1} \cdot \frac{2}{3}$$

$$x = \frac{18}{3}$$

$$x = 6$$

571. C. $\frac{x+1}{x-3}$

Factor the numerator and denominator:

$$\frac{x^2 - 6x - 7}{x^2 - 10x + 21} = \frac{(x-7)(x+1)}{(x-7)(x-3)}$$

Cancel out all the factors you can to reduce the fraction to its lowest terms:

$$\frac{\cancel{(x-7)}(x+1)}{\cancel{(x-7)}(x-3)}$$

572. A. $a + (b + c)$

According to the associative property of addition, $(a+b)+c = a+(b+c)$. It doesn't matter which two factors you combine first, because you'll get the same answer either way.

573. A. $4y$

Pay close attention to detail — this problem is asking you to solve for x. That means your answer can (and should) have the other variable (y) in it. Subtract $4x$ from both sides:

$$4x - 4x + 8y = 6x - 4x$$

$$8y = 2x$$

Because you need to solve for x, flip the equation (most people like the variable they're solving for on the left) and divide both sides by 2:

$$2x = 8y$$
$$\frac{2x}{2} = \frac{8y}{2}$$
$$x = 4y$$

574. C. $-\frac{8}{9}$

Simplify the equation:

$$5x + 7 = (5)(x) + (5)(-2) + (-3)(3x) + (-3)(-3)$$
$$5x + 7 = 5x - 10 - 9x + 9$$
$$5x + 7 = -4x - 1$$

Add $4x$ to both sides, and then subtract 7 from both sides. Divide both sides by 9 to isolate x:

$$5x + 4 + 4x = -4x - 1 + 4x$$
$$9x + 7 = -1$$
$$9x + 7 - 7 = -1 - 7$$
$$9x = -8$$
$$\frac{9x}{9} = -\frac{8}{9}$$
$$x = -\frac{8}{9}$$

575. D. All of the above

Each answer is true if a and b are equal. The choices show the addition, subtraction, and multiplication properties of equality.

576. B. 3

Subtract 38 from both sides; then divide both sides by 475.5 to isolate a:

$$475.5a + 38 - 38 = 1,464.5 - 38$$
$$475.5a = 1,426.5$$
$$\frac{475.5a}{475.5} = \frac{1,426.5}{475.5}$$
$$a = 3$$

577. **C.** $3x^2 + 30x + 63$

Distribute the terms in parentheses using FOIL, or the formula $(a+b)(c+d) = ac + ad + bc + bd$:

$$(x+7)(3x+9) = x(3x) + x(9) + 7(3x) + 7(9)$$
$$= 3x^2 + 9x + 21x + 63$$
$$= 3x^2 + 30x + 63$$

578. **D.** $17 - 5i$

Group the real and imaginary parts of the complex number, because $(a+bi) \pm (c+di) = (a \pm c) + (b \pm d)i$. Then simplify:

$$(1+4i) - (-16+9i) = (1+16) + (4-9)i$$
$$= 17 - 5i$$

579. **C.** 1

Plug in the numbers you know and simplify:

$$z = 4(7) - 3(9)$$
$$z = 28 - 27$$
$$z = 1$$

580. **B.** 6 or −6

Evaluate the expressions in the parentheses first:

$$(9 \times 1)(10-8)(-6+8) = x^2$$
$$x^2 = 9 \times 2 \times 2$$
$$x^2 = 36$$

Find the square root:

$$x = \pm\sqrt{36}$$
$$x = 6 \text{ or } x = -6$$

581. **B.** 3

Combine like terms:

$$12c + 18c = 90$$
$$30c = 90$$

Divide both sides by 30 to isolate c:

$$\frac{30c}{30} = \frac{90}{30}$$
$$c = 3$$

582. **B.** $72x^5 - x - 2$

Multiply the numbers 12 and 6, and then apply the exponent rule, which is $a^b \cdot a^c = a^{b+c}$ (to multiply powers that have the same base, add their exponents):

$$12x^3\left(6x^2\right) - x - 2 = 72x^3x^2 - x - 2$$
$$= 72x^5 - x - 2$$

That's as much as you can simplify.

583. **D.** 2

Multiply the binomials, remembering that $i^2 = -1$:

$$(1+i)(1-i) = 1^2 - 1i + 1i - i^2$$
$$= 1 - i^2$$
$$= 1 - (-1)$$
$$= 2$$

584. **B.** $4x \ln(2)$

Simplify and apply the log rule that says $\log_a\left(x^b\right) = b \cdot \log_a(x)$:

$$\ln\left(4^{2x}\right) = 2x \ln(4)$$

Rewrite the 4 in parentheses in power-base form:

$$2x \ln\left(2^2\right)$$

Apply the log rule again and multiply the whole numbers:

$$2x \ln\left(2^2\right) = (2)2x \ln(2)$$
$$= 4x \ln(2)$$

585. **A.** x^5

Remove the parentheses because $(a) = a$. Apply the exponent rule, which says $a^b \cdot a^c = a^{b+c}$:

$$x^3 x^2 = x^{2+3}$$
$$= x^5$$

586.   B. 2

Multiply both sides by x, and then multiply both sides by $\frac{8}{3}$ (the multiplicative inverse of $\frac{3}{8}$):

$$\frac{3}{4} \div x = \frac{3}{8}$$

$$\frac{3}{4} = \frac{3}{8}x$$

$$\frac{3}{4}\left(\frac{8}{3}\right) = x$$

$$\frac{8}{4} = x$$

$$2 = x$$

587.   B. $\frac{a}{c} = \frac{b}{c}$

The division property of equality says that if $a = b$ and $c \neq 0$, then $\frac{a}{c} = \frac{b}{c}$.

Choice (A) can't be right, because the problem tells you that $a = b$. That means the value of a is the exact same value as b, so look at it this way: a times a divided by c would have to equal one-half of the value of c times a. The equation would look like this:

$$\frac{a \cdot a}{c} = \frac{1}{2}ca$$

Let $a = 1$ and $c = 2$ to find out what happens (remember, the question says $c \neq 0$):

$$\frac{1 \cdot 1}{2} = \frac{1}{2}(2 \cdot 1)$$

$$\frac{1}{2} \neq 1$$

You know that $\frac{1}{2}$ doesn't equal 1, so the equation doesn't work. It's impossible (and it makes Choice (C) wrong, too).

Be careful when you see ASVAB questions that deal in absolutes, such as Choice (D). Although sometimes they'll be correct, nearly every problem you encounter on the ASVAB has a solution.

588.   A. 9

Refine:

$$2x - 2 = 3(x - 1) - 8$$
$$2x - 2 = 3x - 11$$

Add 2 to both sides and subtract $3x$ from both sides to isolate the x term:

$$2x - 2 + 2 = 3x - 11 + 2$$
$$2x = 3x - 9$$
$$2x - 3x = 3x - 9 - 3x$$
$$-x = -9$$

Divide both sides by -1 (or just drop the negative sign):

$$\frac{-x}{-1} = \frac{-9}{-1}$$
$$x = 9$$

589. B. $x = 4$ and $y = 1$

When you solve a system, it's given that x is the same in both equations; so is y.

One approach is to isolate one variable in one equation by solving $x - y = 3$:

$$x - y = 3$$
$$x - y + y = 3 + y$$
$$x = 3 + y$$

Replace x in the first equation with $3 + y$:

$$(3 + y) + y = 5$$
$$3 + 2y = 5$$
$$3 + 2y - 3 = 5 - 3$$
$$2y = 2$$
$$\frac{2y}{2} = \frac{2}{2}$$
$$y = 1$$

Because $y = 1$, you can substitute 1 for y in the original equation to find x:

$$x + 1 = 5$$
$$x + 1 - 1 = 5 - 1$$
$$x = 4$$

590. B. 6

Simplify the equation:

$$1,200y + 4y = 7,224$$
$$1,204y = 7,224$$

Divide both sides by 1,204 to isolate y:

$$\frac{1,204y}{1,204} = \frac{7,224}{1,204}$$
$$y = 6$$

Instead of spending your time doing long division, try scratching off answers that most likely don't make any sense — such as Choices (C) and (D), which would result in numbers far too great for this problem — and substituting your remaining answer choices for y.

591. **B. 3**

Rewrite 64 as a power of 4 and put it in the equation:

$$\log_4 64 = x$$
$$\log_4 (4^3) = x$$

Flip the sides of the equation and apply the log power rule, which says $\log_a(x^b) = b \cdot \log_a(x)$. In other words, bring the 3 down and put it in front of the log:

$$x = \log_4 (4^3)$$
$$x = 3\log_4 (4)$$

Apply the log rule that says $\log_a(a) = 1$ — that is, replace $\log_4(4)$ with 1:

$$x = 3(1)$$
$$= 3$$

Another approach is to change the log to exponential form:

$$\log_4 64 = x$$
$$4^x = 64$$

Rewrite 64 as a power with a base of 4:

$$4^x = 4^3$$

The bases are the same, so the exponents must be equal. Therefore, $x = 3$.

592. **A.** $y = -\frac{2}{3}x + \frac{8}{3}$

First use the slope formula, which says $m = \frac{y_2 - y_1}{x_2 - x_1}$ for the points (x_1, y_1) and (x_2, y_2):

$$m = \frac{2-4}{1+2}$$
$$m = -\frac{2}{3}$$

Find the y-intercept using slope-intercept form $(y = mx + b)$. You can use either set of points:

$$y = -\frac{2}{3}x + b$$
$$2 = -\frac{2}{3}(1) + b$$
$$2 = b - \frac{2}{3}$$
$$2 + \frac{2}{3} = b - \frac{2}{3} + \frac{2}{3}$$
$$b = 2 + \frac{2}{3}$$
$$b = \frac{8}{3}$$

Fill in the values of m and b in the slope-intercept form of an equation:

$$y = -\frac{2}{3}x + \frac{8}{3}$$

593. **C.** $|a + bi| = |a + bi^2|$

Make sure you're reading the questions thoroughly; this one asks you which answer is *not* true. Choice (C) is an incorrect statement because $i \neq i^2$.

594. **D.** $6b + 5$

Multiply the factors in the expression:

$$2a - 6 + 4b - 2a + 2b + 6 + 5$$

Combine like terms:

$$(-2a + 2a) + (4b + 2b) + (-6 + 6 + 5)$$
$$= 6b + 5$$

595. **B.** $y = 50x + 32$

Use slope-intercept form, which says $y = mx + b$, where m is the slope and b represents the y-intercept, and insert the values you are given: $y = 50x + 32$.

596. **C.**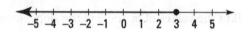

Simplify both sides and solve for x:

$$3(4x-7)\le 15$$
$$12x-21\le 15$$
$$12x-21+21\le 15+21$$
$$12x\le 36$$
$$\frac{12x}{12}\le\frac{36}{12}$$
$$x\le 3$$

As shown on a graph, $x\le 3$ looks like this:

597. **A. 30**

You already know what the variables are, so put them into the formula:

$$x=a(a-b)$$
$$=-15\big(-15-(-13)\big)$$
$$=-15(-15+13)$$
$$=-15(-2)$$
$$=30$$

598. **A. 58**

Work with the numbers you know, filling in the values of a, b, and x:

$$y=4(3)+10(7)-6(4)$$
$$=12+70-24$$
$$=58$$

599. **B. {3, 0}**

Because this problem deals with absolute value, you know that $2x+3=4x-3$ or $2x+3=-(4x-3)$. Solve the first possibility for x:

$$2x+3=4x-3$$
$$2x+2-4x=4x-3-4x$$
$$-2x+3=-3$$
$$-2x+3-3=-3-3$$
$$-2x=-6$$
$$\frac{-2x}{-2}=\frac{-6}{-2}$$
$$x=3$$

Then solve the other possibility for *x:*

$$2x + 3 = -(4x - 3)$$
$$2x + 3 = -4x + 3$$
$$2x + 3 + 4x = -4x + 3 + 4x$$
$$6x + 3 = 3$$
$$6x + 3 - 3 = 3 - 3$$
$$6x = 0$$
$$\frac{6x}{6} = \frac{0}{6}$$
$$x = 0$$

600. A. 2, 3, 5

A prime number is a whole number that's greater than 1 and can be divided evenly only by 1 or itself.

Choice (B) is wrong because the number 9 can be divided evenly by 1, 3, and 9. Choice (C) is incorrect because the 4 is divisible by 1, 2, and 4, and 6 is divisible by 1, 2, 3, and 6. Choice (D) is incorrect because 6 is divisible by 1, 2, 3, and 6, while 9 is divisible by 1, 3, and 9.

601. D. 2

Isolate *x* by subtracting 6 from both sides of the equation and dividing both sides by 2:

$$2x + 6 = 10$$
$$2x + 6 - 6 = 10 - 6$$
$$2x = 4$$
$$\frac{2x}{2} = \frac{4}{2}$$
$$x = 2$$

602. A. 10

The greatest common factor is the greatest number that divides evenly into a set of numbers. In this case, 10 is the greatest number that divides evenly into both 10 and 100.

603. D. 5

In some cases, choosing an answer and seeing whether it works is faster than working out the problem. If you want to solve this problem using algebra rather than the guess-and-check strategy, first get a *p* term by itself on one side of the equation. Then divide to find *p.*

$$5p + 14 = 29 + 2p$$
$$5p + 14 - 14 = 29 + 2p - 14$$
$$5p = 15 + 2p$$
$$5p - 2p = 15 + 2p - 2p$$
$$3p = 15$$
$$\frac{3p}{3} = \frac{15}{3}$$
$$p = 5$$

---

604. **B. −60**

Substitute 3 for x in the equation:

$$y = x^2 + 4x - x^4$$
$$= 3^2 + 4(3) - 3^4$$
$$= 9 + 12 - 81$$
$$= -60$$

---

605. **B. −1**

Isolate x:

$$5x - 6 = 3x - 8$$
$$5x - 6 + 6 = 3x - 8 + 6$$
$$5x = 3x - 2$$
$$5x - 3x = 3x - 2 - 3x$$
$$2x = -2$$
$$\frac{2x}{2} = \frac{-2}{2}$$
$$x = -1$$

---

606. **C. 2**

Combine like terms and isolate the variable:

$$-20 = -4a - 6a$$
$$-20 = -10a$$
$$\frac{-20}{-10} = \frac{-10a}{-10}$$
$$-2 = a$$

---

607. **D. All of the above**

simplify the equation and isolate x to solve:

$$(5(5x))+7=25x+7$$
$$25x+7=25x+7$$
$$25x+7-7=25x+7-7$$
$$25x=25x$$

You don't need to go any further than that. This equation is an *identity* because the numbers on both sides are identical. All real numbers are solutions.

608. A. 1

Apply the factorial rule, $n! = 1 \times 2 \times 3 \times \cdots \times n$:

$$6x = 3!$$
$$6x = 1 \cdot 2 \cdot 3$$
$$6x = 6$$
$$x = 1$$

Another way to use the factorial rule is to multiply n by the next lower number, then the next, and so on until you reach 1. In this case, n is 3: Multiply 3 by 2, and then multiply that number by 1 to reach 6.

609. C. x^{10}

Remove the parentheses and combine the terms:

$$(xxx)x^7 = xxxx^7$$

Apply the exponent rule, which says $a^b \cdot a^c = a^{b+c}$. Remember that each x that doesn't have a written exponent actually has an exponent of 1:

$$xxxx^7 = x^{1+1+1+7} = x^{10}$$

610. A. 2

First evaluate the terms with exponents:

$$6^3 = 6 \times 6 \times 6 = 216$$
$$4^3 = 4 \times 4 \times 4 = 64$$

Replace those values in the equation, and then isolate x to solve:

$$216 + 64 + x = 282$$
$$280 + x = 282$$
$$x + 280 - 280 = 282 - 280$$
$$x = 2$$

611. **B.** $10x^{\frac{3}{2}}y^2z$

Apply the exponent rule, which says $\sqrt{a \cdot b} = \sqrt{a}\sqrt{b}$, and simplify:

$$\sqrt{100x^3y^4z^2}$$
$$= \sqrt{100}\sqrt{y^4}\sqrt{x^3}\sqrt{z^2}$$
$$= 10\sqrt{y^4}\sqrt{x^3}\sqrt{z^2}$$

Remember that $\sqrt{a} = a^{\frac{1}{2}}$, and apply that rule to $\sqrt{y^4}$, $\sqrt{x^3}$, and $\sqrt{z^2}$:

$$\sqrt{y^4} = y^2$$
$$\sqrt{x^3} = x^{\frac{3}{2}}$$
$$\sqrt{z^2} = z$$

Combine the variables to find the solution:

$$10x^{\frac{3}{2}}y^2z$$

612. **C.** $\frac{3}{4}$

Solve this simple inequality the same way you'd solve an equation with only one variable:

$$8x \geq 6$$
$$\frac{8x}{8} \geq \frac{6}{8}$$
$$x \geq \frac{6}{8}$$
$$x \geq \frac{3}{4}$$

Don't forget to simplify the fraction. Sometimes not seeing the answer you've arrived at in the choices can throw you off — but you can avoid reworking the problem if you make sure you're thorough.

613. **C.** $(-3, 4)$

Solve this system by using the elimination method. Multiply each factor in the second equation by −1 and then add the equations:

$$\begin{aligned} x + y &= 1 \\ -x - 3y &= -9 \\ \hline -2y &= -8 \end{aligned}$$

The solution is $-2y = -8$, which you can solve normally:

$$-2y = -8$$
$$\frac{-2y}{-2} = \frac{-8}{-2}$$
$$y = 4$$

Put y into the simplest equation (although either equation will work) to solve for x:

$$x + 4 = 1$$
$$x + 4 - 4 = 1 - 4$$
$$x = -3$$

Express your answer as (x, y). In this case, the answer is $(-3, 4)$.

614. **B. 8**

Combine like terms before you solve:

$$x + 12 = 20$$
$$x + 12 - 12 = 20 - 12$$
$$x = 8$$

615. **A. $15x^3 + x + 7$**

Combine all the like terms:

$$6x^3 + 5x^3 + 4x^3 + x + 7$$
$$= \left(6x^3 + 5x^3 + 4x^3\right) + x + 7$$
$$= 15x^3 + x + 7$$

616. **D. $14x^{17} + 3$**

Combine like terms to simplify:

$$38x^{17} - 24x^{17} + 3$$
$$= \left(38x^{17} - 24x^{17}\right) + 3$$
$$= 14x^{17} + 3$$

617. **A. $x = \dfrac{-3 \pm \sqrt{-19}}{14}$**

Substitute the numbers for the variables:

$$7x^2 + 3x + 1 = 0$$

This equation doesn't factor, so use the quadratic formula. For an equation of the form $ax^2 + bx + c = 0$, $x = \dfrac{-b \pm \sqrt{b^2 - 4ac}}{2a}$:

$$x = \frac{-3 \pm \sqrt{3^2 - 4(7)(1)}}{2(7)}$$
$$= \frac{-3 \pm \sqrt{9 - 28}}{14}$$
$$= \frac{-3 \pm \sqrt{-19}}{14}$$

618.   **A.** $y = 4x - 2$

The slope-intercept form for an equation of a line is $y = mx + b$, with m representing slope and b representing the y-intercept. Use the values given in the problem and solve for b:

$$y = mx + b$$
$$-6 = (4)(-1) + b$$
$$-6 = -4 + b$$
$$-6 + 4 = -4 + b + 4$$
$$-2 = b$$

Because you know the value of b, you can write the equation for the line:

$$y = 4x - 2$$

It always pays to save time on the ASVAB, so you can quickly rule out Choice (B) and Choice (D) because the slopes of those lines will be 6 or –6 when the problem tells you it needs to be 4.

619.   **B.** $y = 2x$

You need to find the equation of a line without being given the slope. To find the slope, m, use the formula $m = \dfrac{y_2 - y_1}{x_2 - x_1}$, where (x_1, y_1) and (x_2, y_2) are the given points on the line:

$$m = \frac{8 - 4}{4 - 2} = \frac{4}{2} = 2$$

Put the values you know into the equation $y = mx + b$, where m represents the slope and x and y are the coordinates of one of the given points. Then, solve for b:

$$y = mx + b$$
$$4 = 2(2) + b$$
$$4 = 4 + b$$
$$4 - 4 = 4 + b - 4$$
$$0 = b$$

It doesn't matter which set of points you choose; the answer will be the same:

$$y = mx + b$$
$$8 = 2(4) + b$$
$$8 = 8 + b$$
$$8 - 8 = 8 + b - 8$$
$$0 = b$$

You know all the values you need to create an equation in the form $y = mx + b$. Fill in the values of m and b:

$$y = 2x + 0$$
$$y = 2x$$

620. D. $(x - 2)(x - 3)$

First, write out the two binomials with an x as the first term of each:

$$(x \quad)(x \quad)$$

Next, insert negative signs in each binominal, because when there's a positive sign in front of the constant term (here, 6), then the signs in the binomials have to match each other. The middle term in the given expression is negative, so the signs in the binomials must both be negative.

$$(x - \quad)(x - \quad)$$

Then think of two numbers that multiply to get 6 but add to get 5. The only two numbers that work are 3 and 2:

$$(x - 3)(x - 2)$$

Last, you can check your work by distributing (or using the FOIL method):

$$(x - 3)(x - 2) = x^2 - 3x - 2x + 6$$
$$= x^2 - 5x + 6$$

Because you have the original expression, you know you factored correctly.

621. B. $-\frac{1}{2}$

The easiest way to solve this problem is to notice the 1 on the right and recall that any number to the 0 power equals 1. Therefore, you can set the exponent on the left equal to 0 and solve for x:

$$2x + 1 = 0$$
$$2x = -1$$
$$x = -\frac{1}{2}$$

If you don't recall this property, you can take the natural log of both sides of the given equation. Then use $\log_a(x^b) = b \cdot \log_a(x)$ to bring down the exponent on the left:

$$\left(\frac{1}{2}\right)^{2x+1} = 1$$
$$(2x + 1)\ln\left(\frac{1}{2}\right) = \ln(1)$$

Because $\ln(1) = 0$, you can write

$$(2x+1)\ln\left(\tfrac{1}{2}\right) = 0$$

Distribute and move one term to the right side:

$$(2x+1)\ln\left(\tfrac{1}{2}\right) = 0$$

$$2x\ln\left(\tfrac{1}{2}\right) + \ln\left(\tfrac{1}{2}\right) = 0$$

$$2x\ln\left(\tfrac{1}{2}\right) = -\ln\left(\tfrac{1}{2}\right)$$

Divide both sides by $\ln\left(\tfrac{1}{2}\right)$ and solve for x:

$$\frac{2x\ln\left(\tfrac{1}{2}\right)}{\ln\left(\tfrac{1}{2}\right)} = \frac{-\ln\left(\tfrac{1}{2}\right)}{\ln\left(\tfrac{1}{2}\right)}$$

$$2x = -1$$

$$x = -\frac{1}{2}$$

On the ASVAB, you may encounter questions that have "Both A and B" or "Neither A nor B" options. If you aren't sure how to solve the problem, try to rule out one or more options using what you do know. It's okay to guess on the ASVAB, but don't let panic make you rush and guess on a series of questions you might be able to solve. (The CAT-ASVAB is designed to penalize you for mismanaging your time.)

622. A. $\frac{33}{26}$

Solve by subtracting 35 from each side and isolating x:

$$26x + 35 = 68$$

$$26x + 35 - 35 = 68 - 35$$

$$26x = 33$$

$$\frac{26x}{26} = \frac{33}{26}$$

$$x = \frac{33}{26}$$

You could write this as a mixed number, but it's not necessary in this case because your answer appears among your choices. Don't waste time on unnecessary steps.

623. A. $3(x - 2)$

Find a common factor between the two terms; that's a number that can be divided out of each term and moved up front. In this case, the greatest common factor is 3. Move the 3 to the front and divide $3x$ and -6 by 3:

$$3x - 6 = 3(x - 2)$$

624. **D.** $y = \dfrac{62x^3 + 42x^2}{85}$

Combine like terms, and then isolate y:

$$27x^3 + 35x^3 + 42x^2 = 85y$$
$$\left(27x^3 + 35x^3\right) + 42x^2 = 85y$$
$$62x^3 + 42x^2 = 85y$$
$$85y = 62x^3 + 42x^2$$
$$\frac{85y}{85} = \frac{62x^3 + 42x^2}{85}$$
$$y = \frac{62x^3 + 42x^2}{85}$$

625. **A.** $\pm\sqrt{\dfrac{3^y}{5}}$

Use the logarithm rules to simplify this equation:

$$y = 2\log_3 x + \log_3 5$$
$$y = \log_3 x^2 + \log_3 5$$
$$y = \log_3 5x^2$$
$$3^y = 5x^2$$

Now solve as usual:

$$5x^2 = 3^y$$
$$\frac{5}{5}x^2 = \frac{3^y}{5}$$
$$x^2 = \frac{3^y}{5}$$
$$x = \pm\sqrt{\frac{3^y}{5}}$$

If you have no idea how to solve a problem, it's okay to guess. Some of the questions on the ASVAB are extremely difficult. When you answer a hard question correctly, the system will adjust and give you another difficult question to find out whether you had a lucky guess or you're extremely talented in the math department.

626. **B.** 6

Set up your equation so you can isolate x:

$$6x + 10 = 46$$
$$6x + 10 - 10 = 46 - 10$$
$$6x = 36$$
$$\frac{6x}{6} = \frac{36}{6}$$
$$x = 6$$

627. A. 2 or $-\dfrac{16}{15}$

You can automatically rule out Choices (B) and (C), because you know that this problem has two possible solutions. Absolute value simply refers to a number's distance from 0 on the number line.

Solve this as you would any other equation by isolating x. The two equations you need to solve for are $5x + 13 = 10x + 3$ and $5x + 13 = -(10x + 3)$. Here's the first version:

$$5x + 13 = |10x + 3|$$
$$5x + 13 - 13 = 10x + 3 - 13$$
$$5x = 10x - 10$$
$$5x - 10x = 10x - 10 - 10x$$
$$-5x = -10$$
$$\frac{-5x}{-5} = \frac{-10}{-5}$$
$$x = 2$$

Solve for the other value:

$$5x + 13 = -(10x + 3)$$
$$5x + 13 + 10x = -10x - 3 + 10x$$
$$15x + 13 = -3$$
$$15x + 13 - 13 = -3 - 13$$
$$15x = -16$$
$$\frac{15x}{15} = \frac{-16}{15}$$
$$x = -\frac{16}{15}$$

628. D. $x < 3$

Solve each inequality separately. Here's the first one:

$$2x - 4 < 10$$
$$2x - 4 + 4 < 10 + 4$$
$$2x < 14$$
$$\frac{2x}{2} < \frac{14}{2}$$
$$x < 7$$

And here's the second:

$$x + 17 < 20$$
$$x + 17 - 17 < 20 - 17$$
$$x < 3$$

Therefore, $x < 3$ and $x < 7$. Combine the ranges to arrive at the answer, which is $x < 3$.

629. B. $[3, +\infty)$

The square bracket indicates that the value of 3 is closed (you do include it in your interval). You always use a parenthesis with the infinity symbol, because the answer can never equal infinity.

630. A. 7

Combine like terms, and then isolate b:

$$3b + b = 28$$
$$4b = 28$$
$$\frac{4b}{4} = \frac{28}{4}$$
$$b = 7$$

631. D. 5

Isolate x:

$$5x = 25$$
$$\frac{5x}{5} = \frac{25}{5}$$
$$x = 5$$

632. B. 36

First solve for x:

$$4x - 2 = 3x + 4$$
$$4x - 2 + 2 = 3x + 4 + 2$$
$$4x = 3x + 6$$
$$4x - 3x = 3x + 6 - 3x$$
$$x = 6$$

Now that you know the value of x, find $6x$:

$$6(6) = 36$$

Don't let simple things trip you up on the test; make sure you read the whole question before settling on an answer.

633. B. $x = y$

Isolate the variable terms. Get all the x terms on one side of the equation and all the y terms on the other:

$$48x + 27y = 75y$$
$$48x + 27y = 75y - 27y$$
$$48x = 48y$$
$$x = y$$

634. D. $20a^2 + b$

The a terms are the same, and the problem involves only addition, so combine like terms:

$$18a^2 + 2a^2 + b = 20a^2 + b$$

635. C. 3

Isolate x:

$$48 + \frac{1}{3}x = 49$$
$$48 + \frac{1}{3}x - 48 = 49 - 48$$
$$\frac{1}{3}x = 1$$
$$3\left(\frac{1}{3}x\right) = 3(1)$$
$$x = 3$$

If you can solve a problem just by looking at it, you don't have to work through the math.

636. A. 2

Isolate x:

$$2(5x + 1) = 11x$$
$$10x + 2 = 11x$$
$$10x + 2 - 11x = 11x - 11x$$
$$-x + 2 = 0$$
$$-x + 2 - 2 = 0 - 2$$
$$-x = -2$$
$$\frac{-x}{-1} = \frac{-2}{-1}$$
$$x = 2$$

637. B. 3

Combine like terms and isolate c:

$$0.5c + 12c = 37.5$$
$$12.5c = 37.5$$
$$\frac{12.5c}{12.5} = \frac{37.5}{12.5}$$
$$c = 3$$

638. C. $3x\sqrt{5}$

Simplify:

$$\sqrt{45x^2} = \sqrt{5\left(3^2\right)x^2}$$
$$= 3x\sqrt{5}$$

639. C. $3x^5$

A *coefficient* is a number or symbol multiplied by a variable; the *base* (sometimes also called a *radix*) is a digit or letters that represent numbers. An *exponent* tells you how many times to multiply the number (the base) by itself.

640. A. 3

Substitute 2 for b in the equation, and then solve:

$$8a + 9b = ab + 36$$
$$8a + 9(2) = 2a + 36$$
$$8a + 18 - 18 = 2a + 36 - 18$$
$$8a = 2a + 18$$
$$8a - 2a = 2a + 18 - 2a$$
$$6a = 18$$
$$\frac{6a}{6} = \frac{18}{6}$$
$$a = 3$$

641.

C. $\pm i\sqrt{\frac{21}{5}}$

Use inverse operations on both sides of the equation to solve:

$$5x^2 + 7 = -35 - 5x^2$$
$$10x^2 = -42$$
$$\frac{10x^2}{10} = \frac{-42}{10}$$
$$x^2 = \frac{-42}{10}$$
$$x^2 = \frac{-21}{5}$$
$$x = \pm\sqrt{\frac{-21}{5}}$$
$$x = \pm i\sqrt{\frac{21}{5}}$$

642.

B. $3x^2 - 11x - 4 = 0$

A quadratic equation has an x^2 term. When the equation is in standard form, both sides equal 0. Put all the terms on the same side, set the other side equal to 0, and combine like terms:

$$2x^2 - 8x - 4 = 3x - x^2$$
$$2x^2 - 8x - 4 - \left(3x - x^2\right) = 3x - x^2 - \left(3x - x^2\right)$$
$$3x^2 - 11x - 4 = 0$$

643.

D. $x = 3, x = 5$

Factoring is the simplest way to solve this quadratic equation, so factor $x^2 - 8x + 15 = 0$ to $(x-3)(x-5) = 0$, because at least one factor must always be equal to zero. Solve each set of terms:

$$x - 3 = 0 \quad \text{or} \quad x - 5 = 0$$
$$x - 3 + 3 = 0 + 3 \quad\quad x - 5 + 5 = 0 + 5$$
$$x = 3 \quad\quad\quad\quad x = 5$$

The solutions are $x = 3$ and $x = 5$.

644.

B. $x = -6, x = 9$

Whether you solve this (or any) quadratic equation by factoring, completing the square, or using the quadratic formula, you're going to get the same answers. That means when you encounter a question that tells you how to solve a problem, you don't necessarily have to do it. You should do what's easiest for you.

To solve for x by factoring, work out the problem this way:

$$3x^2 - 9x - 162 = 0$$
$$3\left(x^2 - 3x - 54\right) = 0$$
$$3(x+6)(x-9) = 0$$

Set each factor equal to 0 and solve:

$$
\begin{array}{ll}
x + 6 = 0 \quad \text{or} & x - 9 = 0 \\
x + 6 - 6 = 0 - 6 & x - 9 + 9 = 0 + 9 \\
\quad\quad x = -6 & \quad\quad x = 9
\end{array}
$$

The solutions are $x = -6$ and $x = 9$.

645. **A. $x = 0$, $x = 3$**

A quadratic equation's standard form is $ax^2 + bx + c = 0$. Although this equation shows only two terms, x^2 and $-3x$, it's still quadratic because there's an x^2 term (you can assume $c = 0$).

Solve this quadratic equation by factoring:

$$x^2 - 3x = 0$$
$$x(x - 3) = 0$$

Set each factor equal to 0; then solve:

$$
\begin{array}{ll}
x = 0 \quad \text{or} & x - 3 = 0 \\
& x - 3 + 3 = 0 + 3 \\
& \quad\quad x = 3
\end{array}
$$

The solutions are $x = 0$ and $x = 3$.

646. **A. $x = \dfrac{-3 + \sqrt{17}}{2}$, $x = \dfrac{-3 - \sqrt{17}}{2}$**

Subtract $-3x + 2$ from both sides of the equation:

$$x^2 - (-3x + 2) = -3x + 2 - (-3x + 2)$$
$$x^2 + 3x - 2 = 0$$

Using the quadratic equation formula, which tells you that the solutions are $x = \dfrac{-b \pm \sqrt{b^2 - 4ac}}{2a}$, fill in what you know:

$$x = \frac{-3 + \sqrt{3^2 - 4(1)(-2)}}{2(1)}$$

$$x = \frac{-3 + \sqrt{17}}{2} \quad \text{or} \quad x = \frac{-3 - \sqrt{17}}{2}$$

647. **D.** $x = 3, x = 4$

This quadratic equation is already factored for you. Because it's already factored, use the zero factor principle to set the factors equal to 0:

$$x - 3 = 0 \quad \text{or} \quad x - 4 = 0$$

Solve the equations as you normally would to determine that $x = 3$ or $x = 4$.

648. **A.** $x = -2, x = -3$

Solve by factoring:

$$x^2 + 5x + 6 = 0$$
$$(x + 2)(x + 3) = 0$$

Use the zero factor principle to solve each set of terms. Set each factor equal to 0 and solve for x:

$$
\begin{array}{ll}
x + 2 = 0 \quad \text{or} & x + 3 = 0 \\
x + 2 - 2 = 0 - 2 & x + 3 - 3 = 0 - 3 \\
x = -2 & x = -3
\end{array}
$$

649. **C.** $x = 1, x = \dfrac{1}{2}$

Factor $2x^2 - 3x + 1$:

$$2x^2 - 3x + 1 = 0$$
$$(x - 1)(2x - 1) = 0$$

Use the zero factor principle on the terms within the parentheses. Set each factor equal to 0 and solve for x:

$$
\begin{array}{ll}
x - 1 = 0 \quad \text{or} & 2x - 1 = 0 \\
x - 1 + 1 = 0 + 1 & 2x - 1 + 1 = 0 + 1 \\
x = 1 & 2x = 1 \\
& \dfrac{2x}{2} = \dfrac{1}{2} \\
& x = \dfrac{1}{2}
\end{array}
$$

The solutions are $x = 1$ and $x = \dfrac{1}{2}$.

650. **D.** $x = 4, x = \dfrac{3}{4}$

You can solve this problem by factoring, completing the square, or using the quadratic formula. The quadratic formula for equations in the form of $ax^2 + bx + c = 0$ looks like this:

$$x = \frac{-b \pm \sqrt{b^2 - 4ac}}{2a}$$

The variables you need are already in the problem: $a = 4$, $b = -19$, and $c = 12$. Enter these values into the quadratic formula and solve for x:

$$x = \frac{-(-19) \pm \sqrt{(-19)^2 - 4(4)(12)}}{2(4)}$$

$$x = \frac{19 \pm \sqrt{361 - 192}}{8}$$

$$x = \frac{19 \pm \sqrt{169}}{8}$$

$$x = \frac{19 \pm 13}{8}$$

Now find both values of x, adding 13 in one case and subtracting 13 in the other:

$$x = \frac{19 + 13}{8} \quad \text{or} \quad x = \frac{19 - 13}{8}$$

$$x = \frac{32}{8} \qquad\qquad x = \frac{6}{8}$$

$$x = 4 \qquad\qquad x = \frac{3}{4}$$

651. **B. right angle.**

The box at the intersection denotes that you're dealing with a right angle. Parallel lines run in the same direction at the same angles, but they never intersect. Transversal lines are those that pass through two lines in the same plane at two distinct points. Complementary angles are two angles that have a sum of 90°.

652. **B. 36 cm**

Use the Pythagorean theorem, which says $a^2 + b^2 = c^2$, to find the length of the third side:

$$c^2 = 9^2 + 12^2$$

$$c^2 = 81 + 144$$

$$c^2 = 225$$

$$\sqrt{c^2} = \sqrt{225}$$

$$c = 15$$

The length of side c is 15 centimeters, so add that to the other two sides to find the perimeter:

$$9 + 12 + 15 = 36$$

The triangle's perimeter is 36 centimeters.

653. D. ∠*ADB*, ∠*CDB*

Complementary angles add up to 90°, so two angles that meet at a corner of a rectangle are complementary. Line *DB*, which you can express as $\overrightarrow{DB}$, divides the rectangle; you know that the angles that form ∠*B* are complementary, as are the angles that form ∠*D*.

To express which angles are complementary, write the points with the vertex (the actual location of the angle) in the middle: ∠*ADB* and ∠*CDB* are one set of complementary angles (and this pair of angles is listed in the choices). Another pair of complementary angles, ∠*ABD* and ∠*CBD*, isn't listed.

654. D. 56.25 m²

Use the formula to find the area of a trapezoid to solve:

$$A = \frac{1}{2}h(b_1 + b_2)$$
$$= \frac{1}{2}(7.5)(9+6)$$
$$= (3.75)(15)$$
$$= 56.25$$

655. C. complementary

You're dealing with a right angle, which is always 90°. Two angles that add up to 90° must be complementary.

656. D. equilateral

A polygon in which all the sides are the same length is equilateral.

657. A. 72 sq. ft

The formula for the area of a rectangle is $A = lw$, with A representing area, l representing length, and w representing width. Remember that area is measured in square feet.

$$A = lw$$
$$A = 12 \times 6$$
$$A = 72 \text{ sq. ft}$$

658. D. $V = s^3$

The formula for the volume of a cube is $V = s^3$, where s is the length of a side or edge. If you aren't sure about the answer to a geometry question on the ASVAB, rule out obvious no-go answers (that's a little more military terminology for you).

In this case, $V = \left(\frac{4}{3}\right)\pi r^3$ will find you the volume of a sphere, $SA = 6s^2$ leads you to the surface area of a cube, and $A = \pi r^2$ is the formula for the area of a circle. If you knew even one of those, you'd increase your chances of getting the answer right on the real test.

659. C. $a^2 + b^2 = c^2$

The Pythagorean theorem says that $a^2 + b^2 = c^2$, where a and b are legs of a right triangle and c is the hypotenuse. Typically, you use this theorem to find an unknown length of the side of a right triangle.

660. B. 12 cm

Use the Pythagorean theorem, which says $a^2 + b^2 = c^2$, where a and b are legs of a right triangle and c is the hypotenuse:

$$a^2 + b^2 = c^2$$
$$9^2 + b^2 = 15^2$$
$$81 + b^2 = 225$$
$$81 + b^2 - 81 = 225 - 81$$
$$b^2 = 144$$
$$b = \sqrt{144}$$
$$b = 12$$

661. D. 50°

L1 and L2 are parallel and are cut by the transversal L3. Therefore, all the large angles you see are congruent to each other, and all the small angles you see are congruent to each other.

Angles that form a straight line form a linear pair and must add up to 180° (they're supplementary). One large angle is 130°. That means its supplement, which corresponds to angle x, must be 50°.

662. D. 50.6 ft²

To find the area of a sector of a circle, use the formula $A = \frac{n}{360}\pi r^2$, with n representing the central angle. You're essentially multiplying the area of the full circle $\left(\pi r^2\right)$ by the fraction of the circle covered by the sector $\left(\frac{n°}{360°}\right)$:

$$A = \frac{n}{360}\pi r^2$$
$$= \frac{58}{360}\pi(10)^2$$

Multiply and then simplify the fraction:

$$A = \frac{10^2 \cdot 58\pi}{360}$$

$$= \frac{10^2 \cdot 29\pi}{180}$$

$$= \frac{10\cancel{0} \cdot 29\pi}{18\cancel{0}}$$

$$= \frac{290\pi}{18}$$

$$= \frac{145\pi}{9}$$

Pi is approximately 3.14, so fill in that value and solve:

$$A = \frac{145\pi}{9}$$

$$\approx \frac{145(3.14)}{9}$$

$$= \frac{455.3}{9}$$

$$= 50.6$$

663.   B. 25 sq. in.

The formula for finding the area of a square is $A = s^2$, with A representing area and s representing the length of a side. In a square, all the sides are the same length — and although this figure is missing some labels (and one is even labeled with a variable), the problem tells you it's a square.

In this case, the area is

$$A = s^2$$

$$= 5^2$$

$$= 5 \times 5$$

$$= 25$$

664.   C. 26°

A straight line (which you know you have because you're looking at a right triangle) has a straight angle of 180°. Therefore, you know that $x + 154 = 180$. Solve for x:

$$x + 154 = 180$$

$$x + 154 - 154 = 180 - 154$$

$$x = 26$$

665. D. 130°

Angles around a point always add up to 360°. The diagram shows the measurements of all the angles except b, so you can solve this problem in a couple of ways. You can use algebra:

$$b + 68 + 80 + 82 = 360$$
$$b + 230 = 360$$
$$b + 230 - 230 = 360 - 230$$
$$b = 130$$

You can also subtract the angles you know from 360 to find what's left over, which is b:

$$360 - 68 - 80 - 82 = 130$$

666. A. 16 ft

The formula for perimeter of a square is $P = 4s$, with P representing perimeter and s representing the length of a side. In this case,

$$P = 4s = 4(4) = 16$$

667. D. 96 square yards

The formula to find the surface area of a prism is $SA = 2B + Ph$, where B represents the area of the base, P represents the perimeter of the base, and h represents the height of the prism.

First find the area of the triangular base using $A = \frac{1}{2}bh$, where b represents the triangle's base and h represents its height:

$$A = \frac{1}{2}(6)8$$
$$= \frac{1}{2}(48)$$
$$= 24$$

Find its perimeter by adding the length of each leg:

$$6 + 8 + 10 = 24$$

The base's area is 24 square yards, the base's perimeter is 24 yards, and the prism's height is 2 yards, so plug that information into the formula for the surface area of a prism:

$$SA = 2(24) + 24(2)$$
$$SA = 48 + 48$$
$$SA = 96$$

The surface area of the prism is 96 square yards.

668. B. 16°

The sum of all angles in a triangle is 180°, so fill in the values you know using $A + B + C = 180°$ and let x represent the angle you don't know (note that angle A is a right angle, so it's 90°):

$$A = 90°$$
$$B = 74°$$
$$C = x$$

$$90 + 74 + x = 180$$
$$164 + x = 180$$
$$x + 164 - 164 = 180 - 164$$
$$x = 16$$

669. A. It has only one dimension.

A line has only one dimension, and that's length. It has no width, and it continues forever in two directions (it's infinite). Lines don't stop at points, or they become line segments; they carry on forever (much like a ruck march during basic training seems to do).

670. A. 1,050 ft²

The formula for finding the area of a rectangle is $A = lw$, with l representing length and w representing width. You have two rectangles here, so find the area of each and add them together.

Rectangle 1:

$$27 \times 30 = 810$$

Rectangle 2:

$$16 \times 15 = 240$$

The area of Rectangle 1 plus the area of Rectangle 2 equals 1,050 square feet.

Area is measured in square feet, so the answer is 1,050 square feet; you can also express it as 1,050 sq. ft and 1,050 ft².

671. **D. 146 ft**

To find the perimeter, find the sum of the length of each side:

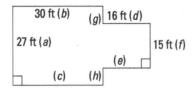

You know that side *a* is 27 feet, side *b* is 30 feet (and so is side *c*), sides *d* and *e* are each 16 feet, and side *f* is 15 feet. Sides *g* and *h* are unknown, but because side *a* is 27 feet and side *f* is 15 feet, you can deduce that, together, they measure 12 feet.

Add everything you know:

$$27 + 30 + 30 + 12 + 16 + 16 + 15 = 146$$

Another approach is to imagine shifting the lines to make a rectangle. In this figure, the rectangle's width is 27 feet, and its length is $30 + 16 = 46$ feet:

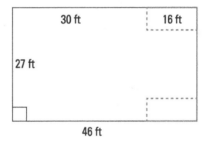

Add the lengths of each side to find the perimeter, and you get the same answer:

$$27 + 46 + 27 + 46 = 146$$

672. **C. 1,050 mm²**

Before you can determine the area of this polygon, you need to know its perimeter. That's because the formula for the area of a regular polygon is $A = \frac{1}{2}ap$, with *a* representing the apothem and *p* representing the perimeter. Because all sides are equal, you can simply add the lengths of the sides or multiply the length by the number of sides to get the perimeter:

$$p = 35 \times 6 = 210$$

Now use what you know in the area formula:

$$A = \frac{1}{2}ap$$
$$= \frac{1}{2}(10)(210)$$
$$= \frac{1}{2}(2,100)$$
$$= 1,050$$

673. **A. 10**

The triangle has two congruent sides (that's what the hash marks represent). That means the two sides are equal. Set their values equal to each other and solve for x:

$$3x - 5 = 2x + 5$$
$$3x - 5 + 5 = 2x + 5 + 5$$
$$3x - 2x = 2x + 10 - 2x$$
$$x = 10$$

674. **B. 60°**

In a triangle, the three interior angles always add up to 180°. Because the figure shows you that two of the angles measure 60°, the remaining angle must also equal 60° so the angles add up to 180°.

This problem is even simpler than that, though. The triangle has three congruent sides, which means the corresponding angles are congruent as well.

675. **A. 35°**

Two of the angles are included in the figure. Let x represent the measure of angle C:

$$\angle A = 55°$$
$$\angle B = 90°$$
$$\angle C = x$$

All the angles inside a triangle must add up to 180°, so write an equation and solve it:

$$A + B + C = 180$$
$$55 + 90 + x = 180$$
$$145 + x - 145 = 180 - 145$$
$$x = 35$$

676. **B. $x = 35°$, $y = 95°$, $z = 50°$**

Supplementary angles together make a straight angle with a measurement of 180°. Find the missing measurements:

$$x + 145 = 180 \qquad\qquad y + 85 = 180$$
$$x + 145 - 145 = 180 - 145 \qquad y + 85 - 85 = 180 - 85$$
$$x = 35 \qquad\qquad\qquad y = 95$$

The interior angles of a triangle always equal 180°, so find z next using $x = 35°$ and $y = 95°$:

$$35 + 95 + z = 180$$
$$130 + z = 180$$
$$z + 130 - 130 = 180 - 130$$
$$z = 50$$

677.   **A. 72°**

A straight line or segment has a straight angle — one that equals 180°. That means the sum of angle y and the angles labeled in the figure must equal 180°:

$$45 + 39 + y + 24 = 180$$
$$y + 108 = 180$$
$$y + 108 - 108 = 180 - 108$$
$$y = 72$$

678.   **A. ∠BAF**

Write the label using the three letters on the shape that define the angle, with the letter of the vertex (where the angle actually is) in the middle.

You could also label this angle ∠FAB or ∠A if you wanted to, but they aren't answer choices.

679.   **C. Acute**

The angle is *acute* because it measures less than 90°. Remember:

- **Acute angles** measure less than 90°.
- **Right angles** measure exactly 90°.
- **Obtuse angles** measure more than 90° but less than 180°.
- **Straight angles** measure exactly 180°.

680.   **D. 75 ft**

The formula for the perimeter of a rectangle is $P = 2l + 2w$ (or $P = 2(l + w)$), with P representing perimeter, l representing length, and w representing width. In this case:

$$P = 2l + 2w$$
$$= 2(12.5) + 2(25)$$
$$= 25 + 50$$
$$= 75$$

681. **A. 70°**

The interior angles of a triangle always add up to 180°, so you know that the missing angle in $\triangle ADB$ must be x in $59 + 73 + x = 180$:

$$59 + 73 + x = 180$$
$$x + 132 = 180$$
$$x + 132 - 132 = 180 - 132$$
$$x = 48$$

The missing angle, x, is 48°. Because the angles are marked as congruent (that's what the hash mark is for at angle x), you know that $\angle JDR$ is 48°. Also, the angles are vertical angles, which are always congruent.

Run through the math again now that you know two angles in $\triangle DRJ$, remembering that all the angles in a triangle add up to 180°:

$$62 + 48 + r = 180$$
$$110 + r = 180$$
$$r + 110 - 110 = 180 - 110$$
$$r = 70$$

682. **B. 230°**

The reflex angle (the one that measures more than 180°) must combine with the obtuse angle in this figure to make a full circle, which measures 360°. Let x represent the measure of the angle you don't know. Then you can express the problem as an equation:

$$x + 130 = 360$$
$$x + 130 - 130 = 360 - 130$$
$$x = 230$$

683. **C. $\angle A$, $\angle C$**

The interior angles of a triangle always add up to 180°, and two angles that add up to 90° are complementary. The figure depicts a right triangle, so you know that the remaining two angles (aside from the right angle, which is marked) must add up to 90°. Therefore, angles A and C are complementary.

684. **A. 165 sq. in.**

The formula to find the area of a triangle is $A = \frac{1}{2}bh$, with b representing the length of the base and h representing the height. Given what you know, replace the variables and solve:

$$A = \frac{1}{2}bh$$
$$= \frac{1}{2}(22)(15)$$
$$= 11(15)$$
$$= 165$$

685. **B. 324 m²**

Don't get tangled up in extra information on the ASVAB. You don't need to know the lengths of the sides to find the answer to this problem; you only need the base and the height, which are 36 meters and 18 meters, respectively.

The formula for the area of a triangle is $A = \frac{1}{2}bh$ or $A = \frac{bh}{2}$, so use what you know to solve the problem:

$$A = \frac{1}{2}bh$$
$$= \frac{1}{2}(36)(18)$$
$$= 18(18)$$
$$= 324$$

686. **D.** $r = \frac{C}{2\pi}$

The formula to solve for the radius of a circle is $r = \frac{C}{2\pi}$, with C representing the circle's circumference (the distance around the outside of a circle). If you don't have this formula memorized, you can start with the circumference formula and solve for r:

$$C = 2\pi r$$
$$\frac{C}{2\pi} = \frac{2\pi r}{2\pi}$$
$$\frac{C}{2\pi} = r$$

687. **A. 28.26 in.²**

The formula for the area of a circle is $A = \pi r^2$, and you know that the circle's radius is 3 inches. Work out the solution, noting that pi is approximately 3.14:

$$A = \pi r^2$$
$$\approx 3.14(3^2)$$
$$= 3.14(9)$$
$$= 28.26$$

688.　B. $\sqrt{8}$

The formula for the area of a circle is $A = \pi r^2$, so create your own equation using the information you already have:

$$\pi r^2 = 8\pi$$
$$\frac{\pi r^2}{\pi} = \frac{8\pi}{\pi}$$
$$r^2 = 8$$
$$r = \sqrt{8}$$

689.　A. $P = 2(l + w)$

In the formula $P = 2(l + w)$, l represents length and w represents width. You can also express the formula as $P = 2l + 2w$.

The other answer choices refer to different shapes:

- $P = s_1 + s_2 + s_3$ is the formula for finding the perimeter of a triangle.

- $P = 2b + 2s$ is the formula for finding the perimeter of a parallelogram.

- $P = s_1 + s_2 + s_3 + s_4$ is the formula for the perimeter of a trapezoid.

690.　B. 78.5 in.²

The formula to find the area of a circle is $A = \pi r^2$. The radius is half the diameter. According to the figure, the diameter is 10 inches; half of that is 5 inches. Pi is approximately equal to 3.14. Put the values you know into the formula:

$$A = \pi r^2$$
$$\approx 3.14\left(5^2\right)$$
$$= 3.14(25)$$
$$= 78.5$$

691.　A. 79 cm

The formula to solve for diameter is $d = 2r$. To find the radius when you know the diameter, divide the diameter by 2:

$$\frac{158}{2} = 79$$

692. D. 62.8 meters

To find the circumference of a circle, you need to know the radius. In this instance, it's 10 meters.

The formula for circumference is $C = 2\pi r$, with r representing the radius. Pi is approximately equal to 3.14. Put what you know into the formula and solve:

$$C = 2\pi r$$
$$= 2\pi(10)$$
$$= 20\pi$$
$$\approx 20(3.14)$$
$$= 62.8$$

693. B. 49 cm

To find the perimeter of an irregular shape (this is actually three rectangles), add the lengths of all its sides:

$$P = 7 + 4 + 3 + 9.5 + 8 + 5.5 + 4 + 8$$
$$= 49$$

694. C. 210π

First, notice that the answer choices are in terms of pi. That means you won't have to multiply by 3.14.

The formula to find the circumference of a circle is $C = 2\pi r$. Because you know the diameter is 210 feet, the radius is 105 feet. Use what you know in the formula:

$$C = 2\pi r$$
$$= 2\pi(105)$$
$$= (2 \cdot 105)\pi$$
$$= 210\pi$$

You can solve the problem more quickly using an alternate formula for the circumference, $C = \pi d$, where d is the diameter. Mentally insert $d = 210$ in for d, and you get $C = 210\pi$.

695.

A. $r = \sqrt{\dfrac{210}{\pi}}$

The answers are in terms of pi, so you won't need to divide by 3.14.

Use the formula for area, $A = \pi r^2$, to determine the radius:

$$A = \pi r^2$$
$$210 = \pi r^2$$
$$\pi r^2 = 210$$
$$\frac{\pi r^2}{\pi} = \frac{210}{\pi}$$
$$r^2 = \frac{210}{\pi}$$

Remember that for $r^2 = f(a)$, the solutions are $r = \sqrt{f(a)}$ and $-\sqrt{f(a)}$.

Because you can't have a negative radius, disregard $-\sqrt{f(a)}$. That means $r = \sqrt{\dfrac{210}{\pi}}$.

696.

A. 17.4 m

All the sides in the hexagon are equal in length, so to find the perimeter, multiply the length of one side by 6 (the number of sides in a hexagon). The formula and the solution look like this:

$$P = 6s$$
$$= 6(2.9)$$
$$= 17.4$$

697.

C. 27 cubic inches

The formula for volume in a cube is $V = s^3$ with s representing the length of an edge. You know that the length of s is 3 inches. Put what you know into the formula:

$$V = 3^3$$
$$= (3)(3)(3)$$
$$= 27$$

698.

D. 240 cm²

Find the area of a parallelogram by using $A = bh$, with b representing the base and h representing the height:

$$A = bh$$
$$= 15(16)$$
$$= 240$$

699. **A. 3,375 cubic feet**

Use the cube volume formula, which is $V = s^3$, to solve this problem:

$$V = s^3$$
$$= (15)(15)(15)$$
$$= 3,375$$

700. **B. 500 cm³**

The formula for the volume of a pyramid is $V = \frac{1}{3}Bh$, where B is the area of the pyramid's base and h is the pyramid's height. You're dealing with a right square pyramid, so the base is a square. Because a square has an area of $A = s^2$ (where s is the length of one side of the base), you can write the formula as $V = \frac{1}{3}s^2h$. Replace the variables with the numbers you know:

$$V = \frac{1}{3}s^2h$$
$$= \frac{1}{3}(10^2)(15)$$
$$= 100(5)$$
$$= 500$$

701. **A. 960 mm³**

The formula for volume of a right rectangular prism is $V = lwh$, with l representing length, w representing width, and h representing height:

$$V = lwh$$
$$= 8 \cdot 6 \cdot 20$$
$$= 960$$

702. **B. Scalene**

A triangle with no equal angles and no equal sides is a scalene triangle.

703. **C. 360°.**

The interior angles of a quadrilateral always add up to 360°, whether you're dealing with a square, a rhombus, a rectangle, a trapezoid, or another quadrilateral.

704. B. 216 cubic feet

To find the volume of a cube, use the formula $V = s^3$, with s representing the length of a side:

$$V = s^3$$
$$= 6^3$$
$$= 216$$

Note that you can express units of volume with an exponent or by using the term *cubic*. In this case, you can use 216 ft³ or 216 cubic feet.

705. B. 7,850 cm³

This multi-step problem gives you all the information you need. Because the formula to find the volume of a cylinder is $V = Bh$, with B representing the area of the base and h representing height, you need to find the area of the base of the cylinder to solve it. However, because the base is a circle and you know the radius is 10 cm, you can find the base area using $A = \pi r^2$ (note that pi is approximately 3.14):

$$A = \pi r^2$$
$$\approx 3.14\left(10^2\right)$$
$$= 3.14(100)$$
$$= 314$$

Now that you know the area of the base, use the formula for the volume of a cylinder:

$$V = Bh$$
$$= 314(25)$$
$$= 7,850$$

706. C. $C = 2\pi r$

To find the circumference of (the distance around) a circle, use the formula $C = 2\pi r$, with r representing the circle's radius. *Note:* Because the diameter is twice the radius, another version of the formula is $C = \pi d$.

707. A. 18.84 meters

The formula for the circumference of a circle is $C = 2\pi r$. The radius in the figure is 3 meters, so plug in what you know. You can use 3.14 as an approximation of pi:

$$C = 2\pi r$$
$$= 2\pi(3)$$
$$= 6\pi$$
$$\approx 6(3.14)$$
$$= 18.84$$

708. **A. 4,069.44 ft³**

The formula for the volume of a right circular cone is $V = \frac{1}{3}Bh$. First replace the B with the formula for the area of circle because a cone has a circle for its base:

$$V = \frac{1}{3}\pi r^2 h$$

Next, replace the variables with the measurements in the diagram:

$$V = \frac{1}{3}\pi r^2 h$$
$$= \frac{1}{3}\pi(12)^2(27)$$
$$= \pi(144)(9)$$
$$= 1,296\pi$$
$$\approx 1,296(3.14)$$
$$= 4,069.44$$

709. **D. 3,750 cubic inches**

To find the volume of a pyramid, you need to know the height and the area of the base. Use the values on the diagram to find the area of the base:

$$A = s^2$$
$$= 25^2$$
$$= 625$$

Now that you have the area of the base, use the formula for the volume of a square pyramid, which is $V = \frac{Bh}{3}$, with B representing the area of the base and h representing the height of the pyramid:

$$V = \frac{Bh}{3}$$
$$= \frac{625 \cdot 18}{3}$$
$$= \frac{11,250}{3}$$
$$= 3,750$$

710. **B. 24 units**

To find the diameter of this circle, work backward. The formula to find the area of a circle is $A = \pi r^2$, so put the information you know in the equation:

$$144\pi = \pi r^2$$

Cancel out what you can and then solve:

$$144\cancel{\pi} = \cancel{\pi}r^2$$
$$144 = r^2$$
$$\sqrt{144} = r$$
$$r = 12$$

You know the radius, and the diameter is two times the radius:

$$d = 2 \cdot 12 = 24$$

711.   **A.** $\dfrac{81\sqrt{3}}{2}$ **cm**^{2}

The formula for the area of a triangle is $A = \dfrac{bh}{2}$. The problem gives you only one leg and the hypotenuse, though, so you need to use the Pythagorean theorem $\left(a^2 + b^2 = c^2\right)$ to figure out how long the base is. If it helps, look at it this way:

$$\text{hypotenuse}^2 = \text{base}^2 + \text{height}^2$$
$$\text{base}^2 = \text{hypotenuse}^2 - \text{height}^2$$
$$\text{base} = \sqrt{\text{hypotenuse}^2 - \text{height}^2}$$

Substitute the values you know to determine the base:

$$\text{base} = \sqrt{18^2 - 9^2}$$
$$= \sqrt{243}$$
$$= 9\sqrt{3}$$

Now you can find the area:

$$A = \frac{9 \cdot 9\sqrt{3}}{2}$$
$$= \frac{81\sqrt{3}}{2}$$

712.   **B. Quadrilateral**

A *quadrilateral* is a four-sided polygon with four angles. Some of the most common quadrilaterals are parallelograms, rectangles, squares, and trapezoids.

713.   **A. Lines** *a* **and** *c*

Parallel lines are lines in a plane that don't meet; they never intersect or touch each other.

714. **D. 16 in.²**

Attention to detail is important on the ASVAB. Notice that the question asks only for the area of the shaded region, which is a rectangle. You can immediately discount the answer choices that involve pi and cube roots, because they definitely don't have anything to do with the area of a rectangle.

You can find the area with $A = lw$, where w represents width and l represents length:

$$A = lw$$
$$= 8 \cdot 2$$
$$= 16$$

715. **B. 1,000 cm²**

The formula to find the area of a parallelogram is $A = bh$, with b representing the length of the base and h representing the height. Replace the variables with what you know:

$$A = bh$$
$$= 50 \cdot 20$$
$$= 1,000$$

716. **B. 45°**

In a parallelogram, opposite angles are congruent. Angle d is 45° because it's opposite the 45° angle in the diagram. Angle c is 115° because it's opposite the 115° angle in the diagram.

717. **D. reflex angle.**

A *reflex angle* is one that's greater than 180°. An *acute angle* is one that's less than 90°, a *straight angle* is a straight line that measures exactly 180°, and an *obtuse angle* is one that's greater than 90° but less than 180°.

718. **B. (2,4), (7,7)**

When you're reading a graph, the x-coordinate is always expressed first in an ordered pair (x, y). The x-coordinate is where the point lies on the x-axis, and the y-coordinate is where the point lies on the y-axis.

719. A. 90°

There are 360° in a circle, so this becomes an algebra problem as soon as you identify the angle you need to calculate.

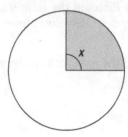

$$x = 0.25(360) = 90$$

720. D. 22.5 in.²

The formula for finding the area of a kite is $A = \frac{pq}{2}$, with p representing the shortest diagonal of the kite and q representing the longest diagonal. Remember, though, that they're interchangeable. Input the values you know:

$$A = \frac{pq}{2}$$
$$= \frac{4.5 \cdot 10}{2}$$
$$= \frac{45}{2}$$
$$= 22.5$$

721. C. 43.2°

The angles in a circle add up to 360°, so when you identify the percent of the region you need to work with, you can use algebra to find the angle. Here, you need 12% of 360°:

$$x = 0.12(360) = 43.2$$

722. A. 67 m

It doesn't matter what irregular shape you're dealing with when you find perimeter. You simply add the lengths of the sides:

$$P = 20 + 7 + 10 + 9 + 21 = 67$$

723. D. 78 m²

One approach is to divide the figure into three rectangles and then add the areas together to find the total area.

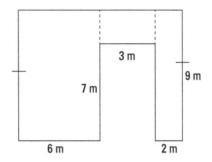

Use the formula $A = lw$, with l representing length and w representing width, to find the area of each rectangle. The first rectangle is 6 m by 9 m:

$$A = 6(9) = 54$$

The second rectangle is 3 m by 2 m (which is 9 m – 7 m):

$$A = 3(2) = 6$$

And the third rectangle is 2 m by 9 m:

$$A = 2(9) = 18$$

Add the areas to get the total:

$$A = 54 + 6 + 18 = 78$$

Another option is to calculate the area as if you were dealing with just one, whole rectangle and then subtract the missing part:

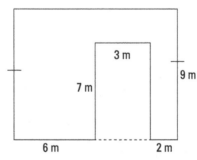

The whole area is

$$A = (6+3+2)(9)$$
$$= (11)(9)$$
$$= 99$$

The area of the missing rectangle is

$$A = 7(3) = 21$$

Subtract:

$$A = 99 - 21$$
$$A = 78$$

724. C. 45°

Ignore line z; it's only there to distract you.

Vertical angles are always congruent, so you know that $\angle a = 45°$ and $\angle d = 135°$.

Further proof is that line x is a straight line, and every straight line has a straight angle — it's 180°. Any line that crosses line x will have angles that add up to 180°. Because one angle on line x measures 135°, the other angle must measure 45°.

725. D. Both A and B

When two lines are parallel and another line intersects them, the angles created on the intersecting line are equal to each other on both lines; here, the acute angles are all congruent to each other, and the obtuse angles are all congruent to each other. Another way to say this: Two lines cut by transversal create congruent corresponding angles.

726. D. 81.96 m²

Find the area of the rectangle by using the formula $A = lw$, with l representing length and w representing width:

$$
\begin{aligned}
A &= lw \\
&= 1,200 \cdot 683 \\
&= 819,600
\end{aligned}
$$

The units on the figure are in centimeters, but the answers are presented in square meters, so remember that 100 cm is equal to 1 m. A square meter equals 100 cm × 100 cm = 10,000 cm², so you need to divide by 10,000; therefore, the answer is 81.96 m². Attention to detail is incredibly important on the ASVAB.

727. D. congruent and obtuse.

The angles have the same measurement (110°), so they're definitely congruent. Their measurement of 110° makes them obtuse as well. An obtuse angle is one that measures between 90° and 180°.

728. A. Right

When you see a half-box tucked into an angle, you know it's a right angle. A right angle's measurement is always 90°.

An acute angle is one that measures less than 90°, a straight angle measures exactly 180° (it's a straight line), and a reflex angle measures more than 180° but less than 360°.

729. C. 2,826 cm²

The formula to find the surface area of a square is $SA = 4\pi r^2$, so use the values you know to solve the problem:

$$SA = 4\pi r^2$$
$$= 4\pi\left(15^2\right)$$
$$= 4\pi\left(225\right)$$
$$= 900\pi$$
$$\approx 900\left(3.14\right)$$
$$= 2,826$$

730. B. *c, d, e, h*

When two parallel lines are crossed by a transversal (a third line), the angles between the parallel lines are considered *interior angles.* The angles created outside the parallel lines are *exterior angles.*

731. C. 137°

There's a straight line running through the circle (you can tell because the two angles below the line are complementary — together, they add up to 180°), and the measurement of angles on a straight line must equal 180°. One angle on that line measures 43°, so subtract 43 from 180 to find the measurement of angle *x:*

$$x = 180 - 43 = 137$$

732. D. 864 in.³

The volume formula for a rectangular prism is $V = lwh$, with *w* representing width, *h* representing height, and *l* representing length:

$$V = lwh$$
$$= 18 \cdot 4 \cdot 12$$
$$= 864$$

733.   B. 108°

The interior angles of a pentagon add up to 540°, but you don't need to know this to solve this problem. All you need to know is that the sides are of equal length; because of that, all the angles are equal.

734.   B. 678.24 m²

The formula to find the surface area of a right cylinder is $SA = 2\pi rh + 2\pi r^2$ — that is, the circumference of a base times the height, plus the areas of the two circular bases. Put in the values you know:

$$SA = 2\pi rh + 2\pi r^2$$
$$= 2\pi(6)(12) + 2\pi\left(6^2\right)$$
$$= 2\pi(72) + 2\pi(36)$$
$$= 144\pi + 72\pi$$
$$= 216\pi$$
$$\approx 216(3.14)$$
$$= 678.24$$

735.   D. 180°

All the interior angles in a triangle add up to 180°.

736.   B. 120°

All the sides in $\triangle BCD$ are congruent, so you know it's an equilateral triangle and that all the angles are equal. Each angle must be 60°.

You know that $\overline{AE}$ creates a straight angle measuring 180°. Because the angles in $\triangle BCD$ all equal 60°, $\angle CDB$ is 60°. To find $\angle CDE$, subtract 60° from 180°:

$$\angle CDE = 180 - 60 = 120$$

737.   A. Isosceles

An *isosceles triangle* has two congruent sides (sides that are the same length) and two congruent angles (angles that have the same measurement).

An *obtuse triangle* has one angle that measures more than 90°, a *right triangle* has one angle that measures exactly 90°, and in an *equilateral triangle*, each angle has a measure of exactly 60°.

738. **D. 25°**

The lines are parallel, which means they must be straight. A straight line has an angle of 180°, so subtract 155 from 180 to find the measurement for angle a:

$$180 - 155 = 25$$

739. **C. 13 cm**

Use the Pythagorean theorem to find the hypotenuse, c, of the triangle:

$$a^2 + b^2 = c^2$$
$$5^2 + 12^2 = c^2$$
$$25 + 144 = c^2$$
$$c^2 = 169$$
$$c = \sqrt{169}$$
$$c = 13$$

740. **B. 289 in.²**

The base of the right square pyramid has 17-inch sides, and the formula for the area of a square is $A = s^2$, with s representing the length of one side.

$$A = 17^2 = 289$$

Don't worry about the height of the pyramid; you don't need it to find the area of the base. (You'll find many problems with distracting elements on the ASVAB, so just make sure you read the question thoroughly and understand what it's asking before you dive into the work.)

741. **D. 50°**

Because this is a parallelogram, angles C and Z are supplementary and their angles add up to 180°. That means angle C must be 50°.

742. **D. 60 ft²**

The easiest way to find the area of a kite is to use the formula $A = \frac{pq}{2}$, with p representing one diagonal and q representing the other:

$$A = \frac{pq}{2}$$
$$= \frac{(10)(12)}{2}$$
$$= \frac{120}{2}$$
$$= 60$$

If you have a tough time remembering all the formulas you need, use the standard method for finding the area of all irregular quadrilaterals: Divide it into triangles, find each triangle's area, and add them all together. In this case, you can break the quadrilateral into two triangles:

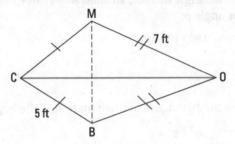

Find the area of one triangle using the formula $A = \frac{1}{2}bh$. Because the sides are the same length on each triangle, you only need to calculate one. Here's the area of $\triangle CMO$, which has a base of 10 (*CO*) and a height of 6 (half of *MB*):

$$A = \frac{1}{2}bh$$
$$= \frac{1}{2}(6)(10)$$
$$= 30$$

Don't forget to double the answer so you have the area for the entire quadrilateral (you're adding the areas of $\triangle CMO$ and $\triangle CBO$). Your answer is 60 square feet.

743.　C. 75 ft²

First find the area of the entire square; then find the area of the unshaded region. Large square:

$$A = s^2$$
$$= 10^2$$
$$= 100$$

Small square:

$$A = s^2$$
$$= 5^2$$
$$= 25$$

Subtract the area of the unshaded region from the area of the shaded region:

$$A = 100 - 25 = 75$$

The area of the shaded region (what's left over after you remove the unshaded region) is 75 ft².

744.   **D. 15.7 cm**

A right triangle with points on the edges of a circle has a hypotenuse that equals the circle's diameter. To find the diameter, find the length of the hypotenuse by using the Pythagorean theorem, where c represents the hypotenuse:

$$a^2 + b^2 = c^2$$
$$4^2 + 3^2 = c^2$$
$$16 + 9 = c^2$$
$$c^2 = 25$$
$$\sqrt{c} = \sqrt{25}$$
$$c = 5$$

You know that the hypotenuse is 5 cm, so that tells you the circle's diameter is also 5 cm. The radius is half that (2.5 cm). Now you can use the formula for finding a circle's circumference, which is $C = 2\pi r$:

$$C = 2\pi r$$
$$= 2\pi(2.5)$$
$$= 5\pi$$
$$\approx 5(3.14)$$
$$= 15.7$$

745.   **A. 45°**

All the angles in a triangle must add up to 180°. One is labeled 45°, and another is a right angle (and right angles always measure 90°). Subtract 45 and 90 from 180 to find the measure of angle A:

$$180 - 45 - 90 = 45$$

Angle A measures 45°.

746.   **B. 96°**

In a *cyclic quadrilateral* — a quadrilateral inside a circle (which has 360°) — opposite angles add up to 180°. To find the measure of angle T, subtract 84 from 180:

$$180 - 84 = 96$$

Angle T is 96°.

747.   **A. 9 in.²**

To find the area of a square, use $A = s^2$, with s representing the length of the side:

$$A = s^2$$
$$= 3^2$$
$$= 9$$

748. **C. 45°**

Count the portions of the circle: There are eight. Every circle has 360°, so to find the arcs over each portion, divide 360 by 8:

$$360 \div 8 = 45$$

749. **B. 28.5°**

The two secants intersect outside a circle, so you can find the angle by using the formula $\angle ACE = \frac{1}{2}\left(\widehat{AE} - \widehat{BD}\right)$, with $\angle ACE$ representing x, the angle formed where the secants intersect (C is the vertex); $\widehat{AE}$ representing the arc at the opposite end of the vertex; and $\widehat{BD}$ representing the inner arc.

When you label the points, it looks like this:

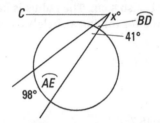

Replace the variables with what you know to solve:

$$\angle ACE = \frac{1}{2}\left(\widehat{AE} - \widehat{BD}\right)$$
$$= \frac{1}{2}(98 - 41)$$
$$= \frac{1}{2}(57)$$
$$= 28.5$$

750. **A. 143.75 in.²**

The formula to find the area of a trapezoid is $A = \frac{1}{2}h(b_1 + b_2)$, with b_1 representing one base, b_2 representing the other, and h representing the height. Replace the variables with what you know:

$$A = \frac{1}{2}h(b_1 + b_2)$$
$$= \frac{1}{2}(12.5)(8 + 15)$$
$$= \frac{1}{2}(12.5)(23)$$
$$= 143.75$$

Arithmetic Reasoning

751.   **A. 5 yards**

Let x represent the team's progress and create an equation:

$$x = -10 + 15$$

Note that it doesn't matter which line the team was on when they lost 10 yards or when they gained 15, because the problem isn't asking you which line they ended up on; it's asking you about their progress.

Solve the equation:

$$x = -10 + 15$$
$$x = 5$$

752.   **C. $4.95**

Remember that Cheryl bought herself a latte, too, so you need to figure out the price of 11 lattes before you determine how much she saved.

Let x equal the total original price of the lattes:

$$x = 4.5 \times 11$$
$$x = 49.5$$

Find out how much Cheryl saved with a 10% discount by multiplying $49.50 by 0.10; let y represent the discount:

$$y = 49.5 \times 0.1$$
$$y = 4.95$$

Attention to detail is important on the ASVAB. Don't miss key words in the problem that can tip you off to the correct answer. In this case, the word *save* could've helped you rule out Choices (B) and (D).

753.   **D. Christina: 12; Angela: 18**

Angela is 6 years older than Christina, so if you let x equal Christina's age now, Angela's current age is $x + 6$. Christina's age 6 years ago would be $x - 6$, and Angela's age 6 years ago would be $(x + 6) - 6$.

Set up an equation showing that Angela's age was double Christina's age 6 years ago; then solve for x to get Christina's current age:

$$(x+6)-6=2(x-6)$$
$$x+6-6=2x-12$$
$$x=2x-12$$
$$x-2x=-12+2x-2x$$
$$x-2x=12$$
$$-x=-12$$
$$\frac{-x}{-1}=\frac{-12}{-1}$$
$$x=12$$

Christina is 12 years old now, and because Angela is 6 years older than Christina is, she's 18.

754.   D. $32.50

Let x represent the toy's original price and write an equation to figure out how much the toy would've cost a civilian:

$$x-15=17.5$$
$$x-15+15=17.5+15$$
$$x=17.5+15$$
$$x=32.5$$

In this problem, you can skip the algebra and add $15 to $17.50 to find out how much the toy originally cost, but it's a good idea to know how to perform the calculations; not all the questions you'll encounter on the ASVAB will be easy enough to answer this way.

755.   D. $5,775

You can solve this simple percentage problem with multiplication. Let x equal Perry's profit and find 3% of the home's price by multiplying the price by 0.03:

$$x=192,500\times0.03$$
$$x=5,775$$

756.   A. 2 dimes, 5 nickels, and 20 pennies

The best way to solve this problem is to create a simple chart, with one column showing the number of each coin and another column showing the monetary value. Don't worry — you're allowed to use as much scratch paper as you need when you take the ASVAB. Let x represent the number of dimes Kim has, and let $x+3$ represent the number of nickels she has. Finally, let $4(x+3)$ equal the number of pennies she has. Your chart should look something like this:

Number of Coins	Value in Cents
x = number of dimes	$10x$ = number of cents in dimes
$x+3$ = number of nickels	$5(x+3)$ = number of cents in nickels
$4(x+3)$ = number of pennies	$4(x+3)$ = number of cents in pennies

Kim has a total of 65 cents, so add the values in cents and set that equal to 65. Now you can solve for x, the number of dimes:

$$10x+5(x+3)+4(x+3)=65$$
$$10x+5x+15+4x+12=65$$
$$19x+27=65$$
$$19x+27-27=65-27$$
$$19x=38$$
$$\frac{19x}{19}=\frac{38}{19}$$
$$x=2$$

Now that you know $x=2$, you can determine that Kim has 2 dimes, 5 nickels, and 16 pennies in her pocket. Check your math by adding up the monetary value of her coins:

$$\$0.20+\$0.25+\$0.20=\$0.65$$

757.   A. −14

Write an algebraic equation to express the problem, and let x equal the number you don't know:

$$x+34=20$$
$$x+34-34=20-34$$
$$x=-14$$

758.   B. 18 dimes, 3 quarters

Let x represent the number of quarters, and let $6x$ represent the number of dimes, because she has 6 times as many dimes.

Together, all the quarters are worth $25x$ cents, and all the dimes are worth $60x$ cents (remember that she has 6 times as many dimes in her piggy bank and that each dime is worth 10 cents).

To make the problem easier, deal only in cents. Therefore, she has 255 cents in her piggy bank. Create your equation based on what you know:

$$25x + 60x = 255$$
$$85x = 255$$
$$\frac{85x}{85} = \frac{255}{85}$$
$$x = 3$$

Now that you know $x = 3$, you know Amy has 3 quarters. She has a total of 21 coins in the bank, so the remaining coins must all be dimes:

$$21 - 3 = 18$$

In this problem, you can deal only in the number of coins. Use the equation $x + 6x = 21$ and let x represent the number of quarters in Amy's piggy bank (she has six times as many dimes as she has quarters, and she has 21 coins). Solve the equation:

$$x + 6x = 21$$
$$7x = 21$$
$$\frac{7x}{7} = \frac{21}{7}$$
$$x = 3$$

Either way you calculate it, Amy has three quarters. The rest are dimes.

759. B. 46

Let x represent the number, and remember that *is* translates to an equals sign in an equation:

$$\frac{1}{2}x + 12 = 35$$
$$\frac{1}{2}x + 12 - 12 = 35 - 12$$
$$\frac{1}{2}x = 23$$
$$\frac{1}{2}x(2) = 23(2)$$
$$x = 46$$

760. A. 8 hours

As with most time, rate, and distance problems, it's often best to create a table to visualize your equations. Let x equal the time, in hours, for Danielle's vehicle. Danielle has a 1-hour head start on Abigail, so Abigail's time is $x - 1$. The distance formula says that rate $\times$ time $=$ distance, so multiply the rate by the time to fill in the distance column. Your table should look something like this:

	Rate	Time	Distance
Danielle	35	x	$35x$
Abigail	40	$x-1$	$40(x-1)$

When the cars are side-by-side, they'll have traveled the same distance. You can create your equation by setting the distance values equal to each other:

$$35x = 40(x-1)$$
$$35x = 40x - 40$$
$$35x = -40 + 40x$$
$$35x - 40x = -40 + 40x - 40x$$
$$-5x = -40$$
$$\frac{-5x}{-5} = \frac{-40}{-5}$$
$$x = 8$$

The women's cars will be at the same point on the expressway in 8 hours after Danielle left.

761.   C. 2 nickels, 10 dimes

Let x equal the number of nickels Matthew has, and let y equal the number of dimes. There are a total of 12 coins, so the number of dimes is $y = 12 - x$. Multiply the number of each coin by its worth (5 or 10 cents), and set the total equal to 110 cents ($1.10):

$$5x + 10(12 - x) = 110$$
$$5x + 120 - 10x = 110$$
$$5x - 10x + 120 - 120 = 110 - 120$$
$$5x - 10x = -10$$
$$-5x = -10$$
$$\frac{-5x}{-5} = \frac{-10}{-5}$$
$$x = 2$$

Matthew has two nickels, so the remaining 10 coins must be dimes.

When you take the ASVAB, try to rule out any answers that don't make sense. In this case, you can rule out any answers that don't total 12 coins (the problem tells you Matthew has "a 12-coin collection"). That means Choices (A) and (D) are automatically wrong, and if you had to guess, you'd have a 50-50 chance of getting the question right with the remaining answer choices.

762. **B. $7 on bait; $14 on tackle**

Determine how much Dan spent on bait and tackle together by subtracting the cost of the fishing pole from his total bill:

$$\$36.95 - \$15.95 = \$21$$

Between bait and tackle, Dan spent $21.00. Let x represent the amount of money Dan spent on bait and $2x$ represent how much he spent on tackle:

$$x + 2x = 21$$
$$3x = 21$$
$$\frac{3x}{3} = \frac{21}{3}$$
$$x = 7$$

Dan spent $7 on bait, so replace x with 7 to find out that he spent $14 on tackle.

763. **A. 3 hours**

Let x represent the amount of time Luke spends reading, and let $2x$ represent the time he spends playing soccer:

$$x + 2x = 4.5$$
$$3x = 4.5$$
$$\frac{3x}{3} = \frac{4.5}{3}$$
$$x = 1.5$$

That tells you that Luke will spend 1.5 hours reading. He'll spend twice that playing soccer:

$$1.5 \times 2 = 3$$

Luke will spend three hours playing soccer.

You can solve more-complex problems the same way if you convert hours into minutes.

764. **C. 2 hours**

Justin has a half-hour (0.5 hour) head start on Bradley because he left MacDill at 12:00 p.m.; Bradley didn't leave until 12:30 p.m.

Let x equal the amount of time Justin flies, and remember that these types of problems are often easiest to solve using tables. Don't forget the formula for distance is $d = rt$, with d representing distance, r representing rate (speed), and t representing time.

	Rate	Time	Distance
Justin	464	x	$464x$
Bradley	580	$x - 0.5$	$580(x - 0.5)$

ANSWERS
701–800

Now you can determine the time (*x*) by making both distances equal in an equation:

$$464x = 580(x - 0.5)$$
$$464x = 580x - 290$$
$$464x + 290 = 580x - 290 + 290$$
$$464x + 290 = 580x$$
$$290 + 464x - 464x = 580x - 464x$$
$$290 = 116x$$
$$116x = 290$$
$$\frac{116x}{116} = \frac{290}{116}$$
$$x = 2.5$$

The variable *x* represents the amount of time Justin flies. However, the question asks how long it will take Bradley to catch up to Justin. Bradley left a half-hour after Justin did, so subtract a half-hour from Justin's time in the air to figure out how long Bradley had to fly:

$$2.5 - 0.5 = 2$$

That means Bradley will catch up to Justin in 2 hours. (Don't let little details like this trip you up on the ASVAB!)

765. C. 6 hours

Note that the question asks you "how long," which means that time is the unknown variable.

The easiest way to solve this problem is with a chart of the trucks' movement. In the chart, *x* equals the time in hours for Truck 1. Because the second truck leaves two hours later, represent its time with $x - 2$. Use the distance formula, $d = rt$, to figure out what goes in the distance column.

	Rate	Time	Distance
Truck 1	40	x	$40x$
Truck 2	60	$x-2$	$60(x-2)$

Use the two distances to create your equation:

$$40x = 60(x - 2)$$
$$40x = 60x - 120$$
$$40x = -120 + 60x$$
$$40x - 60x = -120 + 60x - 60x$$
$$-20x = -120$$
$$\frac{-20x}{-20} = \frac{-120}{-20}$$
$$x = 6$$

The first truck will have been on the road for 6 hours by the time the second truck overtakes it.

766. C. 45 minutes

Use the distance formula, which is $d = rt$, where d represents distance, r represents rate, and t represents time, to figure out the answer to this question. Replace the variables with what you know to isolate and solve for t:

$$6 = 8(t)$$
$$8t = 6$$
$$\frac{8t}{8} = \frac{6}{8}$$
$$t = \frac{6}{8}$$
$$t = \frac{3}{4}$$

The units the problem gives you are hours, which means Ayla will need $\frac{3}{4}$ of an hour, or 45 minutes, to travel 6 miles.

Note: Using mental math, you can reason that 6 miles out of 8 miles is 3 out of 4, which is expressed as $\frac{3}{4}$, so it should take Ayla 45 minutes to bicycle that far — no formulas required!

767. A. 3

One-third of 18 is 6, so that's how many Army Commendation Medals Fani will give to her troops. One-half of 18 is 9, so Fani will give out a total of 9 Army Achievement Medals.

The sum of the Army Commendation Medals and Army Achievement Medals is 15. The remaining awards are Certificates of Achievement, so subtract 15 from 18 to find out how many of those Fani will give her troops: $18 - 15 = 3$.

768. B. 2.7 hours

This is a shared-work problem because Marie and Darl are both filling the pool together. Let a represent the time it takes Marie to fill the pool, let b represent the time it takes Darl to fill the pool, and let c represent the time it will take them to fill it together:

$$\frac{1}{a} + \frac{1}{b} = \frac{1}{c}$$
$$\frac{1}{6} + \frac{1}{5} = \frac{1}{c}$$

Find the least common denominator and solve:

$$(30c)\frac{1}{6} + (30c)\frac{1}{5} = (30c)\frac{1}{c}$$
$$5c + 6c = 30$$
$$11c = 30$$
$$\frac{11c}{11} = \frac{30}{11}$$
$$c \approx 2.7$$

769.   A. $29

The good news: These kinds of problems look a lot trickier than they are. The crafty ASVAB question writers try to dazzle you with loads of information; as long as you know how to pull out what you need, you'll be in good shape.

Let x represent how much money Jesse has. Let $2x$ represent how much Tina has, because she has twice as much as Jesse does, and let $2x - 5$ represent how much David gets (he has $5 less than Tina). The sum is $80, so create an equation that looks like this:

$$x + 2x + (2x - 5) = 80$$

Solve the equation for x to find out how much Jesse has:

$$
\begin{aligned}
x + 2x + (2x - 5) &= 80 \\
x + 2x + 2x - 5 &= 80 \\
5x - 5 + 5 &= 80 + 5 \\
5x &= 85 \\
\frac{5x}{5} &= \frac{85}{5} \\
x &= 17
\end{aligned}
$$

Jesse has $17, and because Tina has twice as much as he does, multiply that by 2; now you know that Tina has $34. David has $5 less than Tina, so subtract 5 from 34 to find out that David has $29.

Check your math by adding up everyone's money:

$$17 + 34 + 29 = 80$$

770.   B. 75 = x(x + 15)

The word *product* means that the problem involves multiplication, and when you see *more than*, you know you're adding. Therefore, you can express this equation this way:

$$75 = x(x + 15)$$

Here, one factor is x and the other factor is $x + 15$, and their product equals 75.

There are several other ways to express the equation, but when you see a question like this on the ASVAB, it's often best to go through the answer choices to see which one fits instead of creating your own formula. (It's faster, too!)

771. D. 31

Let n equal the first odd number, and let $n+2$ represent the second number. Set up your equation based on what you know from the problem; then solve for n:

$$n+(n+2)=60$$
$$2n+2=60$$
$$2n+2-2=60-2$$
$$2n=58$$
$$\frac{2n}{2}=\frac{58}{2}$$
$$n=29$$

The first number is 29, and because the question tells you that the numbers are consecutive (in a row) odd numbers, you know the higher number is 31.

A quick check to see whether $29+31=60$ is wise.

772. C. $21

The unknown number is how much Noah has. Let x represent how much money Noah has, and let $2x+8$ represent how much money Patrick has. (Patrick has $50, which is $8 more than twice what Noah has.)

$$2x+8=50$$
$$2x+8-8=50-8$$
$$2x=42$$
$$\frac{2x}{2}=\frac{42}{2}$$
$$x=21$$

Because x represents Noah's money, you know he has $21.

773. D. $4x=6+\frac{1}{3}x$

Let x represent the number you don't know, and pick out the key terms you need from the problem. When you see the word *is*, think of an equals sign; when you see *times* or *of*, you know you'll need multiplication.

Start with the solution: "four times a number." That means $4x$.

"Six more" means you need to add 6 to $\frac{1}{3}$ times the number:

$$6+\frac{1}{3}x$$

Combine both parts so the whole equation looks like this:

$$4x=6+\frac{1}{3}x$$

774. **C. $155**

Let x represent the amount of money Beto has, and let $2x+36$ represent the amount of money Pili has. Create an equation and solve for x to find out how much Beto has:

$$2x+36 = 346$$
$$2x+36-36 = 346-36$$
$$2x = 310$$
$$\frac{2x}{2} = \frac{310}{2}$$
$$x = 155$$

Beto has $155, which you can check by replacing x in the equation for Pili's money:

$$2(155)+36 = 346$$
$$310+36 = 346$$

775. **A. $750**

First figure out how much Evan is paying by determining 20% of $1,875:

$$1,875 \times 0.2 = 375$$

Evan pays $375 in rent, which contributes to the $1,875 total. Write your equation to include what everyone pays, letting $2x$ represent what Andrew and Kara pay together (remember, they pay equal amounts):

$$2x+375 = 1,875$$
$$2x+375-375 = 1,875-375$$
$$2x = 1,500$$
$$\frac{2x}{2} = \frac{1,500}{2}$$
$$x = 750$$

Andrew pays $750 in rent.

776. **D. $y = 2x + 9$**

To express this problem as an algebraic equation, extract all the information you need. When you see terms like *more*, you know you need to add. *Twice* means you also have to multiply.

The variable x represents the number of green marbles Divana has, so you can set up your equation this way:

$$y = 2x + 9$$

777. C. $44.50

First find out how much Judi spent at the casino based on how much Janice spent. Let x represent Judi's spending:

$$2x = 135$$
$$\frac{2x}{2} = \frac{135}{2}$$
$$x = 67.5$$

(If you read the problem, you could also reason that Judi spent half of $135, which happens to be $67.50, instead of creating an algebraic formula.)

Judi spent $67.50, and then she paid $23 for the taxi ride:

$$67.5 + 23 = 90.5$$

Janice spent $135, so subtract Judi's spending, which was a total of $90.50, from that amount to find out how much more Janice spent than Judi did:

$$135 - 90.5 = 44.5$$

Janice spent $44.50 more than Judi.

778. B. 21

Pat and Gavin are two of the males waiting in line with 48 other people, so there are a total of 50 people. Let x represent the number of males, and let $x - 8$ represent the number of females (remember, there are 8 fewer females than males in the line). Create an equation:

$$x + (x - 8) = 50$$
$$2x - 8 = 50$$
$$2x - 8 + 8 = 50 + 8$$
$$2x = 58$$
$$\frac{2x}{2} = \frac{58}{2}$$
$$x = 29$$

There are 29 males, and the problem tells you that there are 8 fewer females than males. Subtract 8 from 29 to determine that there are 21 females in line.

779. **D. 43.18 hours**

Don't let extra information confuse you on the ASVAB. You don't need to know how much Glenn charges at all; you only need to know how much Charra charges, which is $110 per hour.

The problem tells you how much the project costs ($4,750), but it doesn't tell you how long it takes to complete at $110 per hour. Let x represent the amount of time it takes Charra to complete $4,750 worth of work on a website, and create your equation with what you know:

$$110x = 4,750$$
$$\frac{110x}{110} = \frac{4,750}{110}$$
$$x \approx 43.18$$

It takes Charra about 43.18 hours to complete a website that costs $4,750.

If you needed to know how long it would take Glenn, you could use the same formula with his hourly rate.

780. **A. 224**

Start with the least quantity: the children. Let x represent the number of children, let $5x$ represent the number of men, and let $3x$ represent the number of women. Structure your equation this way, and then isolate x to find out how many children are in the group:

$$x + 5x + 3x = 1,008$$
$$9x = 1,008$$
$$\frac{9x}{9} = \frac{1,008}{9}$$
$$x = 112$$

Now you know there are 112 children, so you can figure out how many men and women are in the group:

Men: $5(112) = 560$

Women: $3(112) = 336$

Don't forget the rest of the problem, which asks you to find out how many more men there are than women. Subtract 336 from 560:

$$560 - 336 = 224$$

There are 224 more men than women in the group.

Check your math by adding all the numbers (men, women, and children) together to get 1,008:

$$560 + 336 + 112 = 1,008$$

781. C. 10 = 4x

The solution to the problem is 10, so that belongs alone on one side of the equals sign. When you read the word *product,* you know that you're dealing with multiplication. Your equation should look like this: $10 = 4x$.

782. B. 54 and 55

Let x represent the first number, and let $x+1$ represent the second number. Then create your equation:

$$x + (x+1) = 109$$
$$2x + 1 = 109$$
$$2x + 1 - 1 = 109 - 1$$
$$2x = 108$$
$$\frac{2x}{2} = \frac{108}{2}$$
$$x = 54$$

The first number is 54, and because the problem tells you that you need consecutive numbers (and because the second number is $x+1$), you know the second number is 55.

Sometimes on the ASVAB, running through the answer choices is a good idea. You can immediately rule out Choice (D) because the numbers aren't consecutive, and you can rule out Choices (A) and (C) because they don't add up to 109.

783. A. 15

Let x represent the first number, $x+1$ represent the second number, $x+2$ represent the third number, and $x+3$ represent the fourth number. The sum is 54, so write your equation using the appropriate terms and then solve for x:

$$x + (x+1) + (x+2) + (x+3) = 54$$
$$4x + 6 = 54$$
$$4x + 6 - 6 = 54 - 6$$
$$4x = 48$$
$$x = 12$$

The first number in the sequence is 12, and the final number is $12 + 3$. That means the greatest number in the sequence is 15.

784.   C. 28

Let x represent the number of pies that Steve and Stan made. Fran made twice as many as they did, so the number of pies she made equals $2x$. Replace x with the number of pies that Steve and Stan made, which the problem says is 14:

$$y = 2x$$
$$y = 2(14)$$
$$y = 28$$

This question is a good place to use mental math. Think: What is twice (or two times) 14?

785.   D. $312,000

Let x represent the amount of money Stacy spent, and let $3x + 48,000$ represent what Jim spent. Create your equation and isolate x to find out how much Stacy spent:

$$x + (3x + 48,000) = 400,000$$
$$4x + 48,000 = 400,000$$
$$4x + 48,000 - 48,000 = 400,000 - 48,000$$
$$4x = 352,000$$
$$\frac{4x}{4} = \frac{352,000}{4}$$
$$x = 88,000$$

You know that Stacy spent $88,000, so replace the variable x in Jim's equation to find out how much he spent:

$$3(88,000) + 48,000$$
$$= 264,000 + 48,000$$
$$= 312,000$$

Jim spent $312,000 of the couple's money. You can check your math by adding $312,000 to what Stacy spent, which was $88,000, to make sure they add up to $400,000:

$$312,000 + 88,000 = 400,000$$

786.   B. 24

Start with the fewest number of colored balls that Bryan bought for Roscoe. According to the problem, Roscoe has the fewest orange balls, so let x represent the number of orange balls. Let $2x$ represent the number of yellow balls, and let $6x$ represent the number of red balls. Write your equation, setting the sum of the colored balls equal to 36:

$$x + 2x + 6x = 36$$
$$9x = 36$$
$$\frac{9x}{9} = \frac{36}{9}$$
$$x = 4$$

That means Roscoe has 4 orange balls. The term that represents how many red balls Roscoe has is $6x$, so replace the variable with 4: $6(4) = 24$, so Roscoe has 24 red balls.

787.   C. $55

Faith has the least money, so let x represent how much she has. Let $2x$ represent how much Chandler has, and let $3x + 4$ represent how much Sadie has. The total money is $106, so write your equation like this:

$$x + 2x + (3x + 4) = \$106$$

Determine how much Faith has by isolating x:

$$x + 2x + (3x + 4) = 106$$
$$6x + 4 = 106$$
$$6x + 4 - 4 = 106 - 4$$
$$6x = 102$$
$$\frac{6x}{6} = \frac{102}{6}$$
$$x = 17$$

Faith has $17, and Sadie has three times that amount plus $4:

$$3(17) + 4 = 55$$

Sadie has $55. (Just for the record, Chandler has $34 because he has twice as much as Faith.)

788.   D. $15

Dani has the least money, so let x represent her share. Mike has two times what Dani has, so let $2x$ represent Mike's portion of the money, and let $2x + 2.5$ represent what Nicklaus has. Their money totals $33.75, so write your equation this way and solve for x, Dani's amount:

$$x + 2x + (2x + 2.5) = 33.75$$
$$5x + 2.5 = 33.75$$
$$5x + 2.5 - 2.5 = 33.75 - 2.5$$
$$5x = 31.25$$
$$\frac{5x}{5} = \frac{31.25}{5}$$
$$x = 6.25$$

Dani has \$6.25, and because the problem tells you that $2x + 2.5$ represents how much Nicklaus has, replace the variable with \$6.25 (remember, x represents Dani's share of the money):

$$= 2(6.25) + 2.5$$
$$= 12.5 + 2.5$$
$$= 15$$

Nicklaus has \$15.

789. **A. 47 − x = 29**

When a problem tells you that someone gave something away, you know you have to subtract. Because this problem doesn't tell you how many books Janae gave to Ellis, that's the unknown variable in your equation. Let x represent the number of books Janae gave to Ellis:

$$47 - x = 29$$

790. **D. 5, 7, and 9**

Let n represent the first odd number. Because the numbers are consecutive odd numbers, let $n + 2$ represent the second consecutive odd number, and then let $n + 4$ represent the third consecutive odd number. Create an equation and solve:

$$n + (n + 2) + (n + 4) = 21$$
$$3n + 6 = 21$$
$$3n + 6 - 6 = 21 - 6$$
$$3n = 15$$
$$\frac{3n}{3} = \frac{15}{3}$$
$$n = 5$$

The first number is 5, which tells you that the next odd numbers in the sequence are 7 and 9.

On problems like this one, plugging in the likely answer choices may be faster. If they add up to the correct amount, you can choose quickly and move to the next problem. You have only 39 minutes to answer 16 questions on the Arithmetic Reasoning subtest of the CAT–ASVAB and 36 minutes to answer 30 questions on the paper-and-pencil version, so save time where you can.

791.   C. $103

Let x represent what Traci made because she made the least. Let $x+11$ represent what Jill made, and let $2(x+11)$ represent what Donna made. Add their earnings and set the total equal to 141; then solve for x:

$$x+(x+11)+2(x+11)=141$$
$$x+x+11+2x+22=141$$
$$4x+33=141$$
$$4x+33-33=141-33$$
$$4x=108$$
$$\frac{4x}{4}=\frac{108}{4}$$
$$x=27$$

Traci made $27, so to determine how much Donna made, replace x in Donna's formula with 27:

$$2(x+11)=2(27+11)=76$$

Donna made $76. The problem asks how much Traci and Donna made together, so add Traci's and Donna's earnings:

$$27+76=103$$

Together, they made $103.

792.   A. $x = \dfrac{b-2}{2}$

The problem tells you that the number of boys is b, and you can let x be the number of girls. The number of boys is two more than twice the number of girls, so let $2x+2$ represent the number of boys. That means $b=2x+2$.

You can express this relationship in an equation, and as with any equation, you need to isolate the variable you want to find. Rearrange the equation to get x by itself:

$$2x+2=b$$
$$2x+2-2=b-2$$
$$2x=b-2$$
$$\frac{2x}{2}=\frac{b-2}{2}$$
$$x=\frac{b-2}{2}$$

793. B. $28

Let x represent how much Private Snuffy spent on tan T-shirts. The problem tells you that Private Snuffy's combat boots cost $14 less than twice what he spent on T-shirts, so double x to get twice the cost of the T-shirts and then subtract 14. Set this amount equal to $42, the cost of the boots, and solve for x:

$$2x - 14 = 42$$
$$2x - 14 + 14 = 42 + 14$$
$$2x = 56$$
$$\frac{2x}{2} = \frac{56}{2}$$
$$x = 28$$

Private Snuffy spent $28 on tan T-shirts (but don't worry — the military will issue you all the combat boots and T-shirts you need).

794. C. $37.50

Write an equation that lets x represent the cost of 1 gallon of unleaded fuel. Ten gallons cost Luz $30, so

$$10x = 30$$
$$\frac{10x}{10} = \frac{30}{10}$$
$$x = 3$$

Because premium fuel costs 25% more, it costs 125% of the price of unleaded fuel, so let $1.25x$ represent the amount Tony spent per gallon. Unleaded gas costs $3 per gallon, so figure out how much Tony spent per gallon by replacing x in his equation with 3:

$$\$3(1.25) = \$3.75$$

Each gallon of premium fuel costs $3.75 and Tony bought 10 gallons, so multiply 3.75 by 10 to find out how much Tony spent:

$$3.75 \times 10 = 37.5$$

Tony spent $37.50 on fuel.

You'll find plenty of multi-step problems on the ASVAB, and the correct answers hinge on paying attention to detail. Make sure you read every question thoroughly before you formulate your answer!

795. C. $x = \frac{y}{5}$

The word *quotient* means you'll be dividing. The word *is* translates to *equals* in math, so your equation will look like this:

$$x = \frac{y}{5}$$

796.   A. 10:12 a.m.

It's a good idea to convert six minutes into 0.1 hours first. Then create a table that shows each dog, its speed, and variables that represent how long it takes them to meet. To fill in the distance column, use the formula $d = rt$, in which d represents distance, r represents rate, and t represents time:

	Rate	Time	Distance
Cujo	5	x	$5x$
Jack	10	$x - 0.1$	$10(x - 0.1)$

Set the distances equal to each other and solve for x to determine how long Cujo ran:

$$5x = 10(x - 0.1)$$
$$5x = 10x - 1$$
$$5x - 10x = -1 + 10x - 10x$$
$$-5x = -1$$
$$\frac{-5x}{-5} = \frac{-1}{-5}$$
$$x = \frac{1}{5}$$

One-fifth of an hour is $\frac{60 \text{ minutes}}{5} = 12$ minutes, which shows you that Cujo had run 1 mile by 10:12 a.m.

Jack left at 10:06 a.m., running at 10 miles per hour. After 6 minutes had elapsed, Jack had run 1 mile. That means Jack caught up with Cujo 6 minutes after he escaped, at 10:12 a.m.

797.   A. 5.24 hours

To find out how much time something takes when you know distance and rate, use the distance formula $(d = rt)$, where d represents the distance, r represents the rate, and t represents the time. Fill in what you know from the question:

$$5t = 26.2$$
$$\frac{5t}{5} = \frac{26.2}{5}$$
$$t = 5.24$$

798.   D. $x = y + 35$

When you see *more than* in a word problem, you know you need to add. The width of the field is y, and its length is 35 yards more than its width. That means $x = y + 35$ is the correct way to express this relationship in mathematical terms.

799. **A. 60 minutes**

Word problems are notorious for including extra information to distract you from pulling out the data you need. To slash through the sludge, find out how long it will take each journalist to arrive on the scene.

Use the distance formula $d = rt$, where d represents distance, r represents rate, and t represents time.

Channel 7:

$$70t = 420$$
$$\frac{70t}{70} = \frac{420}{70}$$
$$t = 6$$

Channel 4:

$$60t = 420$$
$$\frac{60t}{60} = \frac{420}{60}$$
$$t = 7$$

Channel 7's journalist gets to the rally in 6 hours, while Channel 4's journalist arrives in 7 hours (it doesn't matter what time they left; that information is just there to distract you).

The journalist from Channel 7 arrives 60 minutes sooner than the journalist from Channel 4 does.

800. **C.** $xy \geq \dfrac{b}{c}$

When you see *product* in a word problem, you're dealing with multiplication; when you see *quotient*, you're dealing with division. You express the relationship in this problem with an inequality, because it uses the phrase "is greater than or equal to":

$$xy \geq \frac{b}{c}$$

801. **B. $42**

Before you tackle this problem, you must define the variable. Let x represent the amount Abbas starts with, because he starts with less money than Safir does. Let $6x$ represent how much money Safir starts with, and create a table so you can visualize the problem.

	Abbas	*Safir*
Before earning	x	$6x$
After earning	$x + 8$	$6x + 6$

Set up an equation that shows the relationship between their "after" earnings. Safir will have three times as much as Abbas:

$$6x + 6 = 3(x + 8)$$

Solve for x to find out how much money Abbas started with:

$$6x + 6 = 3(x + 8)$$
$$6x + 6 = 3x + 24$$
$$6x + 6 - 6 = 3x + 24 - 6$$
$$6x = 3x + 18$$
$$6x - 3x = 3x + 18 - 3x$$
$$3x = 18$$
$$\frac{3x}{3} = \frac{18}{3}$$
$$x = 6$$

Go back to your original representations of what each man had. Abbas had $6 before earning an additional $8, so now he has $14.

Safir had six times what Abbas originally had, so Safir had $36. He's earned another $6, though, so now he has $42.

Now, Abbas has $14 and Safir has $42. Check your math by making sure that $14 \times 3 = 42$. (It does!)

---

802. **C. 164 and 401**

When you see the word *sum* in a word problem, you know it involves addition. Let x represent one number you're looking for, and let $x + 164$ represent the other number. Create an equation that looks like this:

$$x + (x + 164) = 638$$

Solve that equation for x:

$$x + (x + 164) = 638$$
$$x + x + 164 = 638$$
$$2x + 164 = 638$$
$$2x + 164 - 164 = 638 - 164$$
$$2x = 474$$
$$\frac{2x}{2} = \frac{474}{2}$$
$$x = 237$$

You know that one number is 237. To find the second number, add 164:

$$237 + 164 = 401$$

The second number is 401.

Check your math by adding 237 and 401 to make sure they add up to the original sum, which is 638: $237 + 401 = 638$.

803. B. $2,065.15

Let x represent how much money Lillian made. If Lillian's pay is x, Ron's pay is $\frac{3}{4}x + 164$. Together, they made $4,600, so your equation should look like this:

$$x + \left(\frac{3}{4}x + 164\right) = 4,600$$

Solve for x to find out how much money Lillian made:

$$x + \left(\frac{3}{4}x + 164\right) = 4,600$$
$$1\frac{3}{4}x + 164 - 164 = 4,600 - 164$$
$$1\frac{3}{4}x = 4,436$$
$$1.75x = 4,436$$
$$\frac{1.75x}{1.75} = \frac{4,436}{1.75}$$
$$x = 2,534.86$$

Lillian made $2,534.86, which you represented with x. Replace x in the formula for Ron's pay to find out how much he made:

$$\frac{3}{4}x + 164 = 0.75(2,534.86) + 164$$
$$= 1,901.15 + 164$$
$$= 2,065.15$$

Ron made $2,065.15.

804. A. 25 and 26

For a question like this, it's usually faster to run through the answer choices instead of setting up formulas and equations.

However, here's the algebraic approach. This problem deals with the addition of two unknown numbers, and you can express the problem as an equation:

$$x + (x + 1) = 51$$

Solve the equation for x to find the first number:

$$x + (x + 1) = 51$$
$$2x + 1 = 51$$
$$2x + 1 - 1 = 51 - 1$$
$$2x = 50$$
$$\frac{2x}{2} = \frac{50}{2}$$
$$x = 25$$

The first number is 25. Remember, you need the next number in line, which you expressed as $x + 1$. Replace x with 25 and solve for the second number:

$$25 + 1 = 26$$

The two numbers are 25 and 26.

805. C. 654

Let x represent the number of strawberries the women can pick together in one hour. You know that Renee picks 110 strawberries each hour and Jeniece picks 108 per hour, so by adding them together, you can find the value of x.

$$x = 110 + 108$$
$$x = 218$$

Because you need to find out how many strawberries the women can pick together in 3 hours, represent that figure with $3x$:

$$3x = 3(218) = 654$$

Together, the women can pick 654 strawberries in 3 hours.

806. B. 11

Let x represent the number of awards Omar has. That means $2x$ represents Chris's awards and $2x - 3$ represents the number of awards Michael has. Set up an equation that looks like this:

$$x + 2x + (2x - 3) = 32$$
$$5x - 3 = 32$$
$$5x - 3 + 3 = 32 + 3$$
$$5x = 35$$
$$\frac{5x}{5} = \frac{35}{5}$$
$$x = 7$$

Omar has 7 military awards. You don't have to be concerned about how many Chris has in this problem. Find out how many awards Michael has by replacing x in the expression $2x - 3$:

$$2(7) - 3 = 14 - 3 = 11$$

Michael has 11 military awards.

807.   **C. 2.4 cups**

Let x represent the number of cups of coffee in the pot, and set up an equation to show how much each person drank:

$$x = \frac{x}{3} + \frac{x}{4} + 1$$

Find the least common denominator, which is 12, and multiply each expression by 12 to cancel out the denominators:

$$(x \cdot 12) = \left(\frac{x}{3} \cdot 12\right) + \left(\frac{x}{4} \cdot 12\right) + (1 \cdot 12)$$
$$12x = 4x + 3x + 12$$
$$12x = 7x + 12$$

Solve the equation as you normally would:

$$12x = 7x + 12$$
$$12x - 7x = 12 + 7x - 7x$$
$$5x = 12$$
$$\frac{5x}{5} = \frac{12}{5}$$
$$x = 2\frac{2}{5}$$

Convert the fraction to a decimal (because the answer choices are in decimal form); the answer is 2.4 cups.

808.   **C. $180**

Let x represent the amount of money Kathleen started with. Create an equation representing the sum of her purchases and the remaining money:

$$x = \frac{x}{2} + \frac{x}{3} + \frac{x}{10} + 12$$

The least common denominator for all those denominators is 30. Multiply each part of the equation by 30:

$$(x \cdot 30) = \left(\frac{x}{2} \cdot 30\right) + \left(\frac{x}{3} \cdot 30\right) + \left(\frac{x}{10} \cdot 30\right) + (12 \cdot 30)$$
$$30x = 15x + 10x + 3x + 360$$
$$30x = 28x + 360$$

Solve the equation normally to find x:

$$30x = 28x + 360$$
$$30x - 28x = 28x + 360 - 28x$$
$$2x = 360$$
$$\frac{2x}{2} = \frac{360}{2}$$
$$x = 180$$

Kathleen started out with $180.

809.   A. 18

Let n represent the number you need to find. Then create an equation:

$$n = \frac{n}{2} + \frac{1}{3}n + 3$$

Find the least common denominator. The denominators are 2 and 3, so the least common denominator is 6. Multiply each term by 6 to cancel out the denominators and create a new equation:

$$n = \frac{n}{2} + \frac{1}{3}n + 3$$
$$n(6) = \frac{n}{2}(6) + \left(\frac{1}{3}n\right)(6) + 3(6)$$
$$6n = 3n + 2n + 18$$
$$6n = 5n + 18$$
$$6n - 5n = 5n + 18 - 5n$$
$$n = 18$$

810.   C. 20

The problem tells you everything you need to know to create an equation that looks like this:

$$n = 8 + \frac{3}{5}n$$

Find the least common denominator, or LCD (in this case, it's 5). Multiply each term by 5 to cancel out the denominators:

$$\frac{n}{1} = \frac{3}{5}n + \frac{8}{1}$$
$$\frac{n}{1} \cdot 5 = \left(\frac{3}{5}n \cdot 5\right) + \left(\frac{8}{1} \cdot 5\right)$$
$$5n = 3n + 40$$
$$5n - 3n = 3n - 3n + 40$$
$$2n = 40$$
$$\frac{2}{2}n = \frac{40}{2}$$
$$n = 20$$

811.   A. 36 tablespoons

Remember that the whole is equal to the sum of the parts. Let x represent the original amount of sugar in Sgt. 1st Class Stith's container and create an equation that accounts for every tablespoon of sugar like this:

$$x = \frac{x}{2} + \frac{x}{4} + \frac{x}{6} + 3$$

Get rid of all the fractions by finding the least common denominator. In this case, it's 12, so multiply each term by 12 and cancel the denominators:

$$x = \frac{x}{2} + \frac{x}{4} + \frac{x}{6} + 3$$

$$12x = 12\left(\frac{x}{2}\right) + 12\left(\frac{x}{4}\right) + 12\left(\frac{x}{6}\right) + 12(3)$$

$$12x = 6x + 3x + 2x + 36$$

Combine like terms and solve for x, which is the original amount of sugar in Sgt. 1st Class Stith's container:

$$12x = 6x + 3x + 2x + 36$$

$$12x = 11x + 36$$

$$12x - 11x = 11x + 36 - 11x$$

$$x = 36$$

There were originally 36 tablespoons of sugar in the container.

812. C. 3x = 39

Let x represent the number of toys Robbie has. Because Jules has twice as many, let $2x$ represent the number of toys Jules has. Your equation will look like this:

$$x + 2x = 39$$

You can simplify the equation by expressing it this way:

$$3x = 39$$

813. A. 96 miles

Let x represent the boat's speed and create a table using the distance formula, which is $d = rt$, where d represents distance, r represents rate (speed), and t represents time.

You don't know how far the boat traveled, but you do know that it went 3 hours one way and 4 hours the opposite way. You also know that it had a 4-mile-per-hour current going in its favor downstream and a negative 4-mile-per-hour current going against it upstream.

	Rate	Time	Distance
Downstream	$x + 4$	3	$3(x + 4)$
Upstream	$x - 4$	4	$4(x - 4)$

The two distances are the same, so each distance belongs on its own side of one equation. Set up the equation and solve for x:

$$3(x+4) = 4(x-4)$$
$$3x+12 = 4x-16$$
$$3x+12-12 = 4x-16-12$$
$$3x = 4x-28$$
$$3x-4x = -28+4x-4x$$
$$-x = -28$$
$$x = 28$$

The boat's rate with no current is 28 miles per hour, so you can determine how far the boat went one way by using the distance formula and plugging in the facts you have. Here's the distance using the downstream formula, though the upstream one works just as well:

$$3(x+4) = 3(28+4)$$
$$= 3(32)$$
$$= 96$$

The boat traveled 96 miles each way.

814. B. 21 mph

Current problems can be tough if you can't visualize them, so it's often a good idea to sketch out a table (test administrators will provide you with as much scratch paper as you need when you take the ASVAB) based on the formula $d = rt$, where d represents distance, r represents rate (speed), and t represents time. Let x represent the boat's speed.

	Rate	Time	Distance
Downstream	$x+3$	3	$3(x+3)$
Upstream	$x-3$	4	$4(x-3)$

All you need to solve for is x, because you want the boat's speed in calm water. (The current doesn't matter except that it helps you understand how fast the boat is moving.)

To solve for x, base your equation on the boat's distance. The boat traveled the same distance downstream and upstream:

$$3(x+3) = 4(x-3)$$
$$3x+9 = 4x-12$$
$$3x+9-9 = 4x-12-9$$
$$3x = 4x-21$$
$$3x = -21+4x$$
$$3x-4x = -21+4x-4x$$
$$-x = -21$$
$$x = 21$$

The boat's speed in calm water (without any currents acting on it) is 21 miles per hour.

815. C. 85

Let n represent an odd number. The next odd number is 2 higher than that, so let $n+2$ represent the next odd number. The next odd number is $n+4$, and the last is $n+6$, because they're all consecutive odd numbers.

Their sum is 328, so your equation looks like this:

$$(n)+(n+2)+(n+4)+(n+6) = 328$$

Remove the parentheses and solve for n, the first number in the sequence:

$$n+n+2+n+4+n+6 = 328$$
$$4n+12 = 328$$
$$4n+12-12 = 328-12$$
$$4n = 316$$
$$\frac{4n}{4} = \frac{316}{4}$$
$$n = 79$$

There are four consecutive numbers that add up to 328, so you can either scrawl out the sequence on the scratch paper the test administrators will give you — 79, 81, 83, 85 — or you can work out the greatest number by replacing n in the last expression $(n+6)$. Either way, you come up with 85.

ANSWERS
801–900

816. **C. 6 pounds**

Mixture problems require you to define a variable before you begin. In this case, let s represent the number of pounds of salted caramel (because it costs less than the chocolate does). Create a table that allows you to visualize the problem.

	Pounds	Price	Total
Salted caramel	s	$5	$5s$
Chocolate	$10 - s$	$10	$10(10 - s)$
Total	10		$80

Use the "Total" column to create your equation. Charlie spent $80 on candy altogether, so the other two figures belong on one side of the equation, and the amount he spent belongs on the other:

$$5s + 10(10 - s) = 80$$
$$5s + 100 - 10s = 80$$
$$-5s + 100 - 100 = 80 - 100$$
$$-5s = -20$$
$$\frac{-5s}{-5} = \frac{-20}{-5}$$
$$s = 4$$

Four pounds of the candy was salted caramel, so the remaining 6 pounds was all chocolate.

817. **C. 240**

In this problem, you're concerned only with the three-fourths of 400 students who go to the National Mall. There are a total of 300 students heading to the National Mall, and of those 300, there are four times as many boys as there are girls. You can express the relationship this way by letting x represent the number of girls and $4x$ represent the number of boys:

$$x + 4x = 300$$
$$5x = 300$$
$$\frac{5x}{5} = \frac{300}{5}$$
$$x = 60$$

That means 60 girls went to the National Mall; because $4x$ represents the number of boys who went, substitute 60 for x and solve:

$$4x = 4(60) = 240$$

Therefore, 240 boys went to the National Mall.

818. D. $228

Define the variable first by letting x represent the first person's share of the money. If x represents the first person's share, $2x$ represents the second person's share. Finally, $2x + 4$ represents the third person's share. Create an equation that looks like this and solve for x:

$$x + (2x) + (2x + 4) = 564$$
$$x + 2x + 2x + 4 = 564$$
$$5x + 4 = 564$$
$$5x + 4 - 4 = 564 - 4$$
$$5x = 560$$
$$\frac{5x}{5} = \frac{560}{5}$$
$$x = 112$$

The first person has $112. Double that to find out how much the second person has:

$$2 \times 112 = 224$$

The second person has $224, so because the third person has $4 more, the third person has $228.

819. B. 25

Define the variable first by letting x represent the number of apples Jakson can buy. Set up an equation to find out how many he can buy at $0.20 while spending $5; then solve for x:

$$0.2x = 5$$
$$\frac{0.2x}{0.2} = \frac{5}{0.2}$$
$$x = 25$$

Jakson can buy 25 apples for $5 if they're $0.20 each.

820. D. $1,440

This problem requires you to do two things: Find the area of the floor, and find the total cost of the flooring. To find the area, multiply the length by the width:

$$12 \times 15 = 180$$

The floor's area is 180 square feet, so multiply that by $8 so you can determine the entire cost:

$$180 \times 8 = 1,440$$

It will cost Quintin $1,440 to buy enough hardwood flooring for the room.

821.   C. 14 laps

A hexagon has six sides, so figure out the entire length of the track first:

$$880 \times 6 = 5{,}280$$

Each lap was 5,280 feet, so now you can let x represent the number of laps Heather needs to run for a total of 73,920 feet. Your equation should look like this:

$$5{,}280x = 73{,}920$$
$$\frac{5{,}280x}{5{,}280} = \frac{73{,}920}{5{,}280}$$
$$x = 14$$

Heather needs to run 14 laps to have that many feet under her belt. (Remember, too, that 5,280 feet equals 1 mile; that means Heather needs to run 14 miles, but don't worry — you'll probably have to do that only once or twice during your military career, unless you become a Special Forces operator.)

822.   A. 270

In a problem such as this one, the first thing you need to do is define the variable. Let x represent the number of minutes Julian used on his international calling plan, because that's the number you don't know. Set up your equation like this (don't forget about the $15 monthly fee) and solve for x:

$$0.21x + 15 = 71.7$$
$$0.21x + 15 - 15 = 71.7 - 15$$
$$0.21x = 56.7$$
$$\frac{0.21x}{0.21} = \frac{56.7}{0.21}$$
$$x = 270$$

Julian used 270 international minutes if his bill was $71.70.

You may want to use quick mental calculations instead of setting up equations. For this question, if you're a bill payer, you'll know to subtract 15 from $71.70 and divide the difference by $0.21 to find how many minutes were used. Doing the calculations without first writing out an equation may be quicker, but you may sacrifice accuracy for speed if you're not careful to look over your work and reread the question.

823.   D. 28 + n = 412

When you see *more* in a word problem, you know you'll have to add. Because the end result is 412 ("after Fred gave Omar n paperclips, Omar had 412"), you know what belongs after the equals sign.

824. **C. 51 square feet**

Let x represent the size of the banner Gabriela bought from Rose, because that's the unknown. Set up an equation that looks like this, and solve for x:

$$2.32x = 118.32$$
$$\frac{2.32x}{2.32} = \frac{118.32}{2.32}$$
$$x = 51$$

The banner Gabriela bought from Rose was 51 square feet.

825. **B. 57 minutes**

This problem requires you to use the same variable twice, once for the car and once for the train. Let t represent how much time will pass before the car and the train are 100 miles apart. Use the distance formula, which says $d = rt$ (where d is distance, r is rate, and t is time), and plug in what you know from the problem. The car traveled $45t$, and the train traveled $60t$, for a total of 100 miles:

$$100 = 45t + 60t$$

Solve for t to figure out how many hours it will take the two vehicles to put 100 miles between them:

$$100 = 45t + 60t$$
$$45t + 60t = 100$$
$$105t = 100$$
$$\frac{105t}{105} = \frac{100}{105}$$
$$t \approx 0.95$$

Because the answer choices are listed in minutes, you'll need to figure out how many minutes equal 95% of an hour:

$$60 \times 0.95 = 57$$

That means that it will take 57 minutes for the two vehicles to be 100 miles apart.

826. **D. $60**

You know that each donation sheet has room for 25 names, and you know that Nathan's goal is $1,500. Let x represent the amount of money each donor would have to pitch in to help Nathan reach his goal. Create an equation and solve for x:

$$25x = 1,500$$
$$\frac{25x}{25} = \frac{1,500}{25}$$
$$x = 60$$

If each donor gives $60 (or if the average donation is $60), Nathan will meet his goal without having to use another donation sheet.

827.   B. $15.00

The problem gives you enough information to find out how much a tie costs. Let t represent the cost of a tie, p represent the cost of a pair of pants, and s represent the cost of a shirt. Then build an equation based on what you already know:

$$4s + 4p + t = 235$$

Replace the variables with the prices listed in the problem; then isolate t:

$$4(25) + 4(30) + t = 235$$
$$100 + 120 + t = 235$$
$$220 + t = 235$$
$$t + 220 - 220 = 235 - 220$$
$$t = 15$$

One tie costs $15.

828.   D. 12

Divide 288 by 24 to find out how many groups of kids needed supervision: $288 \div 24 = 12$. Because there are 12 groups of students and each group of students must be supervised by a teacher, there are 12 teachers.

829.   C. 27 hours

You can express Benjamin's situation with an inequality, letting h represent the number of hours he needs to study. The problem says "the minimum number," so your inequality will look like this:

$$h + 12 \geq 15$$

Solve the inequality just as you would any other:

$$h - 12 \geq 15$$
$$h - 12 + 12 \geq 15 + 12$$
$$h \geq 27$$

That tells you Benjamin needs to study at least 27 hours each week. (You can also use your own arithmetic reasoning to add 15 and 12 — the number of hours Benjamin has to work, plus the number of hours he has to study — in your head to arrive at the correct answer.)

830. D. 50 minutes

Use the distance formula, which says distance = rate × time, to create your equation. Let t represent the amount of time, in hours, that each person is driving. Solve for t:

$$38t + 22t = 50$$
$$60t = 50$$
$$\frac{60t}{60} = \frac{50}{60}$$
$$t = \frac{50}{60}$$
$$t = \frac{5}{6}$$

It will take $\frac{5}{6}$ of an hour for the two to put 50 miles between them. The answer choices are presented in minutes, so convert $\frac{5}{6}$ hour into minutes:

$$\frac{5}{6} \times 60 = \frac{5}{6} \times \frac{60}{1} = \frac{300}{5} = 50$$

That tells you it will take 50 minutes.

831. A. 34

As with most mixture word problems, it's easiest to create a table. Let p represent the number of paperbacks Tysha bought, because they cost less than hardcovers do.

	Amount	Price	Total
Paperback books	p	$15.95	$15.95p$
Hardcover books	$37 - p$	$27.95	$27.95(37 - p)$
Total	37		$626.15

Create an equation using the "Total" column:

$$15.95p + 27.95(37 - p) = 626.15$$
$$15.95p + 1{,}034.15 - 27.95p = 626.15$$
$$-12p + 1{,}034.15 = 626.15$$
$$-12p + 1{,}034.15 - 1{,}034.15 = 626.15 - 1{,}034.15$$
$$-12p = -408$$
$$\frac{-12p}{-12} = \frac{-408}{-12}$$
$$p = 34$$

Tysha bought 34 paperbacks. The remaining three were hardcovers.

832. D. 60 gallons

Define your variable first. Let x represent the number of gallons Olivia needs from the 20% concentrate. That means $80 - x$ will represent the number of gallons she needs of the 60% concentrate.

A table can help you visualize the problem:

	Amount	Percent	Total
20 percent concentrate	x	0.2	$0.2x$
60 percent concentrate	$80 - x$	0.6	$0.6(80 - x)$
Total	80 gallons	0.3	

You don't know what belongs where the "Total" row and the "Total" column intersect. If you multiply across the "Total" row, the answer is 24, so that goes on one side of your equation. Add down the "Total" column and put the sum on the other side of the equation:

$$0.2x + 0.6(80 - x) = 24$$
$$0.2x + 48 - 0.6x = 24$$
$$-0.4x + 48 - 48 = 24 - 48$$
$$-0.4x = -24$$
$$\frac{-0.4x}{-0.4} = \frac{-24}{-0.4}$$
$$-x = -60$$
$$x = 60$$

Olivia needs 60 gallons of the 20% concentrate to make her solution.

833. A. 17z = 340

To find out how much a certain number of items weighs, you multiply. Each loaf weighs z ounces, and there are 17 loaves, which you can represent with the expression $17z$. The problem tells you that together, all 17 loaves weigh 340 ounces. Your equation looks like this:

$$17z = 340$$

Because the question only asks you to create an equation, you can stop there. Don't create more work for yourself on the ASVAB — you already have plenty to do!

834. **C. 44**

Let x represent Sylvia's age now. That means $x+9$ represents Robert's age (remember, he's 9 years older than she is).

That means that in 7 years, Sylvia's age will be $x+7$.

It also means that in 7 years, Robert's age will be $x+16$ (you need to add his original 9-year age gap to 7).

You know that in 7 years, their ages will equal 93. That leaves you with a simple equation to solve using the information from the problem:

$$(x+7)+(x+16)=93$$

Combine like terms to simplify the equation:

$$2x+23=93$$
$$2x+23-23=93-23$$
$$2x=70$$
$$\frac{2x}{2}=\frac{70}{2}$$
$$x=35$$

Because x represents Sylvia's age, and you know $x+9$ represents Robert's age, solve by replacing the variable with the value for x: $35+9=44$.

835. **B. 30 boxes**

Many mathematicians find it's helpful to create a table to figure out a problem like this one. Let x equal the number of boxes of candy Deb bought and enter what you know into a table:

	Number of Boxes	*Price*	*Total*
Sold	$x-20$	$30	$30(x-20)$
Bought	x	$15	$15x$
Profit			150

Deb's profit was $15 per box, because she purchased them for $15 but sold them for $30. Now you know that your equation must look like this:

$$30(x-20)-15x=150$$

When you solve for x, you'll have the number of boxes of candy she bought originally:

$$30(x-20)-15x=150$$
$$30x-600-15x=150$$
$$15x-600+600=150+600$$
$$15x=750$$
$$\frac{15x}{15}=\frac{750}{15}$$
$$x=50$$

Deb bought 50 boxes of candy. You know from the problem that she sold all but 20 boxes, so she *sold* 30 boxes.

836. B. 1,600 bacteria

Use the exponential equation $y=ab^{\frac{t}{p}}$, with a representing the beginning number of bacteria and b representing the growth factor (which is 4, because the number of bacteria quadruples). Let t represent the time Connor is running the experiment, and let p represent the time in which the bacteria population quadruples:

$$y=ab^{\frac{t}{p}}$$
$$y=(200)(4)^{\frac{12}{8}}$$

To find $(4)^{\frac{12}{8}}$ without using a calculator, reduce the fractional exponent:

$$(4)^{\frac{3}{2}}$$

When you read the fractional exponent, you know to find the square root of 4 and cube that answer:

$$\left(\sqrt[2]{4}\right)^3=\left(\sqrt{4}\right)^3=2^3=8$$

Continue solving the problem:

$$y=200\times8$$
$$y=1,600$$

837. A. 22 hours

Define the variable first. Let x represent the number of hours Dorothy needs to groom the horses. Because the problem says "at least," you know that you're dealing with an inequality with a solid minimum; that means you'll use $\geq$ in the problem. Your inequality should look like this:

$$x-10\geq12$$
$$x-10+10\geq12+10$$
$$x\geq22$$

Dorothy needs to groom the horses for at least 22 hours per week.

Although this explanation shows you the algebra involved in solving, you may be able to calculate the correct answer in your head by adding 10 and 12. (If you can answer questions without writing equations when you take the ASVAB, you'll save time.)

838. A. 46

Cats and dogs each have four legs, and chickens have two. Let x represent the number of cats and dogs together, and let y represent the number of chickens. Let z represent the total number of legs among all the animals. Your formula looks like this, because you know how many legs each animal has:

$$4x + 2y = z$$

Now replace the variables with what you know about the number of cats and dogs (there are 10 total) and the number of chickens:

$$z = 4(10) + 2(3)$$
$$= 40 + 6$$
$$= 46$$

The animals have a total of 46 legs.

839. C. 500

Let x represent the number of balloons that Rossalyn originally bought. She sold all but 10, so the number she sold is $x - 10$. Set up a table so you can find the appropriate formula:

	Number of Balloons	Price	Total Income/Spending
Sold	$x - 10$	$5	$5(x - 10)$
Bought	x	$2.50	$2.5x$

To get the profit, subtract the spending (total bought) from the income (total sold). Set the profit equal to $1,225 and then solve for x:

$$5(x - 10) - 2.5x = 1,225$$
$$5x - 50 - 2.5x = 1,225$$
$$5x(10) - 50(10) - 2.5x(10) = 1,225(10)$$
$$50x - 500 - 25x = 12,250$$
$$25x - 500 = 12,250$$
$$25x - 500 + 500 = 12,250 + 500$$
$$25x = 12,750$$
$$\frac{25x}{25} = \frac{12,750}{25}$$
$$x = 510$$

Rossalyn originally bought 510 decorative balloons, but she didn't sell 10 of them. That means she sold 500 balloons to make a profit of $1,225.

840. D. 99

Let x represent what Kathy needs to score on the final exam. There are six tests that count toward her grade — the four she has already taken and the final exam, which is worth two test grades — which means you're dealing with a weighted average problem. Your equation should look like this:

$$\frac{78+83+89+92+x+x}{6}=90$$

Simplify the equation and solve for x:

$$\frac{78+83+89+92+2x}{6}=90$$

$$\frac{78+83+89+92+2x}{6}\times\frac{6}{1}=\frac{90}{1}\times\frac{6}{1}$$

$$\frac{342+2x}{6}\times\frac{6}{1}=540$$

$$342+2x=540$$

$$2x+342-342=540-342$$

$$2x=198$$

$$\frac{2x}{2}=\frac{198}{2}$$

$$x=99$$

Kathy needs to score 99 on both tests to get an A in her geometry class. Fortunately, she's been using this book to study for the ASVAB, so she'll be in great shape.

841. C. 3.5

A good way to solve this problem is to use matrices because there are so many inputs. Put Jazmine and Jeneva in the same matrix, and then create a matrix that represents how much each portion of the class is worth. Your final matrix will show you each girl's total:

$$\begin{bmatrix} 92 & 100 & 89 & 180 \\ 88 & 78 & 85 & 92 \end{bmatrix} \times \begin{bmatrix} 0.4 \\ 0.15 \\ 0.25 \\ 0.2 \end{bmatrix} = \begin{bmatrix} x \\ y \end{bmatrix}$$

Jazmine's average is

$$(92\times0.4)+(100\times0.15)+(89\times0.25)+(80\times0.2)$$
$$=36.8+15+22.25+16$$
$$=90.05$$

And Jeneva's average is

$$(88 \times 0.4) + (78 \times 0.15) + (85 \times 0.25) + (92 \times 0.2)$$
$$= 35.2 + 11.7 + 21.25 + 18.4$$
$$= 86.55$$

Subtract Jeneva's final score from Jazmine's to find out how many percentage points Jazmine came out ahead:

$$90.05 - 86.55 = 3.5$$

Jazmine beat Jeneva by 3.5 percentage points.

If matrices confuse you, you can organize the data in a table, which will allow you to write the same calculations you would with a matrix:

	Tests (worth 40%)	Projects (worth 15%)	Homework (worth 25%)	Quizzes (worth 20%)
Jazmine	92	100	89	80
Jeneva	88	78	85	92

Convert each percent into a decimal and complete the calculations as before.

Matrices and tables are both great ways to organize data, so when you take the ASVAB, do what works best for you.

842. D. $110.29

The shirt cost Alejandra $34.20, but she sold it at a 5% loss. To find out Alejandra's loss, multiply $34.20 by 0.05:

$$34.2 \times 0.05 = 1.71$$

Now subtract her loss, $1.71, from the total she had to start with (she recouped all her money except that amount, which she lost in the sale to Tatiana):

$$112 - 1.71 = 110.29$$

Alejandra now has $110.29.

843. D. 7

Let q equal the number of quarters Bonnie has. Because she has 15 coins and those that aren't quarters are dimes, let $15 - q$ represent the number of dimes Bonnie has. A quarter is worth $0.25 and a dime is worth $0.10, so you can create an equation that reflects Bonnie's change this way:

$$0.25q + 0.1(15 - q) = 2.7$$

Solve for q to find out how many quarters Bonnie has (it's easier if you multiply both sides by 100 so you can get rid of all the decimals):

$$0.25q + 0.1(15 - q) = 2.7$$
$$0.25q + 1.5 - 0.1q = 2.7$$
$$0.15q + 1.5 = 2.7$$
$$0.15q(100) + 1.5(100) = 2.7(100)$$
$$15q + 150 = 270$$
$$15q + 150 - 150 = 270 - 150$$
$$15q = 120$$
$$\frac{15q}{15} = \frac{120}{15}$$
$$q = 8$$

That tells you that Bonnie has 8 quarters. The remaining coins are dimes, and you know she has 15 coins altogether. That means she has 7 dimes.

844. B. 2

This scenario lets you create a simple system of equations that you can solve using substitution. To get your equations, let s represent the number of single-layer cakes Bobby will buy, and let d represent the number of double-layer cakes he'll buy. He needs to buy six cakes and has $200 to spend:

$$\begin{cases} s + d = 6 \\ 25s + 50d = 200 \end{cases}$$

Solve the first equation for s:

$$s + d = 6$$
$$s + d - d = 6 - d$$
$$s = 6 - d$$

Substitute the value of s in the second equation:

$$25s + 50d = 200$$
$$25(6 - d) + 50d = 200$$
$$150 - 25d + 50d = 200$$
$$150 + 25d = 200$$
$$25d = 50$$
$$d = 2$$

Bobby can buy 2 double-layer cakes, but he must leave with 6 cakes. That means he needs to buy 4 single-layer cakes.

ANSWERS
801–900

348   PART 2 The Answers

845. **A. $1,460**

With so many factors at play, you may want to organize a chart to solve this problem.

	Small	Medium	Large
Yellow	3	5	2
Red	10	2	3
Blue	13	3	4
Total	26	10	9

Set up and solve an equation that allows you to calculate the resale value of the mats:

$$26s + 10m + 9l$$
$$= 26(20) + 10(40) + 9(60)$$
$$= 520 + 400 + 540$$
$$= 1,460$$

The total value of all the mats is $1,460.

846. **B. $9,450**

Use the formula $A = P(1-r)^t$ for exponential decay, with P representing the principal (starting amount), r representing the depreciation rate, and t representing the time in years.

$$A = P(1-r)^t$$
$$= 10,500(1-0.1)^1$$
$$= 10,500 \times 0.9$$
$$= 9,450$$

The car will be worth approximately $9,450 after one year.

It's helpful to know the math for these types of problems when you take the ASVAB, but in this case, you could've skipped the formula by subtracting 10% of the car's purchase price ($1,050) from the purchase price: $10,500 - $1,050 = $9,450. (You're dealing with only one year of depreciation.)

847. **D. $11,250**

$15,000 is 75% of $20,000, so you know the car has depreciated at a rate of 25% in one year.

Your new starting amount is $15,000 (that's how much the car was worth after it had depreciated 25% from its original purchase price).

Use the formula $A = P(1-r)^t$, with P representing the principal (starting amount), r representing the depreciation rate, and t representing the time in years:

$$\begin{aligned} A &= P(1-r)^t \\ &= 15,000(1-0.25)^1 \\ &= 15,000 \times 0.75 \\ &= 11,250 \end{aligned}$$

The vehicle is worth \$11,250 after another year has elapsed because it depreciates at a rate of 25% per year.

848.   **D. 385 miles**

To find out how far Captain Mike has traveled, let t represent the number of hours he's been on the go. Use the distance formula, $d = rt$, where d represents distance, r represents rate (speed), and t represents time. You know that Captain Mike leaves the dock at 10 a.m. and is traveling until 5:00 p.m., so he's on the move for 7 hours.

$$d = rt = 55(7) = 385$$

After 7 hours, Captain Mike has logged 385 miles in his boat.

849.   **C. \$1,790.67**

Use the formula $A = P\left(1 + \dfrac{r}{n}\right)^{nt}$ with P representing principal (the beginning investment), r representing the growth rate per year, n representing the number of times interest is compounded per year, and t representing the number of years that have passed. Replace the variables in the formula to find out how much money Matt will have after one year has passed:

$$\begin{aligned} A &= P\left(1 + \frac{r}{n}\right)^{nt} \\ &= 35,000\left(1 + \frac{0.05}{12}\right)^{(12 \times 1)} \\ &= 35,000\left(1\frac{0.05}{12}\right)^{12} \\ &= 35,000(1.05116) \\ &= 36,790.67 \end{aligned}$$

Remember that the question asks you how much Matt had earned in interest, which automatically makes Choices (A) and (D) incorrect, so subtract his original amount from his total amount at the end of the year:

$$36,790.67 - 35,000 = 1,790.67$$

Matt earned \$1,790.67 in interest.

850. B. 1 ounce

This problem requires you to use the formula $y = ab^{\frac{t}{p}}$ because you're working with a time period during which the lemonade divides in two. Let a represent how much lemonade Bill started with (8 ounces), and let b represent the rate of decay (in this case, evaporation), which is 0.5. Let t represent how much time has elapsed, and let p represent the period of time in which half the lemonade evaporates.

$$y = ab^{\frac{t}{p}}$$
$$= 8(0.5)^{\frac{18}{6}}$$
$$= 8(0.5)^3$$
$$= 8(0.125)$$
$$= 1$$

Bill must live in the desert! He'll have only 1 ounce of lemonade left after 18 hours. (*Note:* This formula also works to find the half-life of radioactive materials.)

You may have noticed that there are 3 sets of 6-hour periods in an 18-hour period, so you can use mental math to halve the quantity three times: 8 halved to 4, 4 halved to 2, and 2 halved to 1 ounce.

851. C. 36

This problem looks tough, but it doesn't have to be. First, define the variable by letting m represent Melanie's age now. Right now, Jeanne is three times Melanie's age, so let $3m$ represent Jeanne's age.

You have to add 12 years to both ages because the problem tells you that in 12 years, Melanie will be half Jeanne's age. Your equation looks like this:

$$m + 12 = \tfrac{1}{2}(3m + 12)$$

To find out how old Melanie is right now, solve for m, working your way through the equation as you normally would. Start by multiplying both sides by 2 to get rid of the fraction (and save some time):

$$m + 12 = \tfrac{1}{2}(3m + 12)$$
$$2(m + 12) = (2)\tfrac{1}{2}(3m + 12)$$
$$2m + 24 = 3m + 12$$
$$2m + 24 - 2m = 3m + 12 - 2m$$
$$24 = m + 12$$
$$24 - 12 = m + 12 - 12$$
$$12 = m$$

Melanie is 12 now. Jeanne is three times Melanie's age, so multiply 12 by 3 to discover that Jeanne is 36.

852. C. $76

Let c represent the total cost and create an equation that multiplies the total cost of membership and visits by 2; then solve:

$$c = 2(7+31)$$
$$c = 2(38)$$
$$c = 76$$

The total cost for Starla and Phoenix to buy museum memberships and each visit 31 times throughout the year is $76.

You can work out this problem without creating an equation. Add 31 and 7 (the total cost of membership and 31 visits), and then multiply by 2 to figure out how much it costs for both people.

If you can solve ASVAB problems such as this one quickly, you'll have more time to work on others.

853. A. $25.80

You can figure out exactly how much money Emmanuel has based on the information in the problem. Make a quick chart so you can keep track:

Denomination	Number of Bills/Coins	Total Worth
$10	11	$110
$1	9	$9
$0.25	17	$4.25
$0.10	8	$0.80
$0.05	3	$0.15

Add the total worth together to find out how much Emmanuel has:

```
  110.00
    9.00
    4.25
    0.80
+   0.15
  124.20
```

Emmanuel has $124.20, but he needs $150 to purchase the software program. Subtract $124.20 from $150:

$$150 - 124.2 = 25.8$$

Emmanuel still needs $25.80 to buy the program.

854. A. 12 pounds

It may be helpful to create a table so you know what equation to use. Let c represent the amount of cheese you're buying:

	Amount	Price per Pound	Total
Cheese	c	8	$8c$
Turkey	$19 - c$	12	$12(19 - c)$
Total	19		200

Use the "Total" column on the right to create your equation, and then solve for c:

$$8c + 12(19 - c) = 200$$
$$8c + 228 - 12c = 200$$
$$-4c + 228 = 200$$
$$-4c + 228 - 228 = 200 - 228$$
$$-4c = -28$$
$$\frac{-4c}{-4} = \frac{-28}{-4}$$
$$c = 7$$

That tells you that you'll need 7 pounds of cheese in your 19-pound mixture. The remaining 12 pounds must be turkey.

855. D. Both A and C are correct.

Let x be the variable and create an equation that looks like this:

$$\frac{1}{x} = 2x + -x$$

You can also simplify the equation so it looks like this:

$$\frac{1}{x} = 2x - x$$

Therefore, both Choice (A) and Choice (C) are correct.

Remember, when the ASVAB asks you to express an equation, key words tell you what to do. A *reciprocal* is the opposite of a number (the reciprocal of $\frac{1}{2}$ is $\frac{2}{1}$). *Equal* means you need to use an equals sign, and *sum* means you'll be adding.

856.   D. 2 hours

Let x equal the number of hours both Marines need to work together to fill 56 sandbags. Create an equation that looks like this and solve for h:

$$(12+16)h = 56$$
$$28h = 56$$
$$\frac{28h}{28} = \frac{56}{28}$$
$$h = 2$$

The two Marines can fill 56 sandbags in 2 hours.

857.   B. $3\frac{3}{7}$ hours

Let $\frac{1}{6}$ represent the time it takes the new machine to fill a mold, because in one hour, $\frac{1}{6}$ of the job will be done. Let $\frac{1}{8}$ represent the amount of time it takes the old machine to fill a mold, because in one hour, $\frac{1}{8}$ of the job will be done.

Your equation looks like this, with t representing the amount of time the two machines working together need to fill a full set of crayon molds:

$$\frac{1}{6} + \frac{1}{8} = \frac{1}{t}$$

Find the least common denominator for the entire equation. In this case, it's $24t$. Solve for t:

$$(24t)\frac{1}{6} + (24t)\frac{1}{8} = (24t)\frac{1}{t}$$
$$4t + 3t = 24$$
$$7t = 24$$
$$\frac{7t}{7} = \frac{24}{7}$$
$$t = \frac{24}{7}$$
$$t = 3\frac{3}{7}$$

The two machines can fill up one full set of crayon molds in $3\frac{3}{7}$ hours.

858.   C. $\frac{x+9}{3x} = y$

Watch for the word *quantity*. It indicates that more than one term will be involved. The word *increased* is the first clue that you'll need to add. When you see *times* and *equals*, you know that you'll multiply and use the equals sign. *Quotient* means division (which you may represent as a fraction or a fractional expression). Therefore, your equation looks like this:

$$\frac{x+9}{3x} = y$$

859. **C. 2.1 seconds**

This is a classic distance word problem that you can solve by using the distance formula, which is $d = rt$, with d representing distance, r representing rate (speed), and t representing time.

Create a table that shows you how to set up your equations:

	Distance	Rate	Time
Navy Runner	500	8.3	t_1
Army Runner	500	8.6	t_2
Total	500		

Distance equals rate times time, so use the formula for each runner to find out how quickly she'll reach her team's second participant over a 500-meter distance.

Navy runner:

$$500 = 8.3t$$
$$8.3t = 500$$
$$\frac{8.3t}{8.3} = \frac{500}{8.3}$$
$$t \approx 60.24$$

Army runner:

$$500 = 8.6t$$
$$8.6t = 500$$
$$\frac{8.6t}{8.6} = \frac{500}{8.6}$$
$$t \approx 58.14$$

Remember that the problem wants to know how much sooner the Army runner will reach her team's second participant, so subtract the Army runner's time from the Navy runner's time:

$$60.24 - 58.14 = 2.1$$

The Army runner will reach her team's second participant 2.1 seconds before the Navy runner will.

860. **D. −9**

All the clues you need to create your equation are in the problem. Let x represent the number you're trying to find:

$$x(-3) - 4 = -x + 14$$

Solve for x to find the number:

$$x(-3)-4=-x+14$$
$$-3x-4=-x+14$$
$$-3x-4+4=-x+14+4$$
$$-3x=-x+18$$
$$-3x+x=18+-x+x$$
$$-2x=18$$
$$\frac{-2x}{-2}=\frac{18}{-2}$$
$$x=-9$$

Check your work by replacing x in the original equation with -9:

$$x(-3)-4=-x+14$$
$$-9(-3)-4=-(-9)+14$$
$$27-4=9+14$$
$$23=23$$

861.   C. 6

Let x represent the unknown number (the number of pounds of apples Shane is going to buy). The total cost equals the number of pounds times the price per pound. Because you know apples sell for $4.50 per pound, and because you know he'll spend $27.50 on apples, your equation looks like this:

$$4.5x=27$$

Solve for x:

$$4.5x=27$$
$$\frac{4.5x}{4.5}=\frac{27}{4.5}$$
$$x=6$$

Shane will buy 6 pounds of apples.

862.   D. $960

Because the computer depreciates by 20% each year, after the first year it's worth only 80% of its original price ($1,500). You can find out how much the computer is worth after one year by multiplying 0.8 (for 80%) by the original price:

$$1,500\times0.8=1,200$$

The problem asks you to figure out how much the computer is worth after two years, so multiply 0.8 by the first depreciated price to find out:

$$1,200\times0.8=960$$

The computer is worth $960 after two years.

863.   D. 30

When you see *sum* in a word problem, that means you'll be adding. Another tip-off is the word *is*, which you can express mathematically with an equals sign. Because the problem says *twice a number*, you'll also have to use multiplication.

Let *n* represent the number you need to find. Your equation looks like this:

$$2n + n = 90$$

Solve for *n*:

$$2n + n = 90$$
$$3n = 90$$
$$\frac{3n}{3} = \frac{90}{3}$$
$$n = 30$$

Sometimes it's easiest to plug-and-play the answer choices to find out which is correct. In this case, you need to figure out which of the answer choices times 3 equals 90.

864.   B. 1 hour, 20 minutes

Let *t* represent the amount of time Nichole can spend on English and history. Let 2*t* represent how much time she needs to spend on chemistry and physics, and add them together so they total 2 hours. Solve for *t*:

$$t + 2t = 2$$
$$3t = 2$$
$$\frac{3t}{3} = \frac{2}{3}$$
$$t = \frac{2}{3}$$

Nichole needs $\frac{2}{3}$ of an hour, or 40 minutes, to study English and history. She has two hours total to study, so subtract 40 minutes from two hours, or 120 minutes:

$$120 \text{ minutes} - 40 \text{ minutes} = 80 \text{ minutes}$$

Eighty minutes is 1 hour, 20 minutes.

865.   C. $2,375

Let *x* represent John Q. Private's gross pay, before taxes and other deductions were taken out. Remember that 20% of his gross pay comes out, and he takes home $1,900.

Set up an equation that reflects John Q. Private's situation:

$$x - 0.2x = 1,900$$

Solve for x to find out how much his gross pay is, remembering that the coefficient of x alone is 1:

$$x - 0.2x = 1,900$$
$$0.8x = 1,900$$
$$\frac{0.8x}{0.8} = \frac{1,900}{0.8}$$
$$x = 2,375$$

You can double-check your math by finding 20% of $2,375 and subtracting that figure:

$$2,375 \times 0.2 = 475$$
$$2,375 - 475 = 1,900$$

John Q. Private makes $2,375 per paycheck before taxes and deductions.

866.   A. $2,093

There are at least two ways to solve this problem.

First, you can multiply the original amount by 1.15 $(100\% + 15\%)$ to reflect the new price. Let x represent the new price and convert your percentages to decimals:

$$x = 1,820(1 + 0.15)$$
$$= 1,820(1.15)$$
$$= 2,093$$

The second way to solve this problem requires another step. First find 15% of the original amount by multiplying 15% by $1,820; then add it to the old price:

$$x = 1,820 + (0.15 \times 1,820)$$
$$= 1,870 + 273$$
$$= 2,093$$

Either way, you know that the piano now costs $2,093.

867.   B. 40 milliliters

If you're a visual learner, you'll probably find it helpful to create a table so you can see what you're doing. Let x represent the number of milliliters you need from the 15% concentrate. Let $100 - x$ represent how much you need of the 45% concentrate (remember, you need a total of 100 milliliters of the mixture).

	Amount of Concentrate	Percent	Total
15% Concentrate	x	0.15	0.15x
45% Concentrate	100 – x	0.45	0.45(100 – x)
Total	100	0.27	

When you create your table, you need to fill in the box where the "Total" column and "Total" row intersect so you can create your equation. You get that number by multiplying the amount of concentrate by the percentage (in this case, it's $100 \times 0.27 = 27$).

Your equation should look like this:

$$0.15x + 0.45(100 - x) = 27$$

Solve by isolating x:

$$0.15x + 0.45(100 - x) = 27$$
$$0.15x + 45 - 0.45x = 27$$
$$-0.3x + 45 = 27$$
$$-0.3x + 45 - 45 = 27 - 45$$
$$-0.3x = -18$$
$$\frac{-0.3x}{-0.3} = \frac{-18}{-0.3}$$
$$-x = -60$$
$$x = 60$$

That means you need 60 milliliters of the 15% concentrate in your solution. However, the problem asks you how much of the 45% concentrate you need — but don't worry. You already know that the expression $100 - x$ represents the amount of 45% concentrate you and your lab partner need to create the new mixture. Subtract 60 from 100, and you'll find out that you need 40 milliliters of the 45% concentrate to make your new solution with 27% concentrate.

868. A. About 71.5 hours

The problem is asking you how many hours Rod needs to work, so let h represent the necessary hours. To find out how much his salary is, you multiply h by his hourly wage; that's $20h$. You have to subtract the 30% he pays in taxes and insurance, so convert that to a decimal and multiply it by his salary. Create an equation that looks like this:

$$20h - 0.30(20h) = 1,000$$

Solve the equation to find out how many hours Rod needs to work:

$$20h - 0.30(20h) = 1,000$$
$$20h - 6h = 1,000$$
$$14h = 1,000$$
$$\frac{14h}{14} = \frac{1,000}{14}$$
$$h \approx 71.43$$

You can see that Rod needs to work about 71.43 hours to make $1,000 after taxes and insurance are paid.

Look back at your answer choices; 71.43 isn't one of them, so round up and settle on Choice (A), which is about 71.5 hours.

869. **C. 10 mph**

Create a table that helps you use the formula $d = rt$, where d represents distance, r represents rate (speed), and t represents time. Let p be the plane speed, and let w be the wind speed.

	Distance	Rate	Time
Tailwind	1,120	$p + w$	7 hours
Headwind	1,120	$p - w$	8 hours
Total	2,240		15 hours

When you use the distance formula, your equation looks like this for the tailwind:

$$1,120 = 7(p + w)$$

Your equation for headwind looks like this:

$$1,120 = 8(p - w)$$

The first thing you need to do is get rid of one of the variables, so solve the first equation for p (the plane's speed):

$$1,120 = 7(p + w)$$
$$\frac{1,120}{7} = \frac{7(p + w)}{7}$$
$$160 = p + w$$
$$p + w = 160$$
$$p + w - w = 160 - w$$
$$p = 160 - w$$

Now that you know $p = 160 - w$, replace the variable p in the second equation with that expression:

$$1,120 = 8(p - w)$$
$$1,120 = 8((160 - w) - w)$$
$$1,120 = 8(160 - 2w)$$
$$1,120 = 1,280 - 16w$$
$$1,120 = -16w + 1,280$$
$$1,120 - 1,280 = -16w + 1,280 - 1,280$$
$$-160 = -16w$$
$$-16w = -160$$
$$\frac{-16w}{-16} = \frac{-160}{-16}$$
$$w = 10$$

The wind speed is 10 miles per hour.

870. **D. 60 miles**

You need to find out how many miles each recruiter drove, but there's extra information that can throw you off; it doesn't matter how long either recruiter was on the road.

Let x represent how far the second recruiter drove. Write an equation that reflects how far they drove and the total miles they drove, like this:

$$x + 2x = 90$$

Solve the equation:

$$x + 2x = 90$$
$$3x = 90$$
$$\frac{3x}{3} = \frac{90}{3}$$
$$x = 30$$

Because x represents how far the second recruiter drove, double it to find out how far the first recruiter drove:

$$30(2) = 60$$

The first recruiter drove 60 miles.

871. **A. 280**

Let t represent the number of female airmen going on the field training exercise. Let $\frac{4}{3}t$ represent the number of male airmen who are also going on the field exercise. Because the total number of airmen is 490, your equation looks like this:

$$t + \frac{4}{3}t = 490$$
$$(t \cdot 3) + \left(\frac{4}{3}t \cdot 3\right) = (490 \cdot 3)$$
$$3t + 4t = 1{,}470$$
$$7t = 1{,}470$$
$$\frac{7t}{7} = \frac{1{,}470}{7}$$
$$t = 210$$

There are 210 female airmen on the field exercise, so you can solve the mystery of how many males are going in one of two ways. You can subtract 210 from the total (490 airmen) to find out that there are 280 male airmen, or you can replace t in the expression $\frac{4}{3}t$:

$$\frac{4}{3}(210)$$
$$=\frac{4(210)}{3}$$
$$=\frac{840}{3}$$
$$=280$$

No matter how you look at it, there are 280 male airmen going on the field training exercise.

872.   B. 58

Consecutive integers require you to assign the variable n to the least number in the sequence. Because n represents the least number, and because you need to find the next three even numbers, let $n+2$ represent the next number in the sequence, let $n+4$ represent the next number, and let $n+6$ represent the final number. Create an equation that looks like this:

$$n+(n+2)+(n+4)+(n+6)=220$$

Remove the parentheses and solve for n to find the least number:

$$n+(n+2)+(n+4)+(n+6)=220$$
$$4n+12=220$$
$$4n+12-12=220-12$$
$$4n=208$$
$$\frac{4n}{4}=\frac{208}{4}$$
$$n=52$$

The least number is 52. Because the greatest number is represented by $n+6$, replace n with 52 to find out what it is:

$$52+6=58$$

The largest number in the sequence is 58.

You can use a shortcut that can save you time when these types of questions pop up on the ASVAB. If you have four consecutive even numbers, each one will contribute about a quarter of the sum. In this case, $220 \div 4 = 55$. Two of the numbers in the sequence will be above 55, and two will be below. The next two even numbers above 55 are 56 and 58, so the largest number is 58.

873. A. 13

Let d represent the number of dimes in Misty's purse. You know that she has 21 coins, so represent the number of nickels as $21 - d$ (because the coins that aren't dimes must be nickels).

The total value, $1.70, equals the value of all the dimes plus the value of all the nickels. Each dime is worth $0.10, and each nickel is worth $0.05. Create an equation that looks like this:

$$0.1d + 0.05(21 - d) = 1.7$$

Solve the equation for d to find out how many dimes are in Misty's purse. Remember that in money problems, it's often helpful to multiply by 100:

$$0.1d + 0.05(21 - d) = 1.7$$
$$(0.1d \times 100) + (0.05(21 - d) \times 100) = (1.7 \times 100)$$
$$10d + 5(-d + 21) = 170$$
$$5d + 105 = 170$$
$$5d + 105 - 105 = 170 - 105$$
$$5d = 65$$
$$\frac{5d}{5} = \frac{65}{5}$$
$$d = 13$$

Misty has 13 dimes in her purse. (If the question had asked you how many nickels she had, you would just subtract 13 from 21. That tells you that Misty has 8 nickels.)

874. B. 2.17 hours

Distance equals rate times time, so let t represent the number of hours it will take for the station wagon and the motorcycle to be 250 miles apart. Figure out the distances separately, and then add the two distances together to reach the total distance (250 miles).

Let $40t$ represent the station wagon's distance, and let $75t$ represent the motorcycle's distance to create your equation. Isolate t to solve:

$$40t + 75t = 250$$
$$115t = 250$$
$$\frac{115t}{115} = \frac{250}{115}$$
$$t \approx 2.17$$

The two vehicles will be 250 miles apart in about 2.17 hours.

875. C.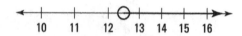

Don't get mixed up on the two instances of "less than" in this word problem. Create an inequality that looks like this, letting x represent the number you don't know, and then solve. Don't forget to reverse the inequality sign whenever you multiply or divide both sides by a negative number.

$$\frac{3}{5}x < x - 5$$
$$\frac{3x}{5} \cdot 5 < 5(x-5)$$
$$3x < 5x - 25$$
$$3x - 5x < 5x - 25 - 5x$$
$$-2x < -25$$
$$2x > 25$$
$$\frac{2x}{2} > \frac{25}{2}$$
$$x > 12.5$$

Your graph will look like this:

876. C. 12π cm

The formula for the circumference of a circle is $C = 2\pi r$, where C represents the circumference and r represents the circle's radius. The problem gives you the radius, so create your equation and solve for C:

$$C = 2\pi r$$
$$= 2\pi(6)$$
$$= 12\pi$$

877. **D. 18 cm**

The formula for the area of a circle is $A = \pi r^2$, where A represents the area and r represents the radius. The radius is half the length of the diameter, which you want to find. Set up the area formula:

$$A = \pi r^2$$
$$81\pi = \pi r^2$$
$$\frac{81\pi}{\pi} = \frac{\pi r^2}{\pi}$$
$$81 = r^2$$
$$\sqrt{81} = r$$
$$r = 9$$

The radius is 9, so double that to find the circle's diameter:

$$9 \times 2 = 18$$

The circle's diameter is 18 centimeters.

878. **B. 93 feet**

The formula for perimeter is $P = 2l + 2w$, where P represents perimeter, l represents length, and w represents width. The formula for area is $A = lw$. You have a system of equations:

$$2l + 2w = 486$$
$$lw = 13,950$$

Solve using substitution: That is, solve one equation for one variable so you can put its value into the other equation. It's simpler to solve the first equation than the second. Here's how to solve for l. You can divide everything by 2 to make the calculations simpler (and so you're working with like terms when you solve the second equation):

$$2l + 2w = 486$$
$$\frac{2l + 2w}{2} = \frac{486}{2}$$
$$l + w = 243$$
$$l + w - w = 243 - w$$
$$l = 243 - w$$

Replace l in the second equation so you can solve for w:

$$lw = 13,950$$
$$(243 - w)w = 13,950$$
$$243w - w^2 = 13,950$$
$$243w - w^2 - 13,950 = 13,950 - 13,950$$
$$243w - w^2 - 13,950 = 0$$

Now you have a quadratic equation that you can solve by factoring:

$$-w^2 + 243w - 13,950 = 0$$
$$-\left(w^2 - 243w + 13,950\right) = 0$$
$$-\left(w - 93\right)\left(w - 150\right) = 0$$

Solve each expression:

$$w - 93 = 0 \qquad \text{or} \qquad w - 150 = 0$$
$$w - 93 + 93 = 0 + 93 \qquad w - 150 + 150 = 0 + 150$$
$$w = 93 \qquad\qquad\qquad w = 150$$

The problem tells you that the narrower side of the garden faces the street, so you know that Woody's Fences Inc. will need to send 93 feet of white fencing with the workers.

879. D. 5 meters

The formula for the area of a square is $A = s^2$, where A represents the area and s represents the length of a side. Replace the variable A with what you know, and then solve:

$$25 = s^2$$
$$\sqrt{25} = s$$
$$s = 5$$

880. A. 85,408 sq. ft.

This question is asking you for the surface area of the water tank. Don't forget that the cylinder has two ends as well. You can find the surface area of a right cylinder with the formula $SA = 2\pi rh + 2\pi r^2$, where SA represents the surface area and r represents the radius. Fill in the variables with what you know and solve:

$$SA = 2\pi rh + 2\pi r^2$$
$$= 2\pi(40)(300) + 2\pi(40)^2$$
$$= 80\pi(300) + 2\pi(1,600)$$
$$= 24,000\pi + 3,200\pi$$
$$= 27,200\pi$$

Pi is approximately equal to 3.14, so to find the answer, multiply 27,200 by 3.14:

$$27,200 \times 3.14 = 85,408$$

The surface area of this massive cylinder is approximately 85,408 square feet.

(In the military, you'll hear the expression, "It's good enough for government work!" That means you're close enough to the right answer, and on the ASVAB, 3.14 is good enough for pi. However, it can't hurt to learn that pi is also approximately equal to $\frac{22}{7}$.)

881. **A. 12 m**

When you take the ASVAB, you get unlimited scrap paper. You may find it helpful to draw a diagram to help you visualize the problem:

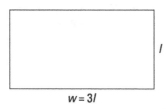

$w = 3l$

The formula for the perimeter of a rectangle is $P = 2l + 2w$, where P represents perimeter, l represents length, and w represents width. The problem gives you the perimeter, and you can figure out the width based on the information given:

$$2l + 2w = P$$
$$2l + 2(3l) = 32$$
$$2l + 6l = 32$$
$$8l = 32$$
$$\frac{8l}{8} = \frac{32}{8}$$
$$l = 4$$

The field's length is 4 meters, so multiply 4 by 3 to find out how wide the field is:

$$4 \times 3 = 12$$

The field is 12 meters wide.

882. **C. 50.24 cm**

The formula to find the circumference of a circle is $C = 2\pi r$, where C represents the circumference and r represents the radius. Replace the variables in the formula with what you know from the problem, recalling that pi is approximately equal to 3.14:

$$C = 2\pi r$$
$$= 2\pi(8)$$
$$= 16\pi$$
$$\approx 16(3.14)$$
$$= 50.24$$

883. D. 162 cm²

There's some extra information in this problem that you don't need. It doesn't matter that the wire is 8-gauge, so ignore that part of the problem. What *does* matter is that the formula for the perimeter of a rectangle is $P = 2l + 2w$, where P represents perimeter, l represents length, and w represents width. The problem tells you that the rectangle's width is twice its length, so you know that $w = 2l$. Put everything you know into the formula to find the answer:

$$2l + 2w = P$$
$$2l + 2(2l) = 54$$
$$2l + 4l = 54$$
$$6l = 54$$
$$\frac{6l}{6} = \frac{54}{6}$$
$$l = 9$$

The length of one of the sides is 9 cm. Remember that a rectangle has four sides. If two of them are each 9 cm and the total perimeter is 54 cm, you can subtract 18 from 54 to find the length of the two remaining sides:

$$54 - 18 = 36$$

Two sides together are 36 centimeters, so each is 18 centimeters.

The dimensions of the rectangle are 9 centimeters by 18 centimeters, so now you can find the area:

$$A = lw$$
$$= 9 \times 18$$
$$= 162$$

The rectangle's area is 162 square centimeters.

884. C. 2 feet

You may want to create a diagram to help you visualize the problem:

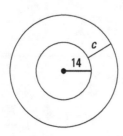

The swimming pool has a radius of 14 feet (the radius is half the diameter), and the width of the concrete surface is c. This problem requires you to find the area of the pool:

$$A = \pi r^2$$
$$= \pi (14)^2$$
$$= 196\pi$$

Knowing the area of the pool (196π) lets you find the area of the pool plus the concrete surface. Remember, the problem tells you the concrete surface's area is 60π square feet:

$$196\pi + 60\pi = 256\pi$$

Find the whole area's radius:

$$256\pi = \pi r^2$$
$$\frac{256\pi}{\pi} = \frac{\pi r^2}{\pi}$$
$$256 = r^2$$
$$\sqrt{256} = r$$
$$r = 16$$

The whole area's radius is 16 feet, so subtract 14 feet (the radius of the pool) from that to find out how wide the concrete surface is:

$$16 - 14 = 2$$

The concrete surface is 2 feet wide.

885. C. 7 cm

The formula to find the area of a square is $A = s^2$, where A represents the area and s represents the length of one side. Replace A in the formula and solve for s:

$$49 = s^2$$
$$\sqrt{49} = s$$
$$s = 7$$

886. D. 729 cubic feet

To find the volume of a cube when you know its edge length, use the formula $V = s^3$, where V represents volume and s represents edge length.

$$V = 9^3 = 729$$

The cube's volume is 729 cubic feet.

887. **B. 22 millimeters**

The formula for the area of a circle is $A = \pi r^2$, where A represents the area and r represents the diameter. Find the radius with the area formula:

$$\pi r^2 = A$$
$$3.14r^2 = 379.94$$
$$\frac{3.14r^2}{3.14} = \frac{379.94}{3.14}$$
$$r^2 = 121$$
$$r = \sqrt{121}$$
$$r = 11$$

The diameter is twice the length of the radius, so if the circle's radius is 11 millimeters, its diameter must be 22 millimeters.

---

888. **B. 4 in.²**

The problem describes a triangle that looks like this:

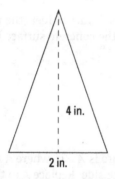

You know the base measures 2 inches and the height measures 4 inches. With this information, use the area formula for a triangle, which is $A = \frac{1}{2}bh$, where A is the area, b is the base, and h is the height:

$$A = \frac{1}{2}bh$$
$$= \frac{1}{2}(2 \cdot 4)$$
$$= \frac{1}{2}(8)$$
$$= 4$$

The triangle's area is 4 square inches.

889. C. 9 inches

When you see *hypotenuse* in a word problem, dust off the Pythagorean theorem, which says $a^2 + b^2 = c^2$. The variable c represents the hypotenuse — the longest side of the triangle — and a and b represent the shorter sides, which are the legs.

First, solve for a in terms of b (you could instead solve for b in terms of a, if you wanted to):

$$a + b = 49$$
$$a + b - b = 49 - b$$
$$a = 49 - b$$

Now you have what you need to use the Pythagorean theorem; replace the variables with what you know:

$$a^2 + b^2 = c^2$$
$$(49 - b)^2 + b^2 = 41^2$$
$$2{,}401 - 98b + b^2 + b^2 = 1{,}681$$
$$2b^2 - 98b + 720 = 0$$
$$b^2 - 49b + 360 = 0$$
$$(b - 9)(b - 40) = 0$$
$$b = 9 \text{ or } 40$$

Solving this quadratic equation gives you both legs of the triangle, although the variable is only b. The shortest is 9 inches.

890. D. 8 in.

The formula to find the perimeter of a rectangle is $P = 2l + 2w$, where P represents the perimeter, l represents the length, and w represents the width.

Find the lengths by using the perimeter formula:

$$P = 2l + 2w$$
$$38 = 2(11) + 2w$$
$$38 = 22 + 2w$$
$$38 = 2w + 22$$
$$38 - 22 = 2w + 22 - 22$$
$$16 = 2w$$
$$2w = 16$$
$$\frac{2w}{2} = \frac{16}{2}$$
$$w = 8$$

The other interior side of the picture frame is 8 inches long.

891.   A. 100°

At first, you may think there isn't enough information to find the answer — but there is, so Choice (D) is out of the question.

You already know that a triangle's angles must add up to 180°. Let β represent the greatest angle and create a formula that looks like this:

$$180 = \beta + (\beta - 65) + (\beta - 55)$$
$$180 = 3\beta - 120$$
$$180 + 120 = 3\beta - 120 + 120$$
$$300 = 3\beta$$
$$3\beta = 300$$
$$\frac{3\beta}{3} = \frac{300}{3}$$
$$\beta = 100$$

The greatest angle measures 100°.

892.   D. 15 cm

Based on what the problem tells you, you can create a sketch to help you visualize the problem:

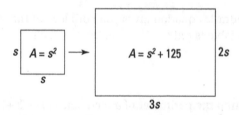

The square's area is s^2, and you can find the rectangle's area by multiplying the length times the width. Create your formula for the area of the rectangle, $(2s)(3s) = s^2 + 125$, and solve for the length of one side of the square first:

$$(2s)(3s) = s^2 + 125$$
$$6s^2 = s^2 + 125$$
$$6s^2 - (s^2 + 125) = s^2 + 125 - (s^2 + 125)$$
$$5s^2 - 125 = 0$$

Now you have a quadratic equation to solve. In this case, factoring is the simplest way to solve it:

$$5s^2 - 125 = 0$$
$$5(s^2 - 25) = 0$$
$$5(s + 5)(s - 5) = 0$$

You know that the length of a side can't be negative, so solve $s - 5 = 0$:

$$s - 5 = 0$$
$$s - 5 + 5 = 0 + 5$$
$$s = 5$$

The length of one side of the square is 5 centimeters. Now you can find the longest side of the rectangle, represented by $3s$:

$$3 \times 5 = 15$$

The longest side of the rectangle is 15 centimeters.

893. **A. 9 feet**

You have enough information to create an equation and solve for the garden's width. Remember that area equals length times width, and solve:

$$18w = 162$$
$$\frac{18w}{18} = \frac{162}{18}$$
$$w = 9$$

Emil needs to build an 18-foot-by-9-foot garden to cover enough space to make Bertha happy.

894. **A. 10 meters**

If drawing diagrams helps you visualize problems, here's what yours should look like:

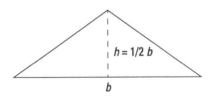

The formula for the area of a triangle is $A = \frac{1}{2}bh$, where A represents area, b represents the length of the base, and h represents height.

The problem tells you that $h = \frac{1}{2}b$, so fill in the formula and replace the variables you know:

$$100 = \frac{1}{2}(b)\left(\frac{1}{2}b\right)$$
$$\left(\frac{1}{2}b\right)\left(\frac{1}{2}b\right) = 100$$
$$\frac{1}{4}b^2 = 100$$
$$\frac{1}{4}(4)b^2 = 100(4)$$
$$b^2 = 400$$
$$\sqrt{b^2} = \pm\sqrt{400}$$
$$b = \pm 20$$

Notice that −20 isn't a solution, because the base of a triangle can't be negative.

The base of the triangle is 20 meters, and the problem says that the height is half that, so the triangle's height is 10 meters.

895.　C. 283.39 square inches

The question is asking you to find the area of a circle with a diameter of 19 inches. You know that because it needs to have a $\frac{1}{2}$-inch overlap all around.

To find the area of a circle, use the formula $A = \pi r^2$. A circle's radius is half its diameter, so in this case, it's 9.5 inches:

$$A = \pi(9.5)^2$$
$$= \pi(90.25)$$
$$= 90.25\pi$$
$$\approx 90.25(3.14)$$
$$= 283.385$$

The manhole cover's area is approximately 283.385 square inches, which you can round up to 283.39 square inches because it's one of the answer choices.

896.　A. 20 cu. ft

The problem deals with the volume of rectangular prisms. To find the volume, use $V = lwh$, where V represents the volume, l represents the length, w represents the width, and h represents the height.

$$V = 2 \times 2.5 \times 1 = 5$$

Each box holds 5 cubic feet of sand, but there are four boxes. Multiply 5 by 4 to find that the soldiers will have to put 20 cubic feet of sand into the boxes.

897.   **D. 942 in.³**

To find the volume of a right cylinder, use $V = \pi r^2 h$, where V represents volume, r represents radius, and h represents height. The canister has a diameter of 10 inches, so its radius is 5 inches.

Plug in the values you know from the question and solve:

$$\begin{aligned} V &= \pi(5)^2(12) \\ &= \pi\left(5^2 \cdot 12\right) \\ &= \pi(25 \cdot 12) \\ &= 300\pi \\ &\approx 300(3.14) \\ &= 942 \end{aligned}$$

Using 3.14 for pi, you can tell that the canister holds approximately 942 cubic inches of pesticide.

898.   **C. 1,099 cm³**

To find the volume of the soda in the can, use the formula $V = \pi r^2 h$, where V represents volume, r represents the radius, and h represents the height. Remember that 1 centimeter of space is left at the top of the can, so the actual height of the soda in the can is only 14 centimeters.

$$\begin{aligned} V &= \pi(5)^2(14) \\ &= \pi(25 \cdot 14) \\ &= 350\pi \\ &\approx 350(3.14) \\ &= 1,099 \end{aligned}$$

The volume of the soda is approximately 1,099 cubic centimeters.

899.   **B. 25 cm**

The perimeter of any figure is the sum of all its sides, so create an equation that represents each side of the triangle, letting x represent the length of the shortest side. Let the second side be $x + 12$ and the longest side be $4x$. Set the sum of the sides equal to 162 and solve for x:

$$\begin{aligned} 4x + (x + 12) + x &= 162 \\ 6x + 12 &= 162 \\ 6x + 12 - 12 &= 162 - 12 \\ 6x &= 150 \\ \frac{6x}{6} &= \frac{150}{6} \\ x &= 25 \end{aligned}$$

The triangle's shortest side is 25 centimeters.

900. D. 33 cm²

This problem requires you to take a few steps to arrive at the answer. Create a table that lets you visualize what to use in your equation, letting x represent the length of one side of the square:

	Square	Rectangle
Length	x	$x+6$
Width	x	$x-2$

The problem gives you the perimeter of the rectangle, so use the perimeter formula to find the dimensions — you'll need them to find the rectangle's area. Remember that $P = 2l + 2w$, where P represents perimeter, l represents length, and w represents width:

$$2l + 2w = P$$
$$2(x+6) + 2(x-2) = 28$$
$$2x + 12 + 2x - 4 = 28$$
$$4x + 8 = 28$$
$$4x + 8 - 8 = 28 - 8$$
$$4x = 20$$
$$\frac{4x}{4} = \frac{20}{4}$$
$$x = 5$$

Now you know that the original square's sides each measured 5 centimeters. As the problem tells you, one side was increased by 6 centimeters to create the rectangle, while the other was decreased by 2 centimeters. That makes one side 11 centimeters and the other 3 centimeters. You can find the area of the rectangle with the formula $A = lw$, where A represents the area, l represents the length, and w represents the width:

$$A = 11 \times 3 = 33$$

The rectangle's area is 33 square centimeters.

901. B. 88°

Let β represent the measure of the largest angle in the triangle, and remember that all the angles in a triangle add up to 180°. Create expressions that represent the other angles:

Second angle: $\beta - 33$

Smallest angle: $\beta - 51$

The measurement for the largest angle is $\beta - 51$ because the sum of 18 and 33 is 51, and the smallest angle therefore has a measure that is 51° less than the largest angle.

Create an angle-sum formula and solve for β:

$$\beta + (\beta - 33) + (\beta - 51) = 180$$
$$3\beta - 84 = 180$$
$$3\beta - 84 + 84 = 180 + 84$$
$$3\beta = 264$$
$$\frac{3\beta}{3} = \frac{264}{3}$$
$$\beta = 88$$

The largest angle is 88°.

You can check your work by finding the smallest and second angles and then adding them together to make sure the sum is 180°:

Second angle: $88 - 33 = 55$
Smallest angle: $88 - 51 = 37$
$88 + 55 + 37 = 180$

902. D. 95°

All the angles in a triangle must add up to 180°, so you can solve this problem with a little algebra:

$$c + 38 + 47 = 180$$
$$c + 85 = 180$$
$$c + 85 - 85 = 180 - 85$$
$$c = 95$$

The missing angle, angle C, is 95°.

903. A. 4,250 square feet

Don't be distracted by extra information in an ASVAB word problem. What time each soldier started sweeping doesn't matter, because the problem only asks you to identify the motor pool's area.

You can draw a sketch of the motor pool so you can visualize the part that each specialist swept:

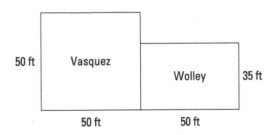

You know that Wolley's portion of the motor pool was 50 feet by 35 feet (the problem tells you that his portion was 15 feet shorter than Vasquez's area).

Figure out the area each soldier swept and add them together:

> Vasquez: $50 \times 50 = 2,500$ square feet
> Wolley: $50 \times 35 = 1,750$ square feet
> $2,500 + 1,750 = 4,250$ square feet

904. A. 96 ft²

This problem asks you for the number of square feet Deedee will have swept, which is the tip-off that you need to find area. The area of a rectangle can be expressed with the formula $A = lw$, where A represents area, l represents length, and w represents width. Replace the variables in the formula with the numbers from the problem:

$$A = 8 \times 12 = 96$$

Deedee will have swept 96 square feet, or 96 ft².

Remember that area is always measured in square units, which makes Choice (C) a no-go right off the bat. (Any time you can automatically rule out answers on the ASVAB, do it.)

905. D. 36

One foot equals 12 inches, and the area of a square is the length of a side squared; that means a 1-foot square's area is 144 square inches $\left(12^2 = 12 \times 12 = 144\right)$.

Each block that Carson and Jolie stack has an area of 4 square inches $(2 \times 2 = 4)$. Divide 144 square inches by 4 square inches to find out how many blocks Carson and Jolie must stack: $144 \div 4 = 36$.

You can check your work by finding the number of blocks they use on each side:

$$\sqrt{36} = 6$$

They'll use 6 2-inch blocks on each side, which adds up to 1 foot on each side.

906. B. 161.25 cm²

To solve for the area of a kite, use $A = \dfrac{(d_1 \times d_2)}{2}$, where d_1 represents the first diagonal and d_2 represents the second diagonal. The problem gives you both measurements, so plug them into the formula and solve:

$$A = \frac{21.5 \times 15}{2}$$
$$= \frac{322.5}{2}$$
$$= 161.25$$

The kite's area is 161.25 square centimeters.

907. **B. 109.8 in.**

To find the perimeter of a kite, use $P = 2a + 2b$, where P represents perimeter, a represents one side, and b represents the adjacent side. Replace the variables in the equation with what you know from the problem to solve for the kite's perimeter:

$$P = 2(24.5) + 2(30.4)$$
$$= 49 + 60.8$$
$$= 109.8$$

The kite's perimeter is 109.8 inches.

Be sure you read the answer choices carefully when you take the ASVAB, because attention to detail is incredibly important on the test (and in the military)! Two of the choices for this question simply have the numbers transposed.

908. **D. 216 square inches**

Sketch the two rectangles and assign variables. Let x represent the original width of the rectangle:

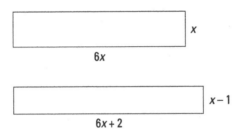

The formula for the area of a rectangle is $A = lw$, where A represents the area, l represents the length, and w represents the width. Figure out the area of the second rectangle by using the values from your sketch:

$$(6x + 2)(x - 1) = 190$$
$$6x^2 - 6x + 2x - 2 = 190$$
$$6x^2 - 4x - 2 = 190$$
$$6x^2 - 4x - 2 - 190 = 190 - 190$$
$$6x^2 - 4x - 192 = 0$$

You can solve this quadratic equation by factoring:

$$6x^2 - 4x - 192$$
$$= 2(3x^2 - 2x - 96)$$
$$= 2(x - 6)(3x + 16)$$

Set each factor equal to zero (the zero factor principle says that if the product of two terms is zero, at least one of the original terms was zero):

$$x - 6 = 0$$
$$x - 6 + 6 = 0 + 6$$
$$x = 6$$

Because you know that the width of a rectangle can't be negative, you don't have to solve the other equation (but if you did, you'd come up with $-\frac{16}{3}$).

The width of the original rectangle is 6 inches, and you know that the rectangle is six times as long as it is wide. Multiply 6 by 6, and you find that the original rectangle measures 36 inches long by 6 inches wide; then find the area: $36 \times 6 = 216$ square inches.

909.   C. 120 m²

The garden is square, so find its dimensions by finding the square root of its area:

$$\sqrt{169} = 13$$

Each side of the garden is 13 meters long.

The walkway needs to measure 2 meters across, so add 2 meters to each side to get the size of the garden and walkway together; each side is 17 meters long.

You can find the area of the entire project — the garden plus the walkway — by squaring 17: $17^2 = 289$.

Now subtract the smaller area (the garden) from the area covering the walkway and the garden: $289 - 169 = 120$. The walkway's area is 120 square meters.

910.   B. 6.28 cm

The problem is asking you to find the circumference of two circles: one with a radius of 5 centimeters and one with a diameter of 12 centimeters.

It's always a good idea to save time when you're taking the ASVAB, so leave the answer in terms of pi until you need to solve with it. You can use the formula $C = \pi d$, where d represents diameter, or the formula $C = 2\pi r$, where r represents radius, to solve this problem. Start with the first circle; its circumference is $2\pi(5)$, or 10π. The second circle's circumference is 12π.

The difference between the two circles is $12\pi - 10\pi = 2\pi$. Now solve by replacing π with 3.14: $2 \times 3.14 = 6.28$. The difference is 6.28 centimeters.

911.   C. 18 cm

The problem tells you that you're dealing with three consecutive integers (n, $n+1$, and $n+2$) and that the triangle's perimeter is equal to eight more than twice the shortest side (n); therefore, your equation will look like this (remember, the perimeter of a triangle is the sum of all its sides):

$$n+(n+1)+(n+2)=2n+8$$
$$3n+3=2n+8$$
$$3n+3-2n=2n+8-2n$$
$$n+3=8$$
$$n+3-3=8-3$$
$$n=5$$

The triangle's shortest side (n) measures 5 centimeters, and the second side ($n+1$) is 6 centimeters. That means the final side ($n+2$) is 7 centimeters. (Because you know they're consecutive integers, you can count to figure out the next two numbers.) Then add the three sides to find the triangle's perimeter:

$$5+6+7=18$$

The triangle's perimeter is 18 centimeters.

912.   A. 4 in.

The formula to find the area of a trapezoid is $A=\frac{1}{2}h(b_1+b_2)$, where A represents the area, b_1 represents length of the first base, b_2 represents the length of the second base, and h represents the height. Replace the variables in the formula and solve:

$$52=\frac{1}{2}h(11+15)$$
$$52=\frac{1}{2}h(26)$$
$$52=13h$$
$$\frac{52}{13}=\frac{13h}{13}$$
$$4=h$$

The trapezoid is 4 inches high.

913. **A. 24 cm²**

The formula to find the area of a triangle is $A = \frac{1}{2}bh$, where A represents area, b represents the length of the triangle's base, and h represents the triangle's height. Replace the variables and solve the problem:

$$A = \frac{1}{2}(12 \cdot 4)$$
$$A = \frac{1}{2}(48)$$
$$A = 24$$

The triangle's area is 24 square centimeters.

914. **B. 12 feet**

You can use the area formula for a right triangle to figure out the mat's height, because you know that the mat needs to fit in a 90° corner. The area formula for a right triangle is $A = \frac{1}{2}bh$, where A represents area, b represents the length of the base, and h represents the triangle's height. Your equation looks like this:

$$18 = \frac{1}{2}(3h)$$

Multiply both sides of the equation by 2 to simplify, and then solve:

$$36 = 3h$$
$$\frac{36}{3} = \frac{3h}{3}$$
$$12 = h$$

Ms. Ruiz's mat needs to have a 12-foot height.

915. **C. 140 square feet**

The formula to find the area of a trapezoid is $A = \frac{1}{2}h(b_1 + b_2)$, where A represents area, b_1 represents one base, b_2 represents the other base, and h represents the height. Replace the variables in the formula and solve:

$$A = \frac{1}{2}(7)(8+12)$$
$$= \frac{1}{2}(7)(20)$$
$$= \frac{140}{2}$$
$$= 70$$

The trapezoid's area is 140 square feet.

916. **B. 180°**

Create a sketch and assign variables that represent what the question is asking. Let x represent the measure of the smallest angles (your sketch doesn't have to be to scale; after all, you don't know the measure of the angles):

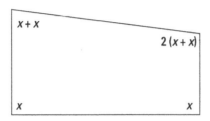

The sum of all the angles in a quadrilateral is 360°, so write your equation based on the values in your sketch:

$$x + x + (x + x) + 2(x + x) = 360$$
$$8x = 360$$
$$\frac{8x}{8} = \frac{360}{8}$$
$$x = 45$$

The smallest angles in the quadrilateral measure 45°, and the problem tells you that the fourth angle is twice the sum of the third angle. The third angle is equal to the sum of the two equal angles. That means $\angle 3$ is $45 + 45 = 90$. Therefore, $\angle 4$ is $90 \times 2 = 180°$.

917. **D. 24π ft**

The formula to find the circumference of a circle is $C = 2\pi r$, where C represents the circumference and r represents the radius. Replace the variable r in the equation with the radius from the problem (12) and solve using pi:

$$C = 2\pi(12) = 24\pi$$

918. **C. 128π cm^3**

Use the formula to find the volume of a cylinder, which is is $V = \pi r^2 h$, where V represents the volume, r represents the radius, and h represents the height. Replace the variables in the equation and solve:

$$V = \pi(4)^2(8)$$
$$= \pi(16 \cdot 8)$$
$$= 128\pi$$

You can also find the area of the base of the cylinder, which you can multiply by the cylinder's height to get its volume.

To find the area of the base of the cylinder, use the formula to find the area of a circle: $A = \pi r^2$, where A represents the area and r represents the radius:

$$A = \pi(4)^2 = 16\pi$$

The base's area is 16π cm².

Multiply the base's area by the cylinder's height to find the volume: $16\pi \text{ cm}^2 \times 8 \text{ cm} = 128\pi \text{ cm}^3$.

919. **D. 28.26 square feet**

Draw a diagram that shows the horse's grazing area:

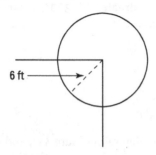

6 ft

From the diagram, you can see that the horse's grazing area is part of a circle with a radius of 6 feet — that's the length of the rope tying the horse to the post. You can also see that because the fence cuts into the circle at a 90° angle, the grazing area takes up 25%, or one-fourth, of the circle.

Find the area of one-fourth of the circle, remembering that $A = \pi r^2$ (and that 25% of 36 is 9):

$$A = 9\pi$$
$$\approx 9 \times 3.14$$
$$= 28.26$$

If you want to take the long route, find 36π (remember, $A = \pi r^2$) to find that the area of the entire circle is approximately 113.04 square feet. Because the horse is confined to only a quarter of that circle, multiply the circle's area by 0.25 to find the horse's grazing area: $113.04 \times 0.25 = 28.26$ square feet.

920. **B. 1,944 cm²**

The formula to find the surface area of a cube is $SA = 6s^3$, where SA represents surface area and s represents the length of one side. Replace the variables in the formula and solve:

$$A = 6\left(18^2\right) = 6\left(324\right) = 1{,}944$$

The cube's surface area is 1,944 square centimeters.

921. **C. 30.25 feet**

The angle-angle similarity postulate lets you solve this problem because when you're dealing with two right triangles that have a shadow cast at the same angle, the proportions of the triangles are the same.

Sketch the problem so you can assign variables and create an equation:

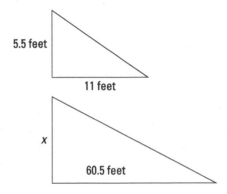

Because the triangles are similar, and because 5.5 is divisible by 11, you can set up a proportion that says 5.5 is to 11 as x is to 60.5, letting x represent the short leg of the larger triangle:

$$\frac{5.5}{11} = \frac{x}{60.5}$$

Isolate x to solve:

$$\frac{5.5}{11} = \frac{x}{60.5}$$
$$0.5\left(60.5\right) = \frac{x}{60.5}\left(60.5\right)$$
$$30.25 = x$$

Vicki's office building is 30.25 feet tall.

922. **C. 198 sq. ft**

To find the area of a parallelogram, use $A = bh$, where A represents the area, b represents the length of the base, and h represents the height.

$$A = 11 \cdot 18 = 198$$

The billboard covers 198 square feet.

923. **A. 14 feet**

The formula to find the area of a parallelogram is $A = bh$, where A represents the area, b represents the length of the base, and h represents the height. You can use this formula to find the missing height; replace the variables with what you know:

$$16h = 224$$
$$\frac{16h}{16} = \frac{224}{16}$$
$$h = 14$$

The vegetable garden is 16 feet long and 14 feet high.

924. **C. 42 in.²**

You can find the area of a triangle with the formula $A = \frac{1}{2}bh$, where A represents the area, b represents the length of the base, and h represents the triangle's height. Replace the variables in the formula and solve:

$$A = \frac{1}{2}(7 \cdot 12)$$
$$= \frac{1}{2}(84)$$
$$= 42$$

The triangle's area is 42 square inches.

925. **A. 35°**

You know that all the angles in a triangle must add up to 180°, so you can create an equation that looks like this, where x represents the measure of the third angle:

$$x + 2x + (2x + 5) = 180$$
$$5x + 5 = 180$$
$$5x + 5 - 5 = 180 - 5$$
$$5x = 175$$
$$\frac{5x}{5} = \frac{175}{5}$$
$$x = 35$$

The third angle measures 35°.

926. B. 34.54 feet

You can start solving this problem with a sketch that represents Cherina's patio with the greatest possible hot tub in place:

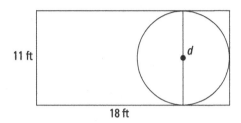

You know that the hot tub can't exceed 11 feet in diameter, because that's the shortest side of Cherina's patio. That means the maximum radius is 5.5 feet, which you can use to determine the circumference of the hot tub. The formula to find the circumference of a circle is $C = 2\pi r$, where C represents circumference and r represents radius:

$$C = 2\pi(5.5)$$
$$= 11\pi$$
$$\approx 11 \times 3.14$$
$$= 34.54$$

The maximum circumference Cherina's hot tub can have is 34.54 feet.

927. B. 255 in.²

The formula to find the area of a triangle is $A = \frac{bh}{2}$, where b represents the length of the base and h represents its height. The triangle's base, in this case, is two times the triangle's height plus 4 inches: $15 \times 2 = 30$, and $30 + 4 = 34$. Replace the variables in the triangle area formula and solve:

$$A = \frac{34 \times 15}{2}$$
$$= \frac{510}{2}$$
$$= 255$$

The triangle is 255 square inches.

928. B. 73°

Sketch the problem, remembering that opposite angles inside a quadrilateral are supplementary; they must add up to 180°. Your sketch doesn't
have to be to scale — it's just a visual aid. You know the two angles in
the problem can't be opposite each other because they add up to more
than 180°.

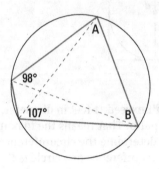

Figure out the missing angles A and B.

Angle A: $180 - 107 = 73°$
Angle B: $180 - 98 = 82°$

The smallest angle in the quadrilateral is $\angle A$, measuring 73°.

929. A. 78.5 m²

Find the area of the *annulus* — the area of the larger circle, minus the
area of the smaller circle — by using the formula $A = \pi\left(R^2 - r^2\right)$, where R
represents the radius of the large circle and r represents the radius of the
small circle. It's just a spin on the formula you already know ($A = \pi r^2$ for
the area of a circle). Remember, pi is approximately equal to 3.14.

$$A = \pi\left(10^2 - 5^2\right)$$
$$A = \pi\left(5^2\right)$$
$$A \approx 25 \times 3.14$$
$$A = 78.5$$

The area of the annulus is 78.5 square meters. (Make sure you're handling like terms before you solve; if you didn't do that on this problem,
you'd reach Choice (D).)

930. **D. 18 square yards**

The formula to find the area of a rectangle is $A = lw$, where A represents the area, l represents the length, and w represents the width. Replace the variables in the formula to find the rectangle's area:

$$A = 6 \cdot 3 = 18$$

The rectangle's area is 18 square yards.

931. **B. complementary.**

When two angles add up to 90°, they're considered complementary angles. The term *supplementary* refers to angles that add up to 180°, and *congruent* refers to angles that have the same measure in degrees or radians.

932. **B. 3 in.²**

Find the area of a triangle with the formula $A = \frac{1}{2}bh$, where A represents the area, b represents the length of the base, and h represents the height:

$$A = \frac{1}{2}(2 \cdot 3)$$
$$= \frac{1}{2}(6)$$
$$= 3$$

The note's area is 3 square inches, so Mandy is safe... this time.

933. **A. 384 in.²**

A cube has six sides, so to find its surface area, use the formula $A = 6s^2$, where A represents the area and s represents the length of one side:

$$A = 6(8)^2$$
$$= 6 \cdot 64$$
$$= 384$$

Remember to take care of the exponent first; don't try to multiply 6 by 8 and square the product. The cube's surface area is 384 square inches.

934. **C. 432 in.** ²

You get all the scrap paper you can handle when you're taking the ASVAB, so if it's helpful, sketch the box. It's a rectangular prism that looks like this:

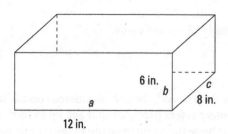

The formula to find the surface area of a rectangular prism is $SA = 2(lw + hl + hw)$, where SA represents surface area, w represents width, h represents height, and l represents length. Replace the variables in the formula to solve Nathan's wrapping paper problem:

$$SA = 2\big((12 \cdot 8) + (6 \cdot 12) + (6 \cdot 8)\big)$$
$$= 2(96 + 72 + 48)$$
$$= 2(216)$$
$$= 432$$

The surface area of the box is 432 square inches.

935. **B. 523.33 in.³**

The formula for the volume of a sphere is $V = \frac{4}{3}\pi r^3$, where r represents the radius. Divide the diameter given in the problem by 2 to find that the sphere's radius is 5 inches. Then replace the variables in the formula and solve:

$$V = \frac{4}{3}\pi(5)^3$$
$$= \frac{4}{3}\pi(125)$$
$$= \frac{4 \cdot 125\pi}{3}$$
$$= \frac{500\pi}{3}$$
$$\approx \frac{500 \cdot 3.14}{3}$$
$$= \frac{1{,}570}{3}$$
$$\approx 523.33$$

The approximate volume of the sphere, using 3.14 for pi, is 523.33 cubic inches.

936. **C. 6 in.**

The formula to find the area of a parallelogram is $A = bh$, where A represents the area, b represents the length of the base, and h represents the height. You can find out how high the parallelogram stands in this problem by filling in what you know and solving for h:

$$bh = A$$
$$4h = 24$$
$$\frac{4h}{4} = \frac{24}{4}$$
$$h = 6$$

The parallelogram is 6 inches high.

937. **A. 50°**

You can find the measurement of an inscribed angle with the formula $m\angle ABC = \frac{1}{2}m\widehat{AC}$, where m represents the measure of the angle. You know that $m\widehat{AC} = 100$, so put that in the formula:

$$m\angle ABC = \frac{1}{2}(100) = 50$$

The measurement of the inscribed angle — the vertex that is on the circle — is 50°.

938. **D. 289 cu. in.**

The formula to find the volume of a square pyramid is $V = \frac{1}{3}Bh$, where B represents the area of the base and h represents the height. Replace the variables in the formula and solve:

$$V = \frac{1}{3}(17 \cdot 51)$$
$$= \frac{1}{3}(867)$$
$$= 289$$

The pyramid can hold 289 cubic inches of colored sand.

939. C. 23°

All the angles in a quadrilateral must add up to 360°, so you can subtract each of the angles from 360 to find out what's left: $360 - 220 - 34 - 83 = 23$.

If you're more comfortable with algebra, you can set up an algebraic equation:

$$d + 220 + 34 + 83 = 360$$
$$d + 337 = 360$$
$$d + 337 - 337 = 360 - 337$$
$$d = 23$$

Either way, you find that the missing angle, $\angle D$, is 23°.

940. A. 9,000 square feet

The problem describes a trapezoid (you can tell because there are two parallel lines, or bases, of different lengths that are connected by a perpendicular border), which you can visualize like this:

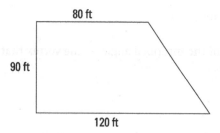

To find the area of a trapezoid, use the formula $A = \frac{1}{2}h(b_1 + b_2)$, where A represents the area, b_1 represents the length of one base, b_2 represents the length of the second base, and h represents the trapezoid's height. Replace the variables in the formula with what you know from the problem and solve:

$$A = \frac{1}{2}90(80 + 120)$$
$$= 45 \cdot 200$$
$$= 9,000$$

The customer's lawn is 9,000 square feet.

941. **A. 30°**

Remember that when you're dealing with angles formed outside a circle, $\angle ACE$ is the intersection of two secants outside of a circle. You can find the angle outside the circle by finding half the difference of the intercepted arcs, so your formula looks like this:

$$m\angle ACE = \tfrac{1}{2}(80 - 20)$$
$$= \tfrac{1}{2}(60)$$
$$= 30$$

The measure of $\angle ACE$ is 30°.

If you need to visualize this problem, draw a sketch that looks like this:

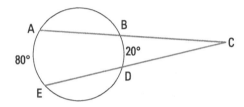

942. **B. 399 ft²**

This problem asks you to find facts, do some arithmetic, and then use the formula for the area of a rectangle, which is $A = lw$, where A represents area, l represents the length, and w represents the width.

First figure out the new rectangle's dimensions by adding 13 to each original side:

$$8 + 13 = 21$$
$$6 + 13 = 19$$

Now put the new dimensions into the area formula:

$$A = 21 \cdot 19 = 399$$

The new rectangle has an area of 399 square feet.

943. **B. 3.4 quarts**

Find the square footage of Josie's room, and remember to subtract some space for the door. Each wall is 80 square feet (they're all 10 feet long and 8 feet high, and the area formula for a rectangle is $A = lw$, where A represents the area, l represents the length, and w represents the width):

$$80 \times 4 = 320$$

Subtract the area of the door (14 square feet):

$$320 - 14 = 306$$

Each quart of paint covers about 90 square feet, so divide the total answer by 90 to find out how many quarts Josie needs:

$$306 \div 90 = 3.4$$

944. C. 8.86π

The formula to find the circumference of a circle is $C = 2\pi r$, where C represents the circumference and r represents the radius. Because the question asks you to find the exact circumference, leave π in your answer:

$$C = 2\pi(4.43)$$
$$= 8.86\pi$$

945. A. 28.26 in.²

There's a lot of extra information to sift through in this problem. The bottom line: You need to find the approximate area of a circle with a radius of 3 inches. The formula for the area of a circle is $A = \pi r^2$, where A represents the area and r represents the circle's radius:

$$A = \pi(3)^2$$
$$= 9\pi$$
$$\approx 9 \cdot 3.14$$
$$= 28.26$$

Each coaster that Mr. Gray carves has an approximate area of 28.26 square inches.

946. C. 4,936 feet

This problem is really only asking you to find the perimeter of a square. To find the perimeter, add the lengths of the sides together; in this case, because each side is the same length, you can just multiply one side by 4 (there are four sides on a square):

$$1,234 \times 4 = 4,936$$

You've walked 4,396 feet. (Now run around the same city block at least two more times so you're in shape for your first physical fitness test in the military!)

Tip: If you're running out of time on the ASVAB, here's a neat shortcut for this problem (and others like it, provided the answer choices aren't rounded): Multiply the ones digits first: $4 \times 4 = 16$. That tells you that the answer has to end in 6, so Choice (C) is most likely correct.

947. **D. 400 feet**

You know that the city can lay 1,200 square feet of concrete each month and that the sidewalks are all 3 feet wide. Use the area formula, which is $A = lw$, where A represents the area, l represents the length, and w represents the width, to find out how long each stretch of sidewalk will be:

$$3l = 1{,}200$$
$$\frac{3l}{3} = \frac{1{,}200}{3}$$
$$l = 400$$

The city can install a 400-foot-long stretch of sidewalk each month.

948. **B. 19.6 in.²**

First find out the diameter of the puddle after an hour and a half; it loses 1 inch each half hour, so after an hour and a half, it has lost 3 inches.

The puddle's diameter is now 5 inches, and you can use that to solve for area using $A = \pi r^2$, where A represents the area and r represents the radius (remember that a circle's radius is half its diameter):

$$A = \pi(2.5)^2$$
$$= 6.25\pi$$
$$\approx 6.25 \times 3.14$$
$$= 19.625$$

The puddle's area is about 19.6 square inches.

949. **D. 80°**

All angles in a triangle must add up to 180°, so use algebra to create an equation. Let a represent the smallest angle in the triangle:

$$a + 3a + (3a + 5) = 180$$
$$7a + 5 = 180$$
$$7a + 5 - 5 = 180 - 5$$
$$7a = 175$$
$$\frac{7a}{7} = \frac{175}{7}$$
$$a = 25$$

The smallest angle in the triangle measures 25°, but the problem asks you for the measurement of the largest angle. In the equation, you represented the largest angle with the expression $3a + 5$, so replace the variable and solve:

$$3(25) + 5 = 75 + 5 = 80$$

The largest angle in the triangle measures 80°.

You can double-check your work by figuring out the value of the second angle, which you represented with the expression $3a$: $3 \times 25 = 75$. Add all the angles together to make sure they add up to $180°$: $25 + 75 + 80 = 180$.

950. **D. Both A and B are correct.**

The formula for the area of a triangle is $A = \frac{1}{2}bh$, which can also be expressed as $A = \frac{bh}{2}$. In both formulas, A represents the area, b represents the length of the base, and h represents the triangle's height. Therefore, Choice (D) is correct.

951. **B. 180°**

Davy completed half a circle, which is $180°$.

952. **A. 31.4 square inches**

First, find the area of the cherry pie. Because the cherry pie's pan measured 9 inches across, it has a radius of 4.5 inches. Use the area formula for a circle, which is $A = \pi r^2$, where A represents area and r represents radius, and leave the answer in terms of pi until the last step to save time:

$$A = \pi (4.5)^2$$
$$= 20.25\pi$$

Do the same with the area of the apple pie:

$$A = \pi (5.5)^2$$
$$= 30.25\pi$$

Now find the difference by subtracting the cherry pie's area from the apple pie's area: $30.25\pi - 20.25\pi = 10\pi$.

Solve, remembering that pi is approximately equal to 3.14:

$$10 \times 3.14 = 31.4$$

The apple pie is 31.4 square inches greater than the cherry pie.

953. **D. 1,805 square feet**

The formula to find the area of a trapezoid is $A = \frac{1}{2}h(b_1 + b_2)$, where A represents the area, b_1 represents the length of the first base, b_2 represents the length of the second base, and h represents the trapezoid's height.

Fill in what you know from the problem and solve for area:

$$A = \frac{1}{2}(38)(40+55)$$
$$= 19(95)$$
$$= 1,805$$

Jesse's soon-to-be laser tag field is 1,805 square feet.

954. **B. 6.25 m²**

The perimeter of any shape is the distance around it. If a square, which has four equal sides, has a perimeter of 10 meters, each side must measure 2.5 meters (divide 10 by 4, and the answer is 2.5).

To find the area of a square, use the formula $A = s^2$, where A represents the area and s represents the length of one side:

$$A = 2.5^2 = 6.25$$

The square's area is 6.25 m².

955. **B. 90°**

A circle has 360°, and when you look at a clock in terms of 3, 6, 9, and 12, you're dividing it into four parts, or quadrants. Each quadrant has a measure of 90°, which is how far the minute hand will have to travel between the number 9 and the number 12.

956. **C. 120°**

Supplementary angles must add up to 180°. Let x represent the measure of $\angle B$ (the smaller angle) and let $2x$ represent the measure of $\angle A$. Create an equation:

$$x + 2x = 180$$
$$3x = 180$$
$$\frac{3x}{3} = \frac{180}{3}$$
$$x = 60$$

Angle B measures 60°, so the measure of $\angle A$ is twice that; it's 120°.

957. **B. 49°**

The term *congruent* means that both angles have the same measure. That means both artists drew 49° angles.

958. **A. −0.2**

When two lines are perpendicular, you know that $m_2 \times m_2 = -1$ — in other words, the slopes are negative reciprocals of each other. In that equation, m_1 represents the slope of the first line, and m_2 represents the slope of the second line.

Replace the variable in the equation and solve:

$$m_1 \times 5 = -1$$
$$\frac{m_1 \times 5}{5} = -\frac{1}{5}$$
$$m_1 = -\frac{1}{5}$$

Convert $-\frac{1}{5}$ to the decimal −0.2; that's Line A's slope.

959. **B. $1,560**

First find the area of the room using $A = lw$, where A represents the area, l represents the length, and w represents the width:

$$A = 13 \times 18 = 234$$

The room's area is 234 square feet. Now convert that to yards, remembering that because 1 yard = 3 feet, a square yard is $(3\ \text{ft})^2 = 9\ \text{ft}^2$:

$$\frac{234}{9} = 26$$

The room is 26 square yards, so now figure out the cost by multiplying 26 by $60:

$$26 \times 60 = \$1,560$$

It will cost $1,560 to put hardwood floors in the room.

960. **C. 65 cm²**

Figure out the area of the larger square by using $A = s^2$, where A represents the area and s represents the length of a side:

$$A = 9^2 = 81$$

The larger square has an area of 81 cm², so subtract the smaller square's area:

$$81 - 16 = 65$$

961.   A. 35 miles

Sergeant Jones rides his bicycle 5 miles each day, and there are 7 days in a week. Multiply:

$$5 \times 7 = 35$$

In one week, Sergeant Jones will ride his bicycle 35 miles.

962.   C. $\frac{20}{33}$

The sample size is 99 (remember, either a motorcycle or pickup truck has already left the parking lot). Let C represent the event of a sports car leaving.

$$n(T) = 99$$
$$n(C) = 60$$

The probability of a sports car leaving next is $\frac{60}{99}$, which you can reduce to $\frac{20}{33}$.

963.   D. All of the above are correct.

A ratio is a way to compare two or more different things. You can express a ratio in three ways: using a colon, using a fraction, or using the word "to" between the numbers.

Make sure the numbers in the ratio appear in the same order as they appear in the question. If the question had asked, "What is the ratio of birthday cakes to wedding cakes," you'd flip the numbers (24:16, and so on).

964.   C. 7.2 cups

This problem requires you to set a proportion using ratios. (Forget the baking powder — the question asks you how much flour the baker needs.)

Out of 24 cups of flour, the baker can make 10 cakes. You can express that this way:

$$\frac{\text{flour}}{\text{cakes}} = \frac{24}{10}$$
$$= \frac{12}{5}$$

To find out how much flour he needs to make only three cakes, create an expression that looks like this:

$$\frac{\text{flour}}{\text{cakes}} = \frac{x}{3}$$

Put your two ratios together, cross-multiply, and solve for x:

$$\frac{12}{5} = \frac{x}{3}$$

$$5x = 36$$

$$\frac{5x}{5} = \frac{36}{5}$$

$$x = 7.2$$

The baker will need 7.2 cups of flour to bake three cakes.

Alternatively, you can solve this problem by figuring out that the baker needs 2.4 cups of flour per cake (he needs 24 cups to bake 10). Multiply that by 3 to find out how much flour he needs in this problem: $2.4 \times 3 = 7.2$.

965. **D. 49°**

You may find it helpful to draw a quick diagram that looks like this (in the military, this diagram is called a *strip map*):

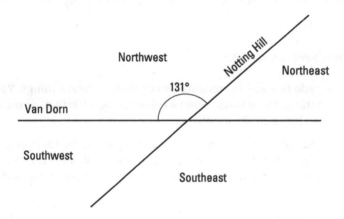

Angles on the same line must be supplementary, which means they need to add up to 180°.

Because the problem asks you to find the measure of the angle on the southwest corner of Notting Hill and Van Dorn, and it tells you the measure of the angle of the northwest corner (131°), subtract that from 180° to find the right measurement: $180 - 131 = 49$.

The angle at the southwest corner of Notting Hill and Van Dorn is 49°.

966. **A.** $\frac{5}{16}$ **hours**

Gordon spent $\frac{1}{4}$ of $1\frac{1}{4}$ hours actually cooking. Convert $1\frac{1}{4}$ into an improper fraction. Now multiply the fractions:

$$\frac{1}{4} \times \frac{5}{4} = \frac{5}{16}$$

Gordon spent $\frac{5}{16}$ of an hour cooking.

967. **C. 6.76 million**

There are 26 letters in the alphabet, and there are 10 possible numbers for each of the last four digits of the password, which you can express this way:

Multiply each of the figures in the diagram:

$$26 \times 26 \times 10 \times 10 \times 10 \times 10 = 6,760,000$$

There are 6.76 million possible passwords.

968. **C. $6.88**

To figure out what fraction is $\frac{5}{6}$ of $\frac{3}{4}$, multiply the fractions:

$$\frac{5}{6} \times \frac{3}{4} = \frac{5 \times 3}{6 \times 4}$$

$$= \frac{5 \times \cancel{3}^{1}}{{}_{2}\cancel{6} \times 4}$$

$$= \frac{5 \times 1}{2 \times 4}$$

$$= \frac{5}{8}$$

Amira spent $\frac{5}{8}$ of the her allowance money on pens, so multiply to find out how much $\frac{5}{8}$ of $11 is:

$$\frac{5}{8} \times \frac{11}{1} = \frac{5 \times 11}{8 \times 1} = \frac{55}{8}$$

Now divide 55 by 8 to find out how much money Amira spent: $55 \div 8 = 6.875$. Because the problem asks for a dollar amount, round up to $6.88.

969. C. 888

To find out how many games the hockey player won, multiply 1,200 by 0.74:

$$1,200 \times 0.74 = 888$$

The hockey player won 888 games over the course of his career.

970. B. 8%

This week, potatoes sell for $0.06 more than they did last week (last week, they were $0.75, and this week, they're $0.81). Find the percent increase over the original price by dividing that $0.06 by $0.75:

$$6 \div 75 = 0.08$$

That's an 8% increase in the price of potatoes.

971. B. 108

Set up a ratio to express the original quantity:

$$\frac{\text{horses}}{\text{dogs}} = \frac{16}{9}$$

You need to figure out how many dogs there will be if there are 192 horses, so create a proportion that uses d to represent the number of dogs while ensuring that both ratios are equal to each other:

$$\frac{16}{9} = \frac{192}{d}$$

Cross-multiply and solve for d:

$$\frac{16}{9} = \frac{192}{d}$$
$$16d = 1,728$$
$$\frac{16d}{16} = \frac{1,728}{16}$$
$$d = 108$$

If there were 192 horses, there would be 108 dogs.

972. D. $35.00

The markup is 40% of the original cost of clothing. The problem tells you that the retailer spent $25 on jeans, so find 40% of $25:

$$25 \times 0.4 = 10$$

The retailer will mark up the price on the jeans by $10, so customers must pay a total of $35 for the jeans ($25 + $10 = $35).

You can also multiply $35 by 1.4 to find the total cost. 100% + 40% means the customer will pay 140% of the original price.

973. B. $55

Let x represent how much the shoe salesman spends on the shoes whole-sale, and let $0.45x$ represent the markup (the salesman marks up the shoes based on the price he pays for them).

Create an equation that reflects the problem and solve for x:

$$x + 0.45x = 79.75$$
$$1.45x = 79.75$$
$$\frac{1.45x}{1.45} = \frac{79.75}{1.45}$$
$$x = 55$$

The salesman spends $55 on each pair of shoes he sells.

974. C. $352.75

Multiply $415 by 0.15 to find out how much money a buyer will save on the TV:

$$415 \times 0.15 = 62.25$$

Now subtract $62.25 from the TV's original price, $415:

$$415 - 62.25 = 352.75$$

The TV is on sale for $352.75.

A faster method is to multiply $415 by 0.85, because the price paid is 85% of the normal price ($100\% - 15\% = 85\%$).

975. B. 10 pounds of white flour at $1.49 each and two 8-ounce bags of wheat flour at $0.90 each

You can immediately rule out Choice (A), because if Mrs. Stevens buys 6 bags of white flour and 4 bags of wheat flour, she'll have only 10 pounds of flour; she won't have enough flour to bake rolls for every student. Now find the costs of the other choices:

» Choice (B) would cost the school $16.70 ($10 \times 1.49 = 14.90$ and $2 \times 0.90 = 1.80$).

» Choice (C) would cost the school $17.83 ($8 \times 0.75 = 6$ and $7 \times 1.69 = 11.83$).

» Choice (D) would cost the school $19.69 ($11 \times 1.79 = 19.69$), making it the most expensive option. (You could rule out this answer immediately because $1.79 is a high price, second only to the pound of wheat flour in Choice (B), so you know the other choices will cost less.)

Choice (B) is the least expensive option, so Mrs. Stevens should choose 10 pounds of white flour and two 8-ounce packages of wheat flour.

976. C. 6

When the candy bin is full, it contains 36 candy bars (a dozen is 12, and $12 \times 3 = 36$). Find $\frac{1}{6}$ of a dozen:

$$12 \div 6 = 2$$

Then multiply by the number of dozens Nuan will have when the bin is full to get the number she'll have when she needs to reorder:

$$2 \times 3 = 6$$

Nuan needs to reorder the candy bars when there are 6 left.

977. C. 23

Sachi isn't a very good roommate.

The alarm clock chimes every five minutes, or 12 times per hour. Sachi's alarm sounded from 6:25 a.m. until 8:15 a.m. That's 1 hour and 50 minutes, or $1\frac{5}{6}$ hours. Multiply the number of alarms by the number of hours:

$$1\frac{5}{6} \times 12 = \frac{11}{6} \times \frac{12}{1}$$
$$= \frac{132}{6}$$
$$= 22$$

Don't forget to add one more; the alarm clock rang at 6:25 as well, which means Sachi's alarm went off 23 times before he got up.

(*Military Tip:* Turn up your alarm clock's volume to its maximum setting and sleep with the clock across the room. The old military saying "If you're 10 minutes early, you're 5 minutes late" has been known to get plenty of new recruits into trouble.)

978. D. 260

There are 10 possibilities on the first reel (remember, 0 is a possibility). There are 26 possibilities on the second reel. Multiply the first set of possibilities by the second set of possibilities:

$$10 \times 26 = 260$$

There are 260 possible combinations standing between Robbie and his birthday presents.

979. B. 81.28 cm

One foot is equal to 12 inches, so your ratio will look like this:

$$\frac{\text{inches}}{\text{centimeters}} = \frac{12}{30.48}$$

Let c represent the number of centimeters you're trying to find and set up a proportion using the information you have from the problem:

$$\frac{12}{30.48} = \frac{32}{c}$$

(You could say, "12 inches is to 30.48 centimeters as 32 inches is to c centimeters.")

Cross-multiply and solve for c:

$$\frac{12}{30.48} = \frac{32}{c}$$
$$12c = 975.36$$
$$\frac{12c}{12} = \frac{975.36}{12}$$
$$c = 81.28$$

There are 81.28 centimeters in 32 inches.

980. C. 108

Sketch a diagram that represents the least fraction in the problem, which is $\frac{1}{9}$ (you'll have nine equal parts):

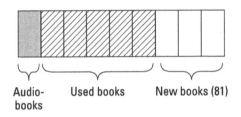

Audio-books   Used books   New books (81)

Now you know that $\frac{3}{9}$ of the books are new. Because there are 81 new books and three blocks in your diagram represents that number, divide 81 by 3 to find out how many books each block represents:

$$\frac{81}{3} = 27$$

Five of the blocks in your diagram represent used books, so multiply 27 by 5 to find out how many used books the bookstore has:

$$27 \times 5 = 135$$

Because only one block in your diagram represents audiobooks, you know that the store has 27 audiobooks. Subtract the number of audiobooks from the number of used books to find the answer to the original question:

$$135 - 27 = 108$$

The bookstore has 108 more used books than audiobooks.

981.   B. 800 miles

This problem is asking you to multiply two separate expressions. First, multiply the speed and the time Javier and Gloria drove the first day:

$$65 \times 8 = 520$$

Next, multiply the speed and the time the pair drove the second day:

$$70 \times 4 = 280$$

Add the distances together: $520 + 280 = 800$, so the beach is 800 miles from Gloria and Javier's home.

982.   D. 160

This ratio problem is simple to solve with a diagram. You have a total of nine parts (4 for females and 5 for males), so sketch two rows:

Females ☐☐☐☐

Males ☐☐☐☐☐

All 9 parts together equal 360 (there are 360 recruits in this cycle). Divide 360 by 9 to figure out how many recruits each block in your diagram represents:

$$\frac{360}{9} = 40$$

Because there are four blocks in your diagram that represent females, and because each block represents 40 recruits, multiply 40 by 4 to find out how many females are in this cycle:

$$40 \times 4 = 160$$

There are 160 females.

You can check your work by simplifying a fraction:

$$\frac{160}{360} = \frac{16}{36} = \frac{4}{9}$$

One hundred sixty recruits out of 360 are females, so reduce that as far as you can; you'll end up with $\frac{4}{9}$, which is the original part-to-total ratio.

983.   D. $2,158.20

The ring cost $1,199, so find out what Oroka's annual insurance costs by finding 15% of the ring's value and multiplying it by 12 (because there are 12 months in a year):

$$1,199 \times 0.15 \times 12$$

Work through the calculations:

$$1,199 \times 0.15 = 179.85$$
$$179.85 \times 12 = 2,158.2$$

Insurance over the course of a year will cost $2,158.20, which means Oroka would probably better off buying an extra ring and skipping the insurance.

984.   A. 100

Sketch out a diagram to help you visualize the problem. You need 12 equal blocks to represent Micah's entire music collection:

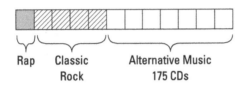

You can see that seven of the blocks represent Micah's 175 alternative music CDs, so divide 175 by 7 to find out how many CDs each block in the diagram represents:

$$\frac{175}{7} = 25$$

Four blocks represent classic rock, so multiply 25 by 4 to find out how many classic rock CDs are in Micah's collection:

$$25 \times 4 = 100$$

Micah has 100 classic rock CDs.

985. C. 35 feet

For many people, it's easier to convert the fraction $1\frac{3}{4}$ into the decimal 1.75 in problems such as this one.

You know that the perimeter formula is $P = 2l + 2w$ (where P represents the perimeter, l represents the length, and w represents the width) and that the chicken coop's length is 1.75 times its width. Set up an equation and solve for width:

$$2(1.75w) + 2w = 192.5$$
$$3.5w + 2w = 192.5$$
$$5.5w = 192.5$$
$$\frac{5.5w}{5.5} = \frac{192.5}{5.5}$$
$$w = 35$$

The chicken coop is 35 feet wide.

986. D. 336

Multiply 42 cups by 8 ounces:

$$42 \times 8 = 336$$

You can hold 336 ounces of liquid in 42 cups.

987. C. $720

Divide the total cost by 52 weeks to find out how much it costs each week:

$$\frac{3,120}{52} = 60$$

You can then multiply 60 by 12 to find out how much housekeeping will cost for 12 weeks:

$$60 \times 12 = 720$$

It will cost $720 for 12 weeks' worth of housekeeping services.

988. D. 3.5 hours

Assuming that Diana keeps up the same pace, figure out how long it takes Diana to run 15 miles by dividing 15 by 7.5 (it's often easier to convert fractions into decimals):

$$\frac{15}{7.5} = 2$$

Diana can run 15 miles in 2 hours. Now you need to figure out how long it takes her to run 1 mile. Divide 2 hours (or 120 minutes) by 15 miles:

$$\frac{120}{15} = 8$$

She's running a mile every 8 minutes, so multiply that by 26:

$$26 \times 8 = 208$$

Diana can run 26 miles in 208 minutes, which translates into about 3.5 hours ($208 \div 60 = 3.466\ldots$).

Just a note on running: The military has strict requirements on running times, and they're based upon gender and age groups. The Navy, Coast Guard, and Air Force require you to run 1.5 miles for your semiannual physical fitness tests, the Army requires you to run 2 miles, and the Marines require you to run 3 miles.

989. A. 72

Divide 36 cups by $\frac{1}{2}$ to find out how many servings are in the bag:

$$36 \div \frac{1}{2} = \frac{36}{1} \times \frac{2}{1}$$
$$= \frac{72}{1}$$
$$= 72$$

There are 72 servings in a 36-cup bag of rice if each serving is $\frac{1}{2}$ cup.

Some people can quickly work out this problem mentally, without going through the steps of division and multiplication. If you can do that on the ASVAB, you should. You have only a few minutes to spend on each question, so the more quickly you can answer easier questions, the better you'll do.

990. D. 12

You have three different categories: beverages, entrées, and desserts. Each is an independent event, so first sketch out the different ways each event could occur:

2	3	2
Beverage	Entrée	Dessert

Multiply all the possible combinations:

$$2 \times 3 \times 2 = 12$$

There are 12 different meal combinations with this menu.

991. C. 7:09 p.m.

Divide 72 pages by 8 (the printer can print 8 pages per minute):

$$\frac{72}{8} = 9$$

It will take the printer 9 minutes to complete the print job, so because Pascual started printing at 7:00 p.m., he'll be finished at 7:09 p.m.

992. A. $650

You have the sale price and the markdown price, but you need to find the markdown amount to find the original price.

Assign variables so you can solve this problem. Let x represent the laptop's original price, and let $0.25x$ represent the markdown of the original price (the new price is 25% off the original price).

Create an equation using the information you have:

$$x - 0.25x = 487.5$$
$$0.75x = 487.5$$
$$\frac{0.75x}{0.75} = \frac{487.5}{0.75}$$
$$x = 650$$

The laptop's original price was $650.

993. A. 2,400 square feet

Figure out the area of the driveway by multiplying 20 by 30:

$$20 \times 30 = 600$$

The driveway is 600 square feet.

That 600-square-foot driveway represents 25% of the yard, so let x represent the original area of the yard, write an equation, and solve for x:

$$0.25x = 600$$
$$\frac{0.25x}{0.25} = \frac{600}{0.25}$$
$$x = 2,400$$

The yard's original size was 2,400 square feet.

994. D. 2 hours

Don't let the extra information in this word problem throw you off. You'll find plenty of questions on the ASVAB that require you to dive in and pull out the facts.

An average giant tortoise moves at 0.17 miles per hour. Divide the giant tortoise's distance (0.34 miles) by its speed (0.17 mph):

$$\frac{0.34}{0.17} = 2$$

It would take the average giant tortoise 2 hours to move 0.34 miles.

995. B. 8

To find out how many tables Kim and Gerry's wedding planner needed to set up, divide 96 by 12:

$$\frac{96}{12} = 8$$

There were 8 guest tables at the wedding.

996. D. 11,893

First find 5% of the population by multiplying 11,327 by 0.05:

$$11,327 \times 0.05 = 566.35$$

Now add that to South Lyon's current population:

$$11,327 + 566.35 = 11,893.35$$

The new population is the old population plus the increase.

One of the town's residents isn't 35% of a person, so round down to 11,893. At the next census, if the growth rate in South Lyon is 5%, that's what the population will be.

997. B. 6,190 meters

This is a multiplication problem. Multiply Mount Everest's height (8,848 meters) by 0.7 (the decimal equivalent of 70%):

$$8,848 \times 0.7 = 6,193.6$$

Rounded to the nearest ten, Denali stands at 6,190 meters high. (Interestingly, it's precisely 6,190 meters, or 20,310 feet, above sea level.)

998. A. 70 gallons

First find out how much water the sprinkler puts out in 35 minutes by multiplying the number of minutes by 12:

$$35 \times 12 = 420$$

In 35 minutes, the sprinkler puts out 420 gallons of water.

Now find out how much water the hose puts out in 35 minutes using the same method:

$$35 \times 14 = 490$$

The hose puts out 490 gallons of water over a 35-minute period.

Subtract the amount of water the sprinkler uses from the amount of water the hose uses to find the answer:

$$490 - 420 = 70$$

The hose puts out 70 more gallons of water than the sprinkler does.

A quicker way to work this problem is to find the difference per minute $(14 - 12 = 2)$ and multiply that by the total time. In 35 minutes, the hose puts out $2 \times 35 = 70$ more gallons than the sprinkler.

999. B. $\frac{3}{8}$

The problem tells you there are 16 marbles in the jar and that 6 of them are blue. You have a 6 out of 16 chance of pulling out a blue marble, which you can express as the fraction $\frac{6}{16}$. Reduce the fraction to $\frac{3}{8}$ — that's the probability of pulling a blue marble out of the jar.

1,000. D. 550 megabits

Multiply the amount of data your Internet connection can transmit (50 mbps) by the number of seconds (11):

$$50 \times 11 = 550$$

Your Internet connection will transfer 550 megabits in 11 seconds.

If you're choosing an IT or communications field in the military, you should know that megabits are different from megabytes; it takes eight megabits to make up a megabyte.

1,001. D. 125

The problem tells you that $\frac{3}{4}$, or 75%, of the children attending a particular school are engaged in extracurricular activities. Find out how many kids are part of these activities by multiplying 500 by 0.75:

$$500 \times 0.75 = 375$$

The remaining children are not participating in extracurricular activities, so to find that number, subtract 375 from the total number of students:

$$500 - 375 = 125$$

One hundred twenty-five kids aren't participating in extracurricular activities.

You can also think of the problem this way: If 75% are participating, then 25% are not, so $0.25 \times 500 = 125$. Or you can find the answer by dividing 500 by 4.

Index

O

1,001 ASVAB Practice Questions For Dummies (Powers), 3
online practice, 2–3

P

Paragraph Comprehension subtest
  about, 29
  answers, 187–231
  practice questions, 30–87
  question types, 29
  what to watch for, 30
percentage questions, 91–92
PIN, for online tool, 2–3
Powers, Rod (author)
  ASVAB AFQT For Dummies, 3
  ASVAB For Dummies, 1, 3
  1,001 ASVAB Practice Questions For Dummies, 3
practice questions
  Arithmetic Reasoning subtest, 124–153
  Mathematics Knowledge subtest, 90–122
  Paragraph Comprehension subtest, 30–87
  Word Knowledge subtest, 8–27

Q

quadratic equation questions, 101–102
question types
  for Arithmetic Reasoning subtest, 123
  for Mathematics Knowledge subtest, 89
  for Paragraph Comprehension subtest, 29
  for Word Knowledge subtest, 7

R

ratio questions, 92–93
registration, 3

S

scientific notation questions, 93
sentence synonym questions, 7, 15–23
square root questions, 93
synonym questions, 7, 8–15

W

websites
  Cheat Sheet, 2
  Wiley Product Technical Support, 3
Wiley Product Technical Support (website), 3
Word Knowledge subtest
  about, 7
  answers, 157–187
  answers: antonyms, 182–187
  answers: synonyms, 157–171
  answers: synonyms in sentences, 171–182
  practice questions: antonyms, 23–27
  practice questions: synonyms, 8–15
  practice questions: synonyms in sentences, 15–23
  question types, 7
  what to watch for, 8

About the Author

Angie Papple Johnston joined the U.S. Army in 2006 as a Chemical, Biological, Radiological, and Nuclear (CBRN) Specialist, ready to tackle chemical weapons in a Level-A HAZMAT suit. During her second deployment as part of Operation Iraqi Freedom, Angie became her battalion's public affairs representative, writing press releases and photographing historic moments from Tikrit to Kirkuk.

Angie also served as the Lead Cadre for the Texas Army National Guard's Recruit Sustainment Program (RSP), teaching brand-new privates how to survive Basic Combat Training, Advanced Individual Training, and the Army.

She's currently the CBRN noncommissioned officer-in-charge of an aviation battalion in Washington, D.C., where her favorite things are teaching her soldiers combatives (the Army's version of hand-to-hand combat), doing the occasional ruck march around the airfield, and setting a positive example for the next generation of leaders. She firmly believes that you can learn something from every leader in the military, even if it's how *not* to lead, and that there's nothing more important than leading soldiers from the front through training and mentoring.

Angie is the proud wife of another noncommissioned officer in the U.S. Army and the mom of a tiny hurricane who keeps her on her toes (no, seriously — he's a climber).

Dedication

This book is for my Davids. You are my favorite people in the whole world, and I love you like crazy!

And Mom. Thanks for teaching me to read and win spelling bees (even if you can't pronounce *ersatz*). Thanks, Mama!

Author's Acknowledgments

To our current, former, and prospective military service members: You have my most sincere gratitude.

I'm exceptionally grateful to Vicki Adang and Lindsay Lefevere for moving me from the back of the book to the front of the book. I cannot imagine a better editor than Vicki, and I'm incredibly lucky to be on the same team as she is.

This book is immeasurably better because of the numerous contributions of Danielle Voirol, Suzanne Langebartels, Devin Hyde, and Caleb Leggett.

Col. Chris Stenman, there's nobody I'd rather follow around Iraq with a camera and a notepad! Thank you for everything.

Lt. Col. Michael Adelberg, thank you for putting me on this path when we were in Kirkuk.

Master Sgt. Tim Gray (Ret.), thank you for trusting me to lead your brand-new recruits.

CW4 Frederick Hall, thank you for recognizing purpose and always putting the mission first.

Publisher's Acknowledgments

Executive Editor: Lindsay Sandman Lefevere

Project Manager: Victoria M. Adang

Copy Editor: Danielle Voirol

Technical Editors: Suzanne Langebartels, Devin Hyde, and Caleb Leggett

Production Editor: Antony Sami

Cover Photos: © Steve Cukrov/Shutterstock

Apple & Mac

iPad For Dummies,
6th Edition
978-1-118-72306-7

iPhone For Dummies,
7th Edition
978-1-118-69083-3

Macs All-in-One
For Dummies, 4th Edition
978-1-118-82210-4

OS X Mavericks
For Dummies
978-1-118-69188-5

Blogging & Social Media

Facebook For Dummies,
5th Edition
978-1-118-63312-0

Social Media Engagement
For Dummies
978-1-118-53019-1

WordPress For Dummies,
6th Edition
978-1-118-79161-5

Business

Stock Investing
For Dummies, 4th Edition
978-1-118-37678-2

Investing For Dummies,
6th Edition
978-0-470-90545-6

Personal Finance
For Dummies, 7th Edition
978-1-118-11785-9

QuickBooks 2014
For Dummies
978-1-118-72005-9

Small Business Marketing Kit
For Dummies, 3rd Edition
978-1-118-31183-7

Careers

Job Interviews For Dummies,
4th Edition
978-1-118-11290-8

Job Searching with Social
Media For Dummies,
2nd Edition
978-1-118-67856-5

Personal Branding
For Dummies
978-1-118-11792-7

Resumes For Dummies,
6th Edition
978-0-470-87361-8

Starting an Etsy Business
For Dummies, 2nd Edition
978-1-118-59024-9

Diet & Nutrition

Belly Fat Diet For Dummies
978-1-118-34585-6

Mediterranean Diet
For Dummies
978-1-118-71525-3

Nutrition For Dummies,
5th Edition
978-0-470-93231-5

Digital Photography

Digital SLR Photography
All-in-One For Dummies,
2nd Edition
978-1-118-59082-9

Digital SLR Video &
Filmmaking For Dummies
978-1-118-36598-4

Photoshop Elements 12
For Dummies
978-1-118-72714-0

Gardening

Herb Gardening
For Dummies, 2nd Edition
978-0-470-61778-6

Gardening with Free-Range
Chickens For Dummies
978-1-118-54754-0

Health

Boosting Your Immunity
For Dummies
978-1-118-40200-9

Diabetes For Dummies,
4th Edition
978-1-118-29447-5

Living Paleo For Dummies
978-1-118-29405-5

Big Data

Big Data For Dummies
978-1-118-50422-2

Data Visualization
For Dummies
978-1-118-50289-1

Hadoop For Dummies
978-1-118-60755-8

Language &
Foreign Language

500 Spanish Verbs
For Dummies
978-1-118-02382-2

English Grammar
For Dummies, 2nd Edition
978-0-470-54664-2

French All-in-One
For Dummies
978-1-118-22815-9

German Essentials
For Dummies
978-1-118-18422-6

Italian For Dummies,
2nd Edition
978-1-118-00465-4

e **Available in print and e-book formats.**

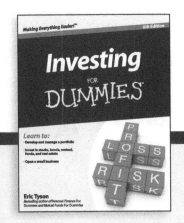

Math & Science

Algebra I For Dummies,
2nd Edition
978-0-470-55964-2

Anatomy and Physiology
For Dummies, 2nd Edition
978-0-470-92326-9

Astronomy For Dummies,
3rd Edition
978-1-118-37697-3

Biology For Dummies,
2nd Edition
978-0-470-59875-7

Chemistry For Dummies,
2nd Edition
978-1-118-00730-3

1001 Algebra II Practice
Problems For Dummies
978-1-118-44662-1

Microsoft Office

Excel 2013 For Dummies
978-1-118-51012-4

Office 2013 All-in-One
For Dummies
978-1-118-51636-2

PowerPoint 2013
For Dummies
978-1-118-50253-2

Word 2013 For Dummies
978-1-118-49123-2

Music

Blues Harmonica
For Dummies
978-1-118-25269-7

Guitar For Dummies,
3rd Edition
978-1-118-11554-1

iPod & iTunes For Dummies,
10th Edition
978-1-118-50864-0

Programming

Beginning Programming
with C For Dummies
978-1-118-73763-7

Excel VBA Programming
For Dummies, 3rd Edition
978-1-118-49037-2

Java For Dummies,
6th Edition
978-1-118-40780-6

Religion & Inspiration

The Bible For Dummies
978-0-7645-5296-0

Buddhism For Dummies,
2nd Edition
978-1-118-02379-2

Catholicism For Dummies,
2nd Edition
978-1-118-07778-8

Self-Help & Relationships

Beating Sugar Addiction
For Dummies
978-1-118-54645-1

Meditation For Dummies,
3rd Edition
978-1-118-29144-3

Seniors

Laptops For Seniors
For Dummies, 3rd Edition
978-1-118-71105-7

Computers For Seniors
For Dummies, 3rd Edition
978-1-118-11553-4

iPad For Seniors
For Dummies, 6th Edition
978-1-118-72826-0

Social Security For Dummies
978-1-118-20573-0

Smartphones & Tablets

Android Phones
For Dummies, 2nd Edition
978-1-118-72030-1

Nexus Tablets For Dummies
978-1-118-77243-0

Samsung Galaxy S 4
For Dummies
978-1-118-64222-1

Samsung Galaxy Tabs
For Dummies
978-1-118-77294-2

Test Prep

ACT For Dummies,
5th Edition
978-1-118-01259-8

ASVAB For Dummies,
3rd Edition
978-0-470-63760-9

GRE For Dummies,
7th Edition
978-0-470-88921-3

Officer Candidate Tests
For Dummies
978-0-470-59876-4

Physician's Assistant Exam
For Dummies
978-1-118-11556-5

Series 7 Exam For Dummies
978-0-470-09932-2

Windows 8

Windows 8.1 All-in-One
For Dummies
978-1-118-82087-2

Windows 8.1 For Dummies
978-1-118-82121-3

Windows 8.1 For Dummies,
Book + DVD Bundle
978-1-118-82107-7

e **Available in print and e-book formats.**

Take Dummies with you everywhere you go!

Whether you are excited about e-books, want more from the web, must have your mobile apps, or are swept up in social media, Dummies makes everything easier.

Leverage the Power

For Dummies is the global leader in the reference category and one of the most trusted and highly regarded brands in the world. No longer just focused on books, customers now have access to the For Dummies content they need in the format they want. Let us help you develop a solution that will fit your brand and help you connect with your customers.

Advertising & Sponsorships

Connect with an engaged audience on a powerful multimedia site, and position your message alongside expert how-to content.

Targeted ads • Video • Email marketing • Microsites • Sweepstakes sponsorship

# of For Dummies

Custom Publishing

Reach a global audience in any language by creating a solution that will differentiate you from competitors, amplify your message, and encourage customers to make a buying decision.

Apps • Books • eBooks • Video • Audio • Webinars

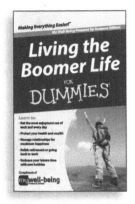

Brand Licensing & Content

Leverage the strength of the world's most popular reference brand to reach new audiences and channels of distribution.

For more information, visit www.Dummies.com/biz

Dummies products make life easier!

- DIY
- Consumer Electronics
- Crafts

- Software
- Cookware
- Hobbies

- Videos
- Music
- Games
- and More!

For more information, go to **Dummies.com·** and search the store by category.

FOR
DUMMIES
A Wiley Brand